Patterns for Parallel Programming

The Software Patterns Series

Series Editor: John M. Vlissides

The Software Patterns Series (SPS) comprises pattern literature of lasting significance to software developers. Software patterns document general solutions to recurring problems in all software-related spheres, from the technology itself, to the organizations that develop and distribute it, to the people who use it. Books in the series distill experience from one or more of these areas into a form that software professionals can apply immediately.

Relevance and *impact* are the tenets of the SPS. Relevance means each book presents patterns that solve real problems. Patterns worthy of the name are intrinsically relevant; they are borne of practitioners' experiences, not theory or speculation. Patterns have impact when they change how people work for the better. A book becomes a part of the series not just because it embraces these tenets, but because it has demonstrated it fulfills them for its audience.

Titles in the series:

Data Access Patterns: Database Interactions in Object-Oriented Applications; Clifton Nock

Design Patterns Explained, Second Edition: A New Perspective on Object-Oriented Design; Alan Shalloway and James Trott

Design Patterns in C#; Steven John Metsker

Design Patterns in Java™; Steven John Metsker and William C. Wake

Design Patterns Java™ Workbook; Steven John Metsker

.NET Patterns: Architecture, Design, and Process; Christian Thilmany

Pattern Hatching: Design Patterns Applied; John M. Vlissides

Pattern Languages of Program Design; James O. Coplien and Douglas C. Schmidt

Pattern Languages of Program Design 2; John M. Vlissides, James O. Coplien, and Norman L. Kerth

Pattern Languages of Program Design 3; Robert C. Martin, Dirk Riehle, and Frank Buschmann

Pattern Languages of Program Design 5; Dragos Manolescu, Markus Voelter, and James Noble

Patterns for Parallel Programming; Timothy G. Mattson, Beverly A. Sanders, and Berna L. Massingill

Software Configuration Management Patterns: Effective Teamwork, Practical Integration; Stephen P. Berczuk and Brad Appleton

The Design Patterns Smalltalk Companion; Sherman Alpert, Kyle Brown, and Bobby Woolf

Use Cases: Patterns and Blueprints; Gunnar Övergaard and Karin Palmkvist

For more information, check out the series web site at www.awprofessional.com/series/swpatterns

Patterns for Parallel Programming

Timothy G. Mattson

Beverly A. Sanders

Berna L. Massingill

✦✦Addison-Wesley

Boston • San Francisco • New York • Toronto • Montreal
London • Munich • Paris • Madrid
Capetown • Sydney • Tokyo • Singapore • Mexico City

Many of the designations used by manufacturers and sellers to distinguish their products are claimed as trademarks. Where those designations appear in this book, and Addison-Wesley was aware of a trademark claim, the designations have been printed with initial capital letters or in all capitals.

The authors and publisher have taken care in the preparation of this book, but make no expressed or implied warranty of any kind and assume no responsibility for errors or omissions. No liability is assumed for incidental or consequential damages in connection with or arising out of the use of the information or programs contained herein.

The publisher offers discounts on this book when ordered in quantity for bulk purchases and special sales. For more information, please contact:

U.S. Corporate and Government Sales
(800) 382-3419
corpsales@pearsontechgroup.com

For sales outside of the U.S., please contact:

International Sales
international@pearsoned.com

Visit Addison-Wesley on the Web: www.awprofessional.com

Library of Congress Cataloging-in-Publication Data

Mattson, Timothy G., 1958-
  Patterns for parallel programming / Timothy G. Mattson, Beverly A. Sanders,
Berna L. Massingill.
        p. cm.
  Includes bibliographical references and index.
  ISBN 0-321-22811-1 (hardback : alk. paper)
  1. Parallel programming (Computer science) I. Sanders, Beverly A.
 II. Massingill, Berna L. III. Title
    QA76.642.M38 2004
    005.2 ' 75—dc22   2004013240

Text printed on recycled and acid-free paper.
ISBN   0321228111
4 5 6 7 8   CRW   09 08
4th Printing   March 2008

To Zorba
  —T. G. M.

To my parents, Marion and Bobbie
  —B. A. S.

To my mother, Billie, and in memory of my father, George
  —B. L. M.

Contents

Preface

"If you build it, they will come."

And so we built them. Multiprocessor workstations, massively parallel supercomputers, a cluster in every department ... and they haven't come. Programmers haven't come to program these wonderful machines. Oh, a few programmers in love with the challenge have shown that most types of problems can be force-fit onto parallel computers, but general programmers, especially professional programmers who "have lives", ignore parallel computers.

And they do so at their own peril. Parallel computers are going mainstream. Multithreaded microprocessors, multicore CPUs, multiprocessor PCs, clusters, parallel game consoles ... parallel computers are taking over the world of computing. The computer industry is ready to flood the market with hardware that will only run at full speed with parallel programs. But who will write these programs?

This is an old problem. Even in the early 1980s, when the "killer micros" started their assault on traditional vector supercomputers, we worried endlessly about how to attract normal programmers. We tried everything we could think of: high-level hardware abstractions, implicitly parallel programming languages, parallel language extensions, and portable message-passing libraries. But after many years of hard work, the fact of the matter is that "they" didn't come. The overwhelming majority of programmers will not invest the effort to write parallel software.

A common view is that you can't teach old programmers new tricks, so the problem will not be solved until the old programmers fade away and a new generation takes over.

But we don't buy into that defeatist attitude. Programmers have shown a remarkable ability to adopt new software technologies over the years. Look at how many old Fortran programmers are now writing elegant Java programs with sophisticated object-oriented designs. The problem isn't with *old programmers*. The problem is with *old parallel computing experts* and the way they've tried to create a pool of capable parallel programmers.

And that's where this book comes in. We want to capture the essence of how expert parallel programmers think about parallel algorithms and communicate that essential understanding in a way professional programmers can readily master. The technology we've adopted to accomplish this task is a *pattern language*. We made this choice not because we started the project as devotees of design patterns looking for a new field to conquer, but because patterns have been shown to work in ways that would be applicable in parallel programming. For example, patterns have been very effective in the field of object-oriented design. They have provided a common language experts can use to talk about the elements of design and have been extremely effective at helping programmers master object-oriented design.

This book contains our pattern language for parallel programming. The book opens with a couple of chapters to introduce the key concepts in parallel computing. These chapters focus on the parallel computing concepts and jargon used in the pattern language as opposed to being an exhaustive introduction to the field.

The pattern language itself is presented in four parts corresponding to the four phases of creating a parallel program:

- *Finding Concurrency*. The programmer works in the problem domain to identify the available concurrency and expose it for use in the algorithm design.

- *Algorithm Structure*. The programmer works with high-level structures for organizing a parallel algorithm.

- *Supporting Structures*. We shift from algorithms to source code and consider how the parallel program will be organized and the techniques used to manage shared data.

- *Implementation Mechanisms*. The final step is to look at specific software constructs for implementing a parallel program.

The patterns making up these four design spaces are tightly linked. You start at the top (*Finding Concurrency*), work through the patterns, and by the time you get to the bottom (*Implementation Mechanisms*), you will have a detailed design for your parallel program.

If the goal is a parallel program, however, you need more than just a parallel algorithm. You also need a programming environment and a notation for expressing the concurrency within the program's source code. Programmers used to be confronted by a large and confusing array of parallel programming environments. Fortunately, over the years the parallel programming community has converged around three programming environments.

- **OpenMP**. A simple language extension to C, C++, or Fortran to write parallel programs for shared-memory computers.

- **MPI**. A message-passing library used on clusters and other distributed-memory computers.

- **Java**. An object-oriented programming language with language features supporting parallel programming on shared-memory computers and standard class libraries supporting distributed computing.

Many readers will already be familiar with one or more of these programming notations, but for readers completely new to parallel computing, we've included a discussion of these programming environments in the appendixes.

In closing, we have been working for many years on this pattern language. Presenting it as a book so people can start using it is an exciting development for us. But we don't see this as the end of this effort. We expect that others will have their own ideas about new and better patterns for parallel programming. We've assuredly missed some important features that really belong in this pattern language. We embrace change and look forward to engaging with the larger parallel computing community to iterate on this language. Over time, we'll update and improve the pattern language until it truly represents the consensus view of the parallel programming community. Then our real work will begin—using the pattern language to guide the creation of better parallel programming environments and helping people to use these technologies to write parallel software. We won't rest until the day sequential software is rare.

ACKNOWLEDGMENTS

We started working together on this pattern language in 1998. It's been a long and twisted road, starting with a vague idea about a new way to think about parallel algorithms and finishing with this book. We couldn't have done this without a great deal of help.

Mani Chandy, who thought we would make a good team, introduced Tim to Beverly and Berna. The National Science Foundation, Intel Corp., and Trinity University have supported this research at various times over the years. Help with the patterns themselves came from the people at the Pattern Languages of Programs (PLoP) workshops held in Illinois each summer. The format of these workshops and the resulting review process was challenging and sometimes difficult, but without them we would have never finished this pattern language. We would also like to thank the reviewers who carefully read early manuscripts and pointed out countless errors and ways to improve the book.

Finally, we thank our families. Writing a book is hard on the authors, but that is to be expected. What we didn't fully appreciate was how hard it would be on our families. We are grateful to Beverly's family (Daniel and Steve), Tim's family (Noah, August, and Martha), and Berna's family (Billie) for the sacrifices they've made to support this project.

    — Tim Mattson, Olympia, Washington, April 2004
    — Beverly Sanders, Gainesville, Florida, April 2004
    — Berna Massingill, San Antonio, Texas, April 2004

CHAPTER 1

A Pattern Language for Parallel Programming

1.1 INTRODUCTION
1.2 PARALLEL PROGRAMMING
1.3 DESIGN PATTERNS AND PATTERN LANGUAGES
1.4 A PATTERN LANGUAGE FOR PARALLEL PROGRAMMING

1.1 INTRODUCTION

Computers are used to model physical systems in many fields of science, medicine, and engineering. Modelers, whether trying to predict the weather or render a scene in the next blockbuster movie, can usually use whatever computing power is available to make ever more detailed simulations. Vast amounts of data, whether customer shopping patterns, telemetry data from space, or DNA sequences, require analysis. To deliver the required power, computer designers combine multiple processing elements into a single larger system. These so-called *parallel computers* run multiple tasks simultaneously and solve bigger problems in less time.

Traditionally, parallel computers were rare and available for only the most critical problems. Since the mid-1990s, however, the availability of parallel computers has changed dramatically. With multithreading support built into the latest microprocessors and the emergence of multiple processor cores on a single silicon die, parallel computers are becoming ubiquitous. Now, almost every university computer science department has at least one parallel computer. Virtually all oil companies, automobile manufacturers, drug development companies, and special effects studios use parallel computing.

For example, in computer animation, rendering is the step where information from the animation files, such as lighting, textures, and shading, is applied to 3D models to generate the 2D image that makes up a frame of the film. Parallel computing is essential to generate the needed number of frames (24 per second) for a feature-length film. *Toy Story,* the first completely computer-generated feature-length film, released by Pixar in 1995, was processed on a "renderfarm" consisting of 100 dual-processor machines [PS00]. By 1999, for *Toy Story 2,* Pixar was using a 1,400-processor system with the improvement in processing power fully reflected in the improved details in textures, clothing, and atmospheric effects. *Monsters, Inc.* (2001) used a system of 250 enterprise servers each containing 14 processors for a total of 3,500 processors. It is interesting that the amount of time required to generate a frame has remained relatively constant—as computing power (both the number of processors and the speed of each processor) has increased, it has been exploited to improve the quality of the animation.

The biological sciences have taken dramatic leaps forward with the availability of DNA sequence information from a variety of organisms, including humans. One approach to sequencing, championed and used with success by Celera Corp., is called the whole genome shotgun algorithm. The idea is to break the genome into small segments, experimentally determine the DNA sequences of the segments, and then use a computer to construct the entire sequence from the segments by finding overlapping areas. The computing facilities used by Celera to sequence the human genome included 150 four-way servers plus a server with 16 processors and 64GB of memory. The calculation involved 500 million trillion base-to-base comparisons [Ein00].

The SETI@home project [SET, ACK+02] provides a fascinating example of the power of parallel computing. The project seeks evidence of extraterrestrial intelligence by scanning the sky with the world's largest radio telescope, the Arecibo Telescope in Puerto Rico. The collected data is then analyzed for candidate signals that might indicate an intelligent source. The computational task is beyond even the largest supercomputer, and certainly beyond the capabilities of the facilities available to the SETI@home project. The problem is solved with *public resource computing,* which turns PCs around the world into a huge parallel computer connected by the Internet. Data is broken up into work units and distributed over the Internet to client computers whose owners donate spare computing time to support the project. Each client periodically connects with the SETI@home server, downloads the data to analyze, and then sends the results back to the server. The client program is typically implemented as a screen saver so that it will devote CPU cycles to the SETI problem only when the computer is otherwise idle. A work unit currently requires an average of between seven and eight hours of CPU time on a client. More than 205,000,000 work units have been processed since the start of the project. More recently, similar technology to that demonstrated by SETI@home has been used for a variety of public resource computing projects as well as internal projects within large companies utilizing their idle PCs to solve problems ranging from drug screening to chip design validation.

Although computing in less time is beneficial, and may enable problems to be solved that couldn't be otherwise, it comes at a cost. Writing software to run on parallel computers can be difficult. Only a small minority of programmers have experience with parallel programming. If all these computers designed to exploit parallelism are going to achieve their potential, more programmers need to learn how to write parallel programs.

This book addresses this need by showing competent programmers of sequential machines how to design programs that can run on parallel computers. Although many excellent books show how to use particular parallel programming environments, this book is unique in that it focuses on how to think about and design parallel algorithms. To accomplish this goal, we will be using the concept of a *pattern language.* This highly structured representation of expert design experience has been heavily used in the object-oriented design community.

The book opens with two introductory chapters. The first gives an overview of the parallel computing landscape and background needed to understand and use the pattern language. This is followed by a more detailed chapter in which we lay out the basic concepts and jargon used by parallel programmers. The book then moves into the pattern language itself.

1.2   PARALLEL PROGRAMMING

The key to parallel computing is *exploitable concurrency*. Concurrency exists in a computational problem when the problem can be decomposed into subproblems that can safely execute at the same time. To be of any use, however, it must be possible to structure the code to expose and later exploit the concurrency and permit the subproblems to actually run concurrently; that is, the concurrency must be *exploitable*.

Most large computational problems contain exploitable concurrency. A programmer works with exploitable concurrency by creating a parallel algorithm and implementing the algorithm using a parallel programming environment. When the resulting parallel program is run on a system with multiple processors, the amount of time we have to wait for the results of the computation is reduced. In addition, multiple processors may allow larger problems to be solved than could be done on a single-processor system.

As a simple example, suppose part of a computation involves computing the summation of a large set of values. If multiple processors are available, instead of adding the values together sequentially, the set can be partitioned and the summations of the subsets computed simultaneously, each on a different processor. The partial sums are then combined to get the final answer. Thus, using multiple processors to compute in parallel may allow us to obtain a solution sooner. Also, if each processor has its own memory, partitioning the data between the processors may allow larger problems to be handled than could be handled on a single processor.

This simple example shows the essence of parallel computing. The goal is to use multiple processors to solve problems in less time and/or to solve bigger problems than would be possible on a single processor. The programmer's task is to identify the concurrency in the problem, structure the algorithm so that this concurrency can be exploited, and then implement the solution using a suitable programming environment. The final step is to solve the problem by executing the code on a parallel system.

Parallel programming presents unique challenges. Often, the concurrent tasks making up the problem include dependencies that must be identified and correctly managed. The order in which the tasks execute may change the answers of the computations in nondeterministic ways. For example, in the parallel summation described earlier, a partial sum cannot be combined with others until its own computation has completed. The algorithm imposes a partial order on the tasks (that is, they must complete before the sums can be combined). More subtly, the numerical value of the summations may change slightly depending on the order of the operations within the sums because floating-point arithmetic is nonassociative. A good parallel programmer must take care to ensure that nondeterministic issues such as these do not affect the quality of the final answer. Creating safe parallel programs can take considerable effort from the programmer.

Even when a parallel program is "correct", it may fail to deliver the anticipated performance improvement from exploiting concurrency. Care must be taken to ensure that the overhead incurred by managing the concurrency does not overwhelm the program runtime. Also, partitioning the work among the processors in a balanced way is often not as easy as the summation example suggests. The effectiveness of a parallel algorithm depends on how well it maps onto the underlying parallel computer, so a parallel algorithm could be very effective on one parallel architecture and a disaster on another.

We will revisit these issues and provide a more quantitative view of parallel computation in the next chapter.

1.3 DESIGN PATTERNS AND PATTERN LANGUAGES

A *design pattern* describes a good solution to a recurring problem in a particular context. The pattern follows a prescribed format that includes the pattern name, a description of the context, the forces (goals and constraints), and the solution. The idea is to record the experience of experts in a way that can be used by others facing a similar problem. In addition to the solution itself, the name of the pattern is important and can form the basis for a domain-specific vocabulary that can significantly enhance communication between designers in the same area.

Design patterns were first proposed by Christopher Alexander. The domain was city planning and architecture [AIS77]. Design patterns were originally introduced to the software engineering community by Beck and Cunningham [BC87] and became prominent in the area of object-oriented programming with the publication of the book by Gamma, Helm, Johnson, and Vlissides [GHJV95], affectionately known as the GoF (Gang of Four) book. This book gives a large collection of design patterns for object-oriented programming. To give one example, the *Visitor pattern* describes a way to structure classes so that the code implementing a heterogeneous data structure can be kept separate from the code to traverse it. Thus, what happens in a traversal depends on both the type of each node and the class that implements the traversal. This allows multiple functionality for data structure traversals, and significant flexibility as new functionality can be added without having to change the data structure class. The patterns in the GoF book have entered the lexicon of object-oriented programming—references to its patterns are found in the academic literature, trade publications, and system documentation. These patterns have by now become part of the expected knowledge of any competent software engineer.

An educational nonprofit organization called the Hillside Group [Hil] was formed in 1993 to promote the use of patterns and pattern languages and, more generally, to improve human communication about computers "by encouraging people to codify common programming and design practice". To develop new patterns and help pattern writers hone their skills, the Hillside Group sponsors an annual Pattern Languages of Programs (PLoP) workshop and several spinoffs in other parts of the world, such as ChiliPLoP (in the western United States), KoalaPLoP

(Australia), EuroPLoP (Europe), and Mensore PLoP (Japan). The proceedings of these workshops [Pat] provide a rich source of patterns covering a vast range of application domains in software development and have been used as a basis for several books [CS95, VCK96, MRB97, HFR99].

In his original work on patterns, Alexander provided not only a catalog of patterns, but also a *pattern language* that introduced a new approach to design. In a pattern language, the patterns are organized into a structure that leads the user through the collection of patterns in such a way that complex systems can be designed using the patterns. At each decision point, the designer selects an appropriate pattern. Each pattern leads to other patterns, resulting in a final design in terms of a web of patterns. Thus, a pattern language embodies a design methodology and provides domain-specific advice to the application designer. (In spite of the overlapping terminology, a pattern language is *not* a programming language.)

1.4   A PATTERN LANGUAGE FOR PARALLEL PROGRAMMING

This book describes a pattern language for parallel programming that provides several benefits. The immediate benefits are a way to disseminate the experience of experts by providing a catalog of good solutions to important problems, an expanded vocabulary, and a methodology for the design of parallel programs. We hope to lower the barrier to parallel programming by providing guidance through the entire process of developing a parallel program. The programmer brings to the process a good understanding of the actual problem to be solved and then works through the pattern language, eventually obtaining a detailed parallel design or possibly working code. In the longer term, we hope that this pattern language can provide a basis for both a disciplined approach to the qualitative evaluation of different programming models and the development of parallel programming tools.

The pattern language is organized into four design spaces—*Finding Concurrency, Algorithm Structure, Supporting Structures,* and *Implementation Mechanisms*—which form a linear hierarchy, with *Finding Concurrency* at the top and *Implementation Mechanisms* at the bottom, as shown in Fig. 1.1.

The *Finding Concurrency* design space is concerned with structuring the problem to expose exploitable concurrency. The designer working at this level focuses

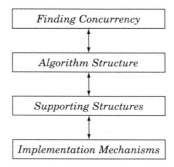

Figure 1.1: Overview of the pattern language

on high-level algorithmic issues and reasons about the problem to expose potential concurrency. The *Algorithm Structure* design space is concerned with structuring the algorithm to take advantage of potential concurrency. That is, the designer working at this level reasons about how to use the concurrency exposed in working with the *Finding Concurrency* patterns. The *Algorithm Structure* patterns describe overall strategies for exploiting concurrency. The *Supporting Structures* design space represents an intermediate stage between the *Algorithm Structure* and *Implementation Mechanisms* design spaces. Two important groups of patterns in this space are those that represent program-structuring approaches and those that represent commonly used shared data structures. The *Implementation Mechanisms* design space is concerned with how the patterns of the higher-level spaces are mapped into particular programming environments. We use it to provide descriptions of common mechanisms for process/thread management (for example, creating or destroying processes/threads) and process/thread interaction (for example, semaphores, barriers, or message passing). The items in this design space are not presented as patterns because in many cases they map directly onto elements within particular parallel programming environments. They are included in the pattern language anyway, however, to provide a complete path from problem description to code.

CHAPTER 2

Background and Jargon of Parallel Computing

2.1 CONCURRENCY IN PARALLEL PROGRAMS VERSUS OPERATING SYSTEMS
2.2 PARALLEL ARCHITECTURES: A BRIEF INTRODUCTION
2.3 PARALLEL PROGRAMMING ENVIRONMENTS
2.4 THE JARGON OF PARALLEL COMPUTING
2.5 A QUANTITATIVE LOOK AT PARALLEL COMPUTATION
2.6 COMMUNICATION
2.7 SUMMARY

In this chapter, we give an overview of the parallel programming landscape, and define any specialized parallel computing terminology that we will use in the patterns. Because many terms in computing are overloaded, taking different meanings in different contexts, we suggest that even readers familiar with parallel programming at least skim this chapter.

2.1 CONCURRENCY IN PARALLEL PROGRAMS VERSUS OPERATING SYSTEMS

Concurrency was first exploited in computing to better utilize or share resources within a computer. Modern operating systems support context switching to allow multiple tasks to appear to execute concurrently, thereby allowing useful work to occur while the processor is stalled on one task. This application of concurrency, for example, allows the processor to stay busy by swapping in a new task to execute while another task is waiting for I/O. By quickly swapping tasks in and out, giving each task a "slice" of the processor time, the operating system can allow multiple users to use the system as if each were using it alone (but with degraded performance).

Most modern operating systems can use multiple processors to increase the throughput of the system. The UNIX shell uses concurrency along with a communication abstraction known as *pipes* to provide a powerful form of modularity: Commands are written to accept a stream of bytes as input (the *consumer*) and produce a stream of bytes as output (the *producer*). Multiple commands can be chained together with a pipe connecting the output of one command to the input of the next, allowing complex commands to be built from simple building blocks. Each command is executed in its own process, with all processes executing concurrently. Because the producer blocks if buffer space in the pipe is not available, and the consumer blocks if data is not available, the job of managing the stream of results moving between commands is greatly simplified. More recently, with operating systems with windows that invite users to do more than one thing at a time, and the Internet, which often introduces I/O delays perceptible to the user, almost every program that contains a GUI incorporates concurrency.

Although the fundamental concepts for safely handling concurrency are the same in parallel programs and operating systems, there are some important differences. For an operating system, the problem is not finding concurrency—the concurrency is inherent in the way the operating system functions in managing a collection of concurrently executing processes (representing users, applications, and background activities such as print spooling) and providing synchronization mechanisms so resources can be safely shared. However, an operating system must support concurrency in a robust and secure way: Processes should not be able to interfere with each other (intentionally or not), and the entire system should not crash if something goes wrong with one process. In a parallel program, finding and exploiting concurrency can be a challenge, while isolating processes from each other is not the critical concern it is with an operating system. Performance goals are different as well. In an operating system, performance goals are normally related to throughput or response time, and it may be acceptable to sacrifice some efficiency to maintain robustness and fairness in resource allocation. In a parallel program, the goal is to minimize the running time of a single program.

2.2 PARALLEL ARCHITECTURES: A BRIEF INTRODUCTION

There are dozens of different parallel architectures, among them networks of workstations, clusters of off-the-shelf PCs, massively parallel supercomputers, tightly coupled symmetric multiprocessors, and multiprocessor workstations. In this section, we give an overview of these systems, focusing on the characteristics relevant to the programmer.

2.2.1 Flynn's Taxonomy

By far the most common way to characterize these architectures is Flynn's taxonomy [Fly72]. He categorizes all computers according to the number of instruction streams and data streams they have, where a stream is a sequence of instructions or data on which a computer operates. In Flynn's taxonomy, there are four possibilities: SISD, SIMD, MISD, and MIMD.

Single Instruction, Single Data (SISD).   In a SISD system, one stream of instructions processes a single stream of data, as shown in Fig. 2.1. This is the common von Neumann model used in virtually all single-processor computers.

Single Instruction, Multiple Data (SIMD).   In a SIMD system, a single instruction stream is concurrently broadcast to multiple processors, each with its own data stream (as shown in Fig. 2.2). The original systems from Thinking Machines and MasPar can be classified as SIMD. The CPP DAP Gamma II and Quadrics Apemille are more recent examples; these are typically deployed in specialized applications, such as digital signal processing, that are suited to fine-grained parallelism and require little interprocess communication. Vector processors, which

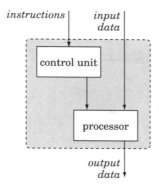

Figure 2.1: The Single Instruction, Single Data (SISD) architecture

operate on vector data in a pipelined fashion, can also be categorized as SIMD. Exploiting this parallelism is usually done by the compiler.

Multiple Instruction, Single Data (MISD).   No well-known systems fit this designation. It is mentioned for the sake of completeness.

Multiple Instruction, Multiple Data (MIMD).   In a MIMD system, each processing element has its own stream of instructions operating on its own data. This architecture, shown in Fig. 2.3, is the most general of the architectures in that each of the other cases can be mapped onto the MIMD architecture. The vast majority of modern parallel systems fit into this category.

2.2.2   A Further Breakdown of MIMD

The MIMD category of Flynn's taxonomy is too broad to be useful on its own; this category is typically decomposed according to memory organization.

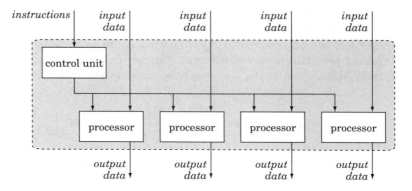

Figure 2.2: The Single Instruction, Multiple Data (SIMD) architecture

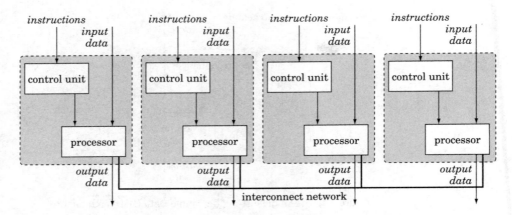

Figure 2.3: The Multiple Instruction, Multiple Data (MIMD) architecture

Shared memory.   In a shared-memory system, all processes share a single address space and communicate with each other by writing and reading shared variables.

One class of shared-memory systems is called SMPs (symmetric multiprocessors). As shown in Fig. 2.4, all processors share a connection to a common memory and access all memory locations at equal speeds. SMP systems are arguably the easiest parallel systems to program because programmers do not need to distribute data structures among processors. Because increasing the number of processors increases contention for the memory, the processor/memory bandwidth is typically a limiting factor. Thus, SMP systems do not scale well and are limited to small numbers of processors.

The other main class of shared-memory systems is called NUMA (nonuniform memory access). As shown in Fig. 2.5, the memory is shared; that is, it is uniformly addressable from all processors, but some blocks of memory may be physically more closely associated with some processors than others. This reduces the memory bandwidth bottleneck and allows systems with more processors; however, as a result, the access time from a processor to a memory location can be significantly different depending on how "close" the memory location is to the processor. To mitigate the effects of nonuniform access, each processor has a cache, along with a protocol to keep cache entries coherent. Hence, another name for these architectures is cachecoherent nonuniform memory access systems (ccNUMA). Logically, programming a ccNUMA system is the same as programming an SMP, but to obtain the best

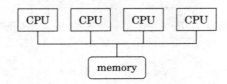

Figure 2.4: The Symmetric Multiprocessor (SMP) architecture

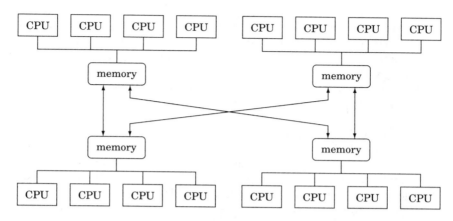

Figure 2.5: An example of the nonuniform memory access (NUMA) architecture

performance, the programmer will need to be more careful about locality issues and cache effects.

Distributed memory.   In a distributed-memory system, each process has its own address space and communicates with other processes by *message passing* (sending and receiving messages). A schematic representation of a distributed memory computer is shown in Fig. 2.6.

Depending on the topology and technology used for the processor interconnection, communication speed can range from almost as fast as shared memory (in tightly integrated supercomputers) to orders of magnitude slower (for example, in a cluster of PCs interconnected with an Ethernet network). The programmer must explicitly program all the communication between processors and be concerned with the distribution of data.

Distributed-memory computers are traditionally divided into two classes: MPP (massively parallel processors) and clusters. In an MPP, the processors and the network infrastructure are tightly coupled and specialized for use in a parallel computer. These systems are extremely scalable, in some cases supporting the use of many thousands of processors in a single system [MSW96, IBM02].

Clusters are distributed-memory systems composed of off-the-shelf computers connected by an off-the-shelf network. When the computers are PCs running the Linux operating system, these clusters are called *Beowulf clusters*. As

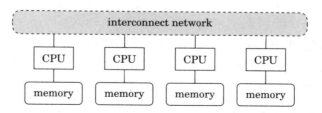

Figure 2.6: The distributed-memory architecture

off-the-shelf networking technology improves, systems of this type are becoming more common and much more powerful. Clusters provide an inexpensive way for an organization to obtain parallel computing capabilities [Beo]. Preconfigured clusters are now available from many vendors. One frugal group even reported constructing a useful parallel system by using a cluster to harness the combined power of obsolete PCs that otherwise would have been discarded [HHS01].

Hybrid systems.   These systems are clusters of nodes with separate address spaces in which each node contains several processors that share memory.

According to van der Steen and Dongarra's "Overview of Recent Supercomputers" [vdSD03], which contains a brief description of the supercomputers currently or soon to be commercially available, hybrid systems formed from clusters of SMPs connected by a fast network are currently the dominant trend in high-performance computing. For example, in late 2003, four of the five fastest computers in the world were hybrid systems [Top].

Grids.   Grids are systems that use distributed, heterogeneous resources connected by LANs and/or WANs [FK03]. Often the interconnection network is the Internet. Grids were originally envisioned as a way to link multiple supercomputers to enable larger problems to be solved, and thus could be viewed as a special type of distributed-memory or hybrid MIMD machine. More recently, the idea of grid computing has evolved into a general way to share heterogeneous resources, such as computation servers, storage, application servers, information services, or even scientific instruments. Grids differ from clusters in that the various resources in the grid need not have a common point of administration. In most cases, the resources on a grid are owned by different organizations that maintain control over the policies governing use of the resources. This affects the way these systems are used, the middleware created to manage them, and most importantly for this discussion, the overhead incurred when communicating between resources within the grid.

2.2.3 Summary

We have classified these systems according to the characteristics of the hardware. These characteristics typically influence the native programming model used to express concurrency on a system; however, this is not always the case. It is possible for a programming environment for a shared-memory machine to provide the programmer with the abstraction of distributed memory and message passing. Virtual distributed shared memory systems contain middleware to provide the opposite: the abstraction of shared memory on a distributed-memory machine.

2.3 PARALLEL PROGRAMMING ENVIRONMENTS

Parallel programming environments provide the basic tools, language features, and *application programming interfaces* (APIs) needed to construct a parallel program. A programming environment implies a particular abstraction of the computer system called a *programming model*. Traditional sequential computers use the well known von Neumann model. Because all sequential computers use this model, software designers can design software to a single abstraction and reasonably expect it to map onto most, if not all, sequential computers.

Unfortunately, there are many possible models for parallel computing, reflecting the different ways processors can be interconnected to construct a parallel system. The most common models are based on one of the widely deployed parallel architectures: shared memory, distributed memory with message passing, or a hybrid combination of the two.

Programming models too closely aligned to a particular parallel system lead to programs that are not portable between parallel computers. Because the effective lifespan of software is longer than that of hardware, many organizations have more than one type of parallel computer, and most programmers insist on programming environments that allow them to write portable parallel programs. Also, explicitly managing large numbers of resources in a parallel computer is difficult, suggesting that higher-level abstractions of the parallel computer might be useful. The result is that as of the mid-1990s, there was a veritable glut of parallel programming environments. A partial list of these is shown in Table 2.1. This created a great deal of confusion for application developers and hindered the adoption of parallel computing for mainstream applications.

Fortunately, by the late 1990s, the parallel programming community converged predominantly on two environments for parallel programming: OpenMP [OMP] for shared memory and MPI [Mesb] for message passing.

OpenMP is a set of language extensions implemented as compiler directives. Implementations are currently available for Fortran, C, and C++. OpenMP is frequently used to incrementally add parallelism to sequential code. By adding a compiler directive around a loop, for example, the compiler can be instructed to generate code to execute the iterations of the loop in parallel. The compiler takes care of most of the details of thread creation and management. OpenMP programs tend to work very well on SMPs, but because its underlying programming model does not include a notion of nonuniform memory access times, it is less ideal for ccNUMA and distributed-memory machines.

MPI is a set of library routines that provide for process management, message passing, and some collective communication operations (these are operations that involve all the processes involved in a program, such as barrier, broadcast, and reduction). MPI programs can be difficult to write because the programmer is responsible for data distribution and explicit interprocess communication using messages. Because the programming model assumes distributed memory, MPI is a good choice for MPPs and other distributed-memory machines.

Neither OpenMP nor MPI is an ideal fit for hybrid architectures that combine multiprocessor nodes, each with multiple processes and a shared memory, into a larger system with separate address spaces for each node: The OpenMP model does not recognize nonuniform memory access times, so its data allocation can lead to poor performance on machines that are not SMPs, while MPI does not include constructs to manage data structures residing in a shared memory. One solution is a hybrid model in which OpenMP is used on each shared-memory node and MPI is used between the nodes. This works well, but it requires the programmer to work with two different programming models within a single program. Another option

Table 2.1: Some Parallel Programming Environments from the Mid-1990s

"C* in C	CUMULVS	Java RMI	P-RIO	Quake
ABCPL	DAGGER	javaPG	P3L	Quark
ACE	DAPPLE	JAVAR	P4-Linda	Quick Threads
ACT++	Data Parallel C	JavaSpaces	Pablo	Sage++
ADDAP	DC++	JIDL	PADE	SAM
Adl	DCE++	Joyce	PADRE	SCANDAL
Adsmith	DDD	Karma	Panda	SCHEDULE
AFAPI	DICE	Khoros	Papers	SciTL
ALWAN	DIPC	KOAN/Fortran-S	Para++	SDDA
AM	Distributed Smalltalk	LAM	Paradigm	SHMEM
AMDC	DOLIB	Legion	Parafrase2	SIMPLE
Amoeba	DOME	Lilac	Paralation	Sina
AppLeS	DOSMOS	Linda	Parallaxis	SISAL
ARTS	DRL	LiPS	Parallel Haskell	SMI
Athapascan-0b	DSM-Threads	Locust	Parallel-C++	SONiC
Aurora	Ease	Lparx	ParC	Split-C
Automap	ECO	Lucid	ParLib++	SR
bb_threads	Eilean	Maisie	ParLin	Sthreads
Blaze	Emerald	Manifold	Parlog	Strand
BlockComm	EPL	Mentat	Parmacs	SUIF
BSP	Excalibur	Meta Chaos	Parti	SuperPascal
C*	Express	Midway	pC	Synergy
C**	Falcon	Millipede	pC++	TCGMSG
C4	Filaments	Mirage	PCN	Telegraphos
CarlOS	FLASH	Modula-2*	PCP:	The FORCE
Cashmere	FM	Modula-P	PCU	Threads.h++
CC++	Fork	MOSIX	PEACE	TRAPPER
Charlotte	Fortran-M	MpC	PENNY	TreadMarks
Charm	FX	MPC++	PET	UC
Charm++	GA	MPI	PETSc	uC++
Chu	GAMMA	Multipol	PH	UNITY
Cid	Glenda	Munin	Phosphorus	V
Cilk	GLU	Nano-Threads	POET	ViC*
CM-Fortran	GUARD	NESL	Polaris	Visifold V-NUS
Code	HAsL	NetClasses++	POOL-T	VPE
Concurrent ML	HORUS	Nexus	POOMA	Win32 threads
Converse	HPC	Nimrod	POSYBL	WinPar
COOL	HPC++	NOW	PRESTO	WWWinda
CORRELATE	HPF	Objective Linda	Prospero	XENOOPS
CparPar	IMPACT	Occam	Proteus	XPC
CPS	ISETL-Linda	Omega	PSDM	Zounds
CRL	ISIS	OOF90	PSI	ZPL
CSP	JADA	Orca	PVM	
Cthreads	JADE	P++	QPC++	

is to use MPI on both the shared-memory and distributed-memory portions of the algorithm and give up the advantages of a shared-memory programming model, even when the hardware directly supports it.

New high-level programming environments that simplify portable parallel programming and more accurately reflect the underlying parallel architectures are topics of current research [Cen]. Another approach more popular in the commercial sector is to extend MPI and OpenMP. In the mid-1990s, the MPI Forum defined an extended MPI called MPI 2.0, although implementations are not widely available at the time this was written. It is a large complex extension to MPI that includes dynamic process creation, parallel I/O, and many other features. Of particular interest to programmers of modern hybrid architectures is the inclusion of one-sided communication. One-sided communication mimics some of the features of a shared-memory system by letting one process write into or read from the memory regions of other processes. The term "one-sided" refers to the fact that the read or write is launched by the initiating process without the explicit involvement of the other participating process. A more sophisticated abstraction of one-sided communication is available as part of the Global Arrays [NHL96, NHK+02, Gloa] package. Global Arrays works together with MPI to help a programmer manage distributed array data. After the programmer defines the array and how it is laid out in memory, the program executes "puts" or "gets" into the array without needing to explicitly manage which MPI process "owns" the particular section of the array. In essence, the global array provides an abstraction of a globally shared array. This only works for arrays, but these are such common data structures in parallel computing that this package, although limited, can be very useful.

Just as MPI has been extended to mimic some of the benefits of a shared-memory environment, OpenMP has been extended to run in distributed-memory environments. The annual WOMPAT (Workshop on OpenMP Applications and Tools) workshops contain many papers discussing various approaches and experiences with OpenMP in clusters and ccNUMA environments.

MPI is implemented as a library of routines to be called from programs written in a sequential programming language, whereas OpenMP is a set of extensions to sequential programming languages. They represent two of the possible categories of parallel programming environments (libraries and language extensions), and these two particular environments account for the overwhelming majority of parallel computing being done today. There is, however, one more category of parallel programming environments, namely languages with built-in features to support parallel programming. Java is such a language. Rather than being designed to support high-performance computing, Java is an object-oriented, general-purpose programming environment with features for explicitly specifying concurrent processing with shared memory. In addition, the standard I/O and network packages provide classes that make it easy for Java to perform interprocess communication between machines, thus making it possible to write programs based on both the shared-memory and the distributed-memory models. The newer `java.nio` packages support I/O in a way that is less convenient for the programmer, but gives significantly better performance, and Java 2 1.5 includes new support for concurrent programming, most significantly in the `java.util.concurrent.*` packages. Additional packages that support different approaches to parallel computing are widely available.

Although there have been other general-purpose languages, both prior to Java and more recent (for example, C#), that contained constructs for specifying concurrency, Java is the first to become widely used. As a result, it may be the first exposure for many programmers to concurrent and parallel programming. Although

Java provides software engineering benefits, currently the performance of parallel Java programs cannot compete with OpenMP or MPI programs for typical scientific computing applications. The Java design has also been criticized for several deficiencies that matter in this domain (for example, a floating-point model that emphasizes portability and more-reproducible results over exploiting the available floating-point hardware to the fullest, inefficient handling of arrays, and lack of a lightweight mechanism to handle complex numbers). The performance difference between Java and other alternatives can be expected to decrease, especially for symbolic or other nonnumeric problems, as compiler technology for Java improves and as new packages and language extensions become available. The Titanium project [Tita] is an example of a Java dialect designed for high-performance computing in a ccNUMA environment.

For the purposes of this book, we have chosen OpenMP, MPI, and Java as the three environments we will use in our examples—OpenMP and MPI for their popularity and Java because it is likely to be many programmers' first exposure to concurrent programming. A brief overview of each can be found in the appendixes.

2.4   THE JARGON OF PARALLEL COMPUTING

In this section, we define some terms that are frequently used throughout the pattern language. Additional definitions can be found in the glossary.

Task.   The first step in designing a parallel program is to break the problem up into tasks. A task is a sequence of instructions that operate together as a group. This group corresponds to some logical part of an algorithm or program. For example, consider the multiplication of two order-N matrices. Depending on how we construct the algorithm, the tasks could be (1) the multiplication of subblocks of the matrices, (2) inner products between rows and columns of the matrices, or (3) individual iterations of the loops involved in the matrix multiplication. These are all legitimate ways to define tasks for matrix multiplication; that is, the task definition follows from the way the algorithm designer thinks about the problem.

Unit of execution (UE).   To be executed, a task needs to be mapped to a UE such as a process or thread. A *process* is a collection of resources that enables the execution of program instructions. These resources can include virtual memory, I/O descriptors, a runtime stack, signal handlers, user and group IDs, and access control tokens. A more high-level view is that a process is a "heavyweight" unit of execution with its own address space. A *thread* is the fundamental UE in modern operating systems. A thread is associated with a process and shares the process's environment. This makes threads lightweight (that is, a context switch between threads takes only a small amount of time). A more high-level view is that a thread is a "lightweight" UE that shares an address space with other threads.

We will use *unit of execution* or UE as a generic term for one of a collection of possibly concurrently executing entities, usually either processes or threads. This is convenient in the early stages of program design when the distinctions between processes and threads are less important.

Processing element (PE). We use the term processing element (PE) as a generic term for a hardware element that executes a stream of instructions. The unit of hardware considered to be a PE depends on the context. For example, some programming environments view each workstation in a cluster of SMP workstations as executing a single instruction stream; in this situation, the PE would be the workstation. A different programming environment running on the same hardware, however, might view each processor of each workstation as executing an individual instruction stream; in this case, the PE is the individual processor, and each workstation contains several PEs.

Load balance and load balancing. To execute a parallel program, the tasks must be mapped to UEs, and the UEs to PEs. How the mappings are done can have a significant impact on the overall performance of a parallel algorithm. It is crucial to avoid the situation in which a subset of the PEs is doing most of the work while others are idle. *Load balance* refers to how well the work is distributed among PEs. *Load balancing* is the process of allocating work to PEs, either statically or dynamically, so that the work is distributed as evenly as possible.

Synchronization. In a parallel program, due to the nondeterminism of task scheduling and other factors, events in the computation might not always occur in the same order. For example, in one run, a task might read variable x before another task reads variable y; in the next run with the same input, the events might occur in the opposite order. In many cases, the order in which two events occur does not matter. In other situations, the order does matter, and to ensure that the program is correct, the programmer must introduce synchronization to enforce the necessary ordering constraints. The primitives provided for this purpose in our selected environments are discussed in the *Implementation Mechanisms* design space (Sec. 6.3).

Synchronous versus asynchronous. We use these two terms to qualitatively refer to how tightly coupled in time two events are. If two events must happen at the same time, they are synchronous; otherwise they are asynchronous. For example, message passing (that is, communication between UEs by sending and receiving messages) is synchronous if a message sent must be received before the sender can continue. Message passing is asynchronous if the sender can continue its computation regardless of what happens at the receiver, or if the receiver can continue computations while waiting for a receive to complete.

Race conditions. A *race condition* is a kind of error peculiar to parallel programs. It occurs when the outcome of a program changes as the relative scheduling of UEs varies. Because the operating system and not the programmer controls the scheduling of the UEs, race conditions result in programs that potentially give different answers even when run on the same system with the same data. Race conditions are particularly difficult errors to debug because by their nature they cannot be reliably reproduced. Testing helps, but is not as effective as with sequential programs: A program may run correctly the first thousand times and then fail catastrophically on the thousand-and-first execution—and then run again correctly when the programmer attempts to reproduce the error as the first step in debugging.

Race conditions result from errors in synchronization. If multiple UEs read and write shared variables, the programmer must protect access to these shared variables so the reads and writes occur in a valid order regardless of how the tasks are interleaved. When many variables are shared or when they are accessed through multiple levels of indirection, verifying by inspection that no race conditions exist can be very difficult. Tools are available that help detect and fix race conditions, such as ThreadChecker from Intel Corporation, and the problem remains an area of active and important research [NM92].

Deadlocks. Deadlocks are another type of error peculiar to parallel programs. A deadlock occurs when there is a cycle of tasks in which each task is blocked waiting for another to proceed. Because all are waiting for another task to do something, they will all be blocked forever. As a simple example, consider two tasks in a message-passing environment. Task A attempts to receive a message from task B, after which A will reply by sending a message of its own to task B. Meanwhile, task B attempts to receive a message from task A, after which B will send a message to A. Because each task is waiting for the other to send it a message first, both tasks will be blocked forever. Fortunately, deadlocks are not difficult to discover, as the tasks will stop at the point of the deadlock.

2.5 A QUANTITATIVE LOOK AT PARALLEL COMPUTATION

The two main reasons for implementing a parallel program are to obtain better performance and to solve larger problems. Performance can be both modeled and measured, so in this section we will take a another look at parallel computations by giving some simple analytical models that illustrate some of the factors that influence the performance of a parallel program.

Consider a computation consisting of three parts: a setup section, a computation section, and a finalization section. The total running time of this program on one PE is then given as the sum of the times for the three parts.

$$T_{total}(1) = T_{setup} + T_{compute} + T_{finalization} \tag{2.1}$$

What happens when we run this computation on a parallel computer with multiple PEs? Suppose that the setup and finalization sections cannot be carried out concurrently with any other activities, but that the computation section could be divided into tasks that would run independently on as many PEs as are available, with the same total number of computation steps as in the original computation. The time for the full computation on P PEs can therefore be given by

$$T_{total}(P) = T_{setup} + \frac{T_{compute}(1)}{P} + T_{finalization} \tag{2.2}$$

Of course, Eq. 2.2 describes a very idealized situation. However, the idea that computations have a serial part (for which additional PEs are useless) and a parallelizable part (for which more PEs decrease the running time) is realistic. Thus, this simple model captures an important relationship.

An important measure of how much additional PEs help is the *relative speedup* S, which describes how much faster a problem runs in a way that normalizes away the actual running time.

$$S(P) = \frac{T_{total}(1)}{T_{total}(P)} \tag{2.3}$$

A related measure is the efficiency E, which is the speedup normalized by the number of PEs.

$$E(P) \quad = \quad \frac{S(P)}{P} \tag{2.4}$$

$$= \quad \frac{T_{total}(1)}{P \, T_{total}(P)} \tag{2.5}$$

Ideally, we would want the speedup to be equal to P, the number of PEs. This is sometimes called *perfect linear speedup*. Unfortunately, this is an ideal that can rarely be achieved because times for setup and finalization are not improved by adding more PEs, limiting the speedup. The terms that cannot be run concurrently are called the *serial terms*. Their running times represent some fraction of the total, called the *serial fraction*, denoted γ.

$$\gamma \quad = \quad \frac{T_{setup} + T_{finalization}}{T_{total}(1)} \tag{2.6}$$

The fraction of time spent in the parallelizable part of the program is then $(1 - \gamma)$. We can thus rewrite the expression for total computation time with P PEs as

$$T_{total}(P) = \gamma \, T_{total}(1) \quad + \quad \frac{(1 - \gamma) \, T_{total}(1)}{P} \tag{2.7}$$

Now, rewriting S in terms of the new expression for $T_{total}(P)$, we obtain the famous Amdahl's law:

$$S(P) \quad = \quad \frac{T_{total}(1)}{(\gamma + \frac{1-\gamma}{P}) \, T_{total}(1)} \tag{2.8}$$

$$= \quad \frac{1}{\gamma + \frac{1-\gamma}{P}} \tag{2.9}$$

Thus, in an ideal parallel algorithm with no overhead in the parallel part, the speedup should follow Eq. 2.9. What happens to the speedup if we take our ideal parallel algorithm and use a very large number of processors? Taking the limit as

P goes to infinity in our expression for S yields

$$S = \frac{1}{\gamma} \tag{2.10}$$

Eq. 2.10 thus gives an upper bound on the speedup obtainable in an algorithm whose serial part represents γ of the total computation.

These concepts are vital to the parallel algorithm designer. In designing a parallel algorithm, it is important to understand the value of the serial fraction so that realistic expectations can be set for performance. It may not make sense to implement a complex, arbitrarily scalable parallel algorithm if 10% or more of the algorithm is serial—and 10% is fairly common.

Of course, Amdahl's law is based on assumptions that may or may not be true in practice. In real life, a number of factors may make the actual running time longer than this formula implies. For example, creating additional parallel tasks may increase overhead and the chances of contention for shared resources. On the other hand, if the original serial computation is limited by resources other than the availability of CPU cycles, the actual performance could be much better than Amdahl's law would predict. For example, a large parallel machine may allow bigger problems to be held in memory, thus reducing virtual memory paging, or multiple processors each with its own cache may allow much more of the problem to remain in the cache. Amdahl's law also rests on the assumption that for any given input, the parallel and serial implementations perform exactly the same number of computational steps. If the serial algorithm being used in the formula is not the best possible algorithm for the problem, then a clever parallel algorithm that structures the computation differently can reduce the total number of computational steps.

It has also been observed [Gus88] that the exercise underlying Amdahl's law, namely running exactly the same problem with varying numbers of processors, is artificial in some circumstances. If, say, the parallel application were a weather simulation, then when new processors were added, one would most likely increase the problem size by adding more details to the model while keeping the total execution time constant. If this is the case, then Amdahl's law, or fixed-size speedup, gives a pessimistic view of the benefits of additional processors.

To see this, we can reformulate the equation to give the speedup in terms of performance on a P-processor system. Earlier in Eq. 2.2, we obtained the execution time for T processors, $T_{total}(P)$, from the execution time of the serial terms and the execution time of the parallelizable part when executed on one processor. Here, we do the opposite and obtain $T_{total}(1)$ from the serial and parallel terms when executed on P processors.

$$T_{total}(1) = T_{setup} + PT_{compute}(P) + T_{finalization} \tag{2.11}$$

Now, we define the so-called *scaled serial fraction*, denoted γ_{scaled}, as

$$\gamma_{scaled} = \frac{T_{setup} + T_{finalization}}{T_{total}(P)} \tag{2.12}$$

and then

$$T_{total}(1) = \gamma_{scaled}T_{total}(P) + P(1 - \gamma_{scaled})T_{total}(P) \qquad (2.13)$$

Rewriting the equation for speedup (Eq. 2.3) and simplifying, we obtain the scaled (or fixed-time) speedup.[1]

$$S(P) = P + (1 - P)\gamma_{scaled}. \qquad (2.14)$$

This gives exactly the same speedup as Amdahl's law, but allows a different question to be asked when the number of processors is increased. Since γ_{scaled} depends on P, the result of taking the limit isn't immediately obvious, but would give the same result as the limit in Amdahl's law. However, suppose we take the limit in P *while holding $T_{compute}$ and thus γ_{scaled} constant.* The interpretation is that we are increasing the size of the problem so that the total running time remains constant when more processors are added. (This contains the implicit assumption that the execution time of the serial terms does not change as the problem size grows.) In this case, the speedup is linear in P. Thus, while adding more processors to solve a fixed problem may hit the speedup limits of Amdahl's law with a relatively small number of processors, if the problem grows as more processors are added, Amdahl's law will be pessimistic. These two models of speedup, along with a fixed-memory version of speedup, are discussed in [SN90].

2.6   COMMUNICATION

2.6.1   Latency and Bandwidth

A simple but useful model characterizes the total time for message transfer as the sum of a fixed cost plus a variable cost that depends on the length of the message.

$$T_{message-transfer} = \alpha + \frac{N}{\beta} \qquad (2.15)$$

The fixed cost α is called *latency* and is essentially the time it takes to send an empty message over the communication medium, from the time the send routine is called to the time the data is received by the recipient. Latency (given in some appropriate time unit) includes overhead due to software and network hardware plus the time it takes for the message to traverse the communication medium. The *bandwidth β* (given in some measure of bytes per time unit) is a measure of the capacity of the communication medium. N is the length of the message.

The latency and bandwidth can vary significantly between systems depending on both the hardware used and the quality of the software implementing the communication protocols. Because these values can be measured with fairly simple benchmarks [DD97], it is sometimes worthwhile to measure values for α and β, as these can help guide optimizations to improve communication performance. For example, in a system in which α is relatively large, it might be worthwhile to try to

---

[1]This equation, sometimes known as Gustafson's law, was attributed in [Gus88] to E. Barsis.

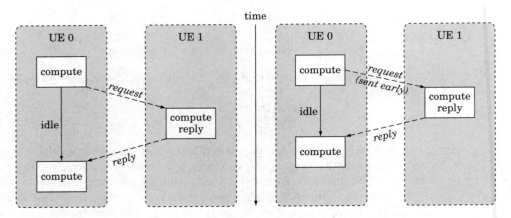

Figure 2.7: Communication without (left) and with (right) support for overlapping communication and computation. Although UE 0 in the computation on the right still has some idle time waiting for the reply from UE 1, the idle time is reduced and the computation requires less total time because of UE 1's earlier start.

restructure a program that sends many small messages to aggregate the communication into a few large messages instead. Data for several recent systems has been presented in [BBC+03].

2.6.2 Overlapping Communication and Computation and Latency Hiding

If we look more closely at the computation time within a single task on a single processor, it can roughly be decomposed into computation time, communication time, and idle time. The communication time is the time spent sending and receiving messages (and thus only applies to distributed-memory machines), whereas the idle time is time that no work is being done because the task is waiting for an event, such as the release of a resource held by another task.

A common situation in which a task may be idle is when it is waiting for a message to be transmitted through the system. This can occur when sending a message (as the UE waits for a reply before proceeding) or when receiving a message. Sometimes it is possible to eliminate this wait by restructuring the task to send the message and/or post the receive (that is, indicate that it wants to receive a message) and then continue the computation. This allows the programmer to overlap communication and computation. We show an example of this technique in Fig. 2.7. This style of message passing is more complicated for the programmer, because the programmer must take care to wait for the receive to complete after any work that can be overlapped with communication is completed.

Another technique used on many parallel computers is to assign multiple UEs to each PE, so that when one UE is waiting for communication, it will be possible to context-switch to another UE and keep the processor busy. This is an example of latency hiding. It is increasingly being used on modern high-performance computing systems, the most famous example being the MTA system from Cray Research [ACC+90].

2.7   SUMMARY

This chapter has given a brief overview of some of the concepts and vocabulary used in parallel computing. Additional terms are defined in the glossary. We also discussed the major programming environments in use for parallel computing: OpenMP, MPI, and Java. Throughout the book, we will use these three programming environments for our examples. More details about OpenMP, MPI, and Java and how to use them to write parallel programs are provided in the appendixes.

CHAPTER 3

The *Finding Concurrency* Design Space

3.1 ABOUT THE DESIGN SPACE
3.2 THE *TASK DECOMPOSITION* PATTERN
3.3 THE *DATA DECOMPOSITION* PATTERN
3.4 THE *GROUP TASKS* PATTERN
3.5 THE *ORDER TASKS* PATTERN
3.6 THE *DATA SHARING* PATTERN
3.7 THE *DESIGN EVALUATION* PATTERN
3.8 SUMMARY

3.1 ABOUT THE DESIGN SPACE

The software designer works in a number of domains. The design process starts in the *problem domain* with design elements directly relevant to the problem being solved (for example, fluid flows, decision trees, atoms, etc.). The ultimate aim of the design is software, so at some point, the design elements change into ones relevant to a program (for example, data structures and software modules). We call this the *program domain*. Although it is often tempting to move into the program domain as soon as possible, a designer who moves out of the problem domain too soon may miss valuable design options.

This is particularly relevant in parallel programming. Parallel programs attempt to solve bigger problems in less time by simultaneously solving different parts of the problem on different processing elements. This can only work, however, if the problem contains exploitable concurrency, that is, multiple activities or *tasks* that can execute at the same time. After a problem has been mapped onto the program domain, however, it can be difficult to see opportunities to exploit concurrency.

Hence, programmers should start their design of a parallel solution by analyzing the problem within the problem domain to expose exploitable concurrency. We call the design space in which this analysis is carried out the *Finding Concurrency* design space. The patterns in this design space will help identify and analyze the exploitable concurrency in a problem. After this is done, one or more patterns from the *Algorithm Structure* space can be chosen to help design the appropriate algorithm structure to exploit the identified concurrency.

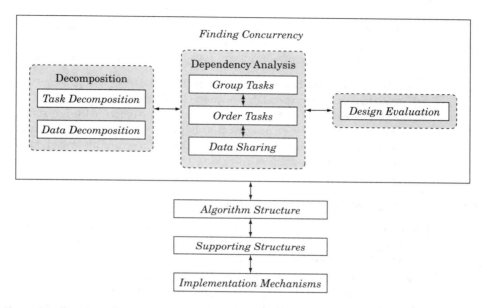

Figure 3.1: Overview of the *Finding Concurrency* design space and its place in the pattern language

An overview of this design space and its place in the pattern language is shown in Fig. 3.1.

Experienced designers working in a familiar domain may see the exploitable concurrency immediately and could move directly to the patterns in the *Algorithm Structure* design space.

3.1.1 Overview

Before starting to work with the patterns in this design space, the algorithm designer must first consider the problem to be solved and make sure the effort to create a parallel program will be justified: Is the problem large enough and the results significant enough to justify expending effort to solve it faster? If so, the next step is to make sure the key features and data elements within the problem are well understood. Finally, the designer needs to understand which parts of the problem are most computationally intensive, because the effort to parallelize the problem should be focused on those parts.

After this analysis is complete, the patterns in the *Finding Concurrency* design space can be used to start designing a parallel algorithm. The patterns in this design space can be organized into three groups.

- **Decomposition Patterns.** The two decomposition patterns, *Task Decomposition* and *Data Decomposition,* are used to decompose the problem into pieces that can execute concurrently.

- **Dependency Analysis Patterns.** This group contains three patterns that help group the tasks and analyze the dependencies among them: *Group Tasks,*

Order Tasks, and *Data Sharing.* Nominally, the patterns are applied in this order. In practice, however, it is often necessary to work back and forth between them, or possibly even revisit the decomposition patterns.

- ***Design Evaluation* Pattern.** The final pattern in this space guides the algorithm designer through an analysis of what has been done so far before moving on to the patterns in the *Algorithm Structure* design space. This pattern is important because it often happens that the best design is not found on the first attempt, and the earlier design flaws are identified, the easier they are to correct. In general, working through the patterns in this space is an iterative process.

3.1.2   Using the Decomposition Patterns

The first step in designing a parallel algorithm is to decompose the problem into elements that can execute concurrently. We can think of this decomposition as occurring in two dimensions.

- The *task-decomposition dimension* views the problem as a stream of instructions that can be broken into sequences called *tasks* that can execute simultaneously. For the computation to be efficient, the operations that make up the task should be largely independent of the operations taking place inside other tasks.

- The *data-decomposition dimension* focuses on the data required by the tasks and how it can be decomposed into distinct chunks. The computation associated with the data chunks will only be efficient if the data chunks can be operated upon relatively independently.

Viewing the problem decomposition in terms of two distinct dimensions is somewhat artificial. A task decomposition implies a data decomposition and vice versa; hence, the two decompositions are really different facets of the same fundamental decomposition. We divide them into separate dimensions, however, because a problem decomposition usually proceeds most naturally by emphasizing one dimension of the decomposition over the other. By making them distinct, we make this design emphasis explicit and easier for the designer to understand.

3.1.3   Background for Examples

In this section, we give background information on some of the examples that are used in several patterns. It can be skipped for the time being and revisited later when reading a pattern that refers to one of the examples.

Medical imaging.   PET (Positron Emission Tomography) scans provide an important diagnostic tool by allowing physicians to observe how a radioactive substance propagates through a patient's body. Unfortunately, the images formed from the distribution of emitted radiation are of low resolution, due in part to the scattering of the radiation as it passes through the body. It is also difficult to reason from the absolute radiation intensities, because different pathways through the body attenuate the radiation differently.

To solve this problem, models of how radiation propagates through the body are used to correct the images. A common approach is to build a Monte Carlo model, as described by Ljungberg and King [LK98]. Randomly selected points within the body are assumed to emit radiation (usually a gamma ray), and the trajectory of each ray is followed. As a particle (ray) passes through the body, it is attenuated by the different organs it traverses, continuing until the particle leaves the body and hits a camera model, thereby defining a full trajectory. To create a statistically significant simulation, thousands, if not millions, of trajectories are followed.

This problem can be parallelized in two ways. Because each trajectory is independent, it is possible to parallelize the application by associating each trajectory with a task. This approach is discussed in the Examples section of the *Task Decomposition* pattern. Another approach would be to partition the body into sections and assign different sections to different processing elements. This approach is discussed in the Examples section of the *Data Decomposition* pattern.

Linear algebra.   Linear algebra is an important tool in applied mathematics: It provides the machinery required to analyze solutions of large systems of linear equations. The classic linear algebra problem asks, for matrix A and vector b, what values for x will solve the equation

$$A \cdot x = b \qquad (3.1)$$

The matrix A in Eq. 3.1 takes on a central role in linear algebra. Many problems are expressed in terms of transformations of this matrix. These transformations are applied by means of a matrix multiplication

$$C = T \cdot A \qquad (3.2)$$

If T, A, and C are square matrices of order N, matrix multiplication is defined such that each element of the resulting matrix C is

$$C_{i,j} = \sum_{k=0}^{N-1} T_{i,k} \cdot A_{k,j} \qquad (3.3)$$

where the subscripts denote particular elements of the matrices. In other words, the element of the product matrix C in row i and column j is the dot product of the i-th row of T and the j-th column of A. Hence, computing each of the N^2 elements of C requires N multiplications and $N - 1$ additions, making the overall complexity of matrix multiplication $O(N^3)$.

There are many ways to parallelize a matrix multiplication operation. It can be parallelized using either a task-based decomposition (as discussed in the Examples section of the *Task Decomposition* pattern) or a data-based decomposition (as discussed in the Examples section of the *Data Decomposition* pattern).

Molecular dynamics.   Molecular dynamics is used to simulate the motions of a large molecular system. For example, molecular dynamics simulations show how a large protein moves around and how differently shaped drugs might interact with the protein. Not surprisingly, molecular dynamics is extremely important in the pharmaceutical industry. It is also a useful test problem for computer scientists working on parallel computing: It is straightforward to understand, relevant to science at large, and difficult to parallelize effectively. As a result, it has been the subject of much research [Mat94, PH95, Pli95].

The basic idea is to treat a molecule as a large collection of balls connected by springs. The balls represent the atoms in the molecule, while the springs represent the chemical bonds between the atoms. The molecular dynamics simulation itself is an explicit time-stepping process. At each time step, the force on each atom is computed and then standard classical mechanics techniques are used to compute how the force moves the atoms. This process is carried out repeatedly to step through time and compute a trajectory for the molecular system.

The forces due to the chemical bonds (the "springs") are relatively simple to compute. These correspond to the vibrations and rotations of the chemical bonds themselves. These are short-range forces that can be computed with knowledge of the handful of atoms that share chemical bonds. The major difficulty arises because the atoms have partial electrical charges. Hence, while atoms only interact with a small neighborhood of atoms through their chemical bonds, the electrical charges cause every atom to apply a force on every other atom.

This is the famous N-body problem. On the order of N^2 terms must be computed to find these nonbonded forces. Because N is large (tens or hundreds of thousands) and the number of time steps in a simulation is huge (tens of thousands), the time required to compute these nonbonded forces dominates the computation. Several ways have been proposed to reduce the effort required to solve the N-body problem. We are only going to discuss the simplest one: the *cutoff method*.

The idea is simple. Even though each atom exerts a force on every other atom, this force decreases with the square of the distance between the atoms. Hence, it should be possible to pick a distance beyond which the force contribution is so small that it can be ignored. By ignoring the atoms that exceed this cutoff, the problem is reduced to one that scales as $O(N \times n)$, where n is the number of atoms within the cutoff volume, usually hundreds. The computation is still huge, and it dominates the overall runtime for the simulation, but at least the problem is tractable.

There are a host of details, but the basic simulation can be summarized as in Fig. 3.2.

The primary data structures hold the atomic positions (`atoms`), the velocities of each atom (`velocity`), the forces exerted on each atom (`forces`), and lists of atoms within the cutoff distance of each atoms (`neighbors`). The program itself is a time-stepping loop, in which each iteration computes the short-range force terms, updates the neighbor lists, and then finds the nonbonded forces. After the force on each atom has been computed, a simple ordinary differential equation is solved to update the positions and velocities. Physical properties based on atomic motions are then updated, and we go to the next time step.

There are many ways to parallelize the molecular dynamics problem. We consider the most common approach, starting with the task decomposition (discussed

```
Int const N // number of atoms

Array of Real :: atoms (3,N) //3D coordinates
Array of Real :: velocities (3,N) //velocity vector
Array of Real :: forces (3,N) //force in each dimension
Array of List :: neighbors(N) //atoms in cutoff volume

loop over time steps
    vibrational_forces (N, atoms, forces)
    rotational_forces (N, atoms, forces)
    neighbor_list (N, atoms, neighbors)
    non_bonded_forces (N, atoms, neighbors, forces)
    update_atom_positions_and_velocities(
                  N, atoms, velocities, forces)
    physical_properties ( ... Lots of stuff ... )
end loop
```

Figure 3.2: Pseudocode for the molecular dynamics example

in the *Task Decomposition* pattern) and following with the associated data decomposition (discussed in the *Data Decomposition* pattern). This example shows how the two decompositions fit together to guide the design of the parallel algorithm.

 ## 3.2   THE *TASK DECOMPOSITION* PATTERN

Problem

How can a problem be decomposed into tasks that can execute concurrently?

Context

Every parallel algorithm design starts from the same point, namely a good understanding of the problem being solved. The programmer must understand which are the computationally intensive parts of the problem, the key data structures, and how the data is used as the problem's solution unfolds.

The next step is to define the tasks that make up the problem and the data decomposition implied by the tasks. Fundamentally, every parallel algorithm involves a collection of tasks that can execute concurrently. The challenge is to find these tasks and craft an algorithm that lets them run concurrently.

In some cases, the problem will naturally break down into a collection of independent (or nearly independent) tasks, and it is easiest to start with a *task-based decomposition*. In other cases, the tasks are difficult to isolate and the decomposition of the data (as discussed in the *Data Decomposition* pattern) is a better starting point. It is not always clear which approach is best, and often the algorithm designer needs to consider both.

Regardless of whether the starting point is a task-based or a data-based decomposition, however, a parallel algorithm ultimately needs tasks that will execute concurrently, so these tasks must be identified.

Forces

The main forces influencing the design at this point are flexibility, efficiency, and simplicity.

- **Flexibility.** Flexibility in the design will allow it to be adapted to different implementation requirements. For example, it is usually not a good idea to narrow the options to a single computer system or style of programming at this stage of the design.

- **Efficiency.** A parallel program is only useful if it scales efficiently with the size of the parallel computer (in terms of reduced runtime and/or memory utilization). For a task decomposition, this means we need enough tasks to keep all the PEs busy, with enough work per task to compensate for overhead incurred to manage dependencies. However, the drive for efficiency can lead to complex decompositions that lack flexibility.

- **Simplicity.** The task decomposition needs to be complex enough to get the job done, but simple enough to let the program be debugged and maintained with reasonable effort.

Solution

The key to an effective task decomposition is to ensure that the tasks are sufficiently independent so that managing dependencies takes only a small fraction of the program's overall execution time. It is also important to ensure that the execution of the tasks can be evenly distributed among the ensemble of PEs (the load-balancing problem).

In an ideal world, the compiler would find the tasks for the programmer. Unfortunately, this almost never happens. Instead, it must usually be done by hand based on knowledge of the problem and the code required to solve it. In some cases, it might be necessary to completely recast the problem into a form that exposes relatively independent tasks.

In a task-based decomposition, we look at the problem as a collection of distinct tasks, paying particular attention to

- The actions that are carried out to solve the problem. (Are there enough of them to keep the processing elements on the target machines busy?)

- Whether these actions are distinct and relatively independent.

As a first pass, we try to identify as many tasks as possible; it is much easier to start with too many tasks and merge them later on than to start with too few tasks and later try to split them.

Tasks can be found in many different places.

- In some cases, each task corresponds to a distinct call to a function. Defining a task for each function call leads to what is sometimes called a functional decomposition.

- Another place to find tasks is in distinct iterations of the loops within an algorithm. If the iterations are independent and there are enough of them, then it might work well to base a task decomposition on mapping each iteration onto a task. This style of task-based decomposition leads to what are sometimes called loop-splitting algorithms.

- Tasks also play a key role in data-driven decompositions. In this case, a large data structure is decomposed and multiple units of execution concurrently update different chunks of the data structure. In this case, the tasks are those updates on individual chunks.

Also keep in mind the forces given in the Forces section:

- **Flexibility.** The design needs to be flexible in the number of tasks generated. Usually this is done by parameterizing the number and size of tasks on some appropriate dimension. This will let the design be adapted to a wide range of parallel computers with different numbers of processors.

- **Efficiency.** There are two major efficiency issues to consider in the task decomposition. First, each task must include enough work to compensate for the overhead incurred by creating the tasks and managing their dependencies. Second, the number of tasks should be large enough so that all the units of execution are busy with useful work throughout the computation.

- **Simplicity.** Tasks should be defined in a way that makes debugging and maintenance simple. When possible, tasks should be defined so they reuse code from existing sequential programs that solve related problems.

After the tasks have been identified, the next step is to look at the data decomposition implied by the tasks. The *Data Decomposition* pattern may help with this analysis.

Examples

Medical imaging.   Consider the medical imaging problem described in Sec. 3.1.3. In this application, a point inside a model of the body is selected randomly, a radioactive decay is allowed to occur at this point, and the trajectory of the emitted particle is followed. To create a statistically significant simulation, thousands, if not millions, of trajectories are followed.

It is natural to associate a task with each trajectory. These tasks are particularly simple to manage concurrently because they are completely independent. Furthermore, there are large numbers of trajectories, so there will be many tasks, making this decomposition suitable for a large range of computer systems, from a shared-memory system with a small number of processing elements to a large cluster with hundreds of processing elements.

With the basic tasks defined, we now consider the corresponding data decomposition—that is, we define the data associated with each task. Each task needs to hold the information defining the trajectory. But that is not all: The tasks need access to the model of the body as well. Although it might not be apparent from our description of the problem, the body model can be extremely large. Because it is a read-only model, this is no problem if there is an effective shared-memory system; each task can read data as needed. If the target platform is based on a distributed-memory architecture, however, the body model will need to be replicated on each PE. This can be very time-consuming and can waste a great deal of memory. For systems with small memories per PE and/or with slow networks between PEs, a decomposition of the problem based on the body model might be more effective.

This is a common situation in parallel programming: Many problems can be decomposed primarily in terms of data or primarily in terms of tasks. If a task-based decomposition avoids the need to break up and distribute complex data structures, it will be a much simpler program to write and debug. On the other hand, if memory and/or network bandwidth is a limiting factor, a decomposition that focuses on the data might be more effective. It is not so much a matter of one approach being "better" than another as a matter of balancing the needs of the machine with the needs of the programmer. We discuss this in more detail in the *Data Decomposition* pattern.

Matrix multiplication. Consider the multiplication of two matrices $(C = A \cdot B)$, as described in Sec. 3.1.3. We can produce a task-based decomposition of this problem by considering the calculation of each element of the product matrix as a separate task. Each task needs access to one row of A and one column of B. This decomposition has the advantage that all the tasks are independent, and because all the data that is shared among tasks (A and B) is read-only, it will be straightforward to implement in a shared-memory environment.

The performance of this algorithm, however, would be poor. Consider the case where the three matrices are square and of order N. For each element of C, N elements from A and N elements from B would be required, resulting in $2N$ memory references for N multiply/add operations. Memory access time is slow compared to floating-point arithmetic, so the bandwidth of the memory subsystem would limit the performance.

A better approach would be to design an algorithm that maximizes reuse of data loaded into a processor's caches. We can arrive at this algorithm in two different ways. First, we could group together the elementwise tasks we defined earlier so the tasks that use similar elements of the A and B matrices run on the same UE (see the *Group Tasks* pattern). Alternatively, we could start with the data decomposition and design the algorithm from the beginning around the way the matrices fit into the caches. We discuss this example further in the Examples section of the *Data Decomposition* pattern.

Molecular dynamics. Consider the molecular dynamics problem described in Sec. 3.1.3. Pseudocode for this example is shown again in Fig. 3.3.

Before performing the task decomposition, we need to better understand some details of the problem. First, the `neighbor_list()` computation is time-consuming.

```
Int const N // number of atoms

Array of Real :: atoms (3,N) //3D coordinates
Array of Real :: velocities (3,N) //velocity vector
Array of Real :: forces (3,N) //force in each dimension
Array of List :: neighbors(N) //atoms in cutoff volume

loop over time steps
    vibrational_forces (N, atoms, forces)
    rotational_forces (N, atoms, forces)
    neighbor_list (N, atoms, neighbors)
    non_bonded_forces (N, atoms, neighbors, forces)
    update_atom_positions_and_velocities(
                    N, atoms, velocities, forces)
    physical_properties ( ... Lots of stuff ... )
end loop
```

Figure 3.3: Pseudocode for the molecular dynamics example

The gist of the computation is a loop over each atom, inside of which every other atom is checked to determine whether it falls within the indicated cutoff volume. Fortunately, the time steps are very small, and the atoms don't move very much in any given time step. Hence, this time-consuming computation is only carried out every 10 to 100 steps.

Second, the `physical_properties()` function computes energies, correlation coefficients, and a host of interesting physical properties. These computations, however, are simple and do not significantly affect the program's overall runtime, so we will ignore them in this discussion.

Because the bulk of the computation time will be in `non_bonded_forces()`, we must pick a problem decomposition that makes that computation run efficiently in parallel. The problem is made easier by the fact that each of the functions inside the time loop has a similar structure: In the sequential version, each function includes a loop over atoms to compute contributions to the force vector. Thus, a natural task definition is the update required by each atom, which corresponds to a loop iteration in the sequential version. After performing the task decomposition, therefore, we obtain the following tasks.

- Tasks that find the vibrational forces on an atom

- Tasks that find the rotational forces on an atom

- Tasks that find the nonbonded forces on an atom

- Tasks that update the position and velocity of an atom

- A task to update the neighbor list for all the atoms (which we will leave sequential)

With our collection of tasks in hand, we can consider the accompanying data decomposition. The key data structures are the neighbor list, the atomic coordinates, the atomic velocities, and the force vector. Every iteration that updates the force vector needs the coordinates of a neighborhood of atoms. The computation of nonbonded forces, however, potentially needs the coordinates of all the atoms, because the molecule being simulated might fold back on itself in unpredictable ways. We will use this information to carry out the data decomposition (in the *Data Decomposition* pattern) and the data-sharing analysis (in the *Data Sharing* pattern).

Known uses.   Task-based decompositions are extremely common in parallel computing. For example, the distance geometry code DGEOM [Mat96] uses a task-based decomposition, as does the parallel WESDYN molecular dynamics program [MR95].

 3.3   THE *DATA DECOMPOSITION* PATTERN

Problem

How can a problem's data be decomposed into units that can be operated on relatively independently?

Context

The parallel algorithm designer must have a detailed understanding of the problem being solved. In addition, the designer should identify the most computationally intensive parts of the problem, the key data structures required to solve the problem, and how data is used as the problem's solution unfolds.

After the basic problem is understood, the parallel algorithm designer should consider the tasks that make up the problem and the data decomposition implied by the tasks. Both the task and data decompositions need to be addressed to create a parallel algorithm. The question is not which decomposition to do. The question is which one to start with. A data-based decomposition is a good starting point if the following is true.

- The most computationally intensive part of the problem is organized around the manipulation of a large data structure.

- Similar operations are being applied to different parts of the data structure, in such a way that the different parts can be operated on relatively independently.

For example, many linear algebra problems update large matrices, applying a similar set of operations to each element of the matrix. In these cases, it is straightforward to drive the parallel algorithm design by looking at how the matrix can be broken up into blocks that are updated concurrently. The task definitions then follow from how the blocks are defined and mapped onto the processing elements of the parallel computer.

Forces

The main forces influencing the design at this point are flexibility, efficiency, and simplicity.

- **Flexibility.** Flexibility will allow the design to be adapted to different implementation requirements. For example, it is usually not a good idea to narrow the options to a single computer system or style of programming at this stage of the design.

- **Efficiency.** A parallel program is only useful if it scales efficiently with the size of the parallel computer (in terms of reduced runtime and/or memory utilization).

- **Simplicity.** The decomposition needs to be complex enough to get the job done, but simple enough to let the program be debugged and maintained with reasonable effort.

Solution

In shared-memory programming environments such as OpenMP, the data decomposition will frequently be implied by the task decomposition. In most cases, however, the decomposition will need to be done by hand, because the memory is physically distributed, because data dependencies are too complex without explicitly decomposing the data, or to achieve acceptable efficiency on a NUMA computer.

If a task-based decomposition has already been done, the data decomposition is driven by the needs of each task. If well-defined and distinct data can be associated with each task, the decomposition should be simple.

When starting with a data decomposition, however, we need to look not at the tasks, but at the central data structures defining the problem and consider whether they can they be broken down into chunks that can be operated on concurrently. A few common examples include the following.

- **Array-based computations.** Concurrency can be defined in terms of updates of different segments of the array. If the array is multidimensional, it can be decomposed in a variety of ways (rows, columns, or blocks of varying shapes).

- **Recursive data structures.** We can think of, for example, decomposing the parallel update of a large tree data structure by decomposing the data structure into subtrees that can be updated concurrently.

Regardless of the nature of the underlying data structure, if the data decomposition is the primary factor driving the solution to the problem, it serves as the organizing principle of the parallel algorithm.

When considering how to decompose the problem's data structures, keep in mind the competing forces.

- **Flexibility.** The size and number of data chunks should be flexible to support the widest range of parallel systems. One approach is to define chunks whose size and number are controlled by a small number of parameters. These parameters define *granularity knobs* that can be varied to modify the size of the data chunks to match the needs of the underlying hardware. (Note, however, that many designs are not infinitely adaptable with respect to granularity.)

  The easiest place to see the impact of granularity on the data decomposition is in the overhead required to manage dependencies between chunks. The time required to manage dependencies must be small compared to the overall runtime. In a good data decomposition, the dependencies scale at a lower dimension than the computational effort associated with each chunk. For example, in many finite difference programs, the cells at the boundaries between chunks, that is, the surfaces of the chunks, must be shared. The size of the set of dependent cells scales as the surface area, while the effort required in the computation scales as the volume of the chunk. This means that the computational effort can be scaled (based on the chunk's volume) to offset overheads associated with data dependencies (based on the surface area of the chunk).

- **Efficiency.** It is important that the data chunks be large enough that the amount of work to update the chunk offsets the overhead of managing dependencies. A more subtle issue to consider is how the chunks map onto UEs. An effective parallel algorithm must balance the load between UEs. If this isn't done well, some PEs might have a disproportionate amount of work, and the overall scalability will suffer. This may require clever ways to break up the problem. For example, if the problem clears the columns in a matrix from left to right, a column mapping of the matrix will cause problems as the UEs with the leftmost columns will finish their work before the others. A row-based block decomposition or even a block-cyclic decomposition (in which rows are assigned cyclically to PEs) would do a much better job of keeping all the processors fully occupied. These issues are discussed in more detail in the *Distributed Array* pattern.

- **Simplicity.** Overly complex data decompositions can be very difficult to debug. A data decomposition will usually require a mapping of a global index space onto a task-local index space. Making this mapping abstract allows it to be easily isolated and tested.

After the data has been decomposed, if it has not already been done, the next step is to look at the task decomposition implied by the tasks. The *Task Decomposition* pattern may help with this analysis.

Examples

Medical imaging.   Consider the medical imaging problem described in Sec. 3.1.3. In this application, a point inside a model of the body is selected randomly, a radioactive decay is allowed to occur at this point, and the trajectory of the emitted particle is followed. To create a statistically significant simulation, thousands if not millions of trajectories are followed.

In a data-based decomposition of this problem, the body model is the large central data structure around which the computation can be organized. The model is broken into segments, and one or more segments are associated with each processing element. The body segments are only read, not written, during the trajectory computations, so there are no data dependencies created by the decomposition of the body model.

After the data has been decomposed, we need to look at the tasks associated with each data segment. In this case, each trajectory passing through the data segment defines a task. The trajectories are initiated and propagated within a segment. When a segment boundary is encountered, the trajectory must be passed between segments. It is this transfer that defines the dependencies between data chunks.

On the other hand, in a task-based approach to this problem (as discussed in the *Task Decomposition* pattern), the trajectories for each particle drive the algorithm design. Each PE potentially needs to access the full body model to service its set of trajectories. In a shared-memory environment, this is easy because the body model is a read-only data set. In a distributed-memory environment, however, this would require substantial startup overhead as the body model is broadcast across the system.

This is a common situation in parallel programming: Different points of view lead to different algorithms with potentially very different performance characteristics. The task-based algorithm is simple, but it only works if each processing element has access to a large memory and if the overhead incurred loading the data into memory is insignificant compared to the program's runtime. An algorithm driven by a data decomposition, on the other hand, makes efficient use of memory and (in distributed-memory environments) less use of network bandwidth, but it incurs more communication overhead during the concurrent part of computation and is significantly more complex. Choosing which is the appropriate approach can be difficult and is discussed further in the *Design Evaluation* pattern.

Matrix multiplication.   Consider the standard multiplication of two matrices ($C = A \cdot B$), as described in Sec. 3.1.3. Several data-based decompositions are possible for this problem. A straightforward one would be to decompose the product matrix C into a set of row blocks (set of adjacent rows). From the definition of matrix multiplication, computing the elements of a row block of C requires the full A matrix, but only the corresponding row block of B. With such a data decomposition, the basic task in the algorithm becomes the computation of the elements in a row block of C.

An even more effective approach that does not require the replication of the full A matrix is to decompose all three matrices into submatrices or blocks. The basic task then becomes the update of a C block, with the A and B blocks being cycled among the tasks as the computation proceeds. This decomposition, however, is much more complex to program; communication and computation must be carefully coordinated during the most time-critical portions of the problem. We discuss this example further in the *Geometric Decomposition* and *Distributed Array* patterns.

One of the features of the matrix multiplication problem is that the ratio of floating-point operations ($O(N^3)$) to memory references ($O(N^2)$) is small. This implies that it is especially important to take into account the memory access patterns to maximize reuse of data from the cache. The most effective approach is to use the block (submatrix) decomposition and adjust the size of the blocks so the problems fit into cache. We could arrive at the same algorithm by carefully grouping together the elementwise tasks that were identified in the Examples section of the *Task Decomposition* pattern, but starting with a data decomposition and assigning a task to update each submatrix seems easier to understand.

Molecular dynamics. Consider the molecular dynamics problem described in Sec. 3.1.3 and in the Examples section of the *Task Decomposition* pattern. This problem naturally breaks down into a task decomposition with a task being an iteration of the loop over atoms in each of the force computation routines.

Summarizing our problem and its task decomposition, we have the following:

- Tasks that find the vibrational forces on an atom

- Tasks that find the rotational forces on an atom

- Tasks that find the nonbonded forces on an atom

- Tasks that update the position and velocity of an atom

- A task to update the neighbor list for all the atoms (which we will leave sequential)

The key data structures are

- An array of atom coordinates, one element per atom

- An array of atom velocities, one element per atom

- An array of lists, one per atom, each defining the neighborhood of atoms within the cutoff distance of the atom

- An array of forces on atoms, one element per atom

An element of the velocity array is used only by the task owning the corresponding atom. This data does not need to be shared and can remain local to the task. Every task, however, needs access to the full array of coordinates. Thus, it will make sense to replicate this data in a distributed-memory environment or share it among UEs in a shared-memory environment.

More interesting is the array of forces. From Newton's third law, the force from atom i on atom j is the negative of the force from atom j on atom i. We can exploit this symmetry to cut the amount of computation in half as we accumulate the force terms. The values in the force array are not in the computation until the last steps in which the coordinates and velocities are updated. Therefore, the approach used is to initialize the entire force array on each PE and have the tasks accumulate partial sums of the force terms into this array. After all the partial force terms have completed, we sum all the PEs' arrays together to provide the final force array. We discuss this further in the *Data Sharing* pattern.

Known uses. Data decompositions are very common in parallel scientific computing. The parallel linear algebra library ScaLAPACK [Sca, BCC+97] uses block-based decompositions. The PLAPACK environment [vdG97] for dense linear algebra problems uses a slightly different approach to data decomposition. If, for example, an equation of the form $y = Ax$ appears, instead of first partitioning matrix A, the vectors y and x are partitioned in a natural way and then the induced partition on A is determined. The authors report better performance and easier implementation with this approach.

The data decomposition used in our molecular dynamics example is described by Mattson and Ravishanker [MR95]. More sophisticated data decompositions for this problem that scale better for large numbers of nodes are discussed by Plimpton and Hendrickson [PH95, Pli95].

3.4   THE *GROUP TASKS* PATTERN

Problem

How can the tasks that make up a problem be grouped to simplify the job of managing dependencies?

Context

This pattern can be applied after the corresponding task and data decompositions have been identified as discussed in the *Task Decomposition* and *Data Decomposition* patterns.

This pattern describes the first step in analyzing dependencies among the tasks within a problem's decomposition. In developing the problem's task decomposition, we thought in terms of tasks that can execute concurrently. While we did not emphasize it during the task decomposition, it is clear that these tasks do not constitute a flat set. For example, tasks derived from the same high-level operation in the algorithm are naturally grouped together. Other tasks may not be related in terms of the original problem but have similar constraints on their concurrent execution and can thus be grouped together.

In short, there is considerable structure to the set of tasks. These structures—these groupings of tasks—simplify a problem's dependency analysis. If a group shares a temporal constraint (for example, waiting on one group to finish filling a file before another group can begin reading it), we can satisfy that constraint once for the whole group. If a group of tasks must work together on a shared data structure, the required synchronization can be worked out once for the whole group.

If a set of tasks are independent, combining them into a single group and scheduling them for execution as a single large group can simplify the design and increase the available concurrency (thereby letting the solution scale to more PEs).

In each case, the idea is to define groups of tasks that share constraints and simplify the problem of managing constraints by dealing with groups rather than individual tasks.

Solution

Constraints among tasks fall into a few major categories.

- The easiest dependency to understand is a temporal dependency—that is, a constraint on the order in which a collection of tasks executes. If task A depends on the results of task B, for example, then task A must wait until task B completes before it can execute. We can usually think of this case in terms of data flow: Task A is blocked waiting for the data to be ready from task B; when B completes, the data flows into A. In some cases, A can begin computing as soon as data starts to flow from B (for example, pipeline algorithms as described in the *Pipeline* pattern).

- Another type of ordering constraint occurs when a collection of tasks must run at the same time. For example, in many data-parallel problems, the original problem domain is divided into multiple regions that can be updated in parallel. Typically, the update of any given region requires information about the boundaries of its neighboring regions. If all of the regions are not processed at the same time, the parallel program could stall or deadlock as some regions wait for data from inactive regions.

- In some cases, tasks in a group are truly independent of each other. These tasks do not have an ordering constraint among them. This is an important feature of a set of tasks because it means they can execute in any order, including concurrently, and it is important to clearly note when this holds.

The goal of this pattern is to group tasks based on these constraints, because of the following.

- By grouping tasks, we simplify the establishment of partial orders between tasks, since ordering constraints can be applied to groups rather than to individual tasks.

- Grouping tasks makes it easier to identify which tasks must execute concurrently.

For a given problem and decomposition, there may be many ways to group tasks. The goal is to pick a grouping of tasks that simplifies the dependency analysis. To clarify this point, think of the dependency analysis as finding and satisfying constraints on the concurrent execution of a program. When tasks share a set of constraints, it simplifies the dependency analysis to group them together.

There is no single way to find task groups. We suggest the following approach, keeping in mind that while one cannot think about task groups without considering the constraints themselves, at this point in the design, it is best to do so as abstractly as possible—identify the constraints and group tasks to help resolve them, but try not to get bogged down in the details.

- First, look at how the original problem was decomposed. In most cases, a high-level operation (for example, solving a matrix) or a large iterative program structure (for example, a loop) plays a key role in defining the decomposition. This is the first place to look for grouping tasks. The tasks that correspond to a high-level operation naturally group together.

    At this point, there may be many small groups of tasks. In the next step, we will look at the constraints shared between the tasks within a group. If the tasks share a constraint—usually in terms of the update of a shared data structure—keep them as a distinct group. The algorithm design will need to ensure that these tasks execute at the same time. For example, many problems involve the coordinated update of a shared data structure by a set of tasks. If these tasks do not run concurrently, the program could deadlock.

- Next, we ask if any other task groups share the same constraint. If so, merge the groups together. Large task groups provide additional concurrency to keep more PEs busy and also provide extra flexibility in scheduling the execution of the tasks, thereby making it easier to balance the load between PEs (that is, ensure that each of the PEs spends approximately the same amount of time working on the problem).

- The next step is to look at constraints between groups of tasks. This is easy when groups have a clear temporal ordering or when a distinct chain of data moves between groups. The more complex case, however, is when otherwise independent task groups share constraints between groups. In these cases, it can be useful to merge these into a larger group of independent tasks—once again because large task groups usually make for more scheduling flexibility and better scalability.

Examples

Molecular dynamics.   This problem was described in Sec. 3.1.3, and we discussed its decomposition in the *Task Decomposition* and *Data Decomposition* patterns. We identified the following tasks:

- Tasks that find the vibrational forces on an atom

- Tasks that find the rotational forces on an atom

- Tasks that find the nonbonded forces on an atom

- Tasks that update the position and velocity of an atom

- A task to update the neighbor list for all the atoms (a single task because we have decided to leave this part of the computation sequential)

Consider how these can be grouped together. As a first pass, each item in the previous list corresponds to a high-level operation in the original problem and defines a task group. If we were to dig deeper into the problem, however, we would see that in each case the updates implied in the force functions are independent. The only dependency is the summation of the forces into a single force array.

We next want to see if we can merge any of these groups. Going down the list, the tasks in first two groups are independent but share the same constraints. In both cases, coordinates for a small neighborhood of atoms are read and local contributions are made to the force array, so we can merge these into a single group for bonded interactions. The other groups have distinct temporal or ordering constraints and therefore should not be merged.

Matrix multiplication.   In the Examples section of the *Task Decomposition* pattern we discuss decomposing the matrix multiplication $C = A \cdot B$ into tasks, each corresponding to the update of one element in C. The memory organization of most modern computers, however, favors larger-grained tasks such as updating a block of C, as described in the Examples section of the *Data Decomposition* pattern. Mathematically, this is equivalent to grouping the elementwise update tasks into groups corresponding to blocks, and grouping the tasks this way is well suited to an optimum utilization of system memory.

3.5   THE *ORDER TASKS* PATTERN

Problem

Given a way of decomposing a problem into tasks and a way of collecting these tasks into logically related groups, how must these groups of tasks be ordered to satisfy constraints among tasks?

Context

This pattern constitutes the second step in analyzing dependencies among the tasks of a problem decomposition. The first step, addressed in the *Group Tasks* pattern, is to group tasks based on constraints among them. The next step, discussed here, is to find and correctly account for dependencies resulting from constraints on the order of execution of a collection of tasks. Constraints among tasks fall into a few major categories:

- Temporal dependencies, that is, constraints placed on the order in which a collection of tasks executes.

- Requirements that particular tasks must execute at the same time (for example, because each requires information that will be produced by the others).

- Lack of constraint, that is, total independence. Although this is not strictly speaking a constraint, it is an important feature of a set of tasks because it means they can execute in any order, including concurrently, and it is important to clearly note when this holds.

The purpose of this pattern is to help find and correctly account for dependencies resulting from constraints on the order of execution of a collection of tasks.

Solution

There are two goals to be met when identifying ordering constraints among tasks and defining a partial order among task groups.

- The ordering must be restrictive enough to satisfy all the constraints so that the resulting design is correct.

- The ordering should not be more restrictive than it needs to be. Overly constraining the solution limits design options and can impair program efficiency; the fewer the constraints, the more flexibility you have to shift tasks around to balance the computational load among PEs.

To identify ordering constraints, consider the following ways tasks can depend on each other.

- First look at the data required by a group of tasks before they can execute. After this data has been identified, find the task group that creates it and an ordering constraint will be apparent. For example, if one group of tasks (call it A) builds a complex data structure and another group (B) uses it, there is a sequential ordering constraint between these groups. When these two groups are combined in a program, they must execute in sequence, first A and then B.

- Also consider whether external services can impose ordering constraints. For example, if a program must write to a file in a certain order, then these file I/O operations likely impose an ordering constraint.

- Finally, it is equally important to note when an ordering constraint does not exist. If a number of task groups can execute independently, there is a much greater opportunity to exploit parallelism, so we need to note when tasks are independent as well as when they are dependent.

Regardless of the source of the constraint, we must define the constraints that restrict the order of execution and make sure they are handled correctly in the resulting algorithm. At the same time, it is important to note when ordering constraints are absent, since this will give valuable flexibility later in the design.

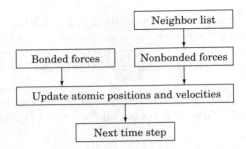

Figure 3.4: Ordering of tasks in molecular dynamics problem

Examples

Molecular dynamics. This problem was described in Sec. 3.1.3, and we discussed its decomposition in the *Task Decomposition* and *Data Decomposition* patterns. In the *Group Tasks* pattern, we described how to organize the tasks for this problem in the following groups:

- A group of tasks to find the "bonded forces" (vibrational forces and rotational forces) on each atom

- A group of tasks to find the nonbonded forces on each atom

- A group of tasks to update the position and velocity of each atom

- A task to update the neighbor list for all the atoms (which trivially constitutes a task group)

Now we are ready to consider ordering constraints between the groups. Clearly, the update of the atomic positions cannot occur until the force computation is complete. Also, the nonbonded forces cannot be computed until the neighbor list is updated. So in each time step, the groups must be ordered as shown in Fig. 3.4.

While it is too early in the design to consider in detail how these ordering constraints will be enforced, eventually we will need to provide some sort of synchronization to ensure that they are strictly followed.

3.6 THE *DATA SHARING* PATTERN

Problem

Given a data and task decomposition for a problem, how is data shared among the tasks?

Context

At a high level, every parallel algorithm consists of

- A collection of tasks that can execute concurrently (see the *Task Decomposition* pattern)

- A data decomposition corresponding to the collection of concurrent tasks (see the *Data Decomposition* pattern)

- Dependencies among the tasks that must be managed to permit safe concurrent execution

As addressed in the *Group Tasks* and *Order Tasks* patterns, the starting point in a dependency analysis is to group tasks based on constraints among them and then determine what ordering constraints apply to groups of tasks. The next step, discussed here, is to analyze how data is shared among groups of tasks, so that access to shared data can be managed correctly.

Although the analysis that led to the grouping of tasks and the ordering constraints among them focuses primarily on the task decomposition, at this stage of the dependency analysis, the focus shifts to the data decomposition, that is, the division of the problem's data into chunks that can be updated independently, each associated with one or more tasks that handle the update of that chunk. This chunk of data is sometimes called task-local data (or just local data), because it is tightly coupled to the task(s) responsible for its update. It is rare, however, that each task can operate using only its own local data; data may need to be shared among tasks in many ways. Two of the most common situations are the following.

- In addition to task-local data, the problem's data decomposition might define some data that must be shared among tasks; for example, the tasks might need to cooperatively update a large shared data structure. Such data cannot be identified with any given task; it is inherently global to the problem. This shared data is modified by multiple tasks and therefore serves as a source of dependencies among the tasks.

- Data dependencies can also occur when one task needs access to some portion of another task's local data. The classic example of this type of data dependency occurs in finite difference methods parallelized using a data decomposition, where each point in the problem space is updated using values from nearby points and therefore updates for one chunk of the decomposition require values from the boundaries of neighboring chunks.

This pattern discusses data sharing in parallel algorithms and how to deal with typical forms of shared data.

Forces

The goal of this pattern is to identify what data is shared among groups of tasks and determine how to manage access to shared data in a way that is both correct and efficient.

Data sharing can have major implications for both correctness and efficiency.

- If the sharing is done incorrectly, a task may get invalid data due to a race condition; this happens often in shared-address-space environments, where a task can read from a memory location before the write of the expected data has completed.

- Guaranteeing that shared data is ready for use can lead to excessive synchronization overhead. For example, an ordering constraint can be enforced by putting barrier operations[1] before reads of shared data. This can be unacceptably inefficient, however, especially in cases where only a small subset of the UEs are actually sharing the data. A much better strategy is to use a combination of copying into local data or restructuring tasks to minimize the number of times shared data must be read.

- Another source of data-sharing overhead is communication. In some parallel systems, any access to shared data implies the passing of a message between UEs. This problem can sometimes be mitigated by overlapping communication and computation, but this isn't always possible. Frequently, a better choice is to structure the algorithm and tasks so that the amount of shared data to communicate is minimized. Another approach is to give each UE its own copy of the shared data; this requires some care to be sure that the copies are kept consistent in value but can be more efficient.

    The goal, therefore, is to manage shared data enough to ensure correctness but not so much as to interfere with efficiency.

Solution

The first step is to identify data that is shared among tasks.

This is most obvious when the decomposition is predominantly a data-based decomposition. For example, in a finite difference problem, the basic data is decomposed into blocks. The nature of the decomposition dictates that the data at the edges of the blocks is shared between neighboring blocks. In essence, the data sharing was worked out when the basic decomposition was done.

In a decomposition that is predominantly task-based, the situation is more complex. At some point in the definition of tasks, it was determined how data is passed into or out of the task and whether any data is updated in the body of the task. These are the sources of potential data sharing.

After the shared data has been identified, it needs to be analyzed to see how it is used. Shared data falls into one of the following three categories.

- **Read-only.** The data is read but not written. Because it is not modified, access to these values does not need to be protected. On some distributed-memory systems, it is worthwhile to replicate the read-only data so each unit of execution has its own copy.

- **Effectively-local.** The data is partitioned into subsets, each of which is accessed (for read or write) by only one of the tasks. (An example of this would be an array shared among tasks in such a way that its elements are effectively partitioned into sets of task-local data.) This case provides some options for handling the dependencies. If the subsets can be accessed independently

---

[1] A barrier is a synchronization construct that defines a point in a program that a group of UEs must all reach before any of them are allowed to proceed.

(as would normally be the case with, say, array elements, but not necessarily with list elements), then it is not necessary to worry about protecting access to this data. On distributed-memory systems, such data would usually be distributed among UEs, with each UE having only the data needed by its tasks. If necessary, the data can be recombined into a single data structure at the end of the computation.

- **Read-write.** The data is both read and written and is accessed by more than one task. This is the general case, and includes arbitrarily complicated situations in which data is read from and written to by any number of tasks. It is the most difficult to deal with, because any access to the data (read or write) must be protected with some type of exclusive-access mechanism (locks, semaphores, etc.), which can be very expensive.

Two special cases of read-write data are common enough to deserve special mention:

- **Accumulate.** The data is being used to accumulate a result (for example, when computing a reduction). For each location in the shared data, the values are updated by multiple tasks, with the update taking place through some sort of associative accumulation operation. The most common accumulation operations are sum, minimum, and maximum, but any associative operation on pairs of operands can be used. For such data, each task (or, usually, each UE) has a separate copy; the accumulations occur into these local copies, which are then accumulated into a single global copy as a final step at the end of the accumulation.

- **Multiple-read/single-write.** The data is read by multiple tasks (all of which need its initial value), but modified by only one task (which can read and write its value arbitrarily often). Such variables occur frequently in algorithms based on data decompositions. For data of this type, at least two copies are needed, one to preserve the initial value and one to be used by the modifying task; the copy containing the initial value can be discarded when no longer needed. On distributed-memory systems, typically a copy is created for each task needing access (read or write) to the data.

Examples

Molecular dynamics.   This problem was described in Sec. 3.1.3, and we discussed its decomposition in the *Task Decomposition* and *Data Decomposition* patterns. We then identified the task groups (in the *Group Tasks* pattern) and considered temporal constraints among the task groups (in the *Order Tasks* pattern). We will ignore the temporal constraints for now and just focus on data sharing for the problem's final task groups:

- The group of tasks to find the "bonded forces" (vibrational forces and rotational forces) on each atom

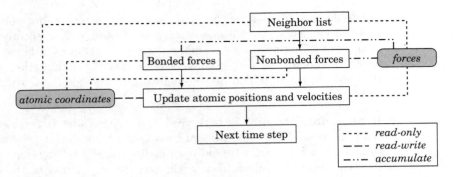

Figure 3.5: Data sharing in molecular dynamics. We distinguish between sharing for reads, read-writes, and accumulations.

- The group of tasks to find the nonbonded forces on each atom

- The group of tasks to update the position and velocity of each atom

- The task to update the neighbor list for all the atoms (which trivially constitutes a task group)

The data sharing in this problem can be complicated. We summarize the data shared between groups in Fig. 3.5. The major shared data items are the following.

- The atomic coordinates, used by each group.

    These coordinates are treated as read-only data by the bonded force group, the nonbonded force group, and the neighbor-list update group. This data is read-write for the position update group. Fortunately, the position update group executes alone after the other three groups are done (based on the ordering constraints developed using the *Order Tasks* pattern). Hence, in the first three groups, we can leave accesses to the position data unprotected or even replicate it. For the position update group, the position data belongs to the read-write category, and access to this data will need to be controlled carefully.

- The force array, used by each group except for the neighbor-list update.

    This array is used as read-only data by the position update group and as accumulate data for the bonded and nonbonded force groups. Because the position update group must follow the force computations (as determined using the *Order Tasks* pattern), we can put this array in the accumulate category for the force groups and in the read-only category for the position update group.

    The standard procedure for molecular dynamics simulations [MR95] begins by initializing the force array as a local array on each UE. Contributions to elements of the force array are then computed by each UE, with the precise terms computed being unpredictable because of the way the molecule folds in space. After all the forces have been computed, the local arrays are reduced into a single array, a copy of which is place on each UE (see the discussion of reduction in Sec. 6.4.2 for more information.)

- The neighbor list, shared between the nonbonded force group and the neighbor-list update group.

    The neighbor list is essentially local data for the neighbor-list update group and read-only data for the nonbonded force computation. The list can be managed in local storage on each UE.

3.7 THE *DESIGN EVALUATION* PATTERN

Problem

Is the decomposition and dependency analysis so far good enough to move on to the next design space, or should the design be revisited?

Context

At this point, the problem has been decomposed into tasks that can execute concurrently (using the *Task Decomposition* and *Data Decomposition* patterns) and the dependencies between them have been identified (using the *Group Tasks, Order Tasks,* and *Data Sharing* patterns). In particular, the original problem has been decomposed and analyzed to produce:

- A task decomposition that identifies tasks that can execute concurrently

- A data decomposition that identifies data local to each task

- A way of grouping tasks and ordering the groups to satisfy temporal constraints

- An analysis of dependencies among tasks

    It is these four items that will guide the designer's work in the next design space (the *Algorithm Structure* patterns). Therefore, getting these items right and finding the best problem decomposition is important for producing a high-quality design.

    In some cases, the concurrency is straightforward and there is clearly a single best way to decompose a problem. More often, however, multiple decompositions are possible. Hence, it is important before proceeding too far into the design process to evaluate the emerging design and make sure it meets the application's needs. Remember that algorithm design is an inherently iterative process, and designers should not expect to produce an optimum design on the first pass through the *Finding Concurrency* patterns.

Forces

The design needs to be evaluated from three perspectives.

- **Suitability for the target platform.** Issues such as number of processors and how data structures are shared will influence the efficiency of any design, but the more the design depends on the target architecture, the less flexible it will be.

- **Design quality.** Simplicity, flexibility, and efficiency are all desirable—but possibly conflicting—attributes.

- **Preparation for the next phase of the design.** Are the tasks and dependencies regular or irregular (that is, are they similar in size, or do they vary)? Is the interaction between tasks synchronous or asynchronous (that is, do the interactions occur at regular intervals or highly variable or even random times)? Are the tasks aggregated in an effective way? Understanding these issues will help choose an appropriate solution from the patterns in the *Algorithm Structure* design space.

Solution

Before moving on to the next phase of the design process, it is helpful to evaluate the work so far from the three perspectives mentioned in the Forces section. The remainder of this pattern consists of questions and discussions to help with the evaluation.

Suitability for target platform. Although it is desirable to delay mapping a program onto a particular target platform as long as possible, the characteristics of the target platform do need to be considered at least minimally while evaluating a design. Following are some issues relevant to the choice of target platform or platforms.

How many PEs are available? With some exceptions, having many more tasks than PEs makes it easier to keep all the PEs busy. Obviously we can't make use of more PEs than we have tasks, but having only one or a few tasks per PE can lead to poor load balance. For example, consider the case of a Monte Carlo simulation in which a calculation is repeated over and over for different sets of randomly chosen data, such that the time taken for the calculation varies considerably depending on the data. A natural approach to developing a parallel algorithm would be to treat each calculation (for a separate set of data) as a task; these tasks are then completely independent and can be scheduled however we like. But because the time for each task can vary considerably, unless there are many more tasks than PEs, it will be difficult to achieve good load balance.

The exceptions to this rule are designs in which the number of tasks can be adjusted to fit the number of PEs in such a way that good load balance is maintained. An example of such a design is the block-based matrix multiplication algorithm described in the Examples section of the *Data Decomposition* pattern: Tasks correspond to blocks, and all the tasks involve roughly the same amount of computation, so adjusting the number of tasks to be equal to the number of PEs produces an algorithm with good load balance. (Note, however, that even in this case it might be advantageous to have more tasks than PEs. This might, for example, allow overlap of computation and communication.)

How are data structures shared among PEs?   A design that involves large-scale or fine-grained data sharing among tasks will be easier to implement and more efficient if all tasks have access to the same memory. Ease of implementation depends on the programming environment; an environment based on a shared-memory model (all UEs share an address space) makes it easier to implement a design requiring extensive data sharing. Efficiency depends also on the target machine; a design involving extensive data-sharing is likely to be more efficient on a symmetric multiprocessor (where access time to memory is uniform across processors) than on a machine that layers a shared-memory environment over physically distributed memory. In contrast, if the plan is to use a message-passing environment running on a distributed-memory architecture, a design involving extensive data sharing is probably not a good choice.

For example, consider the task-based approach to the medical imaging problem described in the Examples section of the *Task Decomposition* pattern. This design requires that all tasks have read access to a potentially very large data structure (the body model). This presents no problems in a shared-memory environment; it is also no problem in a distributed-memory environment in which each PE has a large memory subsystem and there is plenty of network bandwidth to handle broadcasting the large data set. However, in a distributed-memory environment with limited memory or network bandwidth, the more memory-efficient algorithm that emphasizes the data decomposition would be required.

A design that requires fine-grained data-sharing (in which the same data structure is accessed repeatedly by many tasks, particularly when both reads and writes are involved) is also likely to be more efficient on a shared-memory machine, because the overhead required to protect each access is likely to be smaller than for a distributed-memory machine.

The exception to these principles would be a problem in which it is easy to group and schedule tasks in such a way that the only large-scale or fine-grained data sharing is among tasks assigned to the same unit of execution.

What does the target architecture imply about the number of UEs and how structures are shared among them?   In essence, we revisit the preceding two questions, but in terms of UEs rather than PEs.

This can be an important distinction to make if the target system depends on multiple UEs per PE to hide latency. There are two factors to keep in mind when considering whether a design using more than one UE per PE makes sense.

The first factor is whether the target system provides efficient support for multiple UEs per PE. Some systems do provide such support, such as the Cray MTA machines and machines built with Intel processors that utilize hyperthreading. This architectural approach provides hardware support for extremely rapid context switching, making it practical to use in a far wider range of latency-hiding situations. Other systems do not provide good support for multiple UEs per PE.

For example, an MPP system with slow context switching and/or one processor per node might run much better when there is only one UE per PE.

The second factor is whether the design can make good use of multiple UEs per PE. For example, if the design involves communication operations with high latency, it might be possible to mask that latency by assigning multiple UEs to each PE so some UEs can make progress while others are waiting on a high-latency operation. If, however, the design involves communication operations that are tightly synchronized (for example, pairs of blocking send/receives) and relatively efficient, assigning multiple UEs to each PE is more likely to interfere with ease of implementation (by requiring extra effort to avoid deadlock) than to improve efficiency.

On the target platform, will the time spent doing useful work in a task be significantly greater than the time taken to deal with dependencies? A critical factor in determining whether a design is effective is the ratio of time spent doing computation to time spent in communication or synchronization: The higher the ratio, the more efficient the program. This ratio is affected not only by the number and type of coordination events required by the design, but also by the characteristics of the target platform. For example, a message-passing design that is acceptably efficient on an MPP with a fast interconnect network and relatively slow processors will likely be less efficient, perhaps unacceptably so, on an Ethernet-connected network of powerful workstations.

Note that this critical ratio is also affected by problem size relative to the number of available PEs, because for a fixed problem size, the time spent by each processor doing computation decreases with the number of processors, while the time spent by each processor doing coordination might stay the same or even increase as the number of processors increases.

Design quality. Keeping these characteristics of the target platform in mind, we can evaluate the design along the three dimensions of flexibility, efficiency, and simplicity.

Flexibility. It is desirable for the high-level design to be adaptable to a variety of different implementation requirements, and certainly all the important ones. The rest of this section provides a partial checklist of factors that affect flexibility.

- Is the decomposition flexible in the number of tasks generated? Such flexibility allows the design to be adapted to a wide range of parallel computers.

- Is the definition of tasks implied by the task decomposition independent of how they are scheduled for execution? Such independence makes the load balancing problem easier to solve.

- Can the size and number of chunks in the data decomposition be parameterized? Such parameterization makes a design easier to scale for varying numbers of PEs.

- Does the algorithm handle the problem's boundary cases? A good design will handle all relevant cases, even unusual ones. For example, a common operation is to transpose a matrix so that a distribution in terms of blocks of matrix *columns* becomes a distribution in terms of blocks of matrix *rows*. It is easy to write down the algorithm and code it for square matrices where the matrix order is evenly divided by the number of PEs. But what if the matrix is not square, or what if the number of rows is much greater than the number of columns and neither number is evenly divided by the number of PEs? This requires significant changes to the transpose algorithm. For a rectangular matrix, for example, the buffer that will hold the matrix block will need to be large enough to hold the larger of the two blocks. If either the row or column dimension of the matrix is not evenly divisible by the number of PEs, then the blocks will not be the same size on each PE. Can the algorithm deal with the uneven load that will result from having different block sizes on each PE?

Efficiency. The program should effectively utilize the available computing resources. The rest of this section gives a partial list of important factors to check. Note that typically it is not possible to simultaneously optimize all of these factors; design tradeoffs are inevitable.

- Can the computational load be evenly balanced among the PEs? This is easier if the tasks are independent, or if they are roughly the same size.

- Is the overhead minimized? Overhead can come from several sources, including creation and scheduling of the UEs, communication, and synchronization. Creation and scheduling of UEs involves overhead, so each UE needs to have enough work to do to justify this overhead. On the other hand, more UEs allow for better load balance.

- Communication can also be a source of significant overhead, particularly on distributed-memory platforms that depend on message passing. As we discussed in Sec. 2.6, the time to transfer a message has two components: latency cost arising from operating-system overhead and message start-up costs on the network, and a cost that scales with the length of the message. To minimize the latency costs, the number of messages to be sent should be kept to a minimum. In other words, a small number of large messages is better than a large number of small ones. The second term is related to the bandwidth of the network. These costs can sometimes be hidden by overlapping communication with computation.

- On shared-memory machines, synchronization is a major source of overhead. When data is shared between UEs, dependencies arise requiring one task to wait for another to avoid race conditions. The synchronization mechanisms used to control this waiting are expensive compared to many operations carried out by a UE. Furthermore, some synchronization constructs generate significant memory traffic as they flush caches, buffers, and other system resources to make sure UEs see a consistent view of memory. This extra memory traffic can interfere with the explicit data movement within a computation. Synchronization overhead can be reduced by keeping data well-localized to a task, thereby minimizing the frequency of synchronization operations.

Simplicity.   To paraphrase Einstein: Make it as simple as possible, but not simpler.

Keep in mind that practically all programs will eventually need to be debugged, maintained, and often enhanced and ported. A design—even a generally superior design—is not valuable if it is too hard to debug, maintain, and verify the correctness of the final program.

The medical imaging example initially described in Sec. 3.1.3 and then discussed further in the *Task Decomposition* and *Data Decomposition* patterns is an excellent case in point in support of the value of simplicity. In this problem, a large database could be decomposed, but this decomposition would force the parallel algorithm to include complex operations for passing trajectories between UEs and to distribute chunks of the database. This complexity makes the resulting program much more difficult to understand and greatly complicates debugging. The other approach, replicating the database, leads to a vastly simpler parallel program in which completely independent tasks can be passed out to multiple workers as they are read. All complex communication thus goes away, and the parallel part of the program is trivial to debug and reason about.

Preparation for next phase.   The problem decomposition carried out with the *Finding Concurrency* patterns defines the key components that will guide the design in the *Algorithm Structure* design space:

- A task decomposition that identifies tasks that can execute concurrently

- A data decomposition that identifies data local to each task

- A way of grouping tasks and ordering the groups to satisfy temporal constraints

- An analysis of dependencies among tasks

Before moving on in the design, consider these components relative to the following questions.

How regular are the tasks and their data dependencies?   Regular tasks are similar in size and effort. Irregular tasks would vary widely among themselves. If the tasks are irregular, the scheduling of the tasks and their sharing of data will be more complicated and will need to be emphasized in the design. In a regular decomposition, all the tasks are in some sense the same—roughly the same computation (on different sets of data), roughly the same dependencies on data shared with other tasks, etc. Examples include the various matrix multiplication algorithms described in the Examples sections of the *Task Decomposition, Data Decomposition,* and other patterns.

In an irregular decomposition, the work done by each task and/or the data dependencies vary among tasks. For example, consider a discrete-event simulation of a large system consisting of a number of distinct components. We might design a parallel algorithm for this simulation by defining a task for each component and having them interact based on the discrete events of the simulation. This would be a very irregular design in that there would be considerable variation among tasks with regard to work done and dependencies on other tasks.

Are interactions between tasks (or task groups) synchronous or asynchronous?   In some designs, the interaction between tasks is also very regular with regard to time—that is, it is *synchronous*. For example, a typical approach to parallelizing a linear-algebra problem involving the update of a large matrix is to partition the matrix among tasks and have each task update its part of the matrix, using data from both its and other parts of the matrix. Assuming that all the data needed for the update is present at the start of the computation, these tasks will typically first exchange information and then compute independently. Another type of example is a *pipeline computation* (see the *Pipeline* pattern), in which we perform a multi-step operation on a sequence of sets of input data by setting up an assembly line of tasks (one for each step of the operation), with data flowing from one task to the next as each task accomplishes its work. This approach works best if all of the tasks stay more or less in step—that is, if their interaction is synchronous.

In other designs, the interaction between tasks is not so chronologically regular. An example is the discrete-event simulation described previously, in which the events that lead to interaction between tasks can be chronologically irregular.

Are the tasks grouped in the best way?   The temporal relations are easy: Tasks that can run at the same time are naturally grouped together. But an effective design will also group tasks together based on their logical relationship in the overall problem.

As an example of grouping tasks, consider the molecular dynamics problem discussed in the Examples section of the *Group Tasks, Order Tasks,* and *Data Sharing* patterns. The grouping we eventually arrive at (in the *Group Tasks* pattern) is hierarchical: groups of related tasks based on the high-level operations of the problem, further grouped on the basis of which ones can execute concurrently. Such an approach makes it easier to reason about whether the design meets the necessary constraints (because the constraints can be stated in terms of the task groups defined by the high-level operations) while allowing for scheduling flexibility.

3.8   SUMMARY

Working through the patterns in the *Finding Concurrency* design space exposes the concurrency in your problem. The key elements following from that analysis are

- A task decomposition that identifies tasks that can execute concurrently

- A data decomposition that identifies data local to each task

- A way of grouping tasks and ordering the groups to satisfy temporal constraints

- An analysis of dependencies among tasks

A pattern language is traditionally described as a web of patterns with one pattern logically connected to the next. The output from the *Finding Concurrency* design space, however, does not fit into that picture. Rather, the goal of this design space is to help the designer create the design elements that together will lead into the rest of the pattern language.

The *Algorithm Structure* Design Space

4.1   INTRODUCTION

The first phase of designing a parallel algorithm consists of analyzing the problem to identify exploitable concurrency, usually by using the patterns of the *Finding Concurrency* design space. The output from the *Finding Concurrency* design space is a decomposition of the problem into design elements:

- A task decomposition that identifies tasks that can execute concurrently

- A data decomposition that identifies data local to each task

- A way of grouping tasks and ordering the groups to satisfy temporal constraints

- An analysis of dependencies among tasks

These elements provide the connection from the *Finding Concurrency* design space to the *Algorithm Structure* design space. Our goal in the *Algorithm Structure* design space is to refine the design and move it closer to a program that can execute tasks concurrently by mapping the concurrency onto multiple UEs running on a parallel computer.

Of the countless ways to define an algorithm structure, most follow one of six basic design patterns. These patterns make up the *Algorithm Structure* design space. An overview of this design space and its place in the pattern language is shown in Fig. 4.1.

The key issue at this stage is to decide which pattern or patterns are most appropriate for the problem.

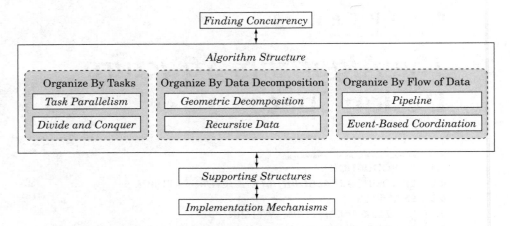

Figure 4.1: Overview of the *Algorithm Structure* design space and its place in the pattern language

First of all, we need to keep in mind that different aspects of the analysis can pull the design in different directions; one aspect might suggest one structure while another suggests a different structure. In nearly every case, however, the following forces should be kept in mind.

- **Efficiency.** It is crucial that a parallel program run quickly and make good use of the computer resources.

- **Simplicity.** A simple algorithm resulting in easy-to-understand code is easier to develop, debug, verify, and modify.

- **Portability.** Ideally, programs should run on the widest range of parallel computers. This will maximize the "market" for a particular program. More importantly, a program is used for many years, while any particular computer system is used for only a few years. Portable programs protect a software investment.

- **Scalability.** Ideally, an algorithm should be effective on a wide range of numbers of processing elements (PEs), from a few up to hundreds or even thousands.

These forces conflict in several ways, however.

Efficiency conflicts with portability: Making a program efficient almost always requires that the code take into account the characteristics of the specific system on which it is intended to run, which limits portability. A design that makes use of the special features of a particular system or programming environment may lead to an efficient program for that particular environment, but be unusable for a different platform, either because it performs poorly or because it is difficult or even impossible to implement for the new platform.

Efficiency also can conflict with simplicity: For example, to write efficient programs that use the *Task Parallelism* pattern, it is sometimes necessary to use complicated scheduling algorithms. These algorithms in many cases, however, make the program very difficult to understand.

Thus, a good algorithm design must strike a balance between (1) abstraction and portability and (2) suitability for a particular target architecture. The challenge faced by the designer, especially at this early phase of the algorithm design, is to leave the parallel algorithm design abstract enough to support portability while ensuring that it can eventually be implemented effectively for the parallel systems on which it will be executed.

4.2   CHOOSING AN *ALGORITHM STRUCTURE* PATTERN

Finding an effective *Algorithm Structure* pattern for a given problem can be accomplished by considering the questions in the following sections.

4.2.1   Target Platform

What constraints are placed on the parallel algorithm by the target machine or programming environment?

In an ideal world, it would not be necessary to consider the details of the target platform at this stage of the design, because doing so works against keeping the program portable and scalable. This is not an ideal world, however, and software designed without considering the major features of the target platform is unlikely to run efficiently.

The primary issue is how many units of execution (UEs) the system will effectively support, because an algorithm that works well for ten UEs may not work well for hundreds of UEs. It is not necessary to decide on a specific number (in fact to do so would overly constrain the applicability of the design), but it is important to have in mind at this point an order of magnitude for the number of UEs.

Another issue is how expensive it is to share information among UEs. If there is hardware support for shared memory, information exchange takes place through shared access to common memory, and frequent data sharing makes sense. If the target is a collection of nodes connected by a slow network, however, the communication required to share information is very expensive and must be avoided wherever possible.

When thinking about both of these issues—the number of UEs and the cost of sharing information—avoid the tendency to over-constrain the design. Software typically outlives hardware, so over the course of a program's life it may be used on a tremendous range of target platforms. The goal is to obtain a design that works well on the original target platform, but at the same time is flexible enough to adapt to different classes of hardware.

Finally, in addition to multiple UEs and some way to share information among them, a parallel computer has one or more programming environments that can be used to implement parallel algorithms. Different programming environments provide different ways to create tasks and share information among UEs, and a design that does not map well onto the characteristics of the target programming environment will be difficult to implement.

4.2.2   Major Organizing Principle

When considering the concurrency in the problem, is there a particular way of looking at it that stands out and provides a high-level mechanism for organizing this concurrency?

The analysis carried out using the patterns of the *Finding Concurrency* design space describes the potential concurrency in terms of tasks and groups of tasks, data (both shared and task-local), and ordering constraints among task groups. The next step is to find an algorithm structure that represents how this concurrency maps onto the UEs. There is usually a *major organizing principle* implied by the concurrency. This usually falls into one of three camps: *organization by tasks, organization by data decomposition,* and *organization by flow of data.* We now consider each of these in more detail.

For some problems, there is really only one group of tasks active at one time, and the way the tasks within this group interact is the major feature of the concurrency. Examples include so-called *embarrassingly parallel* programs in which the tasks are completely independent, as well as programs in which the tasks in a single group cooperate to compute a result.

For other problems, the way data is decomposed and shared among tasks stands out as the major way to organize the concurrency. For example, many problems focus on the update of a few large data structures, and the most productive way to think about the concurrency is in terms of how this structure is decomposed and distributed among UEs. Programs to solve differential equations or carry out linear algebra computations often fall into this category because they are frequently based on updating large data structures.

Finally, for some problems, the major feature of the concurrency is the presence of well-defined interacting groups of tasks, and the key issue is how the data flows among the tasks. For example, in a signal-processing application, data may flow through a sequence of tasks organized as a pipeline, each performing a transformation on successive data elements. Or a discrete-event simulation might be parallelized by decomposing it into a tasks interacting via "events". Here, the major feature of the concurrency is the way in which these distinct task groups interact.

Notice also that the most effective parallel algorithm design might make use of multiple algorithm structures (combined hierarchically, compositionally, or in sequence), and this is the point at which to consider whether such a design makes sense. For example, it often happens that the very top level of the design is a sequential composition of one or more *Algorithm Structure* patterns. Other designs might be organized hierarchically, with one pattern used to organize the interaction of the major task groups and other patterns used to organize tasks within the groups—for example, an instance of the *Pipeline* pattern in which individual stages are instances of the *Task Parallelism* pattern.

4.2.3   The *Algorithm Structure* Decision Tree

For each subset of tasks, which *Algorithm Structure* design pattern most effectively defines how to map the tasks onto UEs?

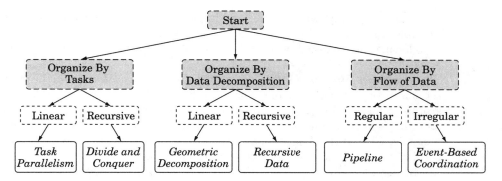

Figure 4.2: Decision tree for the *Algorithm Structure* design space

Having considered the questions raised in the preceding sections, we are now ready to select an algorithm structure, guided by an understanding of constraints imposed by the target platform, an appreciation of the role of hierarchy and composition, and a major organizing principle for the problem. The decision is guided by the decision tree shown in Fig. 4.2. Starting at the top of the tree, consider the concurrency and the major organizing principle, and use this information to select one of the three branches of the tree; then follow the upcoming discussion for the appropriate subtree. Notice again that for some problems, the final design might combine more than one algorithm structure: If no single structure seems suitable, it might be necessary to divide the tasks making up the problem into two or more groups, work through this procedure separately for each group, and then determine how to combine the resulting algorithm structures.

Organize By Tasks.   Select the *Organize By Tasks* branch when the execution of the tasks themselves is the best organizing principle. Then determine how the tasks are enumerated. If they can be gathered into a set linear in any number of dimensions, choose the *Task Parallelism* pattern. This pattern includes both situations in which the tasks are independent of each other (so-called embarrassingly parallel algorithms) and situations in which there are some dependencies among the tasks in the form of access to shared data or a need to exchange messages. If the tasks are enumerated by a recursive procedure, choose the *Divide and Conquer* pattern. In this pattern, the problem is solved by recursively dividing it into subproblems, solving each subproblem independently, and then recombining the subsolutions into a solution to the original problem.

Organize By Data Decomposition.   Select the *Organize By Data Decomposition* branch when the decomposition of the data is the major organizing principle in understanding the concurrency. There are two patterns in this group, differing in how the decomposition is structured—linearly in each dimension or recursively. Choose the *Geometric Decomposition* pattern when the problem space is decomposed into discrete subspaces and the problem is solved by computing solutions for the subspaces, with the solution for each subspace typically requiring data from a small number of other subspaces. Many instances of this pattern can be found in scientific computing, where it is useful in parallelizing grid-based computations, for example. Choose the *Recursive Data* pattern when the problem is defined in terms of following links through a recursive data structure (for example, a binary tree).

Organize By Flow of Data. Select the *Organize By Flow of Data* branch when the major organizing principle is how the flow of data imposes an ordering on the groups of tasks. This pattern group has two members, one that applies when this ordering is regular and static and one that applies when it is irregular and/or dynamic. Choose the *Pipeline* pattern when the flow of data among task groups is regular, one-way, and does not change during the algorithm (that is, the task groups can be arranged into a pipeline through which the data flows). Choose the *Event-Based Coordination* pattern when the flow of data is irregular, dynamic, and/or unpredictable (that is, when the task groups can be thought of as interacting via asynchronous events).

4.2.4 Re-evaluation

Is the *Algorithm Structure* pattern (or patterns) suitable for the target platform? It is important to frequently review decisions made so far to be sure the chosen pattern(s) are a good fit with the target platform.

After choosing one or more *Algorithm Structure* patterns to be used in the design, skim through their descriptions to be sure they are reasonably suitable for the target platform. (For example, if the target platform consists of a large number of workstations connected by a slow network, and one of the chosen *Algorithm Structure* patterns requires frequent communication among tasks, it might be difficult to implement the design efficiently.) If the chosen patterns seem wildly unsuitable for the target platform, try identifying a secondary organizing principle and working through the preceding step again.

4.3 EXAMPLES

4.3.1 Medical Imaging

For example, consider the medical imaging problem described in Sec. 3.1.3. This application simulates a large number of gamma rays as they move through a body and out to a camera. One way to describe the concurrency is to define the simulation of each ray as a task. Because they are all logically equivalent, we put them into a single task group. The only data shared among the tasks is a large data structure representing the body, and since access to this data structure is read-only, the tasks do not depend on each other.

Because there are many independent tasks for this problem, it is less necessary than usual to consider the target platform: The large number of tasks should mean that we can make effective use of any (reasonable) number of UEs; the independence of the tasks should mean that the cost of sharing information among UEs will not have much effect on performance.

Thus, we should be able to choose a suitable structure by working through the decision tree shown previously in Fig. 4.2. Given that in this problem the tasks are independent, the only issue we really need to worry about as we select an algorithm structure is how to map these tasks onto UEs. That is, for this problem, the major organizing principle seems to be the way the tasks are organized, so we start by following the *Organize By Tasks* branch.

We now consider the nature of our set of tasks—whether they are arranged hierarchically or reside in an unstructured or flat set. For this problem, the tasks are in an unstructured set with no obvious hierarchical structure among them, so we choose the *Task Parallelism* pattern. Note that in the problem, the tasks are independent, a fact that we will be able to use to simplify the solution.

Finally, we review this decision in light of possible target-platform considerations. As we observed earlier, the key features of this problem (the large number of tasks and their independence) make it unlikely that we will need to reconsider because the chosen structure will be difficult to implement on the target platform.

4.3.2   Molecular Dynamics

As a second example, consider the molecular dynamics problem described in Sec. 3.1.3. In the *Task Decomposition* pattern, we identified the following groups of tasks associated with this problem:

- Tasks that find the vibrational forces on an atom

- Tasks that find the rotational forces on an atom

- Tasks that find the nonbonded forces on an atom

- Tasks that update the position and velocity of an atom

- A task to update the neighbor list for all the atoms

The tasks within each group are expressed as the iterations of a loop over the atoms within the molecular system.

We can choose a suitable algorithm structure by working through the decision tree shown earlier in Fig. 4.2. One option is to organize the parallel algorithm in terms of the flow of data among the groups of tasks. Note that only the first three task groups (the vibrational, rotational, and nonbonded force calculations) can execute concurrently; that is, they must finish computing the forces before the atomic positions, velocities and neighbor lists can be updated. This is not very much concurrency to work with, so a different branch in Fig. 4.2 should be used for this problem.

Another option is to derive exploitable concurrency from the set of tasks within each group, in this case the iterations of a loop over atoms. This suggests an organization by tasks with a linear arrangement of tasks, or based on Fig. 4.2, the *Task Parallelism* pattern should be used. Total available concurrency is large (on the order of the number of atoms), providing a great deal of flexibility in designing the parallel algorithm.

The target machine can have a major impact on the parallel algorithm for this problem. The dependencies discussed in the *Data Decomposition* pattern (replicated coordinates on each UE and a combination of partial sums from each UE to compute a global force array) suggest that on the order of $2 \cdot 3 \cdot N$ terms (where N is the number of atoms) will need to be passed among the UEs. The computation, however, is of order $n \cdot N$, where n is the number of atoms in the neighborhood of each atom and considerably less than N. Hence, the communication and computation are of the same order and management of communication overhead will be a key factor in designing the algorithm.

4.4   THE *TASK PARALLELISM* PATTERN

Problem

When the problem is best decomposed into a collection of tasks that can execute concurrently, how can this concurrency be exploited efficiently?

Context

Every parallel algorithm is fundamentally a collection of concurrent tasks. These tasks and any dependencies among them can be identified by inspection (for simple problems) or by application of the patterns in the *Finding Concurrency* design space. For some problems, focusing on these tasks and their interaction might not be the best way to organize the algorithm: In some cases it makes sense to organize the tasks in terms of the data (as in the *Geometric Decomposition* pattern) or the flow of data among concurrent tasks (as in the *Pipeline* pattern). However, in many cases it is best to work directly with the tasks themselves. When the design is based directly on the tasks, the algorithm is said to be a *task parallel* algorithm.

The class of task parallel algorithms is very large. Examples include the following.

- Ray-tracing codes such as the medical-imaging example described in the *Task Decomposition* pattern: Here the computation associated with each "ray" becomes a separate and completely independent task.

- The molecular-dynamics example described in the *Task Decomposition* pattern: The update of the nonbonded force on each atom is a task. The dependencies among tasks are managed by replicating the force array on each UE to hold the partial sums for each atom. When all the tasks have completed their contributions to the nonbonded force, the individual force arrays are combined (or "reduced") into a single array holding the full summation of nonbonded forces for each atom.

- Branch-and-bound computations, in which the problem is solved by repeatedly removing a solution space from a list of such spaces, examining it, and either declaring it a solution, discarding it, or dividing it into smaller solution spaces that are then added to the list of spaces to examine. Such computations can be parallelized using this pattern by making each "examine and process a solution space" step a separate task. The tasks weakly depend on each other through the shared queue of tasks.

The common factor is that the problem can be decomposed into a collection of tasks that can execute concurrently. The tasks can be completely independent (as in the medical-imaging example) or there can be dependencies among them (as in the molecular-dynamics example). In most cases, the tasks will be associated with iterations of a loop, but it is possible to associate them with larger-scale program structures as well.

In many cases, all of the tasks are known at the beginning of the computation (the first two examples). However, in some cases, tasks arise dynamically as the computation unfolds, as in the branch-and-bound example.

Also, while it is usually the case that all tasks must be completed before the problem is done, for some problems, it may be possible to reach a solution without completing all of the tasks. For example, in the branch-and-bound example, we have a pool of tasks corresponding to solution spaces to be searched, and we might find an acceptable solution before all the tasks in this pool have been completed.

Forces

- To exploit the potential concurrency in the problem, we must assign tasks to UEs. Ideally we want to do this in a way that is simple, portable, scalable, and efficient. As noted in Sec. 4.1, however, these goals may conflict. A key consideration is balancing the load, that is, ensuring that all UEs have roughly the same amount of work to do.

- If the tasks depend on each other in some way (via either ordering constraints or data dependencies), these dependencies must be managed correctly, again keeping in mind the sometimes-conflicting goals of simplicity, portability, scalability, and efficiency.

Solution

Designs for task-parallel algorithms involve three key elements: the tasks and how they are defined, the dependencies among them, and the *schedule* (how the tasks are assigned to UEs). We discuss them separately, but in fact they are tightly coupled, and all three must be considered before final decisions are made. After these factors are considered, we look at the overall program structure and then at some important special cases of this pattern.

Tasks. Ideally, the tasks into which the problem is decomposed should meet two criteria: First, there should be at least as many tasks as UEs, and preferably many more, to allow greater flexibility in scheduling. Second, the computation associated with each task must be large enough to offset the overhead associated with managing the tasks and handling any dependencies. If the initial decomposition does not meet these criteria, it is worthwhile to consider whether there is another way of decomposing the problem into tasks that does meet the criteria.

For example, in image-processing applications where each pixel update is independent, the task definition can be individual pixels, image lines, or even whole blocks in the image. On a system with a small number of nodes connected by a slow network, tasks should be large to offset high communication latencies, so basing tasks on blocks of the image is appropriate. The same problem on a system containing a large number of nodes connected by a fast (low-latency) network, however, would need smaller tasks to make sure enough work exists to keep all the UEs occupied. Notice that this imposes a requirement for a fast network, because otherwise the smaller amount of work per task will not be enough to compensate for communication overhead.

Dependencies.   Dependencies among tasks have a major impact on the emerging algorithm design. There are two categories of dependencies, ordering constraints and dependencies related to shared data.

For this pattern, ordering constraints apply to task groups and can be handled by forcing the groups to execute in the required order. For example, in a task-parallel multidimensional Fast Fourier Transform, there is a group of tasks for each dimension of the transform, and synchronization or other program constructs are used to make sure computation on one dimension completes before the next dimension begins. Alternatively, we could simply think of such a problem as a sequential composition of task-parallel computations, one for each task group.

Shared-data dependencies are potentially more complicated. In the simplest case, there are no dependencies among the tasks. A surprisingly large number of problems can be cast into this form. Such problems are often called embarrassingly parallel. Their solutions are among the simplest of parallel programs; the main considerations are how the tasks are defined (as discussed previously) and scheduled (as discussed later). When data is shared among tasks, the algorithm can be much more complicated, although there are still some common cases that can be dealt with relatively easily. We can categorize dependencies as follows.

- **Removable dependencies.** In this case, the dependency is not a true dependency between tasks, but an apparent dependency that can be removed by simple code transformations. The simplest case is a temporary variable whose use is completely local to each task; that is, each task initializes the variable without reference to other tasks. This case can be handled by simply creating a copy of the variable local to each UE. In more complicated cases, iterative expressions might need to be transformed into closed-form expressions to remove a loop-carried dependency. For example, consider the following simple loop:

```
int ii = 0, jj = 0;

for(int i = 0; i< N; i++)
{
   ii = ii + 1;
   d[ii] = big_time_consuming_work(ii);
   jj = jj + i;
   a[jj] = other_big_calc(jj);
}
```

The variables `ii` and `jj` create a dependency between tasks and prevent parallelization of the loop. We can remove this dependency by replacing `ii` and `jj` with closed-form expressions (noticing that the values of `ii` and `i` are the same and that the value of `jj` is the sum of the values from 0 through `i`):

```
for(int i = 0; i< N; i++){

   d[i] = big_time_consuming_work(i);
   a[(i*i+i)/2] = other_big_calc((i*i+i)/2));
}
```

- **"Separable" dependencies.** When the dependencies involve accumulation into a shared data structure, they can be separated from the tasks ("pulled outside the concurrent computation") by replicating the data structure at the beginning of the computation, executing the tasks, and then combining the copies into a single data structure after the tasks complete. Often the accumulation is a *reduction* operation, in which a collection of data elements is reduced to a single element by repeatedly applying a binary operation such as addition or multiplication.

  In more detail, these dependencies can be managed as follows: A copy of the data structure used in the accumulation is created on each UE. Each copy is initialized (in the case of a reduction, to the identity element for the binary operation—for example, zero for addition and one for multiplication). Each task then carries out the accumulation into its local data structure, eliminating the shared-data dependency. When all tasks are complete, the local data structures on each UE are combined to produce the final global result (in the case of a reduction, by applying the binary operation again). As an example, consider the following loop to sum the elements of array `f`:

```
for(int i = 0; i< N; i++){
   sum = sum + f(i);
}
```

  This is technically a dependency between loop iterations, but if we recognize that the loop body is just accumulating into a simple scalar variable, it can be handled as a reduction.

  Reductions are so common that both MPI and OpenMP provide support for them as part of the API. Sec. 6.4.2 in the *Implementation Mechanisms* design space discusses reductions in more detail.

- **Other dependencies.** If the shared data cannot be pulled out of the tasks and is both read and written by the tasks, data dependencies must be

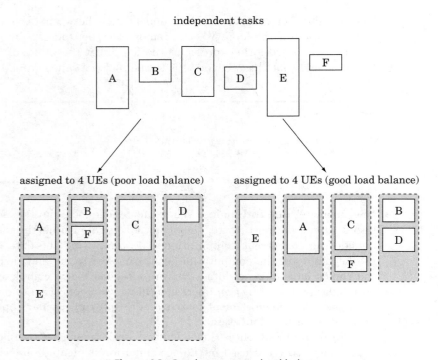

Figure 4.3: Good versus poor load balance

explicitly managed within the tasks. How to do this in a way that gives correct results and also acceptable performance is the subject of the *Shared Data* pattern.

Schedule. The remaining key element to consider is the *schedule*—the way in which tasks are assigned to UEs and scheduled for execution. Load balance (as described in Chapter 2) is a critical consideration in scheduling; a design that balances the computational load among PEs will execute more efficiently than one that does not. Fig. 4.3 illustrates the problem.

Two classes of schedules are used in parallel algorithms: static schedules, in which the distribution of tasks among UEs is determined at the start of the computation and does not change; and dynamic schedules, in which the distribution of tasks among UEs varies as the computation proceeds.

In a static schedule, the tasks are associated into blocks and then assigned to UEs. Block size is adjusted so each UE takes approximately the same amount of time to complete its tasks. In most applications using a static schedule, the computational resources available from the UEs are predictable and stable over the course of the computation, with the most common case being UEs that are identical (that is, the computing system is homogeneous). If the set of times required to complete each task is narrowly distributed about a mean, the sizes of the blocks should be proportional to the relative performance of the UEs (so, in a homogeneous system, they are all the same size). When the effort associated with the tasks varies considerably, a static schedule can still be useful, but now the number of blocks assigned to UEs must be much greater than the number of UEs. By dealing out the blocks in a round-robin manner (much as a deck of cards is dealt among a group of card players), the load is balanced statistically.

Dynamic schedules are used when (1) the effort associated with each task varies widely and is unpredictable and/or (2) when the capabilities of the UEs vary widely and unpredictably. The most common approach used for dynamic load balancing is to define a task queue to be used by all the UEs; when a UE completes its current task and is therefore ready to process more work, it removes a task from the task queue. Faster UEs or those receiving lighter-weight tasks will access the queue more often and thereby be assigned more tasks.

Another dynamic scheduling strategy uses *work stealing,* which works as follows. The tasks are distributed among the UEs at the start of the computation. Each UE has its own work queue. When the queue is empty, the UE will try to steal work from the queue on some other UE (where the other UE is usually randomly selected). In many cases, this produces an optimal dynamic schedule without incurring the overhead of maintaining a single global queue. In programming environments or packages that provide support for the construct, such as Cilk [BJK+96], Hood [BP99], or the FJTask framework [Lea00b, Lea], it is straightforward to use this approach. But with more commonly used programming environments such as OpenMP, MPI, or Java (without support such as the FJTask framework), this approach adds significant complexity and therefore is not often used.

Selecting a schedule for a given problem is not always easy. Static schedules incur the least overhead during the parallel computation and should be used whenever possible.

Before ending the discussion of schedules, we should mention again that while for most problems all of the tasks are known when the computation begins and all must be completed to produce an overall solution, there are problems for which one or both of these is not true. In these cases, a dynamic schedule is probably more appropriate.

Program structure.   Many task-parallel problems can be considered to be loop-based. Loop-based problems are, as the name implies, those in which the tasks are based on the iterations of a loop. The best solutions for such problems use the *Loop Parallelism* pattern. This pattern can be particularly simple to implement in programming environments that provide directives for automatically assigning loop iterations to UEs. For example, in OpenMP a loop can be parallelized by simply adding a "parallel for" directive with an appropriate schedule clause (one that maximizes efficiency). This solution is especially attractive because OpenMP then guarantees that the resulting program is semantically equivalent to the analogous sequential code (within roundoff error associated with different orderings of floating-point operations).

For problems in which the target platform is not a good fit with the *Loop Parallelism* pattern, or for problems in which the model of "all tasks known initially, all tasks must complete" does not apply (either because tasks can be created during the computation or because the computation can terminate without all tasks being complete), this straightforward approach is not the best choice. Instead, the best design makes use of a *task queue;* tasks are placed on the task queue as they are created and removed by UEs until the computation is complete. The overall program structure can be based on either the *Master/Worker* pattern or the *SPMD* pattern. The former is particularly appropriate for problems requiring a dynamic schedule.

In the case in which the computation can terminate before all the tasks are complete, some care must be taken to ensure that the computation ends when it should. If we define the *termination condition* as the condition that when true means the computation is complete—either all tasks are complete or some other condition (for example, an acceptable solution has been found by one task)—then we want to be sure that (1) the termination condition is eventually met (which, if tasks can be created dynamically, might mean building into it a limit on the total number of tasks created), and (2) when the termination condition is met, the program ends. How to ensure the latter is discussed in the *Master/Worker* and *SPMD* patterns.

Common idioms.   Most problems for which this pattern is applicable fall into the following two categories.

Embarrassingly parallel problems are those in which there are no dependencies among the tasks. A wide range of problems fall into this category, ranging from rendering frames in a motion picture to statistical sampling in computational physics. Because there are no dependencies to manage, the focus is on scheduling the tasks to maximize efficiency. In many cases, it is possible to define schedules that automatically and dynamically balance the load among UEs.

Replicated data or reduction problems are those in which dependencies can be managed by "separating them from the tasks" as described earlier—replicating the data at the beginning of computation and combining results when the termination condition is met (usually "all tasks complete"). For these problems, the overall solution consists of three phases, one to replicate the data into local variables, one to solve the now-independent tasks (using the same techniques used for embarrassingly parallel problems), and one to recombine the results into a single result.

Examples

We will consider two examples of this pattern. The first example, an image-construction example, is embarrassingly parallel. The second example will build on the molecular dynamics example used in several of the *Finding Concurrency* patterns.

Image construction.   In many image-construction problems, each pixel in the image is independent of all the other pixels. For example, consider the well known Mandelbrot set [Dou86]. This famous image is constructed by coloring each pixel according to the behavior of the quadratic recurrence relation

$$Z_{n+1} = Z_n^2 + C \qquad\qquad (4.1)$$

where C and Z are complex numbers and the recurrence is started with $Z_0 = C$. The image plots the imaginary part of C on the vertical axis and the real part on the horizontal axis. The color of each pixel is black if the recurrence relation converges to a stable value or is colored depending on how rapidly the relation diverges.

At the lowest level, the task is the update for a single pixel. First consider computing this set on a cluster of PCs connected by an Ethernet. This is a coarse-grained system; that is, the rate of communication is slow relative to the rate of computation. To offset the overhead incurred by the slow network, the task size needs to be large; for this problem, that might mean computing a full row of the image. The work involved in computing each row varies depending on the number of divergent pixels in the row. The variation, however, is modest and distributed closely around a mean value. Therefore, a static schedule with many more tasks than UEs will likely give an effective statistical balance of the load among nodes. The remaining step in applying the pattern is choosing an overall structure for the program. On a shared-memory machine using OpenMP, the *Loop Parallelism* pattern described in the *Supporting Structures* design space is a good fit. On a network of workstations running MPI, the *SPMD* pattern (also in the *Supporting Structures* design space) is appropriate.

Before moving on to the next example, we consider one more target system, a cluster in which the nodes are not heterogeneous—that is, some nodes are much faster than others. Assume also that the speed of each node may not be known when the work is scheduled. Because the time needed to compute the image for a row now depends both on the row and on which node computes it, a dynamic schedule is indicated. This in turn suggests that a general dynamic load-balancing scheme is indicated, which then suggests that the overall program structure should be based on the *Master/Worker* pattern.

Molecular dynamics.   For our second example, we consider the computation of the nonbonded forces in a molecular dynamics computation. This problem is described in Sec. 3.1.3 and in [Mat95, PH95] and is used throughout the patterns in the *Finding Concurrency* design space. Pseudocode for this computation is shown in Fig. 4.4. The physics in this example is not relevant and is buried in code not shown here (the computation of the neighbors list and the force function). The basic computation structure is a loop over atoms, and then for each atom, a loop over interactions with other atoms. The number of interactions per atom is computed separately when the neighbors list is determined. This routine (not shown here) computes the number of atoms within a radius equal to a preset cutoff distance. The neighbor list is also modified to account for Newton's third law: Because the force of atom i on atom j is the negative of the force of atom j on atom i, only half of the potential interactions need actually be computed. Understanding this detail is not important for understanding this example. The key is that this causes each loop over j to vary greatly from one atom to another, thereby greatly complicating the load-balancing problem. Indeed, for the purposes of this example, all that must really be understood is that calculating the force is an expensive operation and that the number of interactions per atom varies greatly. Hence, the computational effort for each iteration over i is difficult to predict in advance.

```
function non_bonded_forces (N, Atoms, neighbors, Forces)

    Int const N // number of atoms

    Array of Real :: atoms (3,N) //3D coordinates
    Array of Real :: forces (3,N) //force in each dimension
    Array of List :: neighbors(N) //atoms in cutoff volume
    Real :: forceX, forceY, forceZ

    loop [i] over atoms

        loop [j] over neighbors(i)
            forceX = non_bond_force(atoms(1,i), atoms(1,j))
            forceY = non_bond_force(atoms(2,i), atoms(2,j))
            forceZ = non_bond_force(atoms(3,i), atoms(3,j))
            force(1,i) += forceX; force(1,j) -= forceX;
            force(2,i) += forceY; force(2,j) -= forceY;
            force(3,i) += forceZ; force(3,j) -= forceZ;
        end loop [j]

    end loop [i]
end function non_bonded_forces
```

Figure 4.4: Pseudocode for the nonbonded computation in a typical molecular dynamics code

Each component of the force term is an independent computation, meaning that each (i, j) pair is fundamentally an independent task. The number of atoms tends to be on the order of thousands, and squaring that gives a number of tasks that is more than enough for all but the largest parallel systems. Therefore, we can take the more convenient approach of defining a task as one iteration of the loop over i. The tasks, however, are not independent: The force array is read and written by each task. Inspection of the code shows that the arrays are only used to accumulate results from the computation, however. Thus, the full array can be replicated on each UE and the local copies combined (reduced) after the tasks complete.

After the replication is defined, the problem is embarrassingly parallel and the same approaches discussed previously apply. We will revisit this example in the *Master/Worker, Loop Parallelism,* and *SPMD* patterns. A choice among these patterns is normally made based on the target platforms.

Known uses.   There are many application areas in which this pattern is useful, including the following.

Many ray-tracing programs use some form of partitioning with individual tasks corresponding to scan lines in the final image [BKS91].

Applications written with coordination languages such as Linda are another rich source of examples of this pattern [BCM+91]. Linda [CG91] is a simple language consisting of only six operations that read and write an associative (that is, content-addressable) shared memory called a *tuple space*. The tuple space provides a natural way to implement a wide variety of shared-queue and master/worker algorithms.

Parallel computational chemistry applications also make heavy use of this pattern. In the quantum chemistry program GAMESS, the loops over two electron integrals are parallelized with the task queue implied by the `Nextval` construct within TCGMSG. An early version of the distance geometry program DGEOM was parallelized with the master/worker form of this pattern. These examples are discussed in [Mat95].

PTEP (Parallel Telemetry Processor) [NBB01], developed by NASA as the downlink processing system for data from a planetary rover or lander, also makes use of this pattern. The system is implemented in Java but can incorporate components implemented in other languages. For each incoming data packet, the system determines which instrument produced the data, and then performs an appropriate sequential pipeline of processing steps. Because the incoming data packets are independent, the processing of individual packets can be done in parallel.

4.5   THE *DIVIDE AND CONQUER* PATTERN

Problem

Suppose the problem is formulated using the sequential divide-and-conquer strategy. How can the potential concurrency be exploited?

Context

The divide-and-conquer strategy is employed in many sequential algorithms. With this strategy, a problem is solved by splitting it into a number of smaller subproblems, solving them independently, and merging the subsolutions into a solution for the whole problem. The subproblems can be solved directly, or they can in turn be solved using the same divide-and-conquer strategy, leading to an overall recursive program structure.

This strategy has proven valuable for a wide range of computationally intensive problems. For many problems, the mathematical description maps well onto a divide-and-conquer algorithm. For example, the famous fast Fourier transform algorithm [PTV93] is essentially a mapping of the doubly nested loops of the discrete Fourier transform into a divide-and-conquer algorithm. Less well known is the fact that many algorithms from computational linear algebra, such as the Cholesky decomposition [ABE+97, PLA], also map well onto divide-and-conquer algorithms.

The potential concurrency in this strategy is not hard to see: Because the subproblems are solved independently, their solutions can be computed concurrently. Fig. 4.5 illustrates the strategy and the potential concurrency. Notice that each "split" doubles the available concurrency. Although the concurrency in a divide-and-conquer algorithm is obvious, the techniques required to exploit it effectively are not always obvious.

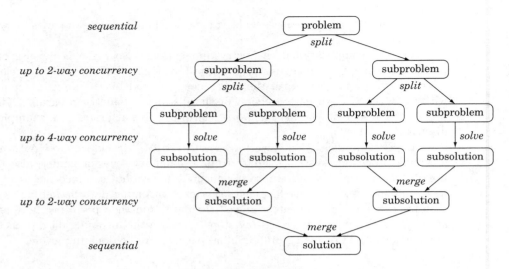

Figure 4.5: The divide-and-conquer strategy

Forces

- The traditional divide-and-conquer strategy is a widely useful approach to algorithm design. Sequential divide-and-conquer algorithms are almost trivial to parallelize based on the obvious exploitable concurrency.

- As Fig. 4.5 suggests, however, the amount of exploitable concurrency varies over the life of the program. At the outermost level of the recursion (initial split and final merge), there is little or no exploitable concurrency, and the subproblems also contain split and merge sections. Amdahl's law (Chapter 2) tells us that the serial parts of a program can significantly constrain the speedup that can be achieved by adding more processors. Thus, if the split and merge computations are nontrivial compared to the amount of computation for the base cases, a program using this pattern might not be able to take advantage of large numbers of processors. Further, if there are many levels of recursion, the number of tasks can grow quite large, perhaps to the point that the overhead of managing the tasks overwhelms any benefit from executing them concurrently.

- In distributed-memory systems, subproblems can be generated on one PE and executed by another, requiring data and results to be moved between the PEs. The algorithm will be more efficient if the amount of data associated with a computation (that is, the size of the parameter set and result for each subproblem) is small. Otherwise, large communication costs can dominate the performance.

- In divide-and-conquer algorithms, the tasks are created dynamically as the computation proceeds, and in some cases, the resulting "task graph" will have an irregular and data-dependent structure. If this is the case, then the solution should employ dynamic load balancing.

```
func solve returns Solution;  // a solution stage
func baseCase returns Boolean;  // direct solution test
func baseSolve returns Solution;  // direct solution
func merge returns Solution;  // combine subsolutions
func split returns Problem[];  // split into subprobs

Solution solve(Problem P) {
    if (baseCase(P))
        return baseSolve(P);
    else {
        Problem subProblems[N];
        Solution subSolutions[N];
        subProblems = split(P);
        for (int i = 0; i < N; i++)
            subSolutions[i] = solve(subProblems[i]);
        return merge(subSolutions);
    }
}
```

Figure 4.6: Sequential pseudocode for the divide-and-conquer algorithm

Solution

A sequential divide-and-conquer algorithm has the structure shown in Fig. 4.6. The cornerstone of this structure is a recursively invoked function (`solve()`) that drives each stage in the solution. Inside `solve`, the problem is either split into smaller subproblems (using `split()`) or it is directly solved (using `baseSolve()`). In the classical strategy, recursion continues until the subproblems are simple enough to be solved directly, often with just a few lines of code each. However, efficiency can be improved by adopting the view that `baseSolve()` should be called when (1) the overhead of performing further splits and merges significantly degrades performance, or (2) the size of the problem is optimal for the target system (for example, when the data required for a `baseSolve()` fits entirely in cache).

The concurrency in a divide-and-conquer problem is obvious when, as is usually the case, the subproblems can be solved independently (and hence, concurrently). The sequential divide-and-conquer algorithm maps directly onto a task-parallel algorithm by defining one task for each invocation of the `solve()` function, as illustrated in Fig. 4.7. Note the recursive nature of the design, with each task in effect dynamically generating and then absorbing a task for each subproblem.

At some level of recursion, the amount of computation required for a subproblems can become so small that it is not worth the overhead of creating a new task to solve it. In this case, a hybrid program that creates new tasks at the higher levels of recursion, then switches to a sequential solution when the subproblems become smaller than some threshold, will be more effective. As discussed next, there are tradeoffs involved in choosing the threshold, which will depend on the specifics of the problem and the number of PEs available. Thus, it is a good idea to design the program so that this "granularity knob" is easy to change.

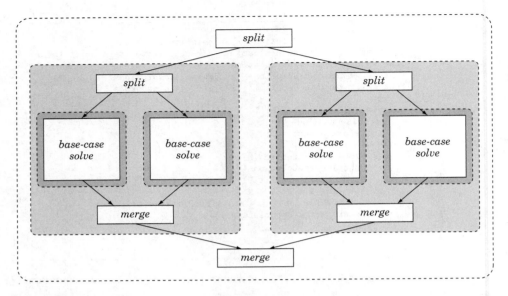

Figure 4.7: Parallelizing the divide-and-conquer strategy. Each dashed-line box represents a task.

Mapping tasks to UEs and PEs. Conceptually, this pattern follows a straightforward fork/join approach (see the *Fork/Join* pattern). One task splits the problem, then forks new tasks to compute the subproblems, waits until the subproblems are computed, and then joins with the subtasks to merge the results.

The easiest situation is when the split phase generates subproblems that are known to be about the same size in terms of needed computation. Then, a straightforward implementation of the fork/join strategy, mapping each task to a UE and stopping the recursion when the number of active subtasks is the same as the number of PEs, works well.

In many situations, the problem will not be regular, and it is best to create more, finer-grained tasks and use a master/worker structure to map tasks to units of execution. This implementation of this approach is described in detail in the *Master/Worker* pattern. The basic idea is to conceptually maintain a queue of tasks and a pool of UEs, typically one per PE. When a subproblem is split, the new tasks are placed in the queue. When a UE finishes a task, it obtains another one from the queue. In this way, all of the UEs tend to remain busy, and the solution shows a good load balance. Finer-grained tasks allow a better load balance at the cost of more overhead for task management.

Many parallel programming environments directly support the fork/join construct. For example, in OpenMP, we could easily produce a parallel application by turning the `for` loop of Fig. 4.6 into an OpenMP `parallel for` construct. Then the subproblems will be solved concurrently rather than in sequence, with the OpenMP runtime environment handling the thread management. Unfortunately, this technique will only work with implementations of OpenMP that support true nesting of parallel regions. Currently, only a few OpenMP implementations do so. Extending OpenMP to better address recursive parallel algorithms is an active area of research in the OpenMP community [Mat03]. One proposal likely to be adopted in a future OpenMP specification is to add an explicit *taskqueue* construct designed to support the expression of recursive algorithms [SHPT00].

The FJTask framework for Java [Lea00b, Lea] provides support for fork/join programs with a pool of threads backing the implementation. Several example programs using a divide-and-conquer strategy are provided with the package.

Communication costs.   Because tasks are generated dynamically from a single top-level task, a task can be executed on a different PE than the one that generated it. In a distributed-memory system, a higher-level task will typically have the data necessary to solve its entire problem, the relevant data must be moved to the subproblem's PE, and the result moved back to the source. Thus it pays to consider how to efficiently represent the parameters and results, and consider whether it makes sense to replicate some data at the beginning of the computation.

Dealing with dependencies.   In most algorithms formulated using the divide-and-conquer strategy, the subproblems can be solved independently from each other. Less commonly, the subproblems require access to a common data structure. These dependencies can be handled using the techniques described in the *Shared Data* pattern.

Other optimizations.   A factor limiting the scalability of this pattern is the serial split and merge sections. Reducing the number of levels of recursion required by splitting each problem into more subproblems can often help, especially if the split and merge phases can be parallelized themselves. This might require restructuring, but can be quite effective, especially in the limiting case of "one-deep divide and conquer", in which the initial split is into P subproblems, where P is the number of available PEs. Examples of this approach are given in [Tho95].

Examples

Mergesort.   Mergesort is a well-known sorting algorithm based on the divide-and-conquer strategy, applied as follows to sort an array of N elements.

- The base case is an array of size less than some threshold. This is sorted using an appropriate sequential sorting algorithm, often quicksort.

- In the split phase, the array is split by simply partitioning it into two contiguous subarrays, each of size $N/2$.

- In the solve-subproblems phase, the two subarrays are sorted (by applying the mergesort procedure recursively).

- In the merge phase, the two (sorted) subarrays are recombined into a single sorted array.

This algorithm is readily parallelized by performing the two recursive mergesorts in parallel.

This example is revisited with more detail in the *Fork/Join* pattern in the *Supporting Structures* design space.

Matrix diagonalization.   Dongarra and Sorensen ([DS87]) describe a parallel algorithm for diagonalizing (computing the eigenvectors and eigenvalues of) a symmetric tridiagonal matrix T. The problem is to find a matrix Q such that $Q^T \cdot T \cdot Q$ is diagonal; the divide-and-conquer strategy goes as follows (omitting the mathematical details).

- The base case is a small matrix which is diagonalized sequentially.

- The split phase consists of finding matrix T' and vectors u, v, such that $T = T' + uv^T$, and T' has the form

$$\begin{bmatrix} T_1 & 0 \\ 0 & T_2 \end{bmatrix}$$

  where T_1 and T_2 are symmetric tridiagonal matrices (which can be diagonalized by recursive calls to the same procedure).

- The merge phase recombines the diagonalizations of T_1 and T_2 into a diagonalization of T.

Details can be found in [DS87] or in [GL96].

Known uses.   Any introductory algorithms text will have many examples of algorithms based on the divide-and-conquer strategy, most of which can be parallelized with this pattern.

Some algorithms frequently parallelized with this strategy include the Barnes-Hut [BH86] and Fast Multipole [GG90] algorithms used in N-body simulations; signal-processing algorithms, such as discrete Fourier transforms; algorithms for banded and tridiagonal linear systems, such as those found in the ScaLAPACK package [CD97, Sca]; and algorithms from computational geometry, such as convex hull and nearest neighbor.

A particularly rich source of problems that use the *Divide and Conquer* pattern is the FLAME project [GGHvdG01]. This is an ambitious project to recast linear algebra problems in recursive algorithms. The motivation is twofold. First, mathematically, these algorithms are naturally recursive; in fact, most pedagogical discussions of these algorithms are recursive. Second, these recursive algorithms have proven to be particularly effective at producing code that is both portable and highly optimized for the cache architectures of modern microprocessors.

Related Patterns

Just because an algorithm is based on a sequential divide-and-conquer strategy does not mean that it must be parallelized with the *Divide and Conquer* pattern. A hallmark of this pattern is the recursive arrangement of the tasks, leading to a varying amount of concurrency and potentially high overheads on machines for which managing the recursion is expensive. If the recursive decomposition into subproblems can be reused, however, it might be more effective to do the recursive decomposition, and then use some other pattern (such as the *Geometric Decomposition* pattern or the *Task Parallelism* pattern) for the actual computation. For example, the first production-level molecular dynamics program to use the fast multipole method, PMD [Win95], used the *Geometric Decomposition* pattern to parallelize the fast multipole algorithm, even though the original fast multipole algorithm used divide and conquer. This worked because the multipole computation was carried out many times for each configuration of atoms.

4.6   THE *GEOMETRIC DECOMPOSITION* PATTERN

Problem

How can an algorithm be organized around a data structure that has been decomposed into concurrently updatable "chunks"?

Context

Many important problems are best understood as a sequence of operations on a core data structure. There may be other work in the computation, but an effective understanding of the full computation can be obtained by understanding how the core data structures are updated. For these types of problems, often the best way to represent the concurrency is in terms of decompositions of these core data structures. (This form of concurrency is sometimes known as domain decomposition, or coarse-grained data parallelism.)

The way these data structures are built is fundamental to the algorithm. If the data structure is recursive, any analysis of the concurrency must take this recursion into account. For recursive data structures, the *Recursive Data* and *Divide and Conquer* patterns are likely candidates. For arrays and other linear data structures, we can often reduce the problem to potentially concurrent components by decomposing the data structure into contiguous substructures, in a manner analogous to dividing a geometric region into subregions—hence the name *Geometric Decomposition*. For arrays, this decomposition is along one or more dimensions, and the resulting subarrays are usually called blocks. We will use the term *chunks* for the substructures or subregions, to allow for the possibility of more general data structures, such as graphs.

This decomposition of data into chunks then implies a decomposition of the update operation into tasks, where each task represents the update of one chunk, and the tasks execute concurrently. If the computations are strictly local, that is, all required information is within the chunk, the concurrency is embarrassingly parallel and the simpler *Task Parallelism* pattern should be used. In many cases, however, the update requires information from points in other chunks (frequently from what we can call *neighboring chunks*—chunks containing data that was nearby in the original global data structure). In these cases, information must be shared between chunks to complete the update.

Example: mesh-computation program.   The problem is to model 1D heat diffusion (that is, diffusion of heat along an infinitely narrow pipe). Initially, the whole pipe is at a stable and fixed temperature. At time 0, we set both ends to different temperatures, which will remain fixed throughout the computation. We then calculate how temperatures change in the rest of the pipe over time. (What we expect is that the temperatures will converge to a smooth gradient from one end of the pipe to the other.) Mathematically, the problem is to solve a 1D differential equation representing heat diffusion:

$$\frac{\partial U}{\partial t} = \frac{\partial^2 U}{\partial x^2} \tag{4.2}$$

The approach used is to discretize the problem space (representing U by a one-dimensional array and computing values for a sequence of discrete time steps). We will output values for each time step as they are computed, so we need only save values for U for two time steps; we will call these arrays `uk` (U at the timestep k) and `ukp1` (U at timestep $k + 1$). At each time step, we then need to compute for each point in array `ukp1` the following:

```
ukp1[i]=uk[i]+ (dt/(dx*dx))*(uk[i+1]-2*uk[i]+uk[i-1]);
```

Variables `dt` and `dx` represent the intervals between discrete time steps and between discrete points, respectively.

Observe that what is being computed is a new value for variable `ukp1` at each point, based on data at that point and its left and right neighbors.

We can begin to design a parallel algorithm for this problem by decomposing the arrays `uk` and `ukp1` into contiguous subarrays (the chunks described earlier). These chunks can be operated on concurrently, giving us exploitable concurrency. Notice that we have a situation in which some elements can be updated using only data from within the chunk, while others require data from neighboring chunks, as illustrated by Fig. 4.8.

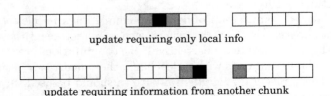

update requiring only local info

update requiring information from another chunk

Figure 4.8: Data dependencies in the heat-equation problem. Solid boxes indicate the element being updated; shaded boxes the elements containing needed data.

Example: matrix-multiplication program.   Consider the multiplication of two square matrices (that is, compute $C = A \cdot B$). As discussed in [FJL+88], the matrices can be decomposed into blocks. The summations in the definition of matrix multiplication are likewise organized into blocks, allowing us to write a blockwise matrix multiplication equation

$$C^{ij} = \sum_k A^{ik} \cdot B^{kj} \tag{4.3}$$

where at each step in the summation, we compute the matrix product $A^{ik} \cdot B^{kj}$ and add it to the running matrix sum.

This equation immediately implies a solution in terms of the *Geometric Decomposition* pattern; that is, one in which the algorithm is based on decomposing the data structure into chunks (square blocks here) that can be operated on concurrently.

To help visualize this algorithm more clearly, consider the case where we decompose all three matrices into square blocks with each task "owning" corresponding blocks of A, B, and C. Each task will run through the sum over k to compute its block of C, with tasks receiving blocks from other tasks as needed. In Fig. 4.9, we illustrate two steps in this process showing a block being updated (the solid block) and the matrix blocks required at two different steps (the shaded blocks), where blocks of the A matrix are passed across a row and blocks of the B matrix are passed around a column.

Forces

- To exploit the potential concurrency in the problem, we must assign chunks of the decomposed data structure to UEs. Ideally, we want to do this in a way that is simple, portable, scalable, and efficient. As noted in Sec. 4.1, however, these goals may conflict. A key consideration is balancing the load, that is, ensuring that all UEs have roughly the same amount of work to do.

- We must also ensure that the data required for the update of each chunk is present when needed. This problem is somewhat analogous to the problem

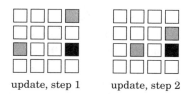

update, step 1   update, step 2

Figure 4.9: Data dependencies in the matrix-multiplication problem. Solid boxes indicate the "chunk" being updated (C); shaded boxes indicate the chunks of A (row) and B (column) required to update C at each of the two steps.

of managing data dependencies in the *Task Parallelism* pattern, and again the design must keep in mind the sometimes-conflicting goals of simplicity, portability, scalability, and efficiency.

Solution

Designs for problems that fit this pattern involve the following key elements: partitioning the global data structure into substructures or "chunks" (the data decomposition), ensuring that each task has access to all the data it needs to perform the update operation for its chunk (the exchange operation), updating the chunks (the update operation), and mapping chunks to UEs in a way that gives good performance (the data distribution and task schedule).

Data decomposition. The granularity of the data decomposition has a significant impact on the efficiency of the program. In a coarse-grained decomposition, there are a smaller number of large chunks. This results in a smaller number of large messages, which can greatly reduce communication overhead. A fine-grained decomposition, on the other hand, results in a larger number of smaller chunks, in many cases leading to many more chunks than PEs. This results in a larger number of smaller messages (and hence increases communication overhead), but it greatly facilitates load balancing.

Although it might be possible in some cases to mathematically derive an optimum granularity for the data decomposition, programmers usually experiment with a range of chunk sizes to empirically determine the best size for a given system. This depends, of course, on the computational performance of the PEs and on the performance characteristics of the communication network. Therefore, the program should be implemented so that the granularity is controlled by parameters that can be easily changed at compile or runtime.

The shape of the chunks can also affect the amount of communication needed between tasks. Often, the data to share between tasks is limited to the boundaries of the chunks. In this case, the amount of shared information scales with the surface area of the chunks. Because the computation scales with the number of points within a chunk, it scales as the volume of the region. This surface-to-volume effect can be exploited to maximize the ratio of computation to communication. Therefore, higher-dimensional decompositions are usually preferred. For example, consider two different decompositions of an N by N matrix into four chunks. In one case, we decompose the problem into four column chunks of size N by $N/4$. In the second case, we decompose the problem into four square chunks of size $N/2$ by $N/2$. For the column block decomposition, the surface area is $2N + 2(N/4)$ or $5N/2$. For the square chunk case, the surface area is $4(N/2)$ or $2N$. Hence, the total amount of data that must be exchanged is less for the square chunk decomposition.

In some cases, the preferred shape of the decomposition can be dictated by other concerns. It may be the case, for example, that existing sequential code can be more easily reused with a lower-dimensional decomposition, and the potential increase in performance is not worth the effort of reworking the code. Also, an instance of this pattern can be used as a sequential step in a larger computation. If the decomposition used in an adjacent step differs from the optimal one for this pattern in isolation, it may or may not be worthwhile to redistribute the data for this step. This is especially an issue in distributed-memory systems where redistributing the data can require significant communication that will delay the computation. Therefore, data decomposition decisions must take into account the capability to reuse sequential code and the need to interface with other steps in the computation. Notice that these considerations might lead to a decomposition that would be suboptimal under other circumstances.

Communication can often be more effectively managed by replicating the non-local data needed to update the data in a chunk. For example, if the data structure is an array representing the points on a mesh and the update operation uses a local neighborhood of points on the mesh, a common communication-management technique is to surround the data structure for the block with a *ghost boundary* to contain duplicates of data at the boundaries of neighboring blocks. So now each chunk has two parts: a primary copy owned by the UE (that will be updated directly) and zero or more ghost copies (also referred to as shadow copies). These ghost copies provide two benefits. First, their use may consolidate communication into potentially fewer, larger messages. On latency-sensitive networks, this can greatly reduce communication overhead. Second, communication of the ghost copies can be *overlapped* (that is, it can be done concurrently) with the update of parts of the array that don't depend on data within the ghost copy. In essence, this hides the communication cost behind useful computation, thereby reducing the observed communication overhead.

For example, in the case of the mesh-computation example discussed earlier, each of the chunks would be extended by one cell on each side. These extra cells would be used as ghost copies of the cells on the boundaries of the chunks. Fig. 4.10 illustrates this scheme.

The exchange operation.   A key factor in using this pattern correctly is ensuring that nonlocal data required for the update operation is obtained before it is needed.

If all the data needed is present before the beginning of the update operation, the simplest approach is to perform the entire exchange before beginning the update, storing the required nonlocal data in a local data structure designed for that purpose (for example, the ghost boundary in a mesh computation). This approach is relatively straightforward to implement using either copying or message passing.

More sophisticated approaches in which computation and communication overlap are also possible. Such approaches are necessary if some data needed for the update is not initially available, and may improve performance in other cases

Figure 4.10: A data distribution with ghost boundaries. Shaded cells are ghost copies; arrows point from primary copies to corresponding secondary copies.

as well. For example, in the example of a mesh computation, the exchange of ghost cells and the update of cells in the interior region (which do not depend on the ghost cells) can proceed concurrently. After the exchange is complete, the boundary layer (the values that do depend on the ghost cells) can be updated. On systems where communication and computation occur in parallel, the savings from such an approach can be significant. This is such a common feature of parallel algorithms that standard communication APIs (such as MPI) include whole classes of message-passing routines to overlap computation and communication. These are discussed in more detail in the MPI appendix.

The low-level details of how the exchange operation is implemented can have a large impact on efficiency. Programmers should seek out optimized implementations of communication patterns used in their programs. In many applications, for example, the collective communication routines in message-passing libraries such as MPI are useful. These have been carefully optimized using techniques beyond the ability of many parallel programmers (we discuss some of these in Sec. 6.4.2) and should be used whenever possible.

The update operation.   Updating the data structure is done by executing the corresponding tasks (each responsible for the update of one chunk of the data structures) concurrently. If all the needed data is present at the beginning of the update operation, and if none of this data is modified during the course of the update, parallelization is easier and more likely to be efficient.

If the required exchange of information has been performed before beginning the update operation, the update itself is usually straightforward to implement—it is essentially identical to the analogous update in an equivalent sequential program, particularly if good choices have been made about how to represent nonlocal data.

If the exchange and update operations overlap, more care is needed to ensure that the update is performed correctly. If a system supports lightweight threads that are well integrated with the communication system, then overlap can be achieved via multithreading within a single task, with one thread computing while another handles communication. In this case, synchronization between the threads is required.

In some systems, for example MPI, nonblocking communication is supported by matching communication primitives: one to start the communication (without blocking), and the other (blocking) to complete the operation and use the results. For maximal overlap, communication should be started as soon as possible, and completed as late as possible. Sometimes, operations can be reordered to allow more overlap without changing the algorithm semantics.

Data distribution and task scheduling.   The final step in designing a parallel algorithm for a problem that fits this pattern is deciding how to map the collection of tasks (each corresponding to the update of one chunk) to UEs. Each UE can then be said to "own" a collection of chunks and the data they contain. Thus, we have a two-tiered scheme for distributing data among UEs: partitioning the data into chunks and then assigning these chunks to UEs. This scheme is flexible enough to represent a variety of popular schemes for distributing data among UEs.

In the simplest case, each task can be statically assigned to a separate UE; then all tasks can execute concurrently, and the intertask coordination needed to implement the exchange operation is straightforward. This approach is most appropriate when the computation times of the tasks are uniform and the exchange operation has been implemented to overlap communication and computation within each tasks.

The simple approach can lead to poor load balance in some situations, however. For example, consider a linear algebra problem in which elements of the matrix are successively eliminated as the computation proceeds. Early in the computation, all the rows and columns of the matrix have numerous elements to work with and decompositions based on assigning full rows or columns to UEs are effective. Later in the computation, however, rows or columns become sparse, the work per row becomes uneven, and the computational load becomes poorly balanced between UEs. The solution is to decompose the problem into many more chunks than there are UEs and to scatter them among the UEs with a cyclic or block-cyclic distribution. (Cyclic and block-cyclic distributions are discussed in the *Distributed Array* pattern.) Then, as chunks become sparse, there are (with high probability) other nonsparse chunks for any given UE to work on, and the load becomes well balanced. A rule of thumb is that one needs around ten times as many tasks as UEs for this approach to work well.

It is also possible to use dynamic load-balancing algorithms to periodically redistribute the chunks among the UEs to improve the load balance. These incur overhead that must be traded off against the improvement likely to occur from the improved load balance and increased implementation costs. In addition, the resulting program is more complex than those that use one of the static methods. Generally, one should consider the (static) cyclic allocation strategy first.

Program structure.   The overall program structure for applications of this pattern will normally use either the *Loop Parallelism* pattern or the *SPMD* pattern, with the choice determined largely by the target platform. These patterns are described in the *Supporting Structures* design space.

Examples

We include two examples with this pattern: a mesh computation and matrix multiplication. The challenges in working with the *Geometric Decomposition* pattern are best appreciated in the low-level details of the resulting programs. Therefore, even though the techniques used in these programs are not fully developed until much later in the book, we provide full programs in this section rather than high-level descriptions of the solutions.

Mesh computation.   This problem is described in the Context section of this pattern. Fig. 4.11 presents a simple sequential version of a program (some details omitted) that solves the 1D heat-diffusion problem. The program associated with

```c
#include <stdio.h>
#include <stdlib.h>
#define NX 100
#define LEFTVAL 1.0
#define RIGHTVAL 10.0
#define NSTEPS 10000

void initialize(double uk[], double ukp1[]) {
  uk[0] = LEFTVAL; uk[NX-1] = RIGHTVAL;
  for (int i = 1; i < NX-1; ++i)
    uk[i] = 0.0;
  for (int i = 0; i < NX; ++i)
    ukp1[i] = uk[i];
}

void printValues(double uk[], int step) { /* NOT SHOWN */ }

int main(void) {
  /* pointers to arrays for two iterations of algorithm */
  double *uk = malloc(sizeof(double) * NX);
  double *ukp1 = malloc(sizeof(double) * NX);
  double *temp;

  double dx = 1.0/NX;
  double dt = 0.5*dx*dx;

  initialize(uk, ukp1);

  for (int k = 0; k < NSTEPS; ++k) {

    /* compute new values */
    for (int i = 1; i < NX-1; ++i) {
      ukp1[i]=uk[i]+ (dt/(dx*dx))*(uk[i+1]-2*uk[i]+uk[i-1]);
    }

    /* "copy" ukp1 to uk by swapping pointers */
    temp = ukp1; ukp1 = uk; uk = temp;

    printValues(uk, k);
  }
  return 0;
}
```

Figure 4.11: Sequential heat-diffusion program

this problem is straightforward, although one detail might need further explanation: After computing new values in ukp1 at each step, conceptually what we want to do is copy them to uk for the next iteration. We avoid a time-consuming actual copy by making uk and ukp1 pointers to their respective arrays and simply swapping them at the end of each step. This causes uk to point to the newly computed values and ukp1 to point to the area to use for computing new values in the next iteration.

This program combines a top-level sequential control structure (the time-step loop) with an array-update operation, which can be parallelized using the *Geometric Decomposition* pattern. We show parallel implementations of this program using OpenMP and MPI.

OpenMP solution.   A particularly simple version of the program using OpenMP and the *Loop Parallelism* pattern is shown in Fig. 4.12. Because OpenMP is a shared-memory programming model, there is no need to explicitly partition and distribute the two key arrays (`uk` and `ukp1`). The creation of the threads and distribution of the work among the threads are accomplished with the `parallel for` directive.

```
#pragma parallel for schedule(static)
```

The `schedule(static)` clause decomposes the iterations of the parallel loop into one contiguous block per thread with each block being approximately the same size. This schedule is important for *Loop Parallelism* programs implementing the *Geometric Decomposition* pattern. Good performance for most *Geometric Decomposition* problems (and mesh programs in particular) requires that the data in the processor's cache be used many times before it is displaced by data from new cache lines. Using large blocks of contiguous loop iterations increases the chance that multiple values fetched in a cache line will be utilized and that subsequent loop iterations are likely to find at least some of the required data in cache.

The last detail to discuss for the program in Fig. 4.12 is the synchronization required to safely copy the pointers. It is essential that all of the threads complete their work before the pointers they manipulate are swapped in preparation for the next iteration. In this program, this synchronization happens automatically due to the implied barrier (see Sec. 6.3.2) at the end of the parallel loop.

The program in Fig. 4.12 works well with a small number of threads. When large numbers of threads are involved, however, the overhead incurred by placing the thread creation and destruction inside the loop over `k` would be prohibitive. We can reduce thread-management overhead by splitting the `parallel for` directive into separate `parallel` and `for` directives and moving the thread creation outside the loop over `k`. This approach is shown in Fig. 4.13. Because the whole `k` loop is now inside a parallel region, we must be more careful about how data is shared between threads. The `private` clause causes the loop indices `k` and `i` to be local to each thread. The pointers `uk` and `ukp1` are shared, however, so the swap operation must be protected. The easiest way to do this is to ensure that only one member of the team of threads does the swap. In OpenMP, this is most easily done by placing the update inside a `single` construct. As described in more detail in the OpenMP appendix, Appendix A, the first thread to encounter the construct will carry out the swap while the other threads wait at the end of the construct.

```
#include <stdio.h>
#include <stdlib.h>
#define NX 100
#define LEFTVAL 1.0
#define RIGHTVAL 10.0
#define NSTEPS 10000

void initialize(double uk[], double ukp1[]) {
  uk[0] = LEFTVAL; uk[NX-1] = RIGHTVAL;
  for (int i = 1; i < NX-1; ++i)
    uk[i] = 0.0;
  for (int i = 0; i < NX; ++i)
    ukp1[i] = uk[i];
}

void printValues(double uk[], int step) { /* NOT SHOWN */ }

int main(void) {
  /* pointers to arrays for two iterations of algorithm */
  double *uk = malloc(sizeof(double) * NX);
  double *ukp1 = malloc(sizeof(double) * NX);
  double *temp;

  double dx = 1.0/NX;
  double dt = 0.5*dx*dx;

  initialize(uk, ukp1);

  for (int k = 0; k < NSTEPS; ++k) {

    #pragma omp parallel for schedule(static)
    /* compute new values */
      for (int i = 1; i < NX-1; ++i) {
        ukp1[i]=uk[i]+ (dt/(dx*dx))*(uk[i+1]-2*uk[i]+uk[i-1]);
      }

    /* "copy" ukp1 to uk by swapping pointers */
    temp = ukp1; ukp1 = uk; uk = temp;

    printValues(uk, k);
  }
  return 0;
}
```

Figure 4.12: Parallel heat-diffusion program using OpenMP

MPI solution. An MPI-based program for this example is shown in Figs. 4.14 and 4.15. The approach used in this program uses a data distribution with ghost cells and the *SPMD* pattern.

Each process is given a single chunk of the data domain of size NX/NP, where NX is the total size of the global data array and NP is the number of processes. For simplicity, we assume NX is evenly divided by NP.

The update of the chunk is straightforward and essentially identical to that from the sequential code. The length and greater complexity in this MPI program

```
#include <stdio.h>
#include <stdlib.h>
#include <omp.h>
#define NX 100
#define LEFTVAL 1.0
#define RIGHTVAL 10.0
#define NSTEPS 10000

void initialize(double uk[], double ukp1[]){/* NOT SHOWN */}
void printValues(double uk[], int step) { /* NOT SHOWN */ }

int main(void) {
  /* pointers to arrays for two iterations of algorithm */
  double *uk = malloc(sizeof(double) * NX);
  double *ukp1 = malloc(sizeof(double) * NX);
  double *temp;
  int i,k;

  double dx = 1.0/NX;
  double dt = 0.5*dx*dx;

  #pragma omp parallel private (k, i)
  {
    initialize(uk, ukp1);

    for (k = 0; k < NSTEPS; ++k) {
      #pragma omp for schedule(static)
      for (i = 1; i < NX-1; ++i) {
        ukp1[i]=uk[i]+ (dt/(dx*dx))*(uk[i+1]-2*uk[i]+uk[i-1]);
      }
      /* "copy" ukp1 to uk by swapping pointers */
      #pragma omp single
      { temp = ukp1; ukp1 = uk; uk = temp; }
    }
  }
  return 0;
}
```

Figure 4.13: Parallel heat-diffusion program using OpenMP. This version has less thread-management overhead.

arises from two sources. First, the data initialization is more complex, because it must account for the data values at the edges of the first and last chunks. Second, message-passing routines are required inside the loop over k to exchange ghost cells.

The details of the message-passing functions can be found in the MPI appendix, Appendix B. Briefly, transmitting data consists of one process doing a *send* operation, specifying the buffer containing the data, and another process doing a *receive* operation, specifying the buffer into which the data should be placed. We need several different pairs of sends and receives because the process that owns the leftmost chunk of the array does not have a left neighbor it needs to communicate with, and similarly the process that owns the rightmost chunk does not have a right neighbor to communicate with.

```
#include <stdio.h>
#include <stdlib.h>
#include <string.h>
#include <mpi.h>
#define NX 100
#define LEFTVAL 1.0
#define RIGHTVAL 10.0
#define NSTEPS 10000

void initialize(double uk[], double ukp1[], int numPoints,
        int numProcs, int myID) {
  for (int i = 1; i <= numPoints; ++i)
     uk[i] = 0.0;
  /* left endpoint */
  if (myID == 0) uk[1] = LEFTVAL;
  /* right endpoint */
  if (myID == numProcs-1) uk[numPoints] = RIGHTVAL;
  /* copy values to ukp1 */
  for (int i = 1; i <= numPoints; ++i) ukp1[i] = uk[i];
}

void printValues(double uk[], int step, int numPoints, int myID)
  { /* NOT SHOWN */ }

int main(int argc, char *argv[]) {
  /* pointers to arrays for two iterations of algorithm */
  double *uk, *ukp1, *temp;

  double dx = 1.0/NX; double dt = 0.5*dx*dx;

  int numProcs, myID, leftNbr, rightNbr, numPoints;
  MPI_Status status;

  /* MPI initialization */
  MPI_Init(&argc, &argv);
  MPI_Comm_size (MPI_COMM_WORLD, &numProcs);
  MPI_Comm_rank(MPI_COMM_WORLD, &myID); //get own ID

  /* initialization of other variables */
  leftNbr = myID - 1; // ID of left "neighbor" process
  rightNbr = myID + 1; // ID of right "neighbor" process
  numPoints = (NX / numProcs);
  /* uk, ukp1 include a "ghost cell" at each end */
  uk = malloc(sizeof(double) * (numPoints+2));
  ukp1 = malloc(sizeof(double) * (numPoints+2));

  initialize(uk, ukp1, numPoints, numProcs, myID);
/* continued in next figure */
```

Figure 4.14: Parallel heat-diffusion program using MPI (continued in Fig. 4.15)

We could further modify the code in Figs. 4.14 and 4.15 to use nonblocking communication to overlap computation and communication, as discussed earlier in this pattern. The first part of the program is unchanged from our first mesh computation MPI program (that is, Fig. 4.14). The differences for this case are

```
/* continued from Figure 4.14 */

for (int k = 0; k < NSTEPS; ++k) {

    /* exchange boundary information */
    if (myID != 0)
        MPI_Send(&uk[1], 1, MPI_DOUBLE, leftNbr, 0,
                            MPI_COMM_WORLD);
    if (myID != numProcs-1)
        MPI_Send(&uk[numPoints], 1, MPI_DOUBLE, rightNbr, 0,
                            MPI_COMM_WORLD);
    if (myID != 0)
        MPI_Recv(&uk[0], 1, MPI_DOUBLE, leftNbr, 0,
                            MPI_COMM_WORLD, &status);
    if (myID != numProcs-1)
        MPI_Recv(&uk[numPoints+1],1, MPI_DOUBLE, rightNbr, 0,
                            MPI_COMM_WORLD, &status);

    /* compute new values for interior points */
    for (int i = 2; i < numPoints; ++i) {
      ukp1[i]=uk[i]+ (dt/(dx*dx))*(uk[i+1]-2*uk[i]+uk[i-1]);
    }
    /* compute new values for boundary points */
    if (myID != 0) {
        int i=1;
        ukp1[i]=uk[i]+ (dt/(dx*dx))*(uk[i+1]-2*uk[i]+uk[i-1]);
    }
    if (myID != numProcs-1) {
        int i=numPoints;
        ukp1[i]=uk[i]+ (dt/(dx*dx))*(uk[i+1]-2*uk[i]+uk[i-1]);
    }

    /* "copy" ukp1 to uk by swapping pointers */
    temp = ukp1; ukp1 = uk; uk = temp;

    printValues(uk, k, numPoints, myID);
}

/* clean up and end */
MPI_Finalize();
return 0;
}
```

Figure 4.15: Parallel heat-diffusion program using MPI (continued from Fig. 4.14)

contained in the second part of the program containing the main computation loop. This code is shown in Fig. 4.16.

While the basic algorithm is the same, the communication is quite different. The *immediate-mode* communication routines, `MPI_Isend` and `MPI_Irecv`, are used to set up and then launch the communication events. These functions (described in more detail in the MPI appendix, Appendix B) return immediately. The update operations on the interior points can then take place because they don't depend on the results of the communication. We then call functions to wait until the communication is complete and update the edges of each UE's chunks using the results

```
/* continued */
MPI_Request reqRecvL, reqRecvR, reqSendL, reqSendR; //needed for
                                                    // nonblocking I/O

for (int k = 0; k < NSTEPS; ++k) {
  /* initiate communication to exchange boundary information */
  if (myID != 0) {
    MPI_Irecv(&uk[0], 1, MPI_DOUBLE, leftNbr, 0,
              MPI_COMM_WORLD, &reqRecvL);
    MPI_Isend(&uk[1], 1, MPI_DOUBLE, leftNbr, 0,
              MPI_COMM_WORLD, &reqSendL);
  }
  if (myID != numProcs-1) {
    MPI_Irecv(&uk[numPoints+1],1, MPI_DOUBLE, rightNbr, 0,
              MPI_COMM_WORLD, &reqRecvR);
    MPI_Isend(&uk[numPoints], 1, MPI_DOUBLE, rightNbr, 0,
              MPI_COMM_WORLD, &reqSendR);
  }
  /* compute new values for interior points */
  for (int i = 2; i < numPoints; ++i) {
    ukp1[i]=uk[i]+ (dt/(dx*dx))*(uk[i+1]-2*uk[i]+uk[i-1]);
  }
  /* wait for communication to complete */
  if (myID != 0) {
    MPI_Wait(&reqRecvL, &status); MPI_Wait(&reqSendL, &status);
  }
  if (myID != numProcs-1) {
    MPI_Wait(&reqRecvR, &status); MPI_Wait(&reqSendR, &status);
  }
  /* compute new values for boundary points */
  if (myID != 0) {
    int i=1;
    ukp1[i]=uk[i]+ (dt/(dx*dx))*(uk[i+1]-2*uk[i]+uk[i-1]);
  }
  if (myID != numProcs-1) {
    int i=numPoints;
    ukp1[i]=uk[i]+ (dt/(dx*dx))*(uk[i+1]-2*uk[i]+uk[i-1]);
  }
  /* "copy" ukp1 to uk by swapping pointers */
  temp = ukp1; ukp1 = uk; uk = temp;

  printValues(uk, k, numPoints, myID);
}
/* clean up and end */
MPI_Finalize();
return 0;
}
```

Figure 4.16: Parallel heat-diffusion program using MPI with overlapping communication/computation (continued from Fig. 4.14)

of the communication events. In this case, the messages are small in size, so it is unlikely that this version of the program would be any faster than our first one. But it is easy to imagine cases where large, complex communication events would be involved and being able to do useful work while the messages move across the computer network would result in significantly greater performance.

```
#include <stdio.h>
#include <stdlib.h>
#define N 100
#define NB 4

#define blockstart(M,i,j,rows_per_blk,cols_per_blk,stride) \
  (M + ((i)*(rows_per_blk))*(stride) + (j)*(cols_per_blk))

int main(int argc, char *argv[]) {
  /* matrix dimensions */
  int dimN = N; int dimP = N; int dimM = N;

  /* block dimensions */
  int dimNb = dimN/NB; int dimPb = dimP/NB; int dimMb = dimM/NB;

  /* allocate memory for matrices */
  double *A = malloc(dimN*dimP*sizeof(double));
  double *B = malloc(dimP*dimM*sizeof(double));
  double *C = malloc(dimN*dimM*sizeof(double));

  /* Initialize matrices */

  initialize(A, B, dimN, dimP, dimM);

  /* Do the matrix multiplication */

  for (int ib=0; ib < NB; ++ib) {
    for (int jb=0; jb < NB; ++jb) {
      /* find block[ib][jb] of C */
      double * blockPtr = blockstart(C, ib, jb, dimNb, dimMb, dimM);
      /* clear block[ib][jb] of C (set all elements to zero) */
      matclear(blockPtr, dimNb, dimMb, dimM);
      for (int kb=0; kb < NB; ++kb) {
        /* compute product of block[ib][kb] of A and
           block[kb][jb] of B and add to block[ib][jb] of C */
        matmul_add(blockstart(A, ib, kb, dimNb, dimPb, dimP),
                   blockstart(B, kb, jb, dimPb, dimMb, dimM),
                   blockPtr, dimNb, dimPb, dimMb, dimP, dimM, dimM);
      }
    }
  }

  /* Code to print results not shown */

  return 0;
}
```

Figure 4.17: Sequential matrix multiplication

Matrix multiplication.   The matrix multiplication problem is described in the Context section. Fig. 4.17 presents a simple sequential program to compute the desired result, based on decomposing the N by N matrix into NB*NB square blocks. The notation block[i][j] in comments indicates the (i,j)-th block as described earlier. To simplify the coding in C, we represent the matrices as 1D arrays (internally arranged in row-major order) and define a macro blockstart to find the top-left

```
/* Declarations, initializations, etc. not shown -- same as
   first version */

/* Do the multiply */

matclear(C, dimN, dimM, dimM); /* sets all elements to zero */

for (int kb=0; kb < NB; ++kb) {

  for (int ib=0; ib < NB; ++ib) {
    for (int jb=0; jb < NB; ++jb) {
      /* compute product of block[ib][kb] of A and
         block[kb][jb] of B and add to block[ib][jb] of C */
      matmul_add(blockstart(A, ib, kb, dimNb, dimPb, dimP),
              blockstart(B, kb, jb, dimPb, dimMb, dimM),
              blockstart(C, ib, jb, dimNb, dimMb, dimM),
              dimNb, dimPb, dimMb, dimP, dimM, dimM);
    }
  }
}

/* Remaining code is the same as for the first version */
```

Figure 4.18: Sequential matrix multiplication, revised. We do not show the parts of the program that are not changed from the program in Fig. 4.17.

corner of a submatrix within one of these 1D arrays. We omit code for functions `initialize` (initialize matrices A and B), `printMatrix` (print a matrix's values), `matclear` (clear a matrix—set all values to zero), and `matmul_add` (compute the matrix product of the two input matrices and add it to the output matrix). Parameters to most of these functions include matrix dimensions, plus a stride that denotes the distance from the start of one row of the matrix to the start of the next and allows us to apply the functions to submatrices as well as to whole matrices.

We first observe that we can rearrange the loops without affecting the result of the computation, as shown in Fig. 4.18.

Observe that with this transformation, we have a program that combines a high-level sequential structure (the loop over `kb`) with a loop structure (the nested loops over `ib` and `jb`) that can be parallelized with the *Geometric Decomposition* pattern.

OpenMP solution. We can produce a parallel version of this program for a shared-memory environment by parallelizing the inner nested loops (over `ib` and/or `jb`) with OpenMP loop directives. As with the mesh example, it is important to keep thread-management overhead small, so once again the **parallel** directive should appear outside of the loop over `kb`. A **for** directive would then be placed prior to one of the inner loops. The issues raised by this algorithm and the resulting source code modifications are essentially the same as those arising from the mesh program example, so we do not show program source code here.

MPI solution. A parallel version of the matrix multiplication program using MPI is shown in Figs. 4.19 and 4.20. The natural approach with MPI is to use

```
#include <stdio.h>
#include <stdlib.h>
#include <string.h>
#include <math.h>
#include <mpi.h>
#define N 100

#define blockstart(M,i,j,rows_per_blk,cols_per_blk,stride) \
  (M + ((i)*(rows_per_blk))*(stride) + (j)*(cols_per_blk))

int main(int argc, char *argv[]) {
  /* matrix dimensions */
  int dimN = N; int dimP = N; int dimM = N;

  /* block dimensions */
  int dimNb, dimPb, dimMb;

  /* matrices */
  double *A, *B, *C;

  /* buffers for receiving sections of A, B from other processes */
  double *Abuffer, *Bbuffer;

  int numProcs, myID, myID_i, myID_j, NB;
  MPI_Status status;

  /* MPI initialization */
  MPI_Init(&argc, &argv);
  MPI_Comm_size (MPI_COMM_WORLD, &numProcs);
  MPI_Comm_rank(MPI_COMM_WORLD, &myID);

  /* initialize other variables */
  NB = (int) sqrt((double) numProcs);
  myID_i = myID / NB;
  myID_j = myID % NB;
  dimNb = dimN/NB; dimPb = dimP/NB; dimMb = dimM/NB;
  A = malloc(dimNb*dimPb*sizeof(double));
  B = malloc(dimPb*dimMb*sizeof(double));
  C = malloc(dimNb*dimMb*sizeof(double));
  Abuffer = malloc(dimNb*dimPb*sizeof(double));
  Bbuffer = malloc(dimPb*dimMb*sizeof(double));

  /* Initialize matrices */
  initialize(A, B, dimNb, dimPb, dimMb, NB, myID_i, myID_j);

/* continued in next figure */
```

Figure 4.19: Parallel matrix multiplication with message passing (continued in Fig. 4.20)

the *SPMD* pattern with the *Geometric Decomposition* pattern. We will use the matrix multiplication algorithm described earlier.

The three matrices (A, B, and C) are decomposed into blocks. The UEs (processes in the case of MPI) involved in the computation are organized into a grid such that the indices of the matrix blocks map onto the coordinates of the processes (that is, matrix block (i,j) is associated with the process with row index i and column index j). For simplicity, we assume the number of processes numProcs is a perfect square and its square root evenly divides the order of the matrices (N).

```
/* continued from previous figure */

  /* Do the multiply */

  matclear(C, dimNb, dimMb, dimMb);
  for (int kb=0; kb < NB; ++kb) {

    if (myID_j == kb) {
      /* send A to other processes in the same "row" */
      for (int jb=0; jb < NB; ++jb) {
        if (jb != myID_j)
          MPI_Send(A, dimNb*dimPb, MPI_DOUBLE,
                   myID_i*NB + jb, 0, MPI_COMM_WORLD);
      }
      /* copy A to Abuffer */
      memcpy(Abuffer, A, dimNb*dimPb*sizeof(double));
    }
    else {
      MPI_Recv(Abuffer, dimNb*dimPb, MPI_DOUBLE,
               myID_i*NB + kb, 0, MPI_COMM_WORLD, &status);
    }
    if (myID_i == kb) {
      /* send B to other processes in the same "column" */
      for (int ib=0; ib < NB; ++ib) {
        if (ib != myID_i)
          MPI_Send(B, dimPb*dimMb, MPI_DOUBLE,
                   ib*NB + myID_j, 0, MPI_COMM_WORLD);
      }
      /* copy B to Bbuffer */
      memcpy(Bbuffer, B, dimPb*dimMb*sizeof(double));
    }
    else {
      MPI_Recv(Bbuffer, dimPb*dimMb, MPI_DOUBLE,
               kb*NB + myID_j, 0, MPI_COMM_WORLD, &status);
    }

    /* compute product of block[ib][kb] of A and
       block[kb][jb] of B and add to block[ib][jb] of C */
    matmul_add(Abuffer, Bbuffer, C,
               dimNb, dimPb, dimMb, dimPb, dimMb, dimMb);
  }
  /* Code to print results not shown */

  /* Clean up and end */
  MPI_Finalize();
  return 0;
}
```

Figure 4.20: Parallel matrix multiplication with message-passing (continued from Fig. 4.19)

Although the algorithm may seem complex at first, the overall idea is straightforward. The computation proceeds through a number of phases (the loop over kb). At each phase, the process whose row index equals the kb index sends its blocks of A across the row of processes. Likewise, the process whose column index equals kb sends its blocks of B along the column of processes. Following the communication operations, each process then multiplies the A and B blocks it received and sums the result into its block of C. After NB phases, the block of the C matrix on each process will hold the final product.

These types of algorithms are very common when working with MPI. The key to understanding these algorithms is to think in terms of the set of processes, the data owned by each process, and how data from neighboring processes flows among the processes as the calculation unfolds. We revisit these issues in the *SPMD* and *Distributed Array* patterns as well as in the MPI appendix.

A great deal of research has been carried out on parallel matrix multiplication and related linear algebra algorithms. A more sophisticated approach, in which the blocks of A and B circulate among processes, arriving at each process just in time to be used, is given in [FJL+88].

Known uses. Most problems involving the solution of differential equations use the *Geometric Decomposition* pattern. A finite-differencing scheme directly maps onto this pattern. Another class of problems that use this pattern comes from computational linear algebra. The parallel routines in the ScaLAPACK [Sca, BCC+97] library are for the most part based on this pattern. These two classes of problems cover a large portion of all parallel applications in scientific computing.

Related Patterns

If the update required for each chunk can be done without data from other chunks, then this pattern reduces to the embarrassingly parallel algorithm described in the *Task Parallelism* pattern. As an example of such a computation, consider computing a 2D FFT (Fast Fourier Transform) by first applying a 1D FFT to each row of the matrix and then applying a 1D FFT to each column. Although the decomposition may appear data-based (by rows/by columns), in fact the computation consists of two instances of the *Task Parallelism* pattern.

If the data structure to be distributed is recursive in nature, then the *Divide and Conquer* or *Recursive Data* pattern may be applicable.

4.7   THE *RECURSIVE DATA* PATTERN

Problem

Suppose the problem involves an operation on a recursive data structure (such as a list, tree, or graph) that appears to require sequential processing. How can operations on these data structures be performed in parallel?

Context

Some problems with recursive data structures naturally use the divide-and-conquer strategy described in the *Divide and Conquer* pattern with its inherent potential for concurrency. Other operations on these data structures, however, seem to have little if any potential for concurrency because it appears that the only way to solve the problem is to sequentially move through the data structure, computing a result at one element before moving on to the next. Sometimes, however, it is possible to reshape the operations in a way that a program can operate concurrently on all elements of the data structure.

An example from [J92] illustrates the situation: Suppose we have a forest of rooted directed trees (defined by specifying, for each node, its immediate ancestor, with a root node's ancestor being itself) and want to compute, for each node in the forest, the root of the tree containing that node. To do this in a sequential program, we would probably trace depth-first through each tree from its root to its leaf nodes; as we visit each node, we have the needed information about the corresponding root. Total running time of such a program for a forest of N nodes would be $O(N)$. There is some potential for concurrency (operating on subtrees concurrently), but there is no obvious way to operate on *all* elements concurrently, because it appears that we cannot find the root for a particular node without knowing its parent's root.

However, a rethinking of the problem exposes additional concurrency: We first define for each node a "successor", which initially will be its parent and ultimately will be the root of the tree to which the node belongs. We then calculate for each node its "successor's successor". For nodes one "hop" from the root, this calculation does not change the value of its successor (because a root's parent is itself). For nodes at least two "hops" away from a root, this calculation makes the node's successor its parent's parent. We repeat this calculation until it converges (that is, the values produced by one step are the same as those produced by the preceding step), at which point every node's successor is the desired value. Fig. 4.21 shows

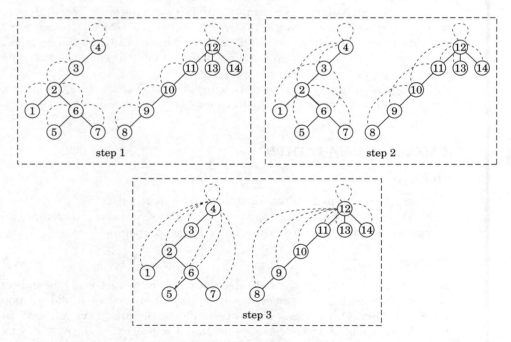

Figure 4.21: Finding roots in a forest. Solid lines represent the original parent-child relationships among nodes; dashed lines point from nodes to their successors.

an example requiring three steps to converge. At each step we can operate on all N nodes in the tree concurrently, and the algorithm converges in at most $\log N$ steps.

What we have done is transform the original sequential calculation (find roots for nodes one "hop" from a root, then find roots for nodes two "hops" from a root, etc.) into a calculation that computes a partial result (successor) for each node and then repeatedly combines these partial results, first with neighboring results, then with results from nodes two hops away, then with results from nodes four hops away, and so on. This strategy can be applied to other problems that at first appear unavoidably sequential; the Examples section presents other examples. This technique is sometimes referred to as *pointer jumping* or *recursive doubling*.

An interesting aspect of this restructuring is that the new algorithm involves substantially more total work than the original sequential one ($O(N \log N)$ versus $O(N)$), but the restructured algorithm contains potential concurrency that if fully exploited reduces total running time to $O(\log N)$ (versus $O(N)$). Most strategies and algorithms based on this pattern similarly trade off an increase in total work for a potential decrease in execution time. Notice also that the exploitable concurrency can be extremely fine-grained (as in the previous example), which may limit the situations in which this pattern yields an efficient algorithm. Nevertheless, the pattern can still serve as an inspiration for lateral thinking about how to parallelize problems that at first glance appear to be inherently sequential.

Forces

- Recasting the problem to transform an inherently sequential traversal of the recursive data structure into one that allows all elements to be operated upon concurrently does so at the cost of increasing the total work of the computation. This must be balanced against the improved performance available from running in parallel.

- This recasting may be difficult to achieve (because it requires looking at the original problem from an unusual perspective) and may lead to a design that is difficult to understand and maintain.

- Whether the concurrency exposed by this pattern can be effectively exploited to improve performance depends on how computationally expensive the operation is and on the cost of communication relative to computation on the target parallel computer system.

Solution

The most challenging part of applying this pattern is restructuring the operations over a recursive data structure into a form that exposes additional concurrency. General guidelines are difficult to construct, but the key ideas should be clear from the examples provided with this pattern.

After the concurrency has been exposed, it is not always the case that this concurrency can be effectively exploited to speed up the solution of a problem. This depends on a number of factors including how much work is involved as each element of the recursive data structure is updated and on the characteristics of the target parallel computer.

Data decomposition.   In this pattern, the recursive data structure is completely decomposed into individual elements and each element is assigned to a separate UE. Ideally each UE would be assigned to a different PE, but it is also possible to assign multiple UEs to each PE. If the number of UEs per PE is too large, however, the overall performance will be poor because there will not be enough concurrency to overcome the increase in the total amount of work.

For example, consider the root-finding problem described earlier. We'll ignore overhead in our computations. If $N = 1024$ and t is the time to perform one step for one data element, then the running time of a sequential algorithm will be about $1024t$. If each UE is assigned its own PE, then the running time of the parallel algorithm will be around $(\log N)t$ or $10t$. If only two PEs are available for the parallel algorithm, however, then all $N \log N$ or 10240 computation steps must be performed on the two PEs, and the execution time will be at least $5120t$, considerably more than the sequential algorithm.

Structure.   Typically the result of applying this pattern is an algorithm whose top-level structure is a sequential composition in the form of a loop, in which each iteration can be described as "perform this operation simultaneously on all (or selected) elements of the recursive data structure". Typical operations include "replace each element's successor with its successor's successor" (as in the example in the Context section) and "replace a value held at this element with the sum of the current value and the value of the predecessor's element."

Synchronization.   Algorithms that fit this pattern are described in terms of *simultaneously* updating all elements of the data structure. Some target platforms (for example, SIMD architectures such as the early Connection Machines) make this trivial to accomplish by assigning each data element to a separate PE (possibly a logical PE) and executing instructions in a lockstep fashion at each PE. MIMD platforms with the right supporting programming environments (for example, High Performance Fortran [HPF97]) provide similar semantics.

If the target platform doesn't provide the required synchronization implicitly, it will be necessary to introduce the synchronization explicitly. For example, if the operation performed during a loop iteration contains the assignment

```
next[k] = next[next[k]]
```

then the parallel algorithm must ensure that `next[k]` is not updated before other UEs that need its value for their computation have received it. One common technique is to introduce a new variable, say `next2`, at each element. Even-numbered iterations then read `next` but update `next2`, while odd-numbered iterations read next2 and update next. The necessary synchronization is accomplished by placing a barrier (as described in the *Implementation Mechanisms* design space) between each successive pair of iterations. Notice that this can substantially increase the overhead associated with the parallel algorithm, which can overwhelm any speedup derived from the additional concurrency. This is most likely to be a factor if the calculation required for each element is trivial (which, alas, for many of the examples it is).

If there are fewer PEs than data elements, the program designer must decide whether to assign each data element to a UE and assign multiple UEs to each PE (thereby simulating some of the parallelism) or whether to assign multiple data elements to each UE and process them serially. The latter is less straightforward (requiring an approach similar to that sketched previously, in which variables involved in the simultaneous update are duplicated), but can be more efficient.

Examples

Partial sums of a linked list.   In this example, adopted from Hillis and Steele [HS86], the problem is to compute the prefix sums of all the elements in a linked list in which each element contains a value x. In other words, after the computation is complete, the first element will contain x_0, the second will contain $x_0 + x_1$, the third $x_0 + x_1 + x_2$, etc.

Fig. 4.22 shows pseudocode for the basic algorithm. Fig. 4.23 shows the evolution of the computation where x_i is the initial value of the $(i + 1)$-th element in the list.

This example can be generalized by replacing addition with any associative operator and is sometime known as a *prefix scan*. It can be used in a variety of situations, including solving various types of recurrence relations.

Known uses.   Algorithms developed with this pattern are a type of *data parallel* algorithm. They are widely used on SIMD platforms and to a lesser extent in languages such as High Performance Fortran [HPF97]. These platforms support the fine-grained concurrency required for the pattern and handle synchronization

```
for all k in parallel
{
    temp[k] = next[k];
    while temp[k] != null
    {
        x[temp[k]] = x[k] + x[temp[k]];
        temp[k] = temp[temp[k]];
    }
}
```

Figure 4.22: Pseudocode for finding partial sums of a list

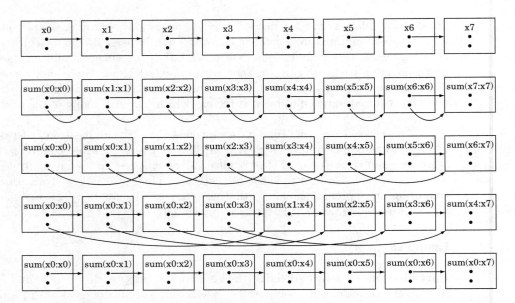

Figure 4.23: Steps in finding partial sums of a list. Straight arrows represent links between elements; curved arrows indicate additions.

automatically because every computation step (logically if not physically) occurs in lockstep on all the processors. Hillis and Steele [HS86] describe several interesting applications of this pattern, including finding the end of a linked list, computing all partial sums of a linked list, region labeling in two-dimensional images, and parsing.

In combinatorial optimization, problems involving traversing all nodes in a graph or tree can often be solved with this pattern by first finding an ordering on the nodes to create a list. Euler tours and ear decomposition [EG88] are well-known techniques to compute this ordering.

JáJá [J92] also describes several applications of this pattern: finding the roots of trees in a forest of rooted directed trees, computing partial sums on a set of rooted directed trees (similar to the preceding example with linked lists), and list-ranking (determining for each element of the list its distance from the start/end of the list).

Related Patterns

With respect to the actual concurrency, this pattern is very much like the *Geometric Decomposition* pattern, a difference being that in this pattern the data structure containing the elements to be operated on concurrently is recursive (at least conceptually). What makes it different is the emphasis on fundamentally rethinking the problem to expose fine-grained concurrency.

4.8 THE *PIPELINE* PATTERN

Problem

Suppose that the overall computation involves performing a calculation on many sets of data, where the calculation can be viewed in terms of data flowing through a sequence of stages. How can the potential concurrency be exploited?

Context

An assembly line is a good analogy for this pattern. Suppose we want to manufacture a number of cars. The manufacturing process can be broken down into a sequence of operations each of which adds some component, say the engine or the windshield, to the car. An assembly line (pipeline) assigns a component to each worker. As each car moves down the assembly line, each worker installs the same component over and over on a succession of cars. After the pipeline is full (and until it starts to empty) the workers can all be busy simultaneously, all performing their operations on the cars that are currently at their stations.

Examples of pipelines are found at many levels of granularity in computer systems, including the CPU hardware itself.

- **Instruction pipeline in modern CPUs.** The stages (fetch instruction, decode, execute, etc.) are done in a pipelined fashion; while one instruction is being decoded, its predecessor is being executed and its successor is being fetched.

- **Vector processing (loop-level pipelining).** Specialized hardware in some supercomputers allows operations on vectors to be performed in a pipelined fashion. Typically, a compiler is expected to recognize that a loop such as

```
for(i = 0; i < N; i++) { a[i] = b[i] + c[i]; }
```

can be vectorized in a way that the special hardware can exploit. After a short startup, one `a[i]` value will be generated each clock cycle.

- **Algorithm-level pipelining.** Many algorithms can be formulated as recurrence relations and implemented using a pipeline or its higher-dimensional generalization, a systolic array. Such implementations often exploit specialized hardware for performance reasons.

- **Signal processing.** Passing a stream of real-time sensor data through a sequence of filters can be modeled as a pipeline, with each filter corresponding to a stage in the pipeline.

- **Graphics.** Processing a sequence of images by applying the same sequence of operations to each image can be modeled as a pipeline, with each operation corresponding to a pipeline stage. Some stages may be implemented by specialized hardware.

- **Shell programs in UNIX.** For example, the shell command

```
cat sampleFile | grep "word" | wc
```

creates a three-stage pipeline, with one process for each command (`cat`, `grep`, and `wc`).

These examples and the assembly-line analogy have several aspects in common. All involve applying a sequence of operations (in the assembly line case it is installing the engine, installing the windshield, etc.) to each element in a sequence of data elements (in the assembly line, the cars). Although there may be ordering constraints on the operations on a single data element (for example, it might be necessary to install the engine before installing the hood), it is possible to perform different operations on different data elements simultaneously (for example, one can install the engine on one car while installing the hood on another.)

The possibility of simultaneously performing different operations on different data elements is the potential concurrency this pattern exploits. In terms of the analysis described in the *Finding Concurrency* patterns, each task consists of repeatedly applying an operation to a data element (analogous to an assembly-line worker installing a component), and the dependencies among tasks are ordering constraints enforcing the order in which operations must be performed on each data element (analogous to installing the engine before the hood).

Forces

- A good solution should make it simple to express the ordering constraints. The ordering constraints in this problem are simple and regular and lend themselves to being expressed in terms of data flowing through a pipeline.

- The target platform can include special-purpose hardware that can perform some of the desired operations.

- In some applications, future additions, modifications, or reordering of the stages in the pipeline are expected.

- In some applications, occasional items in the input sequence can contain errors that prevent their processing.

Solution

The key idea of this pattern is captured by the assembly-line analogy, namely that the potential concurrency can be exploited by assigning each operation (stage

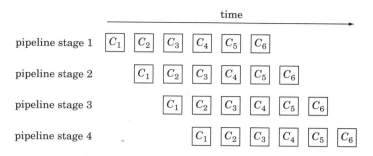

Figure 4.24: Operation of a pipeline. Each pipeline stage *i* computes the *i*-th step of the computation.

of the pipeline) to a different worker and having them work simultaneously, with the data elements passing from one worker to the next as operations are completed. In parallel-programming terms, the idea is to assign each task (stage of the pipeline) to a UE and provide a mechanism whereby each stage of the pipeline can send data elements to the next stage. This strategy is probably the most straightforward way to deal with this type of ordering constraints. It allows the application to take advantage of special-purpose hardware by appropriate mapping of pipeline stages to PEs and provides a reasonable mechanism for handling errors, described later. It also is likely to yield a modular design that can later be extended or modified.

Before going further, it may help to illustrate how the pipeline is supposed to operate. Let C_i represent a multistep computation on data element i. $C_i(j)$ is the jth step of the computation. The idea is to map computation steps to pipeline stages so that each stage of the pipeline computes one step. Initially, the first stage of the pipeline performs $C_1(1)$. After that completes, the second stage of the pipeline receives the first data item and computes $C_1(2)$ while the first stage computes the first step of the second item, $C_2(1)$. Next, the third stage computes $C_1(3)$, while the second stage computes $C_2(2)$ and the first stage $C_3(1)$. Fig. 4.24 illustrates how this works for a pipeline consisting of four stages. Notice that concurrency is initially limited and some resources remain idle until all the stages are occupied with useful work. This is referred to as *filling the pipeline*. At the end of the computation (*draining the pipeline*), again there is limited concurrency and idle resources as the final item works its way through the pipeline. We want the time spent filling or draining the pipeline to be small compared to the total time of the computation. This will be the case if the number of stages is small compared to the number of items to be processed. Notice also that overall throughput/efficiency is maximized if the time taken to process a data element is roughly the same for each stage.

This idea can be extended to include situations more general than a completely linear pipeline. For example, Fig. 4.25 illustrates two pipelines, each with four stages. In the second pipeline, the third stage consists of two operations that can be performed concurrently.

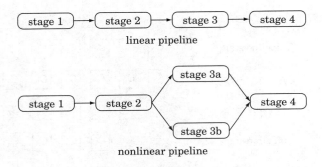

Figure 4.25: Example pipelines

Defining the stages of the pipeline. Normally each pipeline stage will correspond to one task. Fig. 4.26 shows the basic structure of each stage.

If the number of data elements to be processed is known in advance, then each stage can count the number of elements and terminate when these have been processed. Alternatively, a sentinel indicating termination may be sent through the pipeline.

It is worthwhile to consider at this point some factors that affect performance.

- The amount of concurrency in a full pipeline is limited by the number of stages. Thus, a larger number of stages allows more concurrency. However, the data sequence must be transferred between the stages, introducing overhead to the calculation. Thus, we need to organize the computation into stages such that the work done by a stage is large compared to the communication overhead. What is "large enough" is highly dependent on the particular architecture. Specialized hardware (such as vector processors) allows very fine-grained parallelism.

- The pattern works better if the operations performed by the various stages of the pipeline are all about equally computationally intensive. If the stages in the pipeline vary widely in computational effort, the slowest stage creates a bottleneck for the aggregate throughput.

```
initialize
while (more data)
{
    receive data element from previous stage
    perform operation on data element
    send data element to next stage
}
finalize
```

Figure 4.26: Basic structure of a pipeline stage

- The pattern works better if the time required to fill and drain the pipeline is small compared to the overall running time. This time is influenced by the number of stages (more stages means more fill/drain time).

Therefore, it is worthwhile to consider whether the original decomposition into tasks should be revisited at this point, possibly combining lightly-loaded adjacent pipeline stages into a single stage, or decomposing a heavily-loaded stage into multiple stages.

It may also be worthwhile to parallelize a heavily-loaded stage using one of the other *Algorithm Structure* patterns. For example, if the pipeline is processing a sequence of images, it is often the case that each stage can be parallelized using the *Task Parallelism* pattern.

Structuring the computation.   We also need a way to structure the overall computation. One possibility is to use the *SPMD* pattern (described in the *Supporting Structures* design space) and use each UE's ID to select an option in a `case` or `switch` statement, with each case corresponding to a stage of the pipeline.

To increase modularity, object-oriented frameworks can be developed that allow stages to be represented by objects or procedures that can easily be "plugged in" to the pipeline. Such frameworks are not difficult to construct using standard OOP techniques, and several are available as commercial or freely available products.

Representing the dataflow among pipeline elements.   How dataflow between pipeline elements is represented depends on the target platform.

In a message-passing environment, the most natural approach is to assign one process to each operation (stage of the pipeline) and implement each connection between successive stages of the pipeline as a sequence of messages between the corresponding processes. Because the stages are hardly ever perfectly synchronized, and the amount of work carried out at different stages almost always varies, this flow of data between pipeline stages must usually be both buffered and ordered. Most message-passing environments (e.g., MPI) make this easy to do. If the cost of sending individual messages is high, it may be worthwhile to consider sending multiple data elements in each message; this reduces total communication cost at the expense of increasing the time needed to fill the pipeline.

If a message-passing programming environment is not a good fit with the target platform, the stages of the pipeline can be connected explicitly with buffered channels. Such a buffered channel can be implemented as a queue shared between the sending and receiving tasks, using the *Shared Queue* pattern.

If the individual stages are themselves implemented as parallel programs, then more sophisticated approaches may be called for, especially if some sort of data redistribution needs to be performed between the stages. This might be the case if, for example, the data needs to be partitioned along a different dimension or partitioned into a different number of subsets in the same dimension. For example, an application might include one stage in which each data element is partitioned into three subsets and another stage in which it is partitioned into four subsets.

The simplest ways to handle such situations are to aggregate and disaggregate data elements between stages. One approach would be to have only one task in each stage communicate with tasks in other stages; this task would then be responsible for interacting with the other tasks in its stage to distribute input data elements and collect output data elements. Another approach would be to introduce additional pipeline stages to perform aggregation/disaggregation operations. Either of these approaches, however, involves a fair amount of communication. It may be preferable to have the earlier stage "know" about the needs of its successor and communicate with each task receiving part of its data directly rather than aggregating the data at one stage and then disaggregating at the next. This approach improves performance at the cost of reduced simplicity, modularity, and flexibility.

Less traditionally, networked file systems have been used for communication between stages in a pipeline running in a workstation cluster. The data is written to a file by one stage and read from the file by its successor. Network file systems are usually mature and fairly well optimized, and they provide for the visibility of the file at all PEs as well as mechanisms for concurrency control. Higher-level abstractions such as tuple spaces and blackboards implemented over networked file systems can also be used. File-system-based solutions are appropriate in large-grained applications in which the time needed to process the data at each stage is large compared with the time to access the file system.

Handling errors. For some applications, it might be necessary to gracefully handle error conditions. One solution is to create a separate task to handle errors. Each stage of the regular pipeline sends to this task any data elements it cannot process along with error information and then continues with the next item in the pipeline. The error task deals with the faulty data elements appropriately.

Processor allocation and task scheduling. The simplest approach is to allocate one PE to each stage of the pipeline. This gives good load balance if the PEs are similar and the amount of work needed to process a data element is roughly the same for each stage. If the stages have different requirements (for example, one is meant to be run on special-purpose hardware), this should be taken into consideration in assigning stages to PEs.

If there are fewer PEs than pipeline stages, then multiple stages must be assigned to the same PE, preferably in a way that improves or at least does not much reduce overall performance. Stages that do not share many resources can be allocated to the same PE; for example, a stage that writes to a disk and a stage that involves primarily CPU computation might be good candidates to share a PE. If the amount of work to process a data element varies among stages, stages involving less work may be allocated to the same PE, thereby possibly improving load balance. Assigning adjacent stages to the same PE can reduce communication costs. It might also be worthwhile to consider combining adjacent stages of the pipeline into a single stage.

If there are more PEs than pipeline stages, it is worthwhile to consider parallelizing one or more of the pipeline stages using an appropriate *Algorithm Structure* pattern, as discussed previously, and allocating more than one PE to the parallelized stage(s). This is particularly effective if the parallelized stage was previously a bottleneck (taking more time than the other stages and thereby dragging down overall performance).

Another way to make use of more PEs than pipeline stages, *if* there are no temporal constraints among the data items themselves (that is, it doesn't matter if, say, data item 3 is computed before data item 2), is to run multiple independent pipelines in parallel. This can be considered an instance of the *Task Parallelism* pattern. This will improve the throughput of the overall calculation, but does not significantly improve the latency, however, since it still takes the same amount of time for a data element to traverse the pipeline.

Throughput and latency.   There are few more factors to keep in mind when evaluating whether a given design will produce acceptable performance.

In many situations where the *Pipeline* pattern is used, the performance measure of interest is the throughput, the number of data items per time unit that can be processed after the pipeline is already full. For example, if the output of the pipeline is a sequence of rendered images to be viewed as an animation, then the pipeline must have sufficient throughput (number of items processed per time unit) to generate the images at the required frame rate.

In another situation, the input might be generated from real-time sampling of sensor data. In this case, there might be constraints on both the throughput (the pipeline should be able to handle all the data as it comes in without backing up the input queue and possibly losing data) and the latency (the amount of time between the generation of an input and the completion of processing of that input). In this case, it might be desirable to minimize latency subject to a constraint that the throughput is sufficient to handle the incoming data.

Examples

Fourier-transform computations.   A type of calculation widely used in signal processing involves performing the following computations repeatedly on different sets of data.

1. Perform a discrete Fourier transform (DFT) on a set of data.
2. Manipulate the result of the transform elementwise.
3. Perform an inverse DFT on the result of the manipulation.

Examples of such calculations include convolution, correlation, and filtering operations ([PTV93]).

A calculation of this form can easily be performed by a three-stage pipeline.

- The first stage of the pipeline performs the initial Fourier transform; it repeatedly obtains one set of input data, performs the transform, and passes the result to the second stage of the pipeline.

- The second stage of the pipeline performs the desired elementwise manipulation; it repeatedly obtains a partial result (of applying the initial Fourier transform to an input set of data) from the first stage of the pipeline, performs its manipulation, and passes the result to the third stage of the pipeline. This stage can often itself be parallelized using one of the other *Algorithm Structure* patterns.

- The third stage of the pipeline performs the final inverse Fourier transform; it repeatedly obtains a partial result (of applying the initial Fourier transform and then the elementwise manipulation to an input set of data) from the second stage of the pipeline, performs the inverse Fourier transform, and outputs the result.

Each stage of the pipeline processes one set of data at a time. However, except during the initial filling of the pipeline, all stages of the pipeline can operate concurrently; while the first stage is processing the N-th set of data, the second stage is processing the $(N - 1)$-th set of data, and the third stage is processing the $(N - 2)$-th set of data.

Java pipeline framework. The figures for this example show a simple Java framework for pipelines and an example application.

The framework consists of a base class for pipeline stages, `PipelineStage`, shown in Fig. 4.27, and a base class for pipelines, `LinearPipeline`, shown in Fig. 4.28. Applications provide a subclass of `PipelineStage` for each desired stage, implementing its three abstract methods to indicate what the stage should do on the initial step, the computation steps, and the final step, and a subclass of `LinearPipeline` that implements its abstract methods to create an array containing the desired pipeline stages and the desired queues connecting the stages. For the queue connecting the stages, we use `LinkedBlockingQueue`, an implementation of the `BlockingQueue` interface. These classes are found in the `java.util.concurrent` package. These classes use generics to specify the type of objects the queue can hold. For example, `new LinkedBlockingQueue<String>` creates a `BlockingQueue` implemented by an underlying linked list that can hold `Strings`. The operations of interest are `put`, to add an object to the queue, and `take`, to remove an object. `take` blocks if the queue is empty. The class `CountDownLatch`, also found in the `java.util.concurrent` package, is a simple barrier that allows the program to print a message when it has terminated. Barriers in general, and `CountDownLatch` in particular, are discussed in the *Implementation Mechanisms* design space.

The remaining figures show code for an example application, a pipeline to sort integers. Fig. 4.29 is the required subclass of `LinearPipeline`, and Fig. 4.30 is the required subclass of `PipelineStage`. Additional pipeline stages to generate or read the input and to handle the output are not shown.

Known uses. Many applications in signal and image processing are implemented as pipelines.

The OPUS [SR98] system is a pipeline framework developed by the Space Telescope Science Institute originally to process telemetry data from the Hubble

```
import java.util.concurrent.*;

abstract class PipelineStage implements Runnable {

    BlockingQueue in;
    BlockingQueue out;
    CountDownLatch s;

    boolean done;

    //override to specify initialization step
    abstract void firstStep() throws Exception;
    //override to specify compute step
    abstract void step() throws Exception;
    //override to specify finalization step
    abstract void lastStep() throws Exception;


    void handleComputeException(Exception e)
    { e.printStackTrace(); }


    public void run()
    {
     try
       { firstStep();
          while(!done){ step();}
          lastStep();
       }
     catch(Exception e){handleComputeException(e);}
       finally {s.countDown();}
    }

    public void init(BlockingQueue in,
                     BlockingQueue out,
                     CountDownLatch s)
    { this.in = in; this.out = out; this.s = s;}

}
```

Figure 4.27: Base class for pipeline stages

Space Telescope and later employed in other applications. OPUS uses a blackboard architecture built on top of a network file system for interstage communication and includes monitoring tools and support for error handling.

Airborne surveillance radars use space-time adaptive processing (STAP) algorithms, which have been implemented as a parallel pipeline [CLW+00]. Each stage is itself a parallel algorithm, and the pipeline requires data redistribution between some of the stages.

Fx [GOS94], a parallelizing Fortran compiler based on HPF [HPF97], has been used to develop several example applications [DGO+94,SSOG93] that combine data parallelism (similar to the form of parallelism captured in the *Geometric Decomposition* pattern) and pipelining. For example, one application performs 2D Fourier transforms on a sequence of images via a two-stage pipeline (one stage for the row

```
import java.util.concurrent.*;

abstract class LinearPipeline {
    PipelineStage[] stages;
    BlockingQueue[] queues;
    int numStages;
    CountDownLatch s;

    //override method to create desired array of pipeline stage objects
    abstract PipelineStage[] getPipelineStages(String[] args);

    //override method to create desired array of BlockingQueues
    //element i of returned array contains queue between stages i and i+1
    abstract BlockingQueue[] getQueues(String[] args);

    LinearPipeline(String[] args)
    { stages = getPipelineStages(args);
      queues = getQueues(args);
      numStages = stages.length;
      s = new CountDownLatch(numStages);

      BlockingQueue in = null;
      BlockingQueue out = queues[0];
      for (int i = 0; i != numStages; i++)
      { stages[i].init(in,out,s);
        in = out;
        if (i < numStages-2) out = queues[i+1]; else out = null;
        }
    }

    public void start()
    { for (int i = 0; i != numStages; i++)
      { new Thread(stages[i]).start();
        }
    }
}
```

Figure 4.28: Base class for linear pipeline

transforms and one stage for the column transforms), with each stage being itself parallelized using data parallelism. The SIGPLAN paper ([SSOG93]) is especially interesting in that it presents performance figures comparing this approach with a straight data-parallelism approach.

[J92] presents some finer-grained applications of pipelining, including inserting a sequence of elements into a 2-3 tree and pipelined mergesort.

Related Patterns

This pattern is very similar to the *Pipes and Filters* pattern of [BMR+96]; the key difference is that this pattern explicitly discusses concurrency.

For applications in which there are no temporal dependencies between the data inputs, an alternative to this pattern is a design based on multiple sequential pipelines executing in parallel and using the *Task Parallelism* pattern.

```
import java.util.concurrent.*;

class SortingPipeline extends LinearPipeline {

  /*Creates an array of pipeline stages with the
  number of sorting stages given via args. Input
  and output stages are also included at the
  beginning and end of the array. Details are omitted.
  */
  PipelineStage[] getPipelineStages(String[] args)
  { //....
     return stages;
  }


  /* Creates an array of LinkedBlockingQueues to serve as
     communication channels between the stages. For this
     example, the first is restricted to hold Strings,
     the rest can hold Comparables. */
  BlockingQueue[] getQueues(String[] args)
  { BlockingQueue[] queues = new BlockingQueue[totalStages - 1];
     queues[0] = new LinkedBlockingQueue<String>();
     for (int i = 1; i!= totalStages -1; i++)
     { queues[i] = new LinkedBlockingQueue<Comparable>();}
     return queues;
  }


  SortingPipeline(String[] args)
  { super(args);
  }


  public static void main(String[] args)
    throws InterruptedException
  { //create pipeline
     LinearPipeline l = new SortingPipeline(args);
     l.start(); //start threads associated with stages
     l.s.await(); //terminate thread when all stages terminated.
     System.out.println("All threads terminated");
  }
}
```

Figure 4.29: Pipelined sort (main class)

At first glance, one might also expect that sequential solutions built using the *Chain of Responsibility* pattern [GHJV95] could be easily parallelized using the *Pipeline* pattern. In *Chain of Responsibility*, or *COR*, an "event" is passed along a chain of objects until one or more of the objects handle the event. This pattern is directly supported, for example, in the Java Servlet Specification[1] [SER] to enable filtering of HTTP requests. With Servlets, as well as other typical applications of *COR*, however, the reason for using the pattern is to support modular structuring of

---

[1]A Servlet is a Java program invoked by a Web server. The Java Servlets technology is included in the Java 2 Enterprise Edition platform for Web server applications.

```
class SortingStage extends PipelineStage
{
    Comparable val = null;
    Comparable input = null;

    void firstStep() throws InterruptedException
    { input = (Comparable)in.take();
      done = (input.equals("DONE"));
      val = input;
      return;
    }

    void step() throws InterruptedException
    { input = (Comparable)in.take();
        done = (input.equals("DONE"));
        if (!done)
        { if(val.compareTo(input)<0)
            { out.put(val); val = input; }
              else { out.put(input); }
        } else out.put(val);
    }

    void lastStep() throws InterruptedException
    { out.put("DONE"); }
}
```

Figure 4.30: Pipelined sort (sorting stage)

a program that will need to handle *independent* events in *different ways* depending on the event type. It may be that only one object in the chain will even handle the event. We expect that in most cases, the *Task Parallelism* pattern would be more appropriate than the *Pipeline* pattern. Indeed, Servlet container implementations already supporting multithreading to handle independent HTTP requests provide this solution for free.

The *Pipeline* pattern is similar to the *Event-Based Coordination* pattern in that both patterns apply to problems where it is natural to decompose the computation into a collection of semi-independent tasks. The difference is that the *Event-Based Coordination* pattern is irregular and asynchronous where the *Pipeline* pattern is regular and synchronous: In the *Pipeline* pattern, the semi-independent tasks represent the stages of the pipeline, the structure of the pipeline is static, and the interaction between successive stages is regular and loosely synchronous. In the *Event-Based Coordination* pattern, however, the tasks can interact in very irregular and asynchronous ways, and there is no requirement for a static structure.

4.9 THE *EVENT-BASED COORDINATION* PATTERN

Problem

Suppose the application can be decomposed into groups of semi-independent tasks interacting in an irregular fashion. The interaction is determined by the flow of data between them which implies ordering constraints between the tasks. How can these tasks and their interaction be implemented so they can execute concurrently?

Context

Some problems are most naturally represented as a collection of semi-independent entities interacting in an irregular way. What this means is perhaps clearest if we compare this pattern with the *Pipeline* pattern. In the *Pipeline* pattern, the entities form a linear pipeline, each entity interacts only with the entities to either side, the flow of data is one-way, and interaction occurs at fairly regular and predictable intervals. In the *Event-Based Coordination* pattern, in contrast, there is no restriction to a linear structure, no restriction that the flow of data be one-way, and the interaction takes place at irregular and sometimes unpredictable intervals.

As a real-world analogy, consider a newsroom, with reporters, editors, fact-checkers, and other employees collaborating on stories. As reporters finish stories, they send them to the appropriate editors; an editor can decide to send the story to a fact-checker (who would then eventually send it back) or back to the reporter for further revision. Each employee is a semi-independent entity, and their interaction (for example, a reporter sending a story to an editor) is irregular.

Many other examples can be found in the field of discrete-event simulation, that is, simulation of a physical system consisting of a collection of objects whose interaction is represented by a sequence of discrete "events". An example of such a system is the car-wash facility described in [Mis86]: The facility has two car-wash machines and an attendant. Cars arrive at random times at the attendant. Each car is directed by the attendant to a nonbusy car-wash machine if one exists, or queued if both machines are busy. Each car-wash machine processes one car at a time. The goal is to compute, for a given distribution or arrival times, the average time a car spends in the system (time being washed plus any time waiting for a nonbusy machine) and the average length of the queue that builds up at the attendant. The "events" in this system include cars arriving at the attendant, cars being directed to the car-wash machines, and cars leaving the machines. Fig. 4.31 sketches this example. Notice that it includes "source" and "sink" objects to make it easier to model cars arriving and leaving the facility. Notice also that the attendant must be notified when cars leave the car-wash machines so that it knows whether the machines are busy.

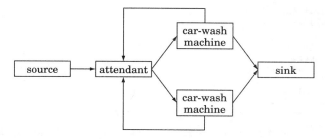

Figure 4.31: Discrete-event simulation of a car-wash facility. Arrows indicate the flow of events.

Also, it is sometimes desirable to compose existing, possibly sequential, program components that interact in possibly irregular ways into a parallel program without changing the internals of the components.

For problems such as this, it might make sense to base a parallel algorithm on defining a task (or a group of tightly coupled tasks) for each component, or in the case of discrete-event simulation, simulation entity. Interaction between these tasks is then based on the ordering constraints determined by the flow of data between them.

Forces

- A good solution should make it simple to express the ordering constraints, which can be numerous and irregular and even arise dynamically. It should also make it possible for as many activities as possible to be performed concurrently.

- Ordering constraints implied by the data dependencies can be expressed by encoding them into the program (for example, via sequential composition) or using shared variables, but neither approach leads to solutions that are simple, capable of expressing complex constraints, and easy to understand.

Solution

A good solution is based on expressing the data flow using abstractions called *events,* with each event having a task that generates it and a task that processes it. Because an event must be generated before it can be processed, events also define ordering constraints between the tasks. Computation within each task consists of processing events.

Defining the tasks.   The basic structure of each task consists of receiving an event, processing it, and possibly generating events, as shown in Fig. 4.32.

If the program is being built from existing components, the task will serve as an instance of the *Facade* pattern [GHJV95] by providing a consistent event-based interface to the component.

The order in which tasks receive events must be consistent with the application's ordering constraints, as discussed later.

```
initialize
while(not done)
{
  receive event
  process event
  send events
}
finalize
```

Figure 4.32: Basic structure of a task in the *Event-Based Coordination* pattern

Representing event flow. To allow communication and computation to overlap, one generally needs a form of asynchronous communication of events in which a task can create (send) an event and then continue without waiting for the recipient to receive it. In a message-passing environment, an event can be represented by a message sent asynchronously from the task generating the event to the task that is to process it. In a shared-memory environment, a queue can be used to simulate message passing. Because each such queue will be accessed by more than one task, it must be implemented in a way that allows safe concurrent access, as described in the *Shared Queue* pattern. Other communication abstractions, such as tuple spaces as found in the Linda coordination language or JavaSpaces [FHA99], can also be used effectively with this pattern. Linda [CG91] is a simple language consisting of only six operations that read and write an associative (that is, content-addressable) shared memory called a *tuple space*. A tuple space is a conceptually shared repository for data containing objects called tuples that tasks use for communication in a distributed system.

Enforcing event ordering. The enforcement of ordering constraints may make it necessary for a task to process events in a different order from the order in which they are sent, or to wait to process an event until some other event from a given task has been received, so it is usually necessary to be able to look ahead in the queue or message buffer and remove elements out of order. For example, consider the situation in Fig. 4.33. Task 1 generates an event and sends it to task 2, which will process it, and also sends it to task 3, which is recording information about all events. Task 2 processes the event from task 1 and generates a new event, a copy of which is also sent to task 3. Suppose that the vagaries of the scheduling and underlying communication layer cause the event from task 2 to arrive before the event from task 1. Depending on what task 3 is doing with the events, this may or may not be problematic. If task 3 is simply tallying the number of events that occur, there is no problem. If task 3 is writing a log entry that should reflect the order in which events are handled, however, simply processing events in the order in which they arrive would in this case produce an incorrect result. If task 3 is controlling a gate, and the event from task 1 results in opening the gate and the event from task 2 in closing the gate, then the out-of-order messages could cause significant problems, and task 3 should not process the first event until after the event from task 1 has arrived and been processed.

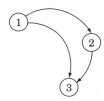

Figure 4.33: Event-based communication among three tasks. Task 2 generates its event in response to the event received from task 1. The two events sent to task 3 can arrive in either order.

In discrete-event simulations, a similar problem can occur because of the semantics of the application domain. An event arrives at a station (task) along with a simulation time when it should be scheduled. An event can arrive at a station before other events with earlier simulation times.

The first step is to determine whether, in a particular situation, out-of-order events can be a problem. There will be no problem if the "event" path is linear so that no out-of-order events will occur, or if, according to the application semantics, out-of-order events do not matter.

If out-of-order events may be a problem, then either an optimistic or pessimistic approach can be chosen. An optimistic approach requires the ability to roll back the effects of events that are mistakenly executed (including the effects of any new events that have been created by the out-of-order execution). In the area of distributed simulation, this approach is called time warp [Jef85]. Optimistic approaches are usually not feasible if an event causes interaction with the outside world. Pessimistic approaches ensure that the events are always executed in order at the expense of increased latency and communication overhead. Pessimistic approaches do not execute events until it can be guaranteed "safe" to do so. In the figure, for example, task 3 cannot process an event from task 2 until it "knows" that no earlier event will arrive from task 1 and vice versa. Providing task 3 with that knowledge may require introducing null events that contain no information useful for anything except the event ordering. Many implementations of pessimistic approaches are based on time stamps that are consistent with the causality in the system [Lam78].

Much research and development effort has gone into frameworks that take care of the details of event ordering in discrete-event simulation for both optimistic [RMC+98] and pessimistic approaches [CLL+99]. Similarly, middleware is available that handles event-ordering problems in process groups caused by the communication system. An example is the Ensemble system developed at Cornell [vRBH+98].

Avoiding deadlocks.   It is possible for systems using this pattern to deadlock at the application level—for some reason the system arrives in a state where no task can proceed without first receiving an event from another task that will never arrive. This can happen because of a programming error; in the case of a simulation, it can also be caused by problems in the model that is being simulated. In the latter case, the developer must rethink the solution.

If pessimistic techniques are used to control the order in which events are processed, then deadlocks can occur when an event is available and actually could be processed, but is not processed because the event is not yet known to be safe. The deadlock can be broken by exchanging enough information that the event can be safely processed. This is a very significant problem as the overhead of dealing with deadlocks can cancel the benefits of parallelism and make the parallel algorithms slower than a sequential simulation. Approaches to dealing with this type of deadlock range from sending frequent enough "null messages" to avoid deadlocks altogether (at the cost of many extra messages) to using deadlock detection schemes to detect the presence of a deadlock and then resolve it (at the cost of possible significant idle time before the deadlock is detected and resolved). The approach of choice will depend on the frequency of deadlock. A middle-ground solution is to use timeouts instead of accurate deadlock detection, and is often the best approach.

Scheduling and processor allocation.   The most straightforward approach is to allocate one task per PE and allow all the tasks to execute concurrently. If insufficient PEs are available to do this, then multiple tasks can be allocated to each PE. This should be done in a way that achieves good load balance. Load balancing is a difficult problem in this pattern due to its potentially irregular structure and possible dynamic nature. Some infrastructures that support this pattern allow task migration so that the load can be balanced dynamically at runtime.

Efficient communication of events.   If the application is to perform well, the mechanism used to communicate events must be as efficient as is feasible. In a shared-memory environment, this means making sure the mechanism does not have the potential to become a bottleneck. In a message-passing environment, there are several efficiency considerations; for example, whether it makes sense to send many short messages between tasks or try to combine them. [YWC⁺96] and [WY95] describe some considerations and solutions.

Examples

Known uses.   A number of discrete-event simulation applications use this pattern. The DPAT simulation used to analyze air traffic control systems [Wie01] is a successful simulation that uses optimistic techniques. It is implemented using the GTW (Georgia Tech Time Warp) System [DFP⁺94]. The paper ([Wie01]) describes application-specific tuning and several general techniques that allow the simulation to work well without excessive overhead for the optimistic synchronization. The Synchronous Parallel Environment for Emulation and Discrete-Event Simulation (SPEEDES) [Met] is another optimistic simulation engine that has been used for large-scale war-gaming exercises. The Scalable Simulation Framework (SSF) [CLL⁺99] is a simulation framework with pessimistic synchronization that has been used for large-scale modeling of the Internet.

The CSWEB application described in [YWC⁺96] simulates the voltage output of combinational digital circuits (that is, circuits without feedback paths). The circuit is partitioned into subcircuits; associated with each are input signal ports and output voltage ports, which are connected to form a representation of the whole circuit. The simulation of each subcircuit proceeds in a timestepped fashion; at each time step, the subcircuit's behavior depends on its previous state and the values read at its input ports (which correspond to values at the corresponding output ports of other subcircuits at previous time steps). Simulation of these subcircuits can proceed concurrently, with ordering constraints imposed by the relationship between values generated for output ports and values read on input ports. The solution described in [YWC⁺96] fits the *Event-Based Coordination* pattern, defining a task for each subcircuit and representing the ordering constraints as events.

Related Patterns

This pattern is similar to the *Pipeline* pattern in that both patterns apply to problems in which it is natural to decompose the computation into a collection of semi-independent entities interacting in terms of a flow of data. There are two key differences. First, in the *Pipeline* pattern, the interaction among entities is fairly regular, with all stages of the pipeline proceeding in a loosely synchronous way, whereas in the *Event-Based Coordination* pattern there is no such requirement, and the entities can interact in very irregular and asynchronous ways. Second, in the *Pipeline* pattern, the overall structure (number of tasks and their interaction) is usually fixed, whereas in the *Event-Based Coordination* pattern, the problem structure can be more dynamic.

CHAPTER 5

The *Supporting Structures* Design Space

5.1 INTRODUCTION

The *Finding Concurrency* and *Algorithm Structure* design spaces focus on algorithm expression. At some point, however, algorithms must be translated into programs. The patterns in the *Supporting Structures* design space address that phase of the parallel program design process, representing an intermediate stage between the problem-oriented patterns of the *Algorithm Structure* design space and the specific programming mechanisms described in the *Implementation Mechanisms* design space. We call these patterns *Supporting Structures* because they describe software constructions or "structures" that support the expression of parallel algorithms. An overview of this design space and its place in the pattern language is shown in Fig. 5.1.

The two groups of patterns in this space are those that represent program-structuring approaches and those that represent commonly used shared data structures. These patterns are briefly described in the next section. In some programming environments, some of these patterns are so well-supported that there is little work for the programmer. We nevertheless document them as patterns for two reasons: First, understanding the low-level details behind these structures is important for effectively using them. Second, describing these structures as patterns provides guidance for programmers who might need to implement them from scratch. The final section of this chapter describes structures that were not deemed important

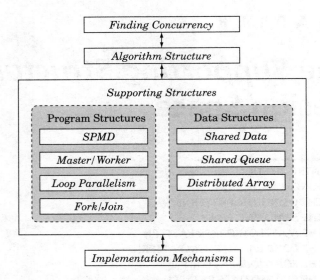

Figure 5.1: Overview of the *Supporting Structures* design space and its place in the pattern language

enough, for various reasons, to warrant a dedicated pattern, but which deserve mention for completeness.

5.1.1   Program Structuring Patterns

Patterns in this first group describe approaches for structuring source code. These patterns include the following.

- **SPMD.** In an *SPMD* (*Single Program, Multiple Data*) program, all UEs execute the same program (*Single Program*) in parallel, but each has its own set of data (*Multiple Data*). Different UEs can follow different paths through the program. In the source code, the logic to control this is expressed using a parameter that uniquely labels each UE (for example a process ID).

- **Master/Worker.** A master process or thread sets up a pool of worker processes or threads and a *bag of tasks*. The workers execute concurrently, with each worker repeatedly removing a task from the bag of tasks and processing it, until all tasks have been processed or some other termination condition has been reached. In some implementations, no explicit master is present.

- **Loop Parallelism.** This pattern addresses the problem of transforming a serial program whose runtime is dominated by a set of compute-intensive loops into a parallel program where the different iterations of the loop are executed in parallel.

- **Fork/Join.** A main UE forks off some number of other UEs that then continue in parallel to accomplish some portion of the overall work. Often the forking UE waits until the child UEs terminate and join.

While we define each of these program structures as a distinct pattern, this is somewhat artificial. It is possible, for example, to implement the *Master/Worker* pattern using the *Fork/Join* pattern or the *SPMD* pattern. These patterns do not represent exclusive, unique ways to structure a parallel program. Rather, they define the major idioms used by experienced parallel programmers.

These patterns also inevitably express a bias rooted in the subset of parallel programming environments we consider in this pattern language. To an MPI programmer, for example, all program structure patterns are essentially a variation on the *SPMD* pattern. To an OpenMP programmer, however, there is a huge difference between programs that utilize thread IDs (that is, the *SPMD* pattern) versus programs that express all concurrency in terms of loop-level worksharing constructs (that is, the *Loop Parallelism* pattern).

Therefore, in using these patterns, don't think of them too rigidly. These patterns express important techniques and are worthy of consideration in isolation, but do not hesitate to combine them in different ways to meet the needs of a particular problem. For example, in the *SPMD* pattern, we will discuss parallel algorithms based on parallelizing loops but expressed with the *SPMD* pattern. It might seem that this indicates that the *SPMD* and *Loop Parallelism* patterns are not really distinct patterns, but in fact it shows how flexible the *SPMD* pattern is.

5.1.2   Patterns Representing Data Structures

Patterns in this second group have to do with managing data dependencies. The *Shared Data* pattern deals with the general case. The others describe specific frequently used data structures.

- ***Shared Data.*** This pattern addresses the general problem of handling data that is shared by more than one UE, discussing both correctness and performance issues.

- ***Shared Queue.*** This pattern represents a "thread-safe" implementation of the familiar queue abstract data type (ADT), that is, an implementation of the queue ADT that maintains the correct semantics even when used by concurrently executing UEs.

- ***Distributed Array.*** This pattern represents a class of data structures often found in parallel scientific computing, namely arrays of one or more dimensions that are decomposed into subarrays and distributed among processes or threads.

5.2   FORCES

All of the program structuring patterns address the same basic problem: how to structure source code to best support algorithm structures of interest. Unique forces are applicable to each pattern, but in designing a program around these structures, there are some common forces to consider in most cases:

- **Clarity of abstraction.** Is the parallel algorithm clearly apparent from the source code?

In a well-structured program, the algorithm leaps from the page. The reader can see the details of the algorithm with little mental effort. We refer to this quality as *clarity of abstraction*. Good clarity of abstraction is always important for writing correct code, but is particularly essential for parallel programs: Parallel programmers must deal with multiple simultaneous tasks that interact in subtle ways. Getting this right can be very difficult, especially if it is hard to figure out what the algorithm is doing by looking at the source code.

- **Scalability.** How many processors can the parallel program effectively utilize?

   The scalability of a program is restricted by three factors. First, there is the amount of concurrency available in the algorithm. If an algorithm only has ten concurrent tasks, then running with more than ten PEs will provide no benefit. Second, the fraction of the runtime spent doing inherently serial work limits how many processors can be used. This is described quantitatively by Amdahl's law as discussed in Chapter 2. Finally, the parallel overhead of the algorithm contributes to the serial fraction mentioned in Amdahl's law and limits scalability.

- **Efficiency.** How close does the program come to fully utilizing the resources of the parallel computer? Recall the quantitative definition of efficiency given in Chapter 2:

$$E(P) = \frac{S(P)}{P} \tag{5.1}$$

$$= \frac{T(1)}{P\,T(P)} \tag{5.2}$$

P is the number of PEs, $T(1)$ is some sequential reference time, and $T(P)$ is the parallel time with P PEs. $S(P)$ is the speedup.

   The most rigorous definition of efficiency sets $T(1)$ to the execution time of the best sequential algorithm corresponding to the parallel algorithm under study. When analyzing parallel programs, "best" sequential algorithms are not always available, and it is common to use the runtime for the parallel program on a single PE as the reference time. This can inflate the efficiency because managing the parallel computation always incurs some overhead, even when executing on a single PE. Efficiency is closely related to scalability because every highly scalable algorithm is also highly efficient. Even when the scalability is limited by the available number of tasks or the parallel hardware, however, algorithms can differ in their efficiency.

- **Maintainability.** Is the program easy to debug, verify, and modify?

   Casting an algorithm into source code is almost never a one-time proposition. Programs need to be debugged, new features added, performance tuned, etc. These changes to the source code are referred to as *maintenance*. Programs are more or less maintainable depending on how hard it is to make these changes and to do them correctly.

- **Environmental affinity.** Is the program well aligned with the programming environment and hardware of choice?

  If the hardware, for example, lacks support for shared memory, an algorithm structure based on shared memory would be a poor choice. This issue also comes up when considering programming environments. When creating a programming environment, the creators usually have a particular style of programming in mind. For example, OpenMP is designed specifically for programs consisting of a series of loops, the iterations of which will be split between multiple threads (loop-based parallelism). It is much easier to write software when the program structure employed is well aligned with the programming environment.

- **Sequential equivalence.** Where appropriate, does a program produce equivalent results when run with many UEs as with one? If not equivalent, is the relationship between them clear?

  It is highly desirable that the results of an execution of a parallel program be the same regardless of the number of PEs used. This is not always possible, especially if bitwise equivalence is desired, because floating-point operations performed in a different order can produce small (or, for ill-conditioned algorithms, not so small) changes in the resulting values. However, if we know that the parallel program gives equivalent results when executed on one processor as many, then we can reason about correctness and do most of the testing on the single-processor version. This is much easier, and thus, when possible, sequential equivalence is a highly desirable goal.

5.3   CHOOSING THE PATTERNS

Choosing which program structure pattern to use is usually straightforward. In most cases, the programming environment selected for the project and the patterns used from the *Algorithm Structure* design space point to the appropriate program structure pattern to use. We will consider these two factors separately.

The relationship between the patterns in the *Algorithm Structure* and *Supporting Structures* design spaces is shown in Table 5.1. Notice that the *Supporting*

Table 5.1: Relationship between *Supporting Structures* patterns and *Algorithm Structure* patterns. The number of stars (ranging from zero to four) is an indication of the likelihood that the given *Supporting Structures* pattern is useful in the implementation of the *Algorithm Structure* pattern.

	Task Parallelism	Divide and Conquer	Geometric Decomposition	Recursive Data	Pipeline	Event-Based Coordination
SPMD	★★★★	★★★	★★★★	★★	★★★	★★
Loop Parallelism	★★★★	★★	★★★			
Master/ Worker	★★★★	★★	★	★	★	★
Fork/Join	★★	★★★★	★★		★★★★	★★★★

Table 5.2: Relationship between *Supporting Structures* patterns and programming environments. The number of stars (ranging from zero to four) is an indication of the likelihood that the given *Supporting Structures* pattern is useful in the programming environment.

	OpenMP	MPI	Java
SPMD	★★★	★★★★	★★
LoopParallelism	★★★★	★	★★★
Master/Worker	★★	★★★	★★★
Fork/Join	★★★		★★★★

Structures patterns can be used with multiple *Algorithm Structure* patterns. For example, consider the range of applications using the *Master/Worker* pattern: In [BCM+91, CG91, CGMS94], it is used to implement everything from embarrassingly parallel programs (a special case of the *Task Parallelism* pattern) to those using the *Geometric Decomposition* pattern. The *SPMD* pattern is even more flexible and covers the most important algorithm structures used in scientific computing (which tends to emphasize the *Geometric Decomposition, Task Parallelism,* and *Divide and Conquer* patterns). This flexibility can make it difficult to choose a program structure pattern solely on the basis of the choice of *Algorithm Structure* pattern(s).

The choice of programming environment, however, helps narrow the choice considerably. In Table 5.2, we show the relationship between programming environments and the *Supporting Structures* patterns. MPI, the programming environment of choice on any distributed-memory computer, strongly favors the *SPMD* pattern. OpenMP, the standard programming model used on virtually every shared-memory computer on the market, is closely aligned with the *Loop Parallelism* pattern. The combination of programming environment and *Algorithm Structure* patterns typically selects which *Supporting Structures* patterns to use.

5.4   THE *SPMD* PATTERN

Problem

The interactions between the various UEs cause most of the problems when writing correct and efficient parallel programs. How can programmers structure their parallel programs to make these interactions more manageable and easier to integrate with the core computations?

Context

A parallel program takes complexity to a new level. There are all the normal challenges of writing any program. On top of those challenges, the programmer must manage multiple tasks running on multiple UEs. In addition, these tasks and UEs interact, either through exchange of messages or by sharing memory. In spite of these complexities, the program must be correct, and the interactions must be well orchestrated if excess overhead is to be avoided.

Fortunately, for most parallel algorithms, the operations carried out on each UE are similar. The data might be different between UEs, or slightly different computations might be needed on a subset of UEs (for example, handling boundary conditions in partial differential equation solvers), but for the most part each UE will carry out similar computations. Hence, in many cases the tasks and their interactions can be made more manageable by bringing them all together into one source tree. This way, the logic for the tasks is side by side with the logic for the interactions between tasks, thereby making it much easier to get them right.

This is the so-called "Single Program, Multiple Data" (SPMD) approach. It emerged as the dominant way to structure parallel programs early in the evolution of scalable computing, and programming environments, notably MPI, have been designed to support this approach.[1]

In addition to the advantages to the programmer, SPMD makes management of the solution much easier. It is much easier to keep a software infrastructure up to date and consistent if there is only one program to manage. This factor becomes especially important on systems with large numbers of PEs. These can grow to huge numbers. For example, the two fastest computers in the world according to the November 2003 top 500 list [Top], the Earth Simulator at the Earth Simulator Center in Japan and the ASCI Q at Los Alamos National Labs, have 5120 and 8192 processors, respectively. If each PE runs a distinct program, managing the application software could quickly become prohibitively difficult.

This pattern is by far the most commonly used pattern for structuring parallel programs. It is particularly relevant for MPI programmers and problems using the Task Parallelism *and* Geometric Decomposition *patterns. It has also proved effective for problems using the* Divide and Conquer *and* Recursive Data *patterns.*

Forces

- Using similar code for each UE is easier for the programmer, but most complex applications require that different operations run on different UEs and with different data.

- Software typically outlives any given parallel computer. Hence, programs should be portable. This compels the programmer to assume the lowest common denominator in programming environments, and to assume that only basic mechanisms for coordinating tasks will be available.

---

[1] It is not that the available programming environments pushed SPMD; the force was the other way around. The programming environments for MIMD machines pushed SPMD because that is the way programmers wanted to write their programs. They wrote them this way because they found it to be the best way to get the logic correct and efficient for what the tasks do and how they interact. For example, the programming environment PVM, sometimes considered a predecessor to MPI, in addition to the SPMD program structure also supported running different programs on different UEs (sometimes called the MPMD program structure). The MPI designers, with the benefit of the PVM experience, chose to support only SPMD.

- Achieving high scalability and good efficiency in a parallel program requires that the program be well aligned with the architecture of the parallel computer. Therefore, the details of the parallel system must be exposed and, where appropriate, under the programmer's control.

Solution

The *SPMD* pattern solves this problem by creating a single source-code image that runs on each of the UEs. The solution consists of the following basic elements.

- **Initialize.** The program is loaded onto each UE and opens with bookkeeping operations to establish a common context. The details of this procedure are tied to the parallel programming environment and typically involve establishing communication channels with other UEs.

- **Obtain a unique identifier.** Near the top of the program, an identifier is set that is unique to each UE. This is usually the UE's rank within the MPI group (that is, a number in the interval from 0 to $N - 1$, where N is the number of UEs) or the thread ID in OpenMP. This unique identifier allows different UEs to make different decisions during program execution.

- **Run the same program on each UE, using the unique ID to differentiate behavior on different UEs.** The same program runs on each UE. Differences in the instructions executed by different UEs are usually driven by the identifier. (They could also depend on the UE's data.) There are many ways to specify that different UEs take different paths through the source code. The most common are (1) branching statements to give specific blocks of code to different UEs and (2) using the UE identifier in loop index calculations to split loop iterations among the UEs.

- **Distribute data.** The data operated on by each UE is specialized to that UE by one of two techniques: (1) decomposing global data into chunks and storing them in the local memory of each UE, and later, if required, recombining them into the globally relevant results or (2) sharing or replicating the program's major data structures and using the UE identifier to associate subsets of the data with particular UEs.

- **Finalize.** The program closes by cleaning up the shared context and shutting down the computation. If globally relevant data was distributed among UEs, it will need to be recombined.

Discussion.   An important issue to keep in mind when developing SPMD programs is the *clarity of abstraction,* that is, how easy it is to understand the algorithm from reading the program's source code. Depending on how the data is handled, this can range from awful to good. If complex index algebra on the UE identifier is needed to determine the data relevant to a UE or the instruction branch, the algorithm can be almost impossible to follow from the source code. (The *Distributed Array* pattern discusses useful techniques for arrays.)

In some cases, a replicated data algorithm combined with simple loop splitting is the best option because it leads to a clear abstraction of the parallel algorithm within the source code and an algorithm with a high degree of sequential equivalence. Unfortunately, this simple approach might not scale well, and more complex solutions might be needed. Indeed, SPMD algorithms can be highly scalable, and algorithms requiring complex coordination between UEs and scaling out to several thousand UEs [PH95] have been written using this pattern. These highly scalable algorithms are usually extremely complicated as they distribute the data across the nodes (that is, no simplifying replicated data techniques), and they generally include complex load-balancing logic. These algorithms, unfortunately, bear little resemblance to their serial counterparts, reflecting a common criticism of the *SPMD* pattern.

An important advantage of the *SPMD* pattern is that overheads associated with startup and termination are segregated at the beginning and end of the program, not inside time-critical loops. This contributes to efficient programs and results in the efficiency issues being driven by the communication overhead, the capability to balance the computational load among the UEs, and the amount of concurrency available in the algorithm itself.

SPMD programs are closely aligned with programming environments based on message passing. For example, most MPI or PVM programs use the *SPMD* pattern. Note, however, that it is possible to use the *SPMD* pattern with OpenMP [CPP01]. With regard to the hardware, the *SPMD* pattern does not assume anything concerning the address space within which the tasks execute. As long as each UE can run its own instruction stream operating on its own data (that is, the computer can be classified as MIMD), the SPMD structure is satisfied. This generality of SPMD programs is one of the strengths of this pattern.

Examples

The issues raised by application of the *SPMD* pattern are best discussed using three specific examples:

- Numerical integration to estimate the value of a definite integral using the trapezoid rule

- Molecular dynamics, force computations

- Mandelbrot set computation

Numerical integration.   We can use a very simple program, frequently used in teaching parallel programming, to explore many of the issues raised by the *SPMD* pattern. Consider the problem of estimating the value of π using Eq. 5.3.

$$\pi = \int_0^1 \frac{4}{1 + x^2} \, dx \tag{5.3}$$

We use trapezoidal integration to numerically solve the integral. The idea is to fill the area under a curve with a series of rectangles. As the width of the rectangles

```
#include <stdio.h>
#include <math.h>

int main () {
    int i;
    int num_steps = 1000000;
    double x, pi, step, sum = 0.0;

    step = 1.0/(double) num_steps;

    for (i=0;i< num_steps; i++)
    {
        x = (i+0.5)*step;
        sum = sum + 4.0/(1.0+x*x);
    }
    pi = step * sum;
    printf("pi %lf\n",pi);
    return 0;
}
```

Figure 5.2: Sequential program to carry out a trapezoid rule integration to compute $\int_0^1 \frac{4}{1+x^2}\,dx$

approaches zero, the sum of the areas of the rectangles approaches the value of the integral.

A program to carry this calculation out on a single processor is shown in Fig. 5.2. To keep the program as simple as possible, we fix the number of steps to use in the integration at 1,000,000. The variable sum is initialized to 0 and the step size is computed as the range in x (equal to 1.0 in this case) divided by the number of steps. The area of each rectangle is the width (the step size) times the height (the value of the integrand at the center of the interval). Because the width is a constant, we pull it out of the summation and multiply the sum of the rectangle heights by the step size, step, to get our estimate of the definite integral.

We will look at several versions of the parallel algorithm. We can see all the elements of a classic SPMD program in the simple MPI version of this program, as shown in Fig. 5.3. The same program is run on each UE. Near the beginning of the program, the MPI environment is initialized and the ID for each UE (my_id) is given by the process rank for each UE in the process group associated with the communicator MPI_COMM_WORLD (for information about communicators and other MPI details, see the MPI appendix, Appendix B). We use the number of UEs and the ID to assign loop ranges (i_start and i_end) to each UE. Because the number of steps may not be evenly divided by the number of UEs, we have to make sure the last UE runs up to the last step in the calculation. After the partial sums have been computed on each UE, we multiply by the step size, step, and then use the MPI_Reduce() routine to combine the partial sums into a global sum. (Reduction operations are described in more detail in the *Implementation Mechanisms* design space.) This global value will only be available in the process with my_id == 0, so we direct that process to print the answer.

In essence, what we have done in the example in Fig. 5.3 is to replicate the key data (in this case, the partial summation value, sum), use the UE's ID to explicitly

```
#include <stdio.h>
#include <math.h>
#include <mpi.h>

int main (int argc, char *argv[]) {
    int i, i_start, i_end;
    int num_steps = 1000000;
    double x, pi, step, sum = 0.0;

    int my_id, numprocs;
    step = 1.0/(double) num_steps;

    MPI_Init(&argc, &argv);
    MPI_Comm_rank(MPI_COMM_WORLD, &my_id);
    MPI_Comm_size(MPI_COMM_WORLD, &numprocs);

    i_start = my_id * (num_steps/numprocs);
    i_end = i_start + (num_steps/numprocs);
    if (my_id == (numprocs-1)) i_end = num_steps;

    for (i=i_start; i< i_end; i++)
    {
        x = (i+0.5)*step;
        sum = sum + 4.0/(1.0+x*x);
    }
    sum *= step;
    MPI_Reduce(&sum, &pi, 1, MPI_DOUBLE, MPI_SUM, 0,
        MPI_COMM_WORLD);
    if (my_id == 0) printf("pi %lf\n",pi);
    MPI_Finalize();
    return 0;
}
```

Figure 5.3: MPI program to carry out a trapezoid rule integration in parallel by assigning one block of loop iterations to each UE and performing a reduction

split up the work into blocks with one block per UE, and then recombine the local results into the final global result. The challenge in applying this pattern is to (1) split up the data correctly, (2) correctly recombine the results, and (3) achieve an even distribution of the work. The first two steps were trivial in this example. The load balance, however, is a bit more difficult. Unfortunately, the simple procedure we used in Fig. 5.3 could result in significantly more work for the last UE if the number of UEs does not evenly divide the number of steps. For a more even distribution of the work, we need to spread out the extra iterations among multiple UEs. We show one way to do this in the program fragment in Fig. 5.4. We compute the number of iterations left over after dividing the number of steps by the number of processors (**rem**). We will increase the number of iterations computed by the first **rem** UEs to cover that amount of work. The code in Fig. 5.4 accomplishes that task. These sorts of index adjustments are the bane of programmers using the *SPMD* pattern. Such code is error-prone and the source of hours of frustration as program readers try to understand the reasoning behind this logic.

Finally, we use a loop-splitting strategy for the numerical integration program. The resulting program is shown in Fig. 5.5. This approach uses a common trick to

```
int rem = num_steps % numprocs;

i_start = my_id * (num_steps/numprocs);
i_end = i_start + (num_steps/numprocs);

if (rem != 0){
   if(my_id < rem){
      i_start += my_id;
      i_end += (my_id + 1);
   }
   else {
      i_start += rem;
      i_end += rem;
   }
}
```

Figure 5.4: Index calculation that more evenly distributes the work when the number of steps is not evenly divided by the number of UEs. The idea is to split up the remaining tasks (rem) among the first rem UEs.

```
#include <stdio.h>
#include <math.h>
#include <mpi.h>

int main (int argc, char *argv[]) {
   int i;
   int num_steps = 1000000;
   double x, pi, step, sum = 0.0;

   int my_id, numprocs;
   step = 1.0/(double) num_steps;

   MPI_Init(&argc, &argv);
   MPI_Comm_rank(MPI_COMM_WORLD, &my_id);
   MPI_Comm_size(MPI_COMM_WORLD, &numprocs);

   for (i=my_id; i< num_steps; i+= numprocs)
   {
      x = (i+0.5)*step;
      sum = sum + 4.0/(1.0+x*x);
   }
   sum *= step;
   MPI_Reduce(&sum, &pi, 1, MPI_DOUBLE, MPI_SUM, 0,
      MPI_COMM_WORLD);
   if (my_id == 0) printf("pi %lf\n",pi);
   MPI_Finalize();
   return 0;
}
```

Figure 5.5: MPI program to carry out a trapezoid rule integration in parallel using a simple loop-splitting algorithm with cyclic distribution of iterations and a reduction

```
#include <stdio.h>
#include <math.h>
#include <omp.h>

int main () {
   int num_steps = 1000000;
   double pi, step, sum = 0.0;

   step = 1.0/(double) num_steps;

#pragma omp parallel reduction(+:sum)
   {
      int i, id = omp_get_thread_num();
      int numthreads = omp_get_num_threads();
      double x;

      for (i=id;i< num_steps; i+=numthreads){
         x = (i+0.5)*step;
         sum += + 4.0/(1.0+x*x);
      }
   } // end of parallel region
   pi = step * sum;
   printf("\n pi is %lf\n",pi);
   return 0;
}
```

Figure 5.6: OpenMP program to carry out a trapezoid rule integration in parallel using the same SPMD algorithm used in Fig. 5.5

achieve a cyclic distribution of the loop iterations: Each UE starts with the iteration equal to its rank, and then marches through the iterations of the loop with a stride equal to the number of UEs. The iterations are interleaved among the UEs, in the same manner as a deck of cards would be dealt. This version of the program evenly distributes the load without resorting to complex index algebra.

SPMD programs can also be written using OpenMP and Java. In Fig. 5.6, we show an OpenMP version of our trapezoidal integration program. This program is very similar to the analogous MPI program. The program has a single parallel region. We start by finding the thread ID and the number of threads in the team. We then use the same trick to interleave iterations among the team of threads. As with the MPI program, we use a reduction to combine partial sums into a single global sum.

Molecular dynamics.   Throughout this pattern language, we have used molecular dynamics as a recurring example. Molecular dynamics simulates the motions of a large molecular system. It uses an explicit time-stepping methodology where at each time step, the force on each atom is computed and standard techniques from classical mechanics are used to compute how the forces change atomic motions.

This problem is ideal for presenting key concepts in parallel algorithms because there are so many ways to approach the problem based on the target computer system and the intended use of the program. In this discussion, we will follow the approach taken in [Mat95] and assume that (1) a sequential version of the program

```
Int const N // number of atoms

Array of Real :: atoms (3,N) //3D coordinates
Array of Real :: velocities (3,N) //velocity vector
Array of Real :: forces (3,N) //force in each dimension
Array of List :: neighbors(N) //atoms in cutoff volume

loop over time steps
    initialize_forces (N, Forces)
    if(time to update neighbor list)
        neighbor_list (N, Atoms, neighbors)
    end if
    vibrational_forces (N, atoms, forces)
    rotational_forces (N, atoms, forces)
    non_bonded_forces (N, atoms, neighbors, forces)
    update_atom_positions_and_velocities(
                    N, atoms, velocities, forces)
    physical_properties ( ... Lots of stuff ... )
end loop
```

Figure 5.7: Pseudocode for molecular dynamics example. This code is very similar to the version discussed earlier, but a few extra details have been included. To support more detailed pseudocode examples, the call to the function that initializes the force arrays has been made explicit. Also, the fact that the neighbor list is only occasionally updated is made explicit.

exists, (2) having a single program for sequential and parallel execution is important, and (3) the target system is a small cluster connected by standard Ethernet LAN. More scalable algorithms for execution on massively parallel systems are discussed in [PH95].

The core algorithm, including pseudocode, was presented in Sec. 3.1.3. While we won't repeat the discussion here, we do provide a copy of the pseudocode in Fig. 5.7.

The parallel algorithm is discussed in several of the patterns in the *Finding Concurrency* and *Algorithm Structure* design spaces. Following are the key points from those discussions that we will need here along with the location of the original discussion.

1. Computing the `non_bonded_forces` takes the overwhelming majority of the runtime (Sec. 3.1.3).

2. In computing the `non_bonded_force`, each atom potentially interacts with all the other atoms. Hence, each UE needs read access to the full atomic position array. Also, due to Newton's third law, each UE will be scattering contributions to the force across the full force array (the Examples section of the *Data Sharing* pattern).

3. One way to decompose the MD problem into tasks is to focus on the computations needed for a particular atom, that is, we can parallelize this problem by assigning atoms to UEs (the Examples section of the *Task Decomposition* pattern).

Given that our target is a small cluster and from point (1) in the preceding list, we will only parallelize the force computations. Because the network is slow for parallel computing and given the data dependency in point (2), we will:

- Keep a copy of the full force and coordinate arrays on each node.

- Have each UE redundantly update positions and velocities for the atoms (that is, we assume it is cheaper to redundantly compute these terms than to do them in parallel and communicate the results).

- Have each UE compute its contributions to the force array and then combine (or reduce) the UEs' contributions into a single global force array copied onto each UE.

The algorithm is a simple transformation from the sequential algorithm. Pseudocode for this SPMD program is shown in Fig. 5.8. As with any MPI program,

```
#include <mpi.h>

    Int const N // number of atoms
    Int const LN // maximum number of atoms assigned to a UE

    Int ID // an ID for each UE
    Int num_UEs // the number of UEs in the parallel computation

    Array of Real :: atoms (3,N) //3D coordinates
    Array of Real :: velocities (3,N) //velocity vector
    Array of Real :: forces (3,N) //force in each dimension
    Array of Real :: final_forces(3,N) //globally summed force
    Array of List :: neighbors(LN) //atoms in cutoff volume
    Array of Int :: local_atoms(LN) //atoms for this UE

    ID = 0 // default ID (used by the serial code)
    num_UEs = 1 // default num_UEs (used by the serial code)
    MPI_Init()
    MPI_Comm_size(MPI_COMM_WORLD, &ID)
    MPI_Comm_rank(MPI_COMM_WORLD, &num_UEs)

    loop over time steps
        initialize_forces (N, forces, final_forces)
        if(time to update neighbor list)
          neighbor_list (N, LN, atoms, neighbors)
        end if
        vibrational_forces (N, LN, local_atoms, atoms, forces)
        rotational_forces (N, LN, local_atoms, atoms, forces)
        non_bonded_forces (N, LN, atoms, local_atoms, neighbors,
          forces)

        MPI_All_reduce{forces, final_forces, 3*N, MPI_REAL,
          MPI_SUM, MPI_COMM_WORLD)

        update_atom_positions_and_velocities(
                    N, atoms, velocities, final_forces)
        physical_properties ( ... Lots of stuff ... )
    end loop

    MPI_Finalize()
```

Figure 5.8: Pseudocode for an SPMD molecular dynamics program using MPI

```
function non_bonded_forces (N, LN, atoms, local_atoms,
                                       neighbors, Forces)

    Int N // number of atoms
    Int LN // maximum number of atoms assigned to a UE

    Array of Real :: atoms (3,N) //3D coordinates
    Array of Real :: forces (3,N) //force in each dimension
    Array of List :: neighbors(LN) //atoms in cutoff volume
    Array of Int :: local_atoms(LN) //atoms assigned to this UE
    real :: forceX, forceY, forceZ

    loop [i] over local_atoms

        loop [j] over neighbors(i)
            forceX = non_bond_force(atoms(1,i), atoms(1,j))
            forceY = non_bond_force(atoms(2,i), atoms(2,j))
            forceZ = non_bond_force(atoms(3,i), atoms(3,j))
            force{1,i) += forceX; force{1,j) -= forceX;
            force(2,i) += forceY; force{2,j) -= forceY;
            force{3,i) += forceZ; force{3,j) -= forceZ;
        end loop [j]

    end loop [i]
end function non_bonded_forces
```

Figure 5.9: Pseudocode for the nonbonded computation in a typical parallel molecular dynamics code. This code is almost identical to the sequential version of the function shown in Fig. 4.4. The only major change is a new array of integers holding the indices for the atoms assigned to this UE, local_atoms. We've also assumed that the neighbor list has been generated to hold only those atoms assigned to this UE. For the sake of allocating space for these arrays, we have added a parameter LN which is the largest number of atoms that can be assigned to a single UE.

the MPI include file is referenced at the top of the program. The MPI environment is initialized and the ID is associated with the rank of the MPI process.

Only a few changes are made to the sequential functions. First, a second force array called **final_forces** is defined to hold the globally consistent force array appropriate for the update of the atomic positions and velocities. Second, a list of atoms assigned to the UE is created and passed to any function that will be parallelized. Finally, the **neighbor_list** is modified to hold the list for only those atoms assigned to the UE.

Finally, within each of the functions to be parallelized (the forces calculations), the loop over atoms is replaced by a loop over the list of local atoms.

We show an example of these simple changes in Fig. 5.9. This is almost identical to the sequential version of this function discussed in the *Task Parallelism* pattern. As discussed earlier, the following are the key changes.

- A new array has been added to hold indices for the atoms assigned to this UE. This array is of length LN where LN is the maximum number of atoms that can be assigned to a single UE.

- The loop over all atoms (loop over i) has been replaced by a loop over the elements of the `local_atoms` list.

- We assume that the neighbor list has been modified to correspond to the atoms listed in the `local_atoms` list.

The resulting code can be used for a sequential version of the program by setting LN to N and by putting the full set of atom indices into `local_atoms`. This feature satisfies one of our design goals: that a single source code would work for both sequential and parallel versions of the program.

The key to this algorithm is in the function to compute the neighbor list. The neighbor list function contains a loop over the atoms. For each atom i, there is a loop over all other atoms and a test to determine which atoms are in the neighborhood of atom i. The indices for these neighboring atoms are saved in **neighbors**, a list of lists. Pseudocode for this code is shown in Fig. 5.10.

```
function neighbor (N, LN, ID, cutoff, atoms, local_atoms,
                   neighbors)

    Int N // number of atoms
    Int LN // max number of atoms assigned to a UE
    Real cutoff // radius of sphere defining neighborhood

    Array of Real :: atoms (3,N) //3D coordinates
    Array of List :: neighbors(LN) //atoms in cutoff volume
    Array of Int :: local_atoms(LN) //atoms assigned to this UE
    real :: dist_squ

    initialize_lists (local_atoms, neighbors)

    loop [i] over atoms on UE //split loop iterations among UEs
        add_to_list (i, local_atoms)
        loop [j] over atoms greater than i
            dist_squ = square(atom(1,i)-atom(1,j)) +
                       square(atom(2,i)-atom(2,j)) +
                       square(atom(3,i)-atom(3,j))
            if(dist_squ < (cutoff * cutoff))
                add_to_list (j, neighbors(i))
            end if
        end loop [j]

    end loop [i]
end function neighbors
```

Figure 5.10: Pseudocode for the neighbor list computation. For each atom i, the indices for atoms within a sphere of radius cutoff are added to the neighbor list for atom i. Notice that the second loop (over j) only considers atoms with indices greater than i. This accounts for the symmetry in the force computation due to Newton's third law of motion, that is, that the force between atom i and atom j is just the negative of the force between atom j and atom i.

The logic defining how the parallelism is distributed among the UEs is captured in the single loop in Fig. 5.10:

```
loop [i] over atoms on UE //split loop iterations among UEs
    add_to_list (i, local_atoms)
```

The details of how this loop is split among UEs depends on the programming environment. An approach that works well with MPI is the cyclic distribution we used in Fig. 5.5:

```
for (i=id;i<number_of_atoms; i+= number_of_UEs){
    add_to_list (i, local_atoms)
}
```

More complex or even dynamic distributions can be handled by creating an *owner-computes filter* [Mat95]. An owner-computes filter provides a flexible and reusable schedule for mapping loop iterations onto UEs. The filter is a boolean function of the ID and the loop iteration. The value of the function depends on whether a UE "owns" a particular iteration of a loop. For example, in a molecular dynamics program, the call to the owner-computes function would be added at the top of the parallelized loops over atoms:

```
for (i=0;i<number_of_atoms; i++){
    if !(is_owner (i)) break

    add_to_list (i, local_atoms)
}
```

No other changes to the loop are needed to support expression of concurrency. If the logic managing the loop is convoluted, this approach partitions the iterations among the UEs without altering that logic, and the index partitioning logic is located clearly in one place in the source code. Another advantage occurs when several loops that should be scheduled the same way are spread out throughout a program. For example, on a NUMA machine or a cluster it is very important that data brought close to a PE be used as many times as possible. Often, this means reusing the same schedule in many loops.

This approach is described further for molecular dynamics applications in [Mat95]. It could be important in this application since the workload captured in the neighbor list generation may not accurately reflect the workload in the various force computations. One could easily collect information about the time required for each atom and then readjust the **is_owner** function to produce more optimal work loads.

```
#include <omp.h>
    Int const N // number of atoms
    Int const LN // maximum number of atoms assigned to a UE
    Int ID // an ID for each UE
    Int num_UEs // number of UEs in the parallel computation
    Array of Real :: atoms(3,N) //3D coordinates
    Array of Real :: velocities(3,N) //velocity vector
    Array of Real :: forces(3,N) //force in each dim
    Array of List :: neighbors(LN) //atoms in cutoff volume
    Array of Int :: local_atoms(LN) //atoms for this UE

    ID = 0
    num_UEs = 1

#pragma omp parallel private (ID, num_UEs, local_atoms, forces) {
    ID = omp_get_thread_num()
    num_UEs = omp_get_num_threads()

    loop over time steps
        initialize_forces (N, forces, final_forces)
        if(time to update neighbor list)
            neighbor_list (N, LN, atoms, neighbors)
        end if
        vibrational_forces (N, LN, local_atoms, atoms, forces)
        rotational_forces (N, LN, local_atoms, atoms, forces)
        non_bonded_forces (N, LN, atoms, local_atoms,
                                          neighbors, forces)
#pragma critical
        final_forces += forces
#barrier

#pragma single
{
        update_atom_positions_and_velocities(
                          N, atoms, velocities, forces)
        physical_properties ( ... Lots of stuff ... )
} // remember, the end of a single implies a barrier

    end loop

} // end of OpenMP parallel region
```

Figure 5.11: Pseudocode for a parallel molecular dynamics program using OpenMP

These SPMD algorithms work for OpenMP programs as well. All of the basic functions remain the same. The top-level program is changed to reflect the needs of OpenMP. This is shown in Fig. 5.11.

The loop over time is placed inside a single parallel region. The parallel region is created with the **parallel** pragma:

```
#pragma omp parallel private (ID, num_UEs, local_atoms, forces)
```

This pragma causes a team of threads to be created with each member of the team executing the loop over time. The `private` clause causes copies of the listed variables to be created for each UE. The reduction is carried out in a critical section:

```
#pragma critical
        final_forces += forces
```

A `reduction` clause on the parallel region cannot be used in this case because the result would not be available until the parallel region completes. The critical section produces the correct result, but the algorithm used has a runtime that is linear in the number of UEs and is hence suboptimal relative to other reduction algorithms as discussed in the *Implementation Mechanisms* design space. On systems with a modest number of processors, however, the reduction with a critical section works adequately.

The barrier following the critical section is required to make sure the reduction completes before the atomic positions and velocities are updated. We then use an OpenMP `single` construct to cause only one UE to do the update. An additional barrier is not needed following the `single` since the close of a `single` construct implies a barrier. The functions used to compute the forces are unchanged between the OpenMP and MPI versions of the program.

Mandelbrot set computation. Consider the well-known Mandelbrot set [Dou86]. We discussed this problem and its parallelization as a task-parallel problem in the *Task Parallelism* pattern. Each pixel is colored based on the behavior of the quadratic recurrence relation in Eq. 5.4.

$$Z_{n+1} = Z_n^2 + C \qquad (5.4)$$

C and Z are complex numbers and the recurrence is started with $Z_0 = C$. The image plots the imaginary part of C on the vertical axis (-1.5 to 1.5) and the real part on the horizontal axis (-1 to 2). The color of each pixel is black if the recurrence relation converges to a stable value or is colored depending on how rapidly the relation diverges.

In the *Task Parallelism* pattern, we described a parallel algorithm where each task corresponds to the computation of a row in the image. A static schedule with more tasks than UEs should be possible that achieves an effective statistical balance of the load among nodes. We will show how to solve this problem using the *SPMD* pattern with MPI.

Pseudocode for the sequential version of this code is shown in Fig. 5.12. The interesting part of the problem is hidden inside the routine `compute_Row()`. Because the details of this routine are not important for understanding the parallel algorithm, we will not show them here, however. At a high level, for each point in the row the following happens.

```
Int const Nrows // number of rows in the image
Int const RowSize // number of pixels in a row
Int const M // number of colors in color map

Real :: conv // divergence rate for a pixel
Array of Int :: color_map (M) // pixel color based on conv rate
Array of Int :: row (RowSize) // Pixels to draw
Array of Real :: ranges(2) // ranges in X and Y dimensions

manage_user_input(ranges, color_map) // input ranges, color map
initialize_graphics(RowSize, Nrows, M, ranges, color_map)

for (int i = 0; i<Nrows; i++){

    compute_Row (RowSize, ranges, row)

    graph(i, RowSize, M, color_map, ranges, row)

} // end loop [i] over rows
```

Figure 5.12: Pseudocode for a sequential version of the Mandelbrot set generation program

- Each pixel corresponds to a value of C in the quadratic recurrence. We compute this value based on the input **range** and the pixel indices.

- We then compute the terms in the recurrence and set the value of the pixel based on whether it converges to a fixed value or diverges. If it diverges, we set the pixel value based on the rate of divergence.

Once computed, the rows are plotted to make the well-known Mandelbrot set images. The colors used for the pixels are determined by mapping divergence rates onto a color map.

An SPMD program based on this algorithm is straightforward; code is shown in Fig. 5.13. We will assume the computation is being carried out on some sort of distributed-memory machine (a cluster or even an MPP) and that there is one machine that serves as the interactive graphics node, while the others are restricted to computation. We will assume that the graphics node is the one with rank 0.

The program starts with the usual MPI setup, as described in the MPI appendix, Appendix B. The UE with rank 0 takes input from the user and then broadcasts this to the other UEs. It then loops over the number of rows in the image, receiving rows as they finish and plotting them. UEs with rank other than 0 use a cyclic distribution of loop iterations and send the rows to the graphics UE as they finish.

Known uses.   The overwhelming majority of MPI programs use this pattern. Pedagogically oriented discussions of SPMD programs and examples can be found in MPI textbooks such as [GLS99] and [Pac96]. Representative applications using this pattern include quantum chemistry [WSG95], finite element methods [ABKP03, KLK+03], and 3D gas dynamics [MHC+99].

```
#include <mpi.h>
    Int const Nrows // number of rows in the image
    Int const RowSize // number of pixels in a row
    Int const M // number of colors in color map
    Real :: conv // divergence rate for a pixel
    Array of Int :: color_map (M) // pixel color based on conv rate
    Array of Int :: row (RowSize) // Pixels to draw
    Array of Real :: ranges(2) // ranges in X and Y dimensions
    Int :: inRowSize // size of received row
    Int :: ID // ID of each UE (process)
    Int :: num_UEs // number of UEs (processes)
    Int :: nworkers // number of UEs computing rows
    MPI_Status :: stat // MPI status parameter

    MPI_Init()
    MPI_Comm_size(MPI_COMM_WORLD, &ID)
    MPI_Comm_rank(MPI_COMM_WORLD, &num_UEs)

// Algorithm requires at least two UEs since we are
// going to dedicate one to graphics
    if (num_UEs < 2) MPI_Abort(MPI_COMM_WORLD, 1)

    if (ID == 0 ){
        manage_user_input(ranges, color_map) // input ranges, color map
        initialize_graphics(RowSize, Nrows, M, ranges, color_map)
    }

// Broadcast data from rank 0 process to all other processes
    MPI_Bcast (ranges, 2, MPI_REAL, 0, MPI_COMM_WORLD);
    if (ID == 0) { // UE with rank 0 does graphics
      for (int i = 0; i<Nrows; i++){
        MPI_Recv(row, &inRowSize, MPI_REAL, MPI_ANY_SOURCE,
                     MPI_ANY_TAG, MPI_COMM_WORLD, &stat)
        row_index = stat(MPI_TAG)
        graph(row_index, RowSize, M, color_map, ranges, Row)
      } // end loop over i
    else { // The other UEs compute the rows
      nworkers = num_UEs - 1
      for (int i = ID-1; i<Nrows; i+=nworkers){
        compute_Row (RowSize, ranges, row)
        MPI_Send (row, RowSize, MPI_REAL, 0, i, MPI_COMM_WORLD);
      } // end loop over i
    }
    MPI_Finalize()
```

Figure 5.13: Pseudocode for a parallel MPI version of the Mandelbrot set generation program

Examples of the *SPMD* pattern in combination with the *Distributed Array* pattern include the GAMESS quantum chemistry program [OSG03] and the ScaLAPACK library [BCC+97, Sca].

Related Patterns

The *SPMD* pattern is very general and can be used to implement other patterns. Many of the examples in the text of this pattern are closely related to the *Loop Parallelism* pattern. Most applications of the *Geometric Decomposition* pattern with

MPI use the *SPMD* pattern as well. The *Distributed Array* pattern is essentially a special case of distributing data for programs using the *SPMD* pattern.

5.5   THE *MASTER/WORKER* PATTERN

Problem

How should a program be organized when the design is dominated by the need to dynamically balance the work on a set of tasks among the UEs?

Context

Parallel efficiency follows from an algorithm's parallel overhead, its serial fraction, and the load balancing. A good parallel algorithm must deal with each of these, but sometimes balancing the load is so difficult that it dominates the design. Problems falling into this category usually share one or more of the following characteristics.

- The workloads associated with the tasks are highly variable and unpredictable. If workloads are predictable, they can be sorted into equal-cost bins, statically assigned to UEs, and parallelized using the *SPMD* or *Loop Parallelism* patterns. But if they are unpredictable, static distributions tend to produce suboptimal load balance.

- The program structure for the computationally intensive portions of the problem doesn't map onto simple loops. If the algorithm is loop-based, one can usually achieve a statistically near-optimal workload by a cyclic distribution of iterations or by using a dynamic schedule on the loop (for example, in OpenMP, by using the `schedule(dynamic)` clause). But if the control structure in the program is more complex than a simple loop, more general approaches are required.

- The capabilities of the PEs available for the parallel computation vary across the parallel system, change over the course of the computation, or are unpredictable.

In some cases, tasks are tightly coupled (that is, they communicate or share read-and-write data) and must be active at the same time. In this case, the *Master/ Worker* pattern is not applicable: The programmer has no choice but to *explicitly* size or group tasks onto UEs dynamically (that is, during the computation) to achieve an effective load balance. The logic to accomplish this can be difficult to implement, and if one is not careful, can add prohibitively large parallel overhead.

If the tasks are independent of each other, however, or if the dependencies can somehow be pulled out from the concurrent computation, the programmer has much greater flexibility in how to balance the load. This allows the load balancing to be done automatically and is the situation we address in this pattern.

This pattern is particularly relevant for problems using the Task Parallelism *pattern when there are no dependencies among the tasks (embarrassingly parallel problems). It can also be used with the* Fork/Join *pattern for the cases where the mapping of tasks onto UEs is indirect.*

Forces

- The work for each task, and in some cases even the capabilities of the PEs, varies unpredictably in these problems. Hence, explicit predictions of the run-time for any given task are not possible and the design must balance the load without them.

- Operations to balance the load impose communication overhead and can be very expensive. This suggests that scheduling should revolve around a smaller number of large tasks. However, large tasks reduce the number of ways tasks can be partitioned among the PEs, thereby making it more difficult to achieve good load balance.

- Logic to produce an optimal load can be convoluted and require error-prone changes to a program. Programmers need to make trade-offs between the desire for an optimal distribution of the load and code that is easy to maintain.

Solution

The well-known *Master/Worker* pattern is a good solution to this problem. This pattern is summarized in Fig. 5.14. The solution consists of two logical elements: a *master* and one or more instances of a *worker*. The master initiates the computation and sets up the problem. It then creates a *bag of tasks*. In the classic algorithm, the master then waits until the job is done, consumes the results, and then shuts down the computation.

A straightforward approach to implementing the bag of tasks is with a single shared queue as described in the *Shared Queue* pattern. Many other mechanisms for creating a globally accessible structure where tasks can be inserted and removed are possible, however. Examples include a tuple space [CG91, FHA99], a distributed queue, or a monotonic counter (when the tasks can be specified with a set of contiguous integers).

Meanwhile, each worker enters a loop. At the top of the loop, the worker takes a task from the bag of tasks, does the indicated work, tests for completion, and then goes to fetch the next task. This continues until the termination condition is met, at which time the master wakes up, collects the results, and finishes the computation.

Master/worker algorithms automatically balance the load. By this, we mean the programmer does not explicitly decide which task is assigned to which UE. This decision is made dynamically by the master as a worker completes one task and accesses the bag of tasks for more work.

Discussion.   Master/worker algorithms have good scalability as long as the number of tasks greatly exceeds the number of workers and the costs of the individual tasks are not so variable that some workers take drastically longer than the others.

Management of the bag of tasks can require global communication, and the overhead for this can limit efficiency. This effect is not a problem when the work associated with the tasks on average is much greater than the time required for management. In some cases, the designer might need to increase the size of each task to decrease the number of times the global task bag needs to be accessed.

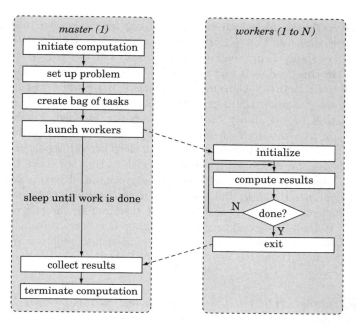

Figure 5.14: The two elements of the *Master/Worker* pattern are the *master* and the *worker*. There is only one master, but there can be one or more workers. Logically, the master sets up the calculation and then manages a bag of tasks. Each worker grabs a task from the bag, carries out the work, and then goes back to the bag, repeating until the termination condition is met.

The *Master/Worker* pattern is not tied to any particular hardware environment. Programs using this pattern work well on everything from clusters to SMP machines. It is, of course, beneficial if the programming environment provides support for managing the bag of tasks.

Detecting completion. One of the challenges in working with master/worker programs is to correctly determine when the entire problem is complete. This needs to be done in a way that is efficient but also guarantees that all of the work is complete before workers shut down.

- In the simplest case, all tasks are placed in the bag before the workers begin. Then each task continues until the bag is empty, at which point the workers terminate.

- Another approach is to use a queue to implement the task bag and arrange for the master or a worker to check for the desired termination condition. When it is detected, a *poison pill*, a special task that tells the workers to terminate, is created. The poison pill must be placed in the bag in such a way that it will be picked up on the next round of work. Depending on how the set of shared tasks are managed, it may be necessary to create one poison pill for each remaining worker to ensure that all workers receive the termination condition.

- Problems for which the set of tasks is not known initially produce unique challenges. This occurs, for example, when workers can add tasks as well as consume them (such as in applications of the *Divide and Conquer* pattern). In this case, it is not necessarily true that when a worker finishes a task and finds the task bag empty that there is no more work to do—another still-active worker could generate a new task. One must therefore ensure that the task bag is empty *and* all workers are finished. Further, in systems based on asynchronous message passing, it must be determined that there are no messages in transit that could, on their arrival, result in the creation of a new task. There are many known algorithms that solve this problem. For example, suppose the tasks are conceptually organized into a tree, where the root is the master task, and the children of a task are the tasks it generates. When all of the children of a task have terminated, the parent task can terminate. When all the children of the master task have terminated, the computation has terminated. Algorithms for termination detection are described in [BT89, Mat87, DS80].

Variations.   There are several variations on this pattern. Because of the simple way it implements dynamic load balancing, this pattern is very popular, especially in embarrassingly parallel problems (as described in the *Task Parallelism* pattern). Here are a few of the more common variations.

- The master may turn into a worker after it has created the tasks. This is an effective technique when the termination condition can be detected without explicit action by the master (that is, the tasks can detect the termination condition on their own from the state of the bag of tasks).

- When the concurrent tasks map onto a simple loop, the master can be implicit and the pattern can be implemented as a loop with dynamic iteration assignment as described in the *Loop Parallelism* pattern.

- A centralized task queue can become a bottleneck, especially in a distributed-memory environment. An optimal solution [FLR98] is based on random work stealing. In this approach, each PE maintains a separate double-ended task queue. New tasks are placed in the front of the task queue of the local PE. When a task is completed, a subproblem is removed from the front of the local task queue. If the local task queue is empty, then another PE is chosen randomly, and a subproblem from the back of its task queue is "stolen". If that queue is also empty, then the PE tries again with another randomly chosen PE. This is particularly effective when used in problems based on the *Divide and Conquer* pattern. In this case, the tasks at the back of the queue were inserted earlier and hence represent larger subproblems. Thus, this approach tends to move large subproblems while handling the finer-grained subproblems at the PE where they were created. This helps the load balance and reduces overhead for the small tasks created in the deeper levels of recursion.

- The *Master/Worker* pattern can be modified to provide a modest level of fault tolerance [BDK95]. The master maintains two queues: one for tasks that still need to be assigned to workers and another for tasks that have already been assigned, but not completed. After the first queue is empty, the master can redundantly assign tasks from the "not completed" queue. Hence, if a worker dies and therefore can't complete its tasks, another worker will cover the unfinished tasks.

Examples

We will start with a generic description of a simple master/worker problem and then provide a detailed example of using the *Master/Worker* pattern in the parallel implementation of a program to generate the Mandelbrot set. Also see the Examples section of the *Shared Queue* pattern, which illustrates the use of shared queues by developing a master/worker implementation of a simple Java framework for programs using the *Fork/Join* pattern.

Generic solutions. The key to the master/worker program is the structure that holds the bag of tasks. The code in this section uses a task queue. We implement the task queue as an instance of the *Shared Queue* pattern.

The master process, shown in Fig. 5.15, initializes the task queue, representing each task by an integer. It then uses the *Fork/Join* pattern to create the worker

```
Int const Ntasks // Number of tasks
Int const Nworkers // Number of workers

SharedQueue :: task_queue; // task queue
SharedQueue :: global_results; // queue to hold results

void master()
{
   void worker()

   // Create and initialize shared data structures
   task_queue = new SharedQueue()
   global_results = new SharedQueue()

   for (int i = 0; i < N; i++)
      enqueue(task_queue, i)

   // Create Nworkers threads executing function Worker()
   ForkJoin (Nworkers, Worker)

   consume_the_results (Ntasks)
}
```

Figure 5.15: Master process for a master/worker program. This assumes a shared address space so the task and results queues are visible to all UEs. In this simple version, the master initializes the queue, launches the workers, and then waits for the workers to finish (that is, the ForkJoin command launches the workers and then waits for them to finish before returning). At that point, results are consumed and the computation completes.

```
void worker()
  {
    Int :: i
    Result :: res

    while (!empty(task_queue) {
        i = dequeue(task_queue)
        res = do_lots_of_work(i)
        enqueue(global_results, res)
    }
  }
```

Figure 5.16: Worker process for a master/worker program. We assume a shared address space thereby making `task_queue` and `global_results` available to the master and all workers. A worker loops over the `task_queue` and exits when the end of the queue is encountered.

processes or threads and wait for them to complete. When they have completed, it consumes the results.

The worker, shown in Fig. 5.16, loops until the task queue is empty. Every time through the loop, it takes the next task and does the indicated work, storing the results in a global results queue. When the task queue is empty, the worker terminates.

Note that we ensure safe access to the key shared variables (`task_queue` and `global_results`) by using instances of the *Shared Queue* pattern.

For programs written in Java, a thread-safe queue can be used to hold `Runnable` objects that are executed by a set of threads whose `run` methods behave like the worker threads described previously: removing a `Runnable` object from the queue and executing its `run` method. The `Executor` interface in the `java.util.concurrent` package in Java 2 1.5 provides direct support for the *Master/Worker* pattern. Classes implementing the interface provide an `execute` method that takes a `Runnable` object and arranges for its execution. Different implementations of the `Executor` interface provide different ways of managing the `Thread` objects that actually do the work. The `ThreadPoolExecutor` implements the *Master/Worker* pattern by using a fixed pool of threads to execute the commands. To use `Executor`, the program instantiates an instance of a class implementing the interface, usually using a factory method in the `Executors` class. For example, the code in Fig. 5.17 sets up a `ThreadPoolExecutor` that creates `num_threads` threads. These threads execute tasks specified by `Runnable` objects that are placed in an unbounded queue.

After the `Executor` has been created, a `Runnable` object whose `run` method specifies the behavior of the task can be passed to the `execute` method, which

```
/*create a ThreadPoolExecutor with an unbounded queue*/
Executor exec = new Executors.newFixedThreadPool(num_threads);
```

Figure 5.17: Instantiating and initializing a pooled executor

arranges for its execution. For example, assume the `Runnable` object is referred to by a variable `task`. Then for the executor defined previously, `exec.execute(task);` will place the task in the queue, where it will eventually be serviced by one of the executor's worker threads.

The *Master/Worker* pattern can also be used with SPMD programs and MPI. Maintaining the global queues is more challenging, but the overall algorithm is the same. A more detailed description of using MPI for shared queues appears in the *Implementation Mechanisms* design space.

Mandelbrot set generation.   Generating the Mandelbrot set is described in detail in the Examples section of the *SPMD* pattern. The basic idea is to explore a quadratic recurrence relation at each point in a complex plane and color the point based on the rate at which the recursion converges or diverges. Each point in the complex plane can be computed independently and hence the problem is embarrassingly parallel (see the *Task Parallelism* pattern).

In Fig. 5.18, we reproduce the pseudocode given in the *SPMD* pattern for a sequential version of this problem. The program loops over the rows of the image displaying one row at a time as they are computed.

On homogeneous clusters or lightly-loaded shared-memory multiprocessor computers, approaches based on the *SPMD* or *Loop Parallelism* patterns are most effective. On a heterogeneous cluster or a multiprocessor system shared among many users (and hence with an unpredictable load on any given PE at any given time), a master/worker approach will be more effective.

We will create a master/worker version of a parallel Mandelbrot program based on the high-level structure described earlier. The master will be responsible for graphing the results. In some problems, the results generated by the workers interact and it can be important for the master to wait until all the workers have

```
Int const Nrows // number of rows in the image
Int const RowSize // number of pixels in a row
Int const M // number of colors in color map

Real :: conv // divergence rate for a pixel
Array of Int :: color_map (M) // pixel color based on Conv rate
Array of Int :: row (RowSize) // Pixels to draw
Array of real :: ranges(2) // ranges in X and Y dimensions

manage_user_input(ranges, color_map) // input ranges, color map
initialize_graphics(RowSize, Nrows, M, ranges, color_map)

for (int i = 0; i<Nrows; i++){

    compute_Row (RowSize, ranges, row)

    graph(i, RowSize, M, color_map, ranges, row)

} // end loop [i] over rows
```

Figure 5.18: Pseudocode for a sequential version of the Mandelbrot set generation program

completed before consuming results. In this case, however, the results do not interact, so we split the fork and join operations and have the master plot results as they
become available. Following the `Fork`, the master must wait for results to appear on
the `global_results` queue. Because we know there will be one result per row, the
master knows in advance how many results to fetch and the termination condition
is expressed simply in terms of the number of iterations of the loop. After all the results have been plotted, the master waits at the `Join` function until all the workers
have completed, at which point the master completes. Code is shown in Fig. 5.19.

```
Int const Ntasks // number of tasks
Int const Nworkers // number of workers
Int const Nrows // number of rows in the image
Int const RowSize // number of pixels in a row
Int const M // number of colors in color map
typedef Row :: struct of {
    int :: index
    array of int :: pixels (RowSize)
} temp_row;
Array of Int :: color_map (M) // pixel color based on conv rate
Array of Real :: ranges(2) // ranges in X and Y dimensions
SharedQueue of Int :: task_queue; // task queue
SharedQueue of Row :: global_results; // queue to hold results

void master()
{
  void worker();

  manage_user_input(ranges, Color_map) // input ranges, color map
  initialize_graphics(RowSize, Nrows, M, ranges, color_map)

  // Create and initialize shared data structures
  task_queue = new SharedQueue();
  global_results = new SharedQueue();

  for (int i = 0; i < Nrows; i++)
    enqueue(task_queue, i);

  // Create Nworkers threads executing function worker()
  Fork (Nworkers, worker);

  // Wait for results and graph them as they appear
  for (int i = 0; i< Nrows; i++) {
      while (empty(task_queue) { // wait for results
        wait
      }
      temp_row = dequeue(global_results)
      graph(temp_row.index, RowSize, M, color_map, ranges, Row.pixels)
  }

  // Terminate the worker UEs
  Join (Nworkers);
}
```

Figure 5.19: Master process for a master/worker parallel version of the Mandelbrot set
generation program

```
void worker()
{
  Int i, irow;
  Row temp_row;

  while (!empty(task_queue) {
     irow = dequeue(task_queue);
     compute_Row (RowSize, ranges, irow, temp_row.pixels)
     temp_row.index = irow
     enqueue(global_results, temp_row);
  }
}
```

Figure 5.20: Worker process for a master/worker parallel version of the Mandelbrot set generation program. We assume a shared address space thereby making `task_queue`, `global_results`, and `ranges` available to the master and the workers.

Notice that this code is similar to the generic case discussed earlier, except that we have overlapped the processing of the results with their computation by splitting the `Fork` and `Join`. As the names imply, `Fork` launches UEs running the indicated function and `Join` causes the master to wait for the workers to cleanly terminate. See the *Shared Queue* pattern for more details about the queue.

The code for the worker is much simpler and is shown in Fig 5.20. First, note that we assume the shared variables such as the queues and computation parameters are globally visible to the master and the workers. Because the queue is filled by the master before forking the workers, the termination condition is simply given by an empty queue. Each worker grabs a row index, does the computation, packs the row index and the computed row into the result queue, and continues until the queue is empty.

Known uses.   This pattern is extensively used with the Linda programming environment. The tuple space in Linda is ideally suited to programs that use the *Master/Worker* pattern, as described in depth in [CG91] and in the survey paper [CGMS94].

The *Master/Worker* pattern is used in many distributed computing environments because these systems must deal with extreme levels of unpredictability in the availability of resources. The SETI@home project [SET] uses the *Master/Worker* pattern to utilize volunteers' Internet-connected computers to download and analyze radio telescope data as part of the Search for Extraterrestrial Intelligence (SETI). Programs constructed with the Calypso system [BDK95], a distributed computing framework which provides system support for dynamic changes in the set of PEs, also use the *Master/Worker* pattern. A parallel algorithm for detecting repeats in genomic data [RHB03] uses the *Master/Worker* pattern with MPI on a cluster of dual-processor PCs.

Related Patterns

This pattern is closely related to the *Loop Parallelism* pattern when the loops utilize some form of dynamic scheduling (such as when the `schedule(dynamic)` clause is used in OpenMP).

Implementations of the *Fork/Join* pattern sometimes use the *Master/Worker* pattern behind the scenes. This pattern is also closely related to algorithms that make use of the `nextval` function from TCGMSG [Har91, WSG95, LDSH95]. The `nextval` function implements a monotonic counter. If the bag of tasks can be mapped onto a fixed range of monotonic indices, the counter provides the bag of tasks and the function of the master is implied by the counter.

Finally, the owner-computes filter discussed in the molecular dynamics example in the *SPMD* pattern is essentially a variation on the master/worker theme. In such an algorithm, all the master would do is set up the bag of tasks (loop iterations) and assign them to UEs, with the assignment of tasks to UEs defined by the filter. Because the UEs can essentially perform this assignment themselves (by examining each task with the filter), no explicit master is needed.

5.6   THE *LOOP PARALLELISM* PATTERN

Problem

Given a serial program whose runtime is dominated by a set of computationally intensive loops, how can it be translated into a parallel program?

Context

The overwhelming majority of programs used in scientific and engineering applications are expressed in terms of iterative constructs; that is, they are loop-based. Optimizing these programs by focusing strictly on the loops is a tradition dating back to the older vector supercomputers. Extending this approach to modern parallel computers suggests a parallel algorithm strategy in which concurrent tasks are identified as iterations of *parallelized* loops.

The advantage of structuring a parallel algorithm around parallelized loops is particularly important in problems for which well-accepted programs already exist. In many cases, it isn't practical to massively restructure an existing program to gain parallel performance. This is particularly important when the program (as is frequently the case) contains convoluted code and poorly understood algorithms.

This pattern addresses ways to structure loop-based programs for parallel computation. When existing code is available, the goal is to "evolve" a sequential program into a parallel program by a series of transformations on the loops. Ideally, all changes are localized to the loops with transformations that remove loop-carried dependencies and leave the overall program semantics unchanged. (Such transformations are called *semantically neutral transformations*).

Not all problems can be approached in this loop-driven manner. Clearly, it will only work when the algorithm structure has most, if not all, of the computationally intensive work buried in a manageable number of distinct loops. Furthermore, the body of the loop must result in loop iterations that work well as parallel tasks (that is, they are computationally intensive, express sufficient concurrency, and are mostly independent).

Not all target computer systems align well with this style of parallel programming. If the code cannot be restructured to create effective distributed data structures, some level of support for a shared address space is essential in all but the most trivial cases. Finally, Amdahl's law and its requirement to minimize a program's serial fraction often means that loop-based approaches are only effective for systems with smaller numbers of PEs.

Even with these restrictions, this class of parallel algorithms is growing rapidly. Because loop-based algorithms are the traditional approach in high-performance computing and are still dominant in new programs, there is a large backlog of loop-based programs that need to be ported to modern parallel computers. The OpenMP API was created primarily to support parallelization of these loop-driven problems. Limitations on the scalability of these algorithms are serious, but acceptable, given that there are orders of magnitude more machines with two or four processors than machines with dozens or hundreds of processors.

This pattern is particularly relevant for OpenMP programs running on shared-memory computers and for problems using the Task Parallelism *and* Geometric Decomposition *patterns.*

Forces

- **Sequential equivalence.** A program that yields identical results (except for round-off errors) when executed with one thread or many threads is said to be *sequentially equivalent* (also known as *serially equivalent*). Sequentially equivalent code is easier to write, easier to maintain, and lets a single program source code work for serial and parallel machines.

- **Incremental parallelism (or refactoring).** When parallelizing an existing program, it is much easier to end up with a correct parallel program if (1) the parallelization is introduced as a sequence of incremental transformations, one loop at a time, and (2) the transformations don't "break" the program, allowing testing to be carried out after each transformation.

- **Memory utilization.** Good performance requires that the data access patterns implied by the loops mesh well with the memory hierarchy of the system. This can be at odds with the previous two forces, causing a programmer to massively restructure loops.

Solution

This pattern is closely aligned with the style of parallel programming implied by OpenMP. The basic approach consists of the following steps.

- **Find the bottlenecks.** Locate the most computationally intensive loops either by inspection of the code, by understanding the performance needs of each subproblem, or through the use of program performance analysis tools. The amount of total runtime on representative data sets contained by these loops will ultimately limit the scalability of the parallel program (see Amdahl's law).

- **Eliminate loop-carried dependencies.** The loop iterations must be nearly independent. Find dependencies between iterations or read/write accesses and transform the code to remove or mitigate them. Finding and removing the dependencies is discussed in the *Task Parallelism* pattern, while protecting dependencies with synchronization constructs is discussed in the *Shared Data* pattern.

- **Parallelize the loops.** Split up the iterations among the UEs. To maintain sequential equivalence, use semantically neutral directives such as those provided with OpenMP (as described in the OpenMP appendix, Appendix A). Ideally, this should be done to one loop at a time with testing and careful inspection carried out at each point to make sure race conditions or other errors have not been introduced.

- **Optimize the loop schedule.** The iterations must be scheduled for execution by the UEs so the load is evenly balanced. Although the right schedule can often be chosen based on a clear understanding of the problem, frequently it is necessary to experiment to find the optimal schedule.

This approach is only effective when the compute times for the loop iterations are large enough to compensate for parallel loop overhead. The number of iterations per loop is also important, because having many iterations per UE provides greater scheduling flexibility. In some cases, it might be necessary to transform the code to address these issues.

Two transformations commonly used are the following:

- **Merge loops.** If a problem consists of a sequence of loops that have consistent loop limits, the loops can often be merged into a single loop with more complex loop iterations, as shown in Fig. 5.21.

- **Coalesce nested loops.** Nested loops can often be combined into a single loop with a larger combined iteration count, as shown in Fig. 5.22. The larger number of iterations can help overcome parallel loop overhead, by (1) creating more concurrency to better utilize larger numbers of UEs, and (2) providing additional options for how the iterations are scheduled onto UEs.

Parallelizing the loops is easily done with OpenMP by using the `omp parallel for` directive. This directive tells the compiler to create a team of threads (the UEs in a shared-memory environment) and to split up loop iterations among the team. The last loop in Fig. 5.22 is an example of a loop parallelized with OpenMP. We describe this directive at a high level in the *Implementation Mechanisms* design space. Syntactic details are included in the OpenMP appendix, Appendix A.

Notice that in Fig. 5.22 we had to direct the system to create copies of the indices i and j local to each thread. The single most common error in using this pattern is to neglect to "privatize" key variables. If i and j are shared, then updates of i and j by different UEs can collide and lead to unpredictable results (that is, the program will contain a race condition). Compilers usually will not detect these errors, so programmers must take great care to make sure they avoid these situations.

```
#define N 20
#define Npoints 512

void FFT(); // a function to apply an FFT
void invFFT(); // a function to apply an inverse FFT
void filter(); // a frequency space filter
void setH(); // Set values of filter, H

int main() {
  int i, j;
  double A[Npoints], B[Npoints], C[Npoints], H[Npoints];

  setH(Npoints, H);

  // do a bunch of work resulting in values for A and C

  // method one: distinct loops to compute A and C
  for(i=0; i<N; i++){
    FFT (Npoints, A, B); // B = transformed A
    filter(Npoints, B, H); // B = B filtered with H
    invFFT(Npoints, B, A); // A = inv transformed B
  }
  for(i=0; i<N; i++){
    FFT (Npoints, C, B); // B = transformed C
    filter(Npoints, B, H); // B = B filtered with H
    invFFT(Npoints, B, C); // C = inv transformed B
  }

  // method two: the above pair of loops combined into
  // a single loop
  for(i=0; i<N; i++){
    FFT (Npoints, A, B); // B = transformed A
    filter(Npoints, B, H); // B = B filtered with H
    invFFT(Npoints, B, A); // A = inv transformed B
    FFT (Npoints, C, B); // B = transformed C
    filter(Npoints, B, H); // B = B filtered with H
    invFFT(Npoints, B, C); // C = inv transformed B
  }
  return 0;
}
```

Figure 5.21: Program fragment showing merging loops to increase the amount of work per iteration

The key to the application of this pattern is to use *semantically neutral* modifications to produce *sequentially equivalent* code. A semantically neutral modification doesn't change the meaning of the single-threaded program. Techniques for loop merging and coalescing of nested loops described previously, when used appropriately, are examples of semantically neutral modifications. In addition, most of the directives in OpenMP are semantically neutral. This means that adding the directive and running it with a single thread will give the same result as running the original program without the OpenMP directive.

Two programs that are semantically equivalent (when run with a single thread) need not both be sequentially equivalent. Recall that sequentially equivalent means

```
#define N 20
#define M 10

extern double work(); // a time-consuming function

int main() {

    int i, j, ij;
    double A[N][M];

    // method one: nested loops

    for(j=0; j<N; j++){
        for(i=0; i<M; i++){
            A[i][j] = work(i,j);
        }
    }

    // method two: the above pair of nested loops combined into
    // a single loop.

    for(ij=0; ij<N*M; ij++){
        j = ij/N;
        i = ij%M;

        A[i][j] = work(i,j);
    }

    // method three: the above loop parallelized with OpenMP.
    // The omp pragma creates a team of threads and maps
    // loop iterations onto them. The private clause
    // tells each thread to maintain local copies of ij, j, and i.

#pragma omp parallel for private(ij, j, i)
    for(ij=0; ij<N*M; ij++){
        j = ij/N;
        i = ij%M;

        A[i][j] = work(i,j);
    }
    return 0;
}
```

Figure 5.22: Program fragment showing coalescing nested loops to produce a single loop with a larger number of iterations

that the program will give the same result (subject to round-off errors due to changing the order of floating-point operations) whether run with one thread or many. Indeed, the (semantically neutral) transformations that eliminate loop-carried dependencies are motivated by the desire to change a program that is not sequentially equivalent to one that is. When transformations are made to improve performance, even though the transformations are semantically neutral, one must be careful that sequential equivalence has not been lost.

It is much more difficult to define sequentially equivalent programs when the code mentions either a thread ID or the number of threads. Algorithms that reference thread IDs and the number of threads tend to favor particular threads or even particular numbers of threads, a situation that is dangerous when the goal is a sequentially equivalent program.

When an algorithm depends on the thread ID, the programmer is using the *SPMD* pattern. This may be confusing. SPMD programs can be loop-based. In fact, many of the examples in the *SPMD* pattern are indeed loop-based algorithms. But they are not instances of the *Loop Parallelism* pattern, because they display the hallmark trait of an SPMD program—namely, they use the UE ID to guide the algorithm.

Finally, we've assumed that a directive-based system such as OpenMP is available when using this pattern. It is possible, but clearly more difficult, to apply this pattern without such a directive-based programming environment. For example, in object-oriented designs, one can use the *Loop Parallelism* pattern by making clever use of anonymous classes with parallel iterators. Because the parallelism is buried in the iterators, the conditions of sequential equivalence can be met.

Performance considerations. In almost every application of this pattern, especially when used with OpenMP, the assumption is made that the program will execute on a computer that has multiple PEs sharing a single address space. This address space is assumed to provide equal-time access to every element of memory.

Unfortunately, this is usually not the case. Memories on modern computers are hierarchical. There are caches on the PEs, memory modules packaged with subsets of PEs, and other complications. While great effort is made in designing shared-memory multiprocessor computers to make them act like symmetric multiprocessor (SMP) computers, the fact is that all shared-memory computers display some degree of nonuniformity in memory access times across the system. In many cases, these effects are of secondary concern, and we can ignore how a program's memory access patterns match up with the target system's memory hierarchy. In other cases, particularly on larger shared-memory machines, programs must be explicitly organized according to the needs of the memory hierarchy. The most common trick is to make sure the data access patterns during initialization of key data structures match those during later computation using these data structures. This is discussed in more detail in [Mat03, NA01] and later in this pattern as part of the mesh computation example.

Another performance problem is false sharing. This occurs when variables are not shared between UEs, but happen to reside on the same cache line. Hence, even though the program semantics implies independence, each access by each UE requires movement of a cache line between UEs. This can create huge overheads as cache lines are repeatedly invalidated and moved between UEs as these supposedly independent variables are updated. An example of a program fragment that would incur high levels of false sharing is shown in Fig. 5.23. In this code, we have a pair of nested loops. The outermost loop has a small iteration count that will map onto the number of UEs (which we assume is four in this case). The innermost loop runs over a large number of time-consuming iterations. Assuming the iterations of the innermost loop are roughly equal, this loop should parallelize effectively.

```
#include <omp.h>
#define N 4 // Assume this equals the number of UEs
#define M 1000

extern double work(int, int); // a time-consuming function

int main() {

   int i, j;
   double A[N] = {0.0}; // Initialize the array to zero

// method one: a loop with false sharing from A since the elements
// of A are likely to reside in the same cache line.

#pragma omp parallel for private(j,i)
   for(j=0; j<N; j++){
      for(i=0; i<M; i++){
         A[j] += work(i,j);
      }
   }

// method two: remove the false sharing by using a temporary
// private variable in the innermost loop

   double temp;

#pragma omp parallel for private(j,i, temp)
   for(j=0; j<N; j++){
      temp = 0.0;
      for(i=0; i<M; i++){
         temp += work(i,j);
      }
      A[j] += temp;
   }
   return 0;
}
```

Figure 5.23: Program fragment showing an example of false sharing. The small array A is held in one or two cache lines. As the UEs access A inside the innermost loop, they will need to take ownership of the cache line back from the other UEs. This back-and-forth movement of the cache lines destroys performance. The solution is to use a temporary variable inside the innermost loop.

But the updates to the elements of the A array inside the innermost loop mean each update requires the UE in question to own the indicated cache line. Although the elements of A are truly independent between UEs, they likely sit in the same cache line. Hence, every iteration in the innermost loop incurs an expensive cache line invalidate-and-movement operation. It is not uncommon for this to not only destroy all parallel speedup, but to even cause the parallel program to become slower as more PEs are added. The solution is to create a temporary variable on each thread to accumulate values in the innermost loop. False sharing is still a factor, but only for the much smaller outermost loop where the performance impact is negligible.

Examples

As examples of this pattern in action, we will briefly consider the following:

- Numerical integration to estimate the value of a definite integral using the trapezoid rule

- Molecular dynamics, nonbonded energy computation

- Mandelbrot set computation

- Mesh computation

Each of these examples has been described elsewhere in detail. We will restrict our discussion in this pattern to the key loops and how they can be parallelized.

Numerical integration.   Consider the problem of estimating the value of π using Eq. 5.5.

$$\pi = \int_0^1 \frac{4}{1 + x^2}\,dx \tag{5.5}$$

We use trapezoidal integration to numerically solve the integral. The idea is to fill the area under a curve with a series of rectangles. As the width of the rectangles approaches 0, the sum of the areas of the rectangles approaches the value of the integral.

A program to carry out this calculation on a single processor is shown in Fig. 5.24. To keep the program as simple as possible, we fix the number of steps to

```
#include <stdio.h>
#include <math.h>

int main () {
   int i;
   int num_steps = 1000000;
   double x, pi, step, sum = 0.0;

   step = 1.0/(double) num_steps;

   for (i=0;i< num_steps; i++)
   {
      x = (i+0.5)*step;
      sum = sum + 4.0/(1.0+x*x);
   }
   pi = step * sum;
   printf("pi %lf\n",pi);
   return 0;
}
```

Figure 5.24: Sequential program to carry out a trapezoid rule integration to compute $\int_0^1 \frac{4}{1+x^2}\,dx$

use in the integration at 1,000,000. The variable `sum` is initialized to 0 and the step size is computed as the range in `x` (equal to 1.0 in this case) divided by the number of steps. The area of each rectangle is the width (the step size) times the height (the value of the integrand at the center of the interval). The width is a constant, so we pull it out of the summation and multiply the sum of the rectangle heights by the step size, `step`, to get our estimate of the definite integral.

Creating a parallel version of this program using the *Loop Parallelism* pattern is simple. There is only one loop, so the inspection phase is trivial. To make the loop iterations independent, we recognize that (1) the values of the variable `x` are local to each iteration, so this variable can be handled as a thread-local or private variable and (2) the updates to `sum` define a reduction. Reductions are supported by the OpenMP API. Other than adding `#include <omp.h>`[2], only one additional line of code is needed to create a parallel version of the program. The following is placed above the `for` loop:

```
#pragma omp parallel for private(x) reduction(+:sum)
```

The pragma tells an OpenMP compiler to (1) create a team of threads, (2) create a private copy of `x` and `sum` for each thread, (3) initialize `sum` to 0 (the identity operand for addition), (4) map loop iterations onto threads in the team, (5) combine local values of `sum` into a single global value, and (6) join the parallel threads with the single master thread. Each of these steps is described in detail in the *Implementation Mechanisms* design space and the OpenMP appendix, Appendix A. For a non-OpenMP compiler, this pragma is ignored and therefore has no effect on the program's behavior.

Molecular dynamics.   Throughout this book, we have used molecular dynamics as a recurring example. Molecular dynamics simulates the motions of a large molecular system. It uses an explicit time-stepping methodology where at each time step the force on each atom is computed and standard techniques from classical mechanics are used to compute how the forces change atomic motions.

The core algorithm, including pseudocode, was presented in Sec. 3.1.3 and in the *SPMD* pattern. The problem comes down to a collection of computationally expensive loops over the atoms within the molecular system. These are embedded in a top-level loop over time.

The loop over time cannot be parallelized because the coordinates and velocities from time step $t-1$ are the starting point for time step t. The individual loops over atoms, however, can be parallelized. The most important case to address is the nonbonded energy calculation. The code for this computation is shown in Fig. 5.25. Unlike the approach used in the examples from the *SPMD* pattern, we assume that the program and its data structures are unchanged from the serial case.

---

[2]The OpenMP include file defines function prototypes and opaque data types used by OpenMP.

```
function non_bonded_forces (N, Atoms, neighbors, Forces)

    Int N // number of atoms

    Array of Real :: atoms (3,N) //3D coordinates
    Array of Real :: forces (3,N) //force in each dimension
    Array of List :: neighbors(N) //atoms in cutoff volume
    Real :: forceX, forceY, forceZ

    loop [i] over atoms

        loop [j] over neighbors(i)
            forceX = non_bond_force(atoms(1,i), atoms(1,j))
            forceY = non_bond_force(atoms(2,i), atoms(2,j))
            forceZ = non_bond_force(atoms(3,i), atoms(3,j))
            force{1,i) += forceX; force{1,j) -= forceX;
            force(2,i) += forceY; force{2,j) -= forceY;
            force{3,i) += forceZ; force{3,j) -= forceZ;
        end loop [j]

    end loop [i]
end function non_bonded_forces
```

Figure 5.25: Pseudocode for the nonbonded computation in a typical parallel molecular dynamics code. This is code is almost identical to the sequential version of the function shown previously in Fig. 4.4.

We will parallelize the `loop [i] over atoms`. Notice that the variables `forceX`, `forceY`, and `forceZ` are temporary variables used inside an iteration. We will need to create local copies of these private to each UE. The updates to the `force` arrays are reductions. Parallelization of this function would therefore require adding a single directive before the loop over atoms:

```
#pragma omp parallel for private(j, forceX, forceY, forceZ) \
                  reduction (+ : force)
```

The work associated with each atom varies unpredictably depending on how many atoms are in "its neighborhood". Although the compiler might be able to guess an effective schedule, in cases such as this one, it is usually best to try different schedules to find the one that works best. The work per atom is unpredictable, so one of the dynamic schedules available with OpenMP (and described in the OpenMP appendix, Appendix A) should be used. This requires the addition of a single `schedule` clause. Doing so gives us our final pragma for parallelizing this program:

```
#pragma omp parallel for private(j, forceX, forceY, forceZ) \
                  reduction (+ : force) schedule (dynamic,10)
```

This schedule tells the compiler to group the loop iterations into blocks of size 10 and assign them dynamically to the UEs. The size of the blocks is arbitrary and chosen to balance dynamic scheduling overhead versus how effectively the load can be balanced.

OpenMP 2.0 for C/C++ does not support reductions over arrays so the reduction would need to be done explicitly. This is straightforward and is shown in Fig. 5.11. A future release of OpenMP will correct this deficiency and support reductions over arrays for all languages that support OpenMP.

The same method used to parallelize the nonbonded force computation could be used throughout the molecular dynamics program. The performance and scalability will lag the analogous SPMD version of the program. The problem is that each time a parallel directive is encountered, a new team of threads is in principle created. Most OpenMP implementations use a thread pool, rather than actually creating a new team of threads for each parallel region, which minimizes thread creation and destruction overhead. However, this method of parallelizing the computation still adds significant overhead. Also, the reuse of data from caches tends to be poor for these approaches. In principle, each loop can access a different pattern of atoms on each UE. This eliminates the capability for UEs to make effective use of values already in cache.

Even with these shortcomings, however, these approaches are commonly used when the goal is extra parallelism on a small shared-memory system [BBE+99]. For example, one might use an SPMD version of the molecular dynamics program across a cluster and then use OpenMP to gain extra performance from dual processors or from microprocessors utilizing simultaneous multithreading [MPS02].

Mandelbrot set computation.   Consider the well-known Mandelbrot set [Dou86]. We discuss this problem and its parallelization as a task-parallel problem in the *Task Parallelism* and *SPMD* patterns. Each pixel is colored based on the behavior of the quadratic recurrence relation in Eq. 5.6.

$$Z_{n+1} = Z_n^2 + C \qquad (5.6)$$

C and Z are complex numbers and the recurrence is started with $Z_0 = C$. The image plots the imaginary part of C on the vertical axis (-1.5 to 1.5) and the real part on the horizontal axis (-1 to 2). The color of each pixel is black if the recurrence relation converges to a stable value or is colored depending on how rapidly the relation diverges.

Pseudocode for the sequential version of this code is shown in Fig. 5.26. The interesting part of the problem is hidden inside the routine `compute_Row()`. The details of this routine are not important for understanding the parallel algorithm, however, so we will not show them here. At a high level, the following happens for each point in the row.

- Each pixel corresponds to a value of C in the quadratic recurrence. We compute this value based on the input `range` and the pixel indices.

```
Int const Nrows // number of rows in the image
Int const RowSize // number of pixels in a row
Int const M // number of colors in color map

Real :: conv // divergence rate for a pixel
Array of Int :: color_map (M) // pixel color based on conv rate
Array of Int :: row (RowSize) // Pixels to draw
Array of Real :: ranges(2) // ranges in X and Y dimensions

manage_user_input(ranges, color_map) // input ranges, color map
initialize_graphics(RowSize, Nrows, M, ranges, color_map)

for (int i = 0; i<Nrows; i++){

    compute_Row (RowSize, ranges, row)

    graph(i, RowSize, M, color_map, ranges, row)

} // end loop [i] over rows
```

Figure 5.26: Pseudocode for a sequential version of the Mandelbrot set generation program

- We then compute the terms in the recurrence and set the value of the pixel based on whether it converges to a fixed value or diverges. If it diverges, we set the pixel value based on the rate of divergence.

Once computed, the rows are plotted to make the well-known Mandelbrot set images. The colors used for the pixels are determined by mapping divergence rates onto a color map.

Creating a parallel version of this program using the *Loop Parallelism* pattern is trivial. The iterations of the loop over rows are independent. All we need to do is make sure each thread has its own row to work on. We do this with the single pragma:

```
#pragma omp parallel for private(row)
```

The scheduling can be a bit tricky because work associated with each row will vary considerably depending on how many points diverge. The programmer should try several different schedules, but a cyclic distribution is likely to provide an effective load balance. In this schedule, the loop iterations are dealt out like a deck of cards. By interleaving the iterations among a set of threads, we are likely to get a balanced load. Because the scheduling decisions are static, the overhead incurred by this approach is small.

```
#pragma omp parallel for private(Row) schedule(static, 1)
```

For more information about the **schedule** clause and the different options available to the parallel programmer, see the OpenMP appendix, Appendix A.

Notice that we have assumed that the graphics package is thread-safe. This means that multiple threads can simultaneously call the library without causing any problems. The OpenMP specifications require this for the standard I/O library, but not for any other libraries. Therefore, it may be necessary to protect the call to the **graph** function by placing it inside a critical section:

```
#pragma critical
        graph(i, RowSize, M, color_map, ranges, row)
```

We describe this construct in detail in the *Implementation Mechanisms* design space and in the OpenMP appendix, Appendix A. This approach would work well, but it could have serious performance implications if the rows took the same time to compute and the threads all tried to graph their rows at the same time.

Mesh computation.   Consider a simple mesh computation that solves the 1D heat-diffusion equation. The details of this problem and its solution using OpenMP are presented in the *Geometric Decomposition* pattern. We reproduce this solution in Fig. 5.27.

This program would work well on most shared-memory computers. A careful analysis of the program performance, however, would expose two performance problems. First, the **single** directive required to protect the swapping of the shared pointers adds an extra barrier, thereby greatly increasing the synchronization overhead. Second, on NUMA computers, memory access overhead is likely to be high because we've made no effort to keep the arrays near the PEs that will be manipulating them.

We address both of these problems in Fig. 5.28. To eliminate the need for the **single** directive, we modify the program so each thread has its own copy of the pointers uk and ukp1. This can be done with a **private** clause, but to be useful, we need the new, private copies of uk and ukp1 to point to the shared arrays comprising the mesh of values. We do this with the **firstprivate** clause applied to the **parallel** directive that creates the team of threads.

The other performance issue we address, minimizing memory access overhead, is more subtle. As discussed earlier, to reduce memory traffic in the system, it is important to keep the data close to the PEs that will work with the data. On NUMA computers, this corresponds to making sure the pages of memory are allocated and "owned" by the PEs that will be working with the data contained in the page. The most common NUMA page-placement algorithm is the "first touch" algorithm, in which the PE first referencing a region of memory will have the page holding that memory assigned to it. So a very common technique in OpenMP programs is to initialize data in parallel using the same loop schedule as will be used later in the computations.

```
#include <stdio.h>
#include <stdlib.h>
#include <omp.h>
#define NX 100
#define LEFTVAL 1.0
#define RIGHTVAL 10.0
#define NSTEPS 10000

void initialize(double uk[], double ukp1[]) {
    uk[0] = LEFTVAL; uk[NX-1] = RIGHTVAL;
    for (int i = 1; i < NX-1; ++i)
        uk[i] = 0.0;
    for (int i = 0; i < NX; ++i)
        ukp1[i] = uk[i];
}

void printValues(double uk[], int step) { /* NOT SHOWN */ }

int main(void) {
    /* pointers to arrays for two iterations of algorithm */
    double *uk = malloc(sizeof(double) * NX);
    double *ukp1 = malloc(sizeof(double) * NX);
    double *temp;
    int i,k;

    double dx = 1.0/NX; double dt = 0.5*dx*dx;

  #pragma omp parallel private (k, i)
    {
        initialize(uk, ukp1);

        for (k = 0; k < NSTEPS; ++k) {
          #pragma omp for schedule(static)
          for (i = 1; i < NX-1; ++i) {
            ukp1[i]=uk[i]+ (dt/(dx*dx))*(uk[i+1]-2*uk[i]+uk[i-1]);
          }
          /* "copy" ukp1 to uk by swapping pointers */
          #pragma omp single
          {temp = ukp1; ukp1 = uk; uk = temp;}
        }
    }
    return 0;
}
```

Figure 5.27: Parallel heat-diffusion program using OpenMP. This program is described in the Examples section of the *Geometric Decomposition* pattern.

We do this by first changing the initialization slightly so the initialization loop is identical to the computation loop. We then use the same loop parallelization directive on the initialization loop as on the computational loop. This doesn't guarantee an optimal mapping of memory pages onto the PEs, but it is a portable way to improve this mapping and in many cases come quite close to an optimal solution.

```
#include <stdio.h>
#include <stdlib.h>
#include <omp.h>
#define NX 100
#define LEFTVAL 1.0
#define RIGHTVAL 10.0
#define NSTEPS 10000

void initialize(double uk[], double ukp1[]) {
    int i;
    uk[0] = LEFTVAL; uk[NX-1] = RIGHTVAL;
    ukp1[NX-1] = 0.0;
#pragma omp for schedule(static)
    for (i = 1; i < NX-1; ++i){
        uk[i] = 0.0;
        ukp1[i] = 0.0;
    }
}

void printValues(double uk[], int step) { /* NOT SHOWN */ }

int main(void) {
    /* pointers to arrays for two iterations of algorithm */
    double *uk = malloc(sizeof(double) * NX);
    double *ukp1 = malloc(sizeof(double) * NX);
    double *temp;
    int i,k;

    double dx = 1.0/NX; double dt = 0.5*dx*dx;

#pragma omp parallel private (k, i, temp) firstprivate(uk, ukp1)
    {
        initialize(uk, ukp1);

        for (k = 0; k < NSTEPS; ++k) {
            #pragma omp for schedule(static)
            for (i = 1; i < NX-1; ++i) {
              ukp1[i]=uk[i]+ (dt/(dx*dx))*(uk[i+1]-2*uk[i]+uk[i-1]);
            }
            /* "copy" ukp1 to uk by swapping pointers */
            temp = ukp1; ukp1 = uk; uk = temp;
        }
    }
    return 0;
}
```

Figure 5.28: Parallel heat-diffusion program using OpenMP, with reduced thread management overhead and memory management more appropriate for NUMA computers

Known uses.   The *Loop Parallelism* pattern is heavily used by OpenMP programmers. Annual workshops are held in North America (Wompat: Workshop on OpenMP Applications and Tools), Europe (EWOMP: European Workshop on OpenMP), and Japan (WOMPEI: Workshop on OpenMP Experiences and Implementations) to discuss OpenMP and its use. Proceedings from many of these workshops are widely available [VJKT00, Sci03, EV01] and are full of examples of the *Loop Parallelism* pattern.

Most of the work on OpenMP has been restricted to shared-memory multiprocessor machines for problems that work well with a nearly flat memory hierarchy. Work has been done to extend OpenMP applications to more complicated memory hierarchies, including NUMA machines [NA01, SSGF00] and even clusters [HLCZ99, SHTS01].

Related Patterns

The concept of driving parallelism from a collection of loops is general and used with many patterns. In particular, many problems using the *SPMD* pattern are loop-based. They use the UE ID, however, to drive the parallelization of the loop and hence don't perfectly map onto this pattern. Furthermore, problems using the *SPMD* pattern usually include some degree of parallel logic in between the loops. This allows them to decrease their serial fraction and is one of the reasons why SPMD programs tend to scale better than programs using the *Loop Parallelism* pattern.

Algorithms targeted for shared-memory computers that use the *Task Parallelism* or *Geometric Decomposition* patterns frequently use the *Loop Parallelism* pattern.

5.7 THE *FORK/JOIN* PATTERN

Problem

In some programs, the number of concurrent tasks varies as the program executes, and the way these tasks are related prevents the use of simple control structures such as parallel loops. How can a parallel program be constructed around such complicated sets of dynamic tasks?

Context

In some problems, the algorithm imposes a general and dynamic parallel control structure. Tasks are created dynamically (that is, *forked*) and later terminated (that is, *joined* with the forking task) as the program continues to execute. In most cases, the relationships between tasks are simple, and dynamic task creation can be handled with parallel loops (as described in the *Loop Parallelism* pattern) or through task queues (as described in the *Master/Worker* pattern). In other cases, relationships between the tasks within the algorithm must be captured in the way the tasks are managed. Examples include recursively generated task structures, highly irregular sets of connected tasks, and problems where different functions are mapped onto different concurrent tasks. In each of these examples, tasks are forked and later joined with the parent task (that is, the task that executed the fork) and the other tasks created by the same fork. These problems are addressed in the *Fork/Join* pattern.

As an example, consider an algorithm designed using the *Divide and Conquer* pattern. As the program execution proceeds, the problem is split into subproblems and new tasks are recursively created (or forked) to concurrently execute subproblems; each of these tasks may in turn be further split. When all the tasks created to handle a particular split have terminated and joined with the parent task, the parent task continues the computation.

> *This pattern is particularly relevant for Java programs running on shared-memory computers and for problems using the* Divide and Conquer *and* Recursive Data *patterns. OpenMP can be used effectively with this pattern when the OpenMP environment supports nested parallel regions.*

Forces

- Algorithms imply relationships between tasks. In some problems, there are complex or recursive relations between tasks, and these relations need to be created and terminated dynamically. Although these can be mapped onto familiar control structures, the design in many cases is much easier to understand if the structure of the tasks is mimicked by the structure of the UEs.

- A one-to-one mapping of tasks onto UEs is natural in these algorithms, but that must be balanced against the number of UEs a system can handle.

- UE creation and destruction are costly operations. The algorithm might need to be recast to decrease these operations so they don't adversely affect the program's overall performance.

Solution

In problems that use the *Fork/Join* pattern, tasks map onto UEs in different ways. We will discuss two different approaches to the solution: (1) a simple direct mapping where there is one task per UE, and (2) an indirect mapping where a pool of UEs work on sets of tasks.

Direct task/UE mapping.   The simplest case is one where we map each subtask to a UE. As new subtasks are forked, new UEs are created to handle them. This will build up corresponding sets of tasks and UEs. In many cases, there is a synchronization point where the main task waits for its subtasks to finish. This is called a *join*. After a subtask terminates, the UE handling it will be destroyed. We will provide an example of this approach later using Java.

The direct task/UE mapping solution to the *Fork/Join* pattern is the standard programming model in OpenMP. A program begins as a single thread (the *master thread*). A parallel construct forks a team of threads, the threads execute within a shared address space, and at the end of the parallel construct, the threads join back together. The original master thread then continues execution until the end of the program or until the next parallel construct.[3] This structure underlies

---

[3]In principle, nested parallel regions in OpenMP programs also map onto this direct-mapping solution. This approach has been successfully used in [AML+99]. The OpenMP specification, however, lets conforming OpenMP implementations "serialize" nested parallel regions (that is, execute them with a team of size one). Therefore, an OpenMP program cannot depend on nested parallel regions actually forking additional threads, and programmers must be cautious when using OpenMP for all but the simplest fork/join programs.

the implementation of the OpenMP parallel loop constructs described in the *Loop Parallelism* pattern.

Indirect task/UE mapping.   Thread and process creation and destruction is one of the more expensive operations that occur in parallel programs. Thus, if a program contains repeated fork and join sections, the simple solution, which would require repeated destruction and creation of UEs, might not be efficient enough. Also, if at some point there are many more UEs than PEs, the program might incur unacceptable overhead due to the costs of context switches.

In this case, it is desirable to avoid the dynamic UE creation by implementing the fork/join paradigm using a thread pool. The idea is to create a (relatively) static set of UEs before the first fork operation. The number of UEs is usually the same as the number of PEs. The mapping of tasks to UEs then occurs dynamically using a task queue. The UEs themselves are not repeatedly created and destroyed, but simply mapped to dynamically created tasks as the need arises. This approach, although complicated to implement, usually results in efficient programs with good load balance. We will discuss a Java program that uses this approach in the Examples section of this pattern.

In OpenMP, there is some controversy over the best approach to use with this indirect-mapping approach [Mat03]. An approach gaining credibility is one based on a new, proposed OpenMP workshare construct called a `taskqueue` [SHPT00]. The proposal actually defines two new constructs: a `taskqueue` and a `task`. As the name implies, the programmer uses a `taskqueue` construct to create the task queue. Inside the `taskqueue` construct, a `task` construct defines a block of code that will be packaged into a task and placed on the task queue. The team of threads (as usually created with a parallel construct), playing the role of a thread pool, pulls tasks off the queue and executes them until the queue is empty.

Unlike OpenMP parallel regions, `taskqueue`s can be dependably nested to produce a hierarchy of task queues. The threads work across task queues using work-stealing to keep all threads fully occupied until all of the queues are empty. This approach has been shown to work well [SHPT00] and is likely to be adopted in a future OpenMP specification.

Examples

As examples of this pattern, we will consider direct-mapping and indirect-mapping implementations of a parallel mergesort algorithm. The indirect-mapping solution makes use of a Java package FJTasks [Lea00b]. The Examples section of the *Shared Queue* pattern develops a similar, but simpler, framework.

Mergesort using direct mapping.   As an example, consider the straightforward implementation of a method to performs a mergesort in Java shown in Fig. 5.29. The method takes a reference to the array to be sorted and sorts the elements with indices ranging from `lo` (inclusive) to `hi` (exclusive). Sorting the entire array `A` is done by invoking `sort(A,0,A.length)`.

```
static void sort(final int[] A,final int lo, final int hi)
{ int n = hi - lo;

    //if not large enough to do in parallel, sort sequentially
    if (n <= THRESHOLD){ Arrays.sort(A,lo,hi); return; }
    else
    { //split array
        final int pivot = (hi+lo)/2;

        //create and start new thread to sort lower half
        Thread t = new Thread()
        { public void run()
            { sort(A, lo, pivot); }
        };
        t.start();

        //sort upper half in current thread
        sort(A,pivot,hi);

        //wait for other thread
        try{t.join();}
        catch (InterruptedException e){Thread.dumpStack();}

        //merge sorted arrays
        int[] ws = new int[n];
        System.arraycopy(A,lo,ws,0,n);
        int wpivot = pivot - lo;
        int wlo = 0;
        int whi = wpivot;
        for (int i = lo; i != hi; i++)
        { if((wlo < wpivot) && (whi >= n || ws[wlo] <= ws[whi]))
            { A[i] = ws[wlo++]; }
            else { A[i] = ws[whi++]; }
        }
    }
}
```

Figure 5.29: Parallel mergesort where each task corresponds to a thread

The first step of the method is to compute the size of the segment of the array to be sorted. If the size of the problem is too small to make the overhead of sorting it in parallel worthwhile, then a sequential sorting algorithm is used (in this case, the tuned quicksort implementation provided by the **Arrays** class in the **java.util** package). If the sequential algorithm is not used, then a pivot point is computed to divide the segment to be sorted. A new thread is forked to sort the lower half of the array, while the parent thread sorts the upper half. The new task is specified by the **run** method of an anonymous inner subclass of the **Thread** class. When the new thread has finished sorting, it terminates. When the parent thread finishes sorting, it performs a join to wait for the child thread to terminate and then merges the two sorted segments together.

This simple approach may be adequate in fairly regular problems where appropriate threshold values can easily be determined. We stress that it is crucial that the threshold value be chosen appropriately: If too small, the overhead from too

```
int groupSize = 4; //number of threads
FJTaskRunnerGroup group = new FJTaskRunnerGroup(groupSize);
group.invoke(new FJTask()
    { public void run()
        { synchronized(this)
            { sort(A,0, A.length); }


    }
});
```

Figure 5.30: Instantiating `FJTaskRunnerGroup` and invoking the master task

many UEs can make the program run even slower than a sequential version. If too large, potential concurrency remains unexploited.

Mergesort using indirect mapping. This example uses the FJTask framework included as part of the public-domain package EDU.oswego.cs.dl.util. concurrent [Lea00b].[4] Instead of creating a new thread to execute each task, an instance of a (subclass of) FJTask is created. The package then dynamically maps the FJTask objects to a static set of threads for execution. Although less general than a Thread, an FJTask is a much lighter-weight object than a thread and is thus much cheaper to create and destroy. In Fig. 5.30 and Fig. 5.31, we show how to modify the mergesort example to use FJTasks instead of Java threads. The needed classes are imported from package EDU.oswego.cs.dl.util.concurrent. Before starting any FJTasks, a FJTaskRunnerGroup must be instantiated, as shown in Fig. 5.30. This creates the threads that will constitute the thread pool and takes the number of threads (group size) as a parameter. Once instantiated, the master task is invoked using the **invoke** method on the **FJTaskRunnerGroup**.

The sort routine itself is similar to the previous version except that the dynamically created tasks are implemented by the **run** method of an **FJTask** subclass instead of a **Thread** subclass. The **fork** and **join** methods of **FJTask** are used to fork and join the task in place of the **Thread start** and **join** methods. Although the underlying implementation is different, from the programmer's viewpoint, this indirect method is very similar to the direct implementation shown previously.

A more sophisticated parallel implementation of mergesort is provided with the **FJTask** examples in the **util.concurrent** distribution. The package also includes functionality not illustrated by this example.

Known uses. The documentation with the FJTask package includes several applications that use the *Fork/Join* pattern. The most interesting of these include Jacobi iteration, a parallel divide-and-conquer matrix multiplication, a standard

---

[4]This package was the basis for the new facilities to support concurrency introduced via JSR166 in Java 2 1.5. Its author, Doug Lea, was a lead in the JSR effort. The FJTask framework is not part of Java 2 1.5, but remains available in [Lea00b].

```
static void sort(final int[] A,final int lo, final int hi) {
   int n = hi - lo;
   if (n <= THRESHOLD){ Arrays.sort(A,lo,hi); return; }
   else {
      //split array
      final int pivot = (hi+lo)/2;

      //override run method in FJTask to execute run method
      FJTask t = new FJTask()
      { public void run()
         { sort(A, lo, pivot); }
      };

      //fork new task to sort lower half of array
      t.fork();

      //perform sort on upper half in current task
      sort(A,pivot,hi);

      //join with forked task
      t.join();

      //merge sorted arrays as before, code omitted
   }
}
```

Figure 5.31: Mergesort using the FJTask framework

parallel-processing benchmark program that simulates heat diffusion across a mesh, LU matrix decomposition, integral computation using recursive Gaussian Quadrature, and an adaptation of the Microscope game.[5]

Because OpenMP is based on a fork/join programming model, one might expect heavy use of the *Fork/Join* pattern by OpenMP programmers. The reality is, however, that most OpenMP programmers use either the *Loop Parallelism* or *SPMD* patterns because the current OpenMP standard provides poor support for true nesting of parallel regions. One of the few published accounts of using the *Fork/Join* pattern with standard OpenMP is a paper where nested parallelism was used to provide fine-grained parallelism in an implementation of LAPACK [ARv03].

Extending OpenMP so it can use the *Fork/Join* pattern in substantial applications is an active area of research. We've mentioned one of these lines of investigation for the case of the indirect-mapping solution of the *Fork/Join* pattern (the task queue [SHPT00]). Another possibility is to support nested parallel regions with explicit groups of threads for the direct-mapping solution of the *Fork/Join* pattern (the Nanos OpenMP compiler [GAM+00]).

---

[5]According to the documentation for this application, this is the game that is played while looking through the microscope in the laboratory in *The 7th Guest* (T7G; A CD-ROM game for PCs). It is a board game in which two players compete to fill spaces on the board with their tiles, something like Reversi or Othello.

Related Patterns

Algorithms that use the *Divide and Conquer* pattern use the *Fork/Join* pattern.

The *Loop Parallelism* pattern, in which threads are forked just to handle a single parallel loop, is an instance of the *Fork/Join* pattern.

The *Master/Worker* pattern, which in turn uses the *Shared Queue* pattern, can be used to implement the indirect-mapping solution.

 ## 5.8   THE *SHARED DATA* PATTERN

Problem

How does one explicitly manage shared data inside a set of concurrent tasks?

Context

Most of the *Algorithm Structure* patterns simplify the handling of shared data by using techniques to "pull" the shared data "outside" the set of tasks. Examples include replication plus reduction in the *Task Parallelism* pattern and alternating computation and communication in the *Geometric Decomposition* pattern. For certain problems, however, these techniques do not apply, thereby requiring that shared data be explicitly managed inside the set of concurrent tasks.

For example, consider the *phylogeny problem* from molecular biology, as described in [YWC+96]. A phylogeny is a tree showing relationships between organisms. The problem consists of generating large numbers of subtrees as potential solutions and then rejecting those that fail to meet the various consistency criteria. Different sets of subtrees can be examined concurrently, so a natural task definition in a parallel phylogeny algorithm would be the processing required for each set of subtrees. However, not all sets must be examined—if a set S is rejected, all supersets of S can also be rejected. Thus, it makes sense to keep track of the sets still to be examined *and* the sets that have been rejected. Given that the problem naturally decomposes into nearly independent tasks (one per set), the solution to this problem would use the *Task Parallelism* pattern. Using the pattern is complicated, however, by the fact that all tasks need both read and write access to the data structure of rejected sets. Also, because this data structure changes during the computation, we cannot use the replication technique described in the *Task Parallelism* pattern. Partitioning the data structure and basing a solution on this data decomposition, as described in the *Geometric Decomposition* pattern, might seem like a good alternative, but the way in which the elements are rejected is unpredictable, so any data decomposition is likely to lead to a poor load balance.

Similar difficulties can arise any time shared data must be explicitly managed inside a set of concurrent tasks. The common elements for problems that need the *Shared Data* pattern are (1) at least one data structure is accessed by multiple tasks in the course of the program's execution, (2) at least one task modifies the shared data structure, and (3) the tasks potentially need to use the modified value during the concurrent computation.

Forces

- The results of the computation must be correct for *any* ordering of the tasks that could occur during the computation.

- Explicitly managing shared data can incur parallel overhead, which must be kept small if the program is to run efficiently.

- Techniques for managing shared data can limit the number of tasks that can run concurrently, thereby reducing the potential scalability of an algorithm.

- If the constructs used to manage shared data are not easy to understand, the program will be more difficult to maintain.

Solution

Explicitly managing shared data can be one of the more error-prone aspects of designing a parallel algorithm. Therefore, a good approach is to start with a solution that emphasizes simplicity and clarity of abstraction and then try more complex solutions if necessary to obtain acceptable performance. The solution reflects this approach.

Be sure this pattern is needed.   The first step is to confirm that this pattern is truly needed; it might be worthwhile to revisit decisions made earlier in the design process (the decomposition into tasks, for example) to see whether different decisions might lead to a solution that fits one of the *Algorithm Structure* patterns without the need to explicitly manage shared data. For example, if the *Task Parallelism* pattern is a good fit, it is worthwhile to review the design and see if dependencies can be managed by replication and reduction.

Define an abstract data type.   Assuming this pattern must indeed be used, start by viewing the shared data as an abstract data type (ADT) with a fixed set of (possibly complex) operations on the data. For example, if the shared data structure is a queue (see the *Shared Queue* pattern), these operations would consist of *put* (enqueue), *take* (dequeue), and possibly other operations, such as a test for an empty queue or a test to see if a specified element is present. Each task will typically perform a sequence of these operations. These operations should have the property that if they are executed serially (that is, one at a time, without interference from other tasks), each operation will leave the data in a consistent state.

The implementation of the individual operations will most likely involve a sequence of lower-level actions, the results of which should not be visible to other UEs. For example, if we implemented the previously mentioned queue using a linked list, a "take" operation actually involves a sequence of lower-level operations (which may themselves consist of a sequence of even lower-level operations):

1. Use variable `first` to obtain a reference to the first object in the list.
2. From the first object, get a reference to the second object in the list.
3. Replace the value of `first` with the reference to the second object.

4. Update the size of the list.

5. Return the first element.

If two tasks are executing "take" operations concurrently, and these lower-level operations are interleaved (that is, the "take" operations are not being executed atomically), the result could easily be an inconsistent list.

Implement an appropriate concurrency-control protocol.   After the ADT and its operations have been identified, the objective is to implement a concurrency-control protocol to ensure that these operations give the same results as if they were executed serially. There are several ways to do this; start with the first technique, which is the simplest, and then try the other more complex techniques if it does not yield acceptable performance. These more complex techniques can be combined if more than one is applicable.

One-at-a-time execution.   The easiest solution is to ensure that the operations are indeed executed serially.

In a shared-memory environment, the most straightforward way to do this is to treat each operation as part of a single critical section and use a mutual-exclusion protocol to ensure that only one UE at a time is executing its critical section. This means that all of the operations on the data are mutually exclusive. Exactly how this is implemented will depend on the facilities of the target programming environment. Typical choices include mutex locks, synchronized blocks, critical sections, and semaphores. These mechanisms are described in the *Implementation Mechanisms* design space. If the programming language naturally supports the implementation of abstract data types, it is usually appropriate to implement each operation as a procedure or method, with the mutual-exclusion protocol implemented in the method itself.

In a message-passing environment, the most straightforward way to ensure serial execution is to assign the shared data structure to a particular UE. Each operation should correspond to a message type; other processes request operations by sending messages to the UE managing the data structure, which processes them serially.

In either environment, this approach is usually not difficult to implement, but it can be overly conservative (that is, it might disallow concurrent execution of operations that would be safe to execute simultaneously), and it can produce a bottleneck that negatively affects the performance of the program. If this is the case, the remaining approaches described in this section should be reviewed to see whether one of them can reduce or eliminate this bottleneck and give better performance.

Noninterfering sets of operations.   One approach to improving performance begins by analyzing the interference between the operations. We say that operation A *interferes with* operation B if A writes a variable that B reads. Notice that an operation may interfere with itself, which would be a concern if more than one task executes the same operation (for example, more than one task executes "take" operations on a shared queue). It may be the case, for example, that the operations fall into two disjoint sets, where the operations in different sets do not interfere with each other. In this case, the amount of concurrency can be increased by treating each of the sets as a different critical section. That is, within each set, operations execute one a time, but operations in different sets can proceed concurrently.

Readers/writers.   If there is no obvious way to partition the operations into disjoint sets, consider the type of interference. It may be the case that some of the operations modify the data, but others only read it. For example, if operation A is a writer (both reading and writing the data) and operation B is a reader (reading, but not writing, the data), A interferes with itself and with B, but B does not interfere with itself. Thus, if one task is performing operation A, no other task should be able to execute either A or B, but any number of tasks should be able to execute B concurrently. In such cases, it may be worthwhile to implement a readers/writers protocol that will allow this potential concurrency to be exploited. The overhead of managing the readers/writers protocol is greater than that of simple mutex locks, so the length of the readers' computation should be long enough to make this overhead worthwhile. In addition, there should generally be a larger number of concurrent readers than writers.

The `java.util.concurrent` package provides read/write locks to support the readers/writers protocol. The code in Fig. 5.32 illustrates how these locks

```
class X {
  ReadWriteLock rw = new ReentrantReadWriteLock();
  // ...

  /*operation A is a writer*/
  public void A() throws InterruptedException {
    rw.writeLock().lock(); //lock the write lock
    try {
      // ... do operation A
    }
    finally {
      rw.writeLock().unlock(); //unlock the write lock
    }
  }

  /*operation B is a reader*/
  public void B() throws InterruptedException {
    rw.readLock().lock(); //lock the read lock
    try {
      // ... do operation B
    }
    finally {
      rw.readLock().unlock(); //unlock the read lock
    }
  }
}
```

Figure 5.32: Typical use of read/write locks. These locks are defined in the `java.util.concurrent.locks` package. Putting the unlock in the `finally` block ensures that the lock will be unlocked regardless of how the `try` block is exited (normally or with an exception) and is a standard idiom in Java programs that use locks rather than synchronized blocks.

are typically used: First instantiate a `ReadWriteLock`, and then obtain its read and write locks. `ReentrantReadWriteLock` is a class that implements the `ReadWriteLock` interface. To perform a read operation, the read lock must be locked. To perform a write operation, the write lock must be locked. The semantics of the locks are that any number of UEs can simultaneously hold the read lock, but the write lock is exclusive; that is, only one UE can hold the write lock, and if the write lock is held, no UEs can hold the read lock either.

Readers/writers protocols are discussed in [And00] and most operating systems texts.

Reducing the size of the critical section.   Another approach to improving performance begins with analyzing the implementations of the operations in more detail. It may be the case that only part of the operation involves actions that interfere with other operations. If so, the size of the critical section can be reduced to that smaller part. Notice that this sort of optimization is very easy to get wrong, so it should be attempted only if it will give significant performance improvements over simpler approaches, *and* the programmer completely understands the interferences in question.

Nested locks.   This technique is a sort of hybrid between two of the previous approaches, noninterfering operations and reducing the size of the critical section. Suppose we have an ADT with two operations. Operation A does a lot of work both reading and updating variable x and then reads and updates variable y in a single statement. Operation B reads and writes y. Some analysis shows that UEs executing A need to exclude each other, UEs executing B need to exclude each other, and because both operations read and update y, technically, A and B need to mutually exclude each other as well. However, closer inspection shows that the two operations are *almost* noninterfering. If it weren't for that single statement where A reads and updates y, the two operations could be implemented in separate critical sections that would allow one A and one B to execute concurrently. A solution is to use two locks, as shown in Fig. 5.33. A acquires and holds `lockA` for the entire operation. B acquires and holds `lockB` for the entire operation. A acquires `lockB` and holds it only for the statement updating y.

Whenever nested locking is used, the programmer should be aware of the potential for deadlocks and double-check the code. (The classic example of deadlock, stated in terms of the previous example, is as follows: A acquires `lockA` and B acquires `lockB`. A then tries to acquire `lockB` and B tries to acquire `lockA`. Neither operation can now proceed.) Deadlocks can be avoided by assigning a partial order to the locks and ensuring that locks are always acquired in an order that respects the partial order. In the previous example, we would define the order to be `lockA` < `lockB` and ensure that `lockA` is never acquired by a UE already holding `lockB`.

Application-specific semantic relaxation.   Yet another approach is to consider partially replicating shared data (the software caching described in [YWC$^+$96]) and perhaps even allowing the copies to be inconsistent if this can be done without affecting the results of the computation. For example, a distributed-memory solution to the phylogeny problem described earlier might give

```
class Y {
  Object lockA = new Object();
  Object lockB = new Object();

  void A()
  { synchronized(lockA)
    {
      ....compute....
      synchronized(lockB)
      { ....read and update y....
      }
    }
  }

  void B() throws InterruptedException
  { synchronized(lockB)
    { ...compute....
    }
  }
}
```

Figure 5.33: Example of nested locking using synchronized blocks with dummy objects `lockA` and `lockB`

each UE its own copy of the set of sets already rejected and allow these copies to be out of synch; tasks may do extra work (in rejecting a set that has already been rejected by a task assigned to a different UE), but this extra work will not affect the result of the computation, and it may be more efficient overall than the communication cost of keeping all copies in synch.

Review other considerations

Memory synchronization.   Make sure memory is synchronized as required: Caching and compiler optimizations can result in unexpected behavior with respect to shared variables. For example, a stale value of a variable might be read from a cache or register instead of the newest value written by another task, or the latest value might not have been flushed to memory and thus would not be visible to other tasks. In most cases, memory synchronization is performed implicitly by higher-level synchronization primitives, but it is still necessary to be aware of the issue. Unfortunately, memory synchronization techniques are very platform-specific. In OpenMP, the flush directive can be used to synchronize memory explicitly; it is implicitly invoked by several other directives. In Java, memory is implicitly synchronized when entering and leaving a synchronized block, and, in Java 2 1.5, when locking and unlocking locks. Also, variables marked `volatile` are implicitly synchronized with respect to memory. This is discussed in more detail in the *Implementation Mechanisms* design space.

Task scheduling.   Consider whether the explicitly managed data dependencies addressed by this pattern affect task scheduling. A key goal in deciding how to schedule tasks is good load balance; in addition to the considerations described in the *Algorithm Structure* pattern being used, one should also take into account that tasks might be suspended waiting for access to shared data. It makes sense to try to assign tasks in a way that minimizes such waiting, or to assign multiple tasks to each UE in the hope that there will always be one task per UE that is not waiting for access to shared data.

Examples

Shared queues.   The shared queue is a commonly used ADT and an excellent example of the *Shared Data* pattern. The *Shared Queue* pattern discusses concurrency-control protocols and the techniques used to achieve highly efficient shared-queue programs.

Genetic algorithm for nonlinear optimization.   Consider the GAFORT program from the SPEC OMP2001 benchmark suite [ADE+01]. GAFORT is a small Fortran program (around 1,500 lines) that implements a genetic algorithm for nonlinear optimization. The calculations are predominantly integer arithmetic, and the program's performance is dominated by the cost of moving large arrays of data through the memory subsystem.

The details of the genetic algorithm are not important for this discussion. We are going to focus on a single loop within GAFORT. Pseudocode for the sequential version of this loop, based on the discussion of GAFORT in [EM], is shown in Fig. 5.34. This loop shuffles the population of chromosomes and consumes on the order of 36 percent of the runtime in a typical GAFORT job [AE03].

```
Int const NPOP // number of chromosomes (~40000)
Int const NCHROME // length of each chromosome

Real :: tempScalar
Array of Real :: temp(NCHROME)
Array of Int :: iparent(NCHROME, NPOP)
Array of Int :: fitness(NPOP)
Int :: j, iother

loop [j] over NPOP
    iother = rand(j) // returns random value greater
                     // than or equal to zero but not
                     // equal to j and less than NPOP

    // Swap Chromosomes
    temp(1:NCHROME) = iparent(1:NCHROME, iother)
    iparent(1:NCHROME, iother) = iparent(1:NCHROME, j)
    iparent(1:NCHROME, j) = temp(1:NCHROME)

    // Swap fitness metrics
    tempScalar = fitness(iother)
    fitness(iother) = fitness(j)
    fitness(j) = tempScalar

end loop [j]
```

Figure 5.34: Pseudocode for the population shuffle loop from the genetic algorithm program GAFORT

A parallel version of this program will be created by parallelizing the loop, using the *Loop Parallelism* pattern. In this example, the shared data consists of the `iparent` and `fitness` arrays. Within the body of the loop, calculations involving these arrays consist of swapping two elements of `iparent` and then swapping the corresponding elements of `fitness`. Examination of these operations shows that two swap operations interfere when at least one of the locations being swapped is the same in both operations.

Thinking about the shared data as an ADT helps us to identify and analyze the actions taken on the shared data. This does not mean, however, that the implementation itself always needs to reflect this structure. In some cases, especially when the data structure is simple and the programming language does not support ADTs well, it can be more effective to forgo the encapsulation implied in an ADT and work with the data directly. This example illustrates this.

As mentioned earlier, the chromosomes being swapped might interfere with each other; thus the loop over j cannot safely execute in parallel. The most straightforward approach is to enforce a "one at a time" protocol using a critical section, as shown in Fig. 5.35. It is also necessary to modify the random number generator

```
#include <omp.h>
    Int const NPOP // number of chromosomes (~40000)
    Int const NCHROME // length of each chromosome

    Real :: tempScalar
    Array of Real :: temp(NCHROME)
    Array of Int :: iparent(NCHROME, NPOP)
    Array of Int :: fitness(NPOP)
    Int :: j, iother

#pragma omp parallel for
    loop [j] over NPOP
        iother = par_rand(j) // returns random value greater
                             // than or equal to zero but not
                             // equal to j and less than NPOP

#pragma omp critical
{

        // Swap Chromosomes
        temp(1:NCHROME) = iparent(1:NCHROME, iother)
        iparent(1:NCHROME, iother) = iparent(1:NCHROME, j)
        iparent(1:NCHROME, j) = temp(1:NCHROME)

        // Swap fitness metrics
        tempScalar = fitness(iother)
        fitness(iother) = fitness(j)
        fitness(j) = tempScalar
}
    end loop [j]
```

Figure 5.35: Pseudocode for an ineffective approach to parallelizing the population shuffle in the genetic algorithm program GAFORT

so it produces a consistent set of pseudorandom numbers when called in parallel by many threads. The algorithms to accomplish this are well understood [Mas97], but will not be discussed here.

The program in Fig. 5.35 can safely execute with multiple threads, but it will not run any faster as more threads are added. In fact, this program will slow down as more threads are added because the threads will waste system resources as they wait for their turn to execute the critical section. In essence, the concurrency-control protocol eliminates all of the available concurrency.

The solution to this problem is to take advantage of the fact that the swap operations on the shared data only interfere when at least one of the locations being swapped is the same in both operations. Hence, the right concurrency-control protocol uses pairwise synchronization with nested locks, thereby adding only modest overhead when loop iterations do not interfere. The approach used in [ADE+01] is to create an OpenMP lock for each chromosome. Pseudocode for this solution is shown in Fig. 5.36. In the resulting program, most of the loop iterations do not actually interfere with each other. The total number of chromosomes, NPOP (40,000 in the SPEC OMP2001 benchmark), is much larger than the number of UEs, so there is only a slight chance that loop iterations will happen to interfere with another loop iteration.

OpenMP locks are described in the OpenMP appendix, Appendix A. The locks themselves use an opaque type, omp_lock_t, defined in the omp.h header file. The lock array is defined and later initialized in a separate parallel loop. Once inside the chromosome-swapping loop, the locks are set for the pair of swapping chromosomes, the swap is carried out, and the locks are unset. Nested locks are being used, so the possibility of deadlock must be considered. The solution here is to order the locks using the value of the indices of the array element associated with the lock. Always acquiring locks in this order will prevent deadlock when a pair of loop iterations happen to be swapping the same two elements at the same time. After the more efficient concurrency-control protocol is implemented, the program runs well in parallel.

Known uses. A solution to the phylogeny problem described in the Context section is presented in [YWC+96]. The overall approach fits the *Task Parallelism* pattern; the rejected-sets data structure is explicitly managed using replication and periodic updates to reestablish consistency among copies.

Another problem presented in [YWC+96] is the Gröbner basis program. Omitting most of the details, in this application the computation consists of using pairs of polynomials to generate new polynomials, comparing them against a master set of polynomials, and adding those that are not linear combinations of elements of the master set to the master set (where they are used to generate new pairs). Different pairs can be processed concurrently, so one can define a task for each pair and partition them among UEs. The solution described in [YWC+96] fits the *Task Parallelism* pattern (with a task queue consisting of pairs of polynomials), plus explicit management of the master set using an application-specific protocol called *software caching*.

```
#include <omp.h>
    Int const NPOP // number of chromosomes (~40000)
    Int const NCHROME // length of each chromosome

    Array of omp_lock_t :: lck(NPOP)

    Real :: tempScalar
    Array of Real :: temp(NCHROME)
    Array of Int :: iparent(NCHROME, NPOP)
    Array of Int :: fitness(NPOP)
    Int :: j, iother

// Initialize the locks
#pragma omp parallel for
    for (j=0; j<NPOP; j++){ omp_init_lock (&lck(j)) }

#pragma omp parallel for
    for (j=0; j<NPOP; j++){
        iother = par_rand(j) // returns random value >= 0, != j,
                             //  < NPOP
        if (j < iother) {
            set_omp_lock (lck(j)); set_omp_lock (lck(iother))
        }
        else {
            set_omp_lock (lck(iother)); set_omp_lock (lck(j))
        }

        // Swap Chromosomes
        temp(1:NCHROME) = iparent(1:NCHROME, iother);
        iparent(1:NCHROME, iother) = iparent(1:NCHROME, j);
        iparent(1:NCHROME, j) = temp(1:NCHROME);

        // Swap fitness metrics
        tempScalar = fitness(iother)
        fitness(iother) = fitness(j)
        fitness(j) = tempScalar

        if (j < iother) {
            unset_omp_lock (lck(iother)); unset_omp_lock (lck(j))
        }
        else {
            unset_omp_lock (lck(j)); unset_omp_lock (lck(iother))
        }
    } // end loop [j]
```

Figure 5.36: Pseudocode for a parallelized loop to carry out the population shuffle in the genetic algorithm program GAFORT. This version of the loop uses a separate lock for each chromosome and runs effectively in parallel.

Related Patterns

The *Shared Queue* and *Distributed Array* patterns discuss specific types of shared data structures. Many problems that use the *Shared Data* pattern use the *Task Parallelism* pattern for the algorithm structure.

5.9   THE *SHARED QUEUE* PATTERN

Problem

How can concurrently-executing UEs safely share a queue data structure?

Context

Effective implementation of many parallel algorithms requires a queue that is to be shared among UEs. The most common situation is the need for a task queue in programs implementing the *Master/Worker* pattern.

Forces

- Simple concurrency-control protocols provide greater clarity of abstraction and make it easier for the programmer to verify that the shared queue has been correctly implemented.

- Concurrency-control protocols that encompass too much of the shared queue in a single synchronization construct increase the chances UEs will remain blocked waiting to access the queue and will limit available concurrency.

- A concurrency-control protocol finely tuned to the queue and how it will be used increases the available concurrency, but at the cost of much more complicated, and more error-prone, synchronization constructs.

- Maintaining a single queue for systems with complicated memory hierarchies (as found on NUMA machines and clusters) can cause excess communication and increase parallel overhead. Solutions may in some cases need to break with the single-queue abstraction and use multiple or distributed queues.

Solution

Ideally the shared queue would be implemented as part of the target programming environment, either explicitly as an ADT to be used by the programmer, or implicitly as support for the higher-level patterns (such as *Master/Worker*) that use it. In Java 2 1.5, such queues are available in the `java.util.concurrent` package. Here we develop implementations from scratch to illustrate the concepts.

Implementing shared queues can be tricky. Appropriate synchronization must be utilized to avoid race conditions, and performance considerations—especially for problems where large numbers of UEs access the queue—can require sophisticated synchronization. In some cases, a noncentralized queue might be needed to eliminate performance bottlenecks.

However, if it is necessary to implement a shared queue, it can be done as an instance of the *Shared Data* pattern: First, we design an ADT for the queue by defining the values the queue can hold and the set of operations on the queue. Next, we consider the concurrency-control protocols, starting with the simplest "one-at-a-time execution" solution and then applying a series of refinements. To make this discussion more concrete, we will consider the queue in terms of a specific problem:

a queue to hold tasks in a master/worker algorithm. The solutions presented here, however, are general and can be easily extended to cover other applications of a shared queue.

The abstract data type (ADT). An ADT is a set of values and the operations defined on that set of values. In the case of a queue, the values are ordered lists of zero or more objects of some type (for example, integers or task IDs). The operations on the queue are `put` (or *enqueue*) and `take` (or *dequeue*). In some situations, there might be other operations, but for the sake of this discussion, these two are sufficient.

We must also decide what happens when a `take` is attempted on an empty queue. What should be done depends on how termination will be handled by the master/worker algorithm. Suppose, for example, that all the tasks will be created at startup time by the master. In this case, an empty task queue will indicate that the UE should terminate, and we will want the `take` operation on an empty queue to return immediately with an indication that the queue is empty—that is, we want a *nonblocking* queue. Another possible situation is that tasks can be created dynamically and that UEs will terminate when they receive a special *poison-pill* task. In this case, appropriate behavior might be for the `take` operation on an empty queue to wait until the queue is nonempty—that is, we want a *block-on-empty* queue.

Queue with "one at a time" execution

Nonblocking queue. Because the queue will be accessed concurrently, we must define a concurrency-control protocol to ensure that interference by multiple UEs will not occur. As recommended in the *Shared Data* pattern, the simplest solution is to make all operations on the ADT exclude each other. Because none of the operations on the queue can block, a straightforward implementation of mutual exclusion as described in the *Implementation Mechanisms* design spaces suffices. The Java implementation shown in Fig. 5.37 uses a linked list to hold the tasks in the queue. (We develop our own list class rather than using an unsynchronized library class such as `java.util.LinkedList` or a class from the `java.util.concurrent` package to illustrate how to add appropriate synchronization.) `head` refers to an always-present dummy node.[6]

The first task in the queue (if any) is held in the node referred to by `head.next`. The `isEmpty` method is private, and only invoked inside a synchronized method. Thus, it need not be synchronized. (If it were public, it would need to be synchronized as well.) Of course, numerous ways of implementing the structure that holds the tasks are possible.

Block-on-empty queue. The second version of the shared queue is shown in Fig. 5.38. In this version of the queue, the `take` operation is changed so that

---

[6]The code for `take` makes the old head node into a dummy node rather than simply manipulating `next` pointers to allow us to later optimize the code so that `put` and `get` can execute concurrently.

```
public class SharedQueue1
{
    class Node //inner class defines list nodes
    { Object task;
      Node next;

      Node(Object task)
      {this.task = task; next = null;}
    }

    private Node head = new Node(null); //dummy node
    private Node last = head;

    public synchronized void put(Object task)
    { assert task != null: "Cannot insert null task";
      Node p = new Node(task);
      last.next = p;
      last = p;
    }

    public synchronized Object take()
    { //returns first task in queue or null if queue is empty
      Object task = null;
      if (!isEmpty())
      { Node first = head.next;
        task = first.task;
        first.task = null;
        head = first;
      }
      return task;
    }

    private boolean isEmpty(){return head.next == null;}
}
```

Figure 5.37: Queue that ensures that at most one thread can access the data structure at one time. If the queue is empty, `null` is immediately returned.

a thread trying to take from an empty queue will wait for a task rather than returning immediately. The waiting thread needs to release its lock and reacquire it before trying again. This is done in Java using the `wait` and `notify` methods. These are described in the Java appendix, Appendix C. The Java appendix also shows the queue implemented using locks from the `java.util.concurrent.locks` package introduced in Java 2 1.5 instead of `wait` and `notify`. Similar primitives are available with POSIX threads (Pthreads) [But97,IEE], and techniques for implementing this functionality with semaphores and other basic primitives can be found in [And00].

In general, to change a method that returns immediately if a condition is false to one that waits until the condition is true, two changes need to be made: First, we replace a statement of the form

```
if (condition){do_something;}
```

```
public class SharedQueue2
{
   class Node
   { Object task;
     Node next;

     Node(Object task)
     {this.task = task; next = null;}
   }

   private Node head = new Node(null);
   private Node last = head;

   public synchronized void put(Object task)
   { assert task != null: "Cannot insert null task";
     Node p = new Node(task);
     last.next = p;
     last = p;
     notifyAll();
   }

   public synchronized Object take()
   { //returns first task in queue, waits if queue is empty
     Object task = null;
     while (isEmpty())
        {try{wait();}catch(InterruptedException ignore){}}
     { Node first = head.next;
        task = first.task;
        first.task = null;
        head = first;
     }
     return task;
   }

   private boolean isEmpty(){return head.next == null;}
}
```

Figure 5.38: Queue that ensures at most one thread can access the data structure at one time. Unlike the first shared queue example, if the queue is empty, the thread waits. When used in a master/worker algorithm, a poison pill would be required to signal termination to a thread.

with a loop[7]

```
while( !condition){wait();} do_something;
```

Second, we examine the other operations on the shared queue and add a `notifyAll` to any operations that might establish `condition`. The result is an instance of

---

[7]The fact that `wait` can throw an `InterruptedException` must be dealt with; it is ignored here for clarity, but handled properly in the code examples.

the basic idiom for using `wait`, described in more detail in the Java appendix, Appendix C.

Thus, two major changes are made in moving to the code in Fig. 5.38. First, we replace the code

```
if (!isEmpty()){....}
```

with

```
while(isEmpty())
   {try{wait()}catch(InterruptedException ignore){}}{....}
```

Second, we note that the `put` method will make the queue not empty, so we add to it a call to `notifyAll`.

This implementation has a performance problem in that it will generate extraneous calls to `notifyAll`. This does not affect the correctness, but it might degrade the performance. One way this implementation could be optimized would be to minimize the number of invocations of `notifyAll` in `put`. One way to do this is to keep track of the number of waiting threads and only perform a `notifyAll` when there are threads waiting. We would have, for `int w` indicating the number of waiting threads:

```
while( !condition){w++; wait(); w--} do_something;
```

and

```
if (w>0) notifyAll();
```

In this particular example, because only one waiting thread will be able to consume a task, `notifyAll` could be replaced by `notify`, which notifies only one waiting thread. We show code for this refinement in a later example (Fig. 5.40).

Concurrency-control protocols for noninterfering operations.   If the performance of the shared queue is inadequate, we must look for more efficient concurrency-control protocols. As discussed in the *Shared Data* pattern, we need to look for noninterfering sets of operations in our ADT. Careful examination of the operations in our nonblocking shared queue (see Fig. 5.37 and Fig. 5.38) shows that

```
public class SharedQueue3
{
    class Node
    { Object task;
      Node next;

      Node(Object task)
      {this.task = task; next = null;}
    }

    private Node head = new Node(null);
    private Node last = head;

    private Object putLock = new Object();
    private Object takeLock = new Object();

    public void put(Object task)
    { synchronized(putLock)
        { assert task != null: "Cannot insert null task";
          Node p = new Node(task);
          last.next = p;
          last = p;
        }
    }

    public Object take()
    { Object task = null;
      synchronized(takeLock)
        { if (!isEmpty())
            { Node first = head.next;
              task = first.task;
              first.task = null;
              head = first;
            }
        }
        return task;
    }
}
```

Figure 5.39: Shared queue that takes advantage of the fact that put and take are noninterfering and uses separate locks so they can proceed concurrently

the put and take are noninterfering because they do not access the same variables. The put method modifies the reference last and the next member of the object referred to by last. The take method modifies the value of the task member in the object referred to by head.next and the reference head. Thus, put modifies last and the next member of some Node object. The take method modifies head and the task member of some object. These are noninterfering operations, so we can use one lock for put and a different lock for take. This solution is shown in Fig. 5.39.

Concurrency-control protocols using nested locks. The approach shown in Fig. 5.39 isn't as easy to apply to a block-on-empty queue, however. First of all, the wait, notify, and notifyAll methods on an object can only be invoked within a block synchronized on that object. Also, if we have optimized the invocations of notify as described previously, then w, the count of waiting threads, is accessed in both put and take. Therefore, we use putLock both to protect w and to serve as the lock on which a taking thread blocks when the queue is empty. Code is shown in Fig. 5.40. Notice that putLock.wait() in get will release only the lock

```
pubic class SharedQueue4
{
    class Node
    { Object task;
      Node next;

      Node(Object task)
      {this.task = task; next = null;}
    }

    private Node head = new Node(null);
    private Node last = head;
    private int w;
    private Object putLock = new Object();
    private Object takeLock = new Object();

    public void put(Object task)
    { synchronized(putLock)
        { assert task != null: "Cannot insert null task";
          Node p = new Node(task);
          last.next = p;
          last = p;
          if(w>0){putLock.notify();}
        }
    }

    public Object take()
    { Object task = null;
        synchronized(takeLock)
        { //returns first task in queue, waits if queue is empty
          while (isEmpty())
          { try{synchronized(putLock){w++; putLock.wait();w--;} }
            catch(InterruptedException error){assert false;}}
          { Node first = head.next;
            task = first.task;
            first.task = null;
            head = first;
          }
        }
        return task;
    }

    private boolean isEmpty(){return head.next == null;}

}
```

Figure 5.40: Blocking queue with multiple locks to allow concurrent put and take on a nonempty queue

on `putLock`, so a blocked thread will continue to block other takers from the outer block synchronized on `takeLock`. This is okay for this particular problem. This scheme continues to allow putters and takers to execute concurrently; the only exception being when the queue is empty.

Another issue to note is that this solution has nested synchronized blocks in both `take` and `put`. Nested synchronized blocks should always be examined for potential deadlocks. In this case, there will be no deadlock because `put` only acquires one lock, `putLock`. More generally, we would define a partial order over all the locks and ensure that the locks are always acquired in an order consistent with our partial order. For example, here, we could define `takeLock` < `putLock` and make sure that the synchronized blocks are entered in a way that respects that partial order.

As mentioned earlier, several Java-based implementations of queues are included in Java 2 1.5 in the `java.util.concurrent` package, some based on the simple strategies discussed here and some based on more complex strategies that provide additional flexibility and performance.

Distributed shared queues.   A centralized shared queue may cause a hot spot, indicating that performance might be improved by a more distributed implementation. As an example, we will develop a simple package to support fork/join programs using a pool of threads and a distributed task queue in the underlying implementation. The package is a much simplified version of the FJTask package [Lea00b], which in turn uses ideas from [BJK+96]. The idea is to create a fixed pool of threads to execute the tasks that are dynamically created as the program executes. Instead of a single central task queue, we associate a nonblocking queue with each thread. When a thread generates a new task, it is placed in its own queue. When a thread is able to execute a new task, it first tries to obtain a task from its own queue. If its own queue is empty, it randomly chooses another thread and attempts to steal a task from that thread's queue and continues checking the other queues until a task is found. (In [BJK+96], this is called *random work stealing.*)

A thread terminates when it receives a poison-pill task. For the fork/join programs we have in mind, this approach has been shown to work well when threads remove tasks from their own queue in LIFO (last in, first out) order and from other queues in FIFO (first in, first out) order. Therefore, we will add to the ADT an operation that removes the last element, to be used by threads to remove tasks from their own queues. The implementation can then be similar to Fig. 5.40, but with an additional method `takeLast` for the added operation. The result is shown in Fig. 5.41.

The remainder of the package comprises three classes.

- `Task` is an abstract class. Applications extend it and override its `run` method to indicate the functionality of a task in the computation. Methods offered by the class include `fork` and `join`.

- `TaskRunner` extends `Thread` and provides the functionality of the threads in the thread pool. Each instance contains a shared task queue. The task-stealing code is in this class.

```
public class SharedQueue5
{
  class Node
  { Object task;
    Node next;
    Node prev;

    Node(Object task, Node prev)
    {this.task = task; next = null; this.prev = prev;}
  }

  private Node head = new Node(null, null);
  private Node last = head;

  public synchronized void put(Object task)
  { assert task != null: "Cannot insert null task";
    Node p = new Node(task, last);
    last.next = p;
    last = p;
  }

  public synchronized Object take()
  { //returns first task in queue or null if queue is empty
    Object task = null;
    if (!isEmpty())
    { Node first = head.next;
      task = first.task;
      first.task = null;
      head = first;
    }
    return task;
  }

  public synchronized Object takeLast()
  { //returns last task in queue or null if queue is empty
    Object task = null;
    if (!isEmpty())
    { task = last.task; last = last.prev; last.next = null;}
    return task;
  }

  private boolean isEmpty(){return head.next == null;}
}
```

Figure 5.41: Nonblocking shared queue with `takeLast` operation

- **TaskRunnerGroup** manages the **TaskRunners**. It contains methods to initialize and shut down the thread pool. It also has a method **executeAndWait** that starts a task running and waits for its completion. This method is used to get the computation started. (It is needed because the **fork** method in class **Task** can only be invoked from within a **Task**. We describe the reason for this restriction later.)

```
public abstract class Task implements Runnable
{
  //done indicates whether the task is finished
  private volatile boolean done;
  public final void setDone(){done = true;}
  public boolean isDone(){return done;}

  //returns the currently executing TaskRunner thread
  public static TaskRunner getTaskRunner()
  { return (TaskRunner)Thread.currentThread(); }

  //push this task on the local queue of current thread
  public void fork()
  { getTaskRunner().put(this);
  }

  //wait until this task is done
  public void join()
  { getTaskRunner().taskJoin(this);
  }

  //execute the run method of this task
  public void invoke()
  { if (!isDone()){run(); setDone(); }
  }
}
```

Figure 5.42: Abstract base class for tasks

We will now discuss these classes in more detail. **Task** is shown in Fig. 5.42. The only state associated with the abstract class is **done**, which is marked **volatile** to ensure that any thread that tries to access it will obtain a fresh value.

The **TaskRunner** class is shown in Fig. 5.43, Fig. 5.44, and Fig. 5.45. The thread, as specified in the **run** method, loops until the poison task is encountered. First it tries to obtain a task from the back of its local queue. If the local queue is empty, it attempts to steal a task from the front of a queue belonging to another thread.

The code for the **TaskRunnerGroup** class is shown in Fig. 5.46. The constructor for **TaskRunnerGroup** initializes the thread pool, given the number of threads as a parameter. Typically, this value would be chosen to match the number of processors in the system. The **executeAndWait** method starts a task by placing it in the task queue of thread 0.

One use for this method is get a computation started. Something like this is needed because we can't just fork a new **Task** from a main or other non-**TaskRunner** thread—this is what was meant by the earlier remark that the **fork** and **join** methods of **Task** can only be invoked from within another **Task**. This is because these methods require interaction with the **TaskRunner** thread executing

```
import java.util.*;

class TaskRunner extends Thread
{

    private final TaskRunnerGroup g; //managing group
    private final Random chooseToStealFrom; //random number generator
    private final Task poison; //poison task
    protected volatile boolean active; //state of thread
    final int id; //index of task in the TaskRunnerGroup

    private final SharedQueue5 q; //Nonblocking shared queue

    //operations relayed to queue
    public void put(Task t){q.put(t);}
    public Task take(){return (Task)q.take();}
    public Task takeLast(){return (Task)q.takeLast();}

    //constructor
    TaskRunner(TaskRunnerGroup g, int id, Task poison)
    { this.g = g;
       this.id = id;
       this.poison = poison;
       chooseToStealFrom = new Random(System.identityHashCode(this));
       setDaemon(true);
       q = new SharedQueue5();
    }

    protected final TaskRunnerGroup getTaskRunnerGroup(){return g;}
    protected final int getID(){return id;}
/* continued in next figure */
```

Figure 5.43: Class defining behavior of threads in the thread pool (continued in Fig. 5.44 and Fig. 5.45)

the task (for example, `fork` involves adding the task to the thread's task queue); we find the appropriate `TaskRunner` using `Thread.getCurrentThread`, thus `fork` and `join` must be invoked only in code being executed by a thread that is a `TaskRunner`.

We normally also want the program that creates the initial task to wait until it completes before going on. To accomplish this and also meet the restriction on when `fork` can be invoked on a `task`, we create a "wrapper" task whose function is to start the initial task, wait for it to complete, and then notify the main thread (the one that called `executeAndWait`). We then add this wrapper task to thread 0's task queue, making it eligible to be executed, and wait for it to notify us (with `notifyAll`) that it has completed.

All of this may be clearer from the usage of `fork`, `join`, and `executeAndWait` in the Fibonacci example in the Examples section.

```
/* continued from previous figure */
  //Attempts to steal a task from another thread. First chooses a
  //random victim, then continues with other threads until either
  //a task has been found or all have been checked. If a task
  //is found, it is invoked. The parameter waitingFor is a task
  //on which this thread is waiting for a join. If steal is not
  //called as part of a join, use waitingFor = null.
  void steal(final Task waitingFor)
  { Task task = null;

      TaskRunner[] runners = g.getRunners();
      int victim = chooseToStealFrom.nextInt(runners.length);
        for (int i = 0; i != runners.length; ++i)
        { TaskRunner tr = runners[victim];
            if (waitingFor != null && waitingFor.isDone()){break;}
          else
          { if (tr != null && tr != this)
            task = (Task)tr.q.take();
            if(task != null) {break;}
            yield();
            victim = (victim + 1)%runners.length;

        }
      } //have either found a task or have checked all other queues

      //if have a task, invoke it
      if(task != null && ! task.isDone())
      { task.invoke(); }
  }
/* continued in next figure
```

Figure 5.44: Class defining behavior of threads in the thread pool (continued from Fig. 5.43 and continued in Fig. 5.45)

Examples

Computing Fibonacci numbers. We show in Fig. 5.47 and Fig. 5.48 code that uses our distributed queue package.[8] Recall that

$$Fib(0) = 0 \tag{5.7}$$

$$Fib(1) = 1 \tag{5.8}$$

$$Fib(n + 2) = Fib(n) + Fib(n + 1) \tag{5.9}$$

This is a classic divide-and-conquer algorithm. To use our task package, we define a class `Fib` that extends `Task`. Each `Fib` task contains a member `number` that

---

[8] This code is essentially the same as the class to compute Fibonacci numbers that is provided as a demo with the FJTask package, except for the slight modification necessary to use the classes described previously.

```
/* continued from previous figure */
//Main loop of thread. First attempts to find a task on local
//queue and execute it. If not found, then tries to steal a task
//from another thread. Performance may be improved by modifying
//this method to back off using sleep or lowered priorities if the
//thread repeatedly iterates without finding a task. The run
//method, and thus the thread, terminates when it retrieves the
//poison task from the task queue.
 public void run()
 { Task task = null;
    try
     { while (!poison.equals(task))
        { task = (Task)q.takeLast();
          if (task != null) { if (!task.isDone()){task.invoke();}}
          else { steal(null); }
        }
     } finally { active = false; }
  }

  //Looks for another task to run and continues when Task w is done.
  protected final void taskJoin(final Task w)
  { while(!w.isDone())
     { Task task = (Task)q.takeLast();
         if (task != null) { if (!task.isDone()){ task.invoke();}}
         else { steal(w);}
     }
  }
}
```

Figure 5.45: Class defining behavior of threads in the thread pool (continued from Fig. 5.43 and Fig. 5.44)

initially contains the number for which the Fibonacci number should be computed and later is replaced by the result. The **getAnswer** method returns the result after it has been computed. Because this variable will be accessed by multiple threads, it is declared **volatile**.

The **run** method defines the behavior of each task. Recursive parallel decomposition is done by creating a new **Fib** object for each subtask, invoking the **fork** method on each subtask to start their computation, calling the **join** method for each subtask to wait for the subtasks to complete, and then computing the sum of their results.

The **main** method drives the computation. It first reads **proc** (the number of threads to create), **num** (the value for which the Fibonacci number should be computed), and optionally the **sequentialThreshold**. The value of this last, optional parameter (the default is 0) is used to decide when the problem is too small to bother with a parallel decomposition and should therefore use a sequential algorithm. After these parameters have been obtained, the **main** method creates a **TaskRunnerGroup** with the indicated number of threads, and then creates a **Fib** object, initialized with **num**. The computation is initiated by passing the **Fib** object to the **TaskRunnerGroup**'s **invokeAndWait** method. When this returns, the

```
class TaskRunnerGroup
{ protected final TaskRunner[] threads;
  protected final int groupSize;
  protected final Task poison;

  public TaskRunnerGroup(int groupSize)
  { this.groupSize = groupSize;
    threads = new TaskRunner[groupSize];
    poison = new Task(){public void run(){assert false;}};
    poison.setDone();
    for (int i = 0; i!= groupSize; i++)
      {threads[i] = new TaskRunner(this,i,poison);}
    for(int i=0; i!= groupSize; i++){ threads[i].start(); }
  }

  //start executing task t and wait for its completion.
  //The wrapper task is used in order to start t from within
  //a Task (thus allowing fork and join to be used)
  public void executeAndWait(final Task t)
  { final TaskRunnerGroup thisGroup = this;
    Task wrapper = new Task()
      { public void run()
        { t.fork();
          t.join();
          setDone();
          synchronized(thisGroup)
            { thisGroup.notifyAll();} //notify waiting thread
        }
      };
    //add wrapped task to queue of thread[0]
    threads[0].put(wrapper);
    //wait for notification that t has finished.
    synchronized(thisGroup)
    { try{thisGroup.wait();}
      catch(InterruptedException e){return;}
    }
  }

  //cause all threads to terminate. The programmer is responsible
  //for ensuring that the computation is complete.
  public void cancel()
  { for(int i=0; i!= groupSize; i++)
    { threads[i].put(poison); }
  }

  public TaskRunner[] getRunners(){return threads;}
}
```

Figure 5.46: The `TaskRunnerGroup` class. This class initializes and manages the threads in the thread pool.

computation is finished. The thread pool is shut down with the `TaskRunnerGroup`'s `cancel` method. Finally, the result is retrieved from the `Fib` object and displayed.

Related Patterns

The *Shared Queue* pattern is an instance of the *Shared Data* pattern. It is often used to represent the task queues in algorithms that use the *Master/Worker* pattern.

```
public class Fib extends Task
{
  volatile int number; // number holds value to compute initially,
                       //after computation is replaced by answer
  Fib(int n) { number = n; } //task constructor, initializes number

  //behavior of task
  public void run() {
    int n = number;

    // Handle base cases:
    if (n <= 1) { // Do nothing: fib(0) = 0; fib(1) = 1 }
    // Use sequential code for small problems:
    else if (n <= sequentialThreshold) {
      number = seqFib(n);
    }
    // Otherwise use recursive parallel decomposition:
    else {
      // Construct subtasks:
      Fib f1 = new Fib(n - 1);
      Fib f2 = new Fib(n - 2);

      // Run them in parallel:
      f1.fork();f2.fork();
      // Await completion;
      f1.join();f2.join();

      // Combine results:
      number = f1.number + f2.number;
      // (We know numbers are ready, so directly access them.)
    }
  }

  // Sequential version for arguments less than threshold
  static int seqFib(int n) {
    if (n <= 1) return n;
    else return seqFib(n-1) + seqFib(n-2);
  }

  //method to retrieve answer after checking to make sure
  //computation has finished, note that done and isDone are
  //inherited from the Task class. done is set by the executing
  //(TaskRunner) thread when the run method is finished.
  int getAnswer() {
    if (!isDone()) throw new Error("Not yet computed");
    return number;
  }
/* continued in next figure */
```

Figure 5.47: Program to compute Fibonacci numbers (continued in Fig. 5.48)

It can also be used to support thread-pool-based implementations of the *Fork/Join* pattern.

Note that when the tasks in a task queue map onto a consecutive sequence of integers, a monotonic shared counter, which would be much more efficient, can be used in place of a queue.

```
/* continued from previous figure */
  //Performance-tuning constant, sequential algorithm is used to
  //find Fibonacci numbers for values <= this threshold
  static int sequentialThreshold = 0;

  public static void main(String[] args) {
      int procs; //number of threads
      int num; //Fibonacci number to compute
      try {
        //read parameters from command line
        procs = Integer.parseInt(args[0]);
        num = Integer.parseInt(args[1]);
        if (args.length > 2)
          sequentialThreshold = Integer.parseInt(args[2]);
      }
      catch (Exception e) {
        System.out.println("Usage: java Fib <threads> <number> "+
            "[<sequentialThreshold>]");
        return;
      }

      //initialize thread pool
      TaskRunnerGroup g = new TaskRunnerGroup(procs);

      //create first task
      Fib f = new Fib(num);

      //execute it
      g.executeAndWait(f);

      //computation has finished, shutdown thread pool
      g.cancel();

      //show result
      long result;
      {result = f.getAnswer();}
      System.out.println("Fib: Size: " + num + " Answer: " + result);
  }

}
```

Figure 5.48: Program to compute Fibonacci numbers (continued from Fig. 5.47)

5.10 THE *DISTRIBUTED ARRAY* PATTERN

Problem

Arrays often need to be partitioned between multiple UEs. How can we do this so the resulting program that is both readable and efficient?

Context

Large arrays are fundamental data structures in scientific computing problems. Differential equations are at the core of many technical computing problems, and solving these equations requires the use of large arrays that arise naturally when a continuous domain is replaced by a collection of values at discrete points. Large arrays also arise in signal processing, statistical analysis, global optimization, and a host of other problems. Hence, it should come as no surprise that dealing effectively with large arrays is an important problem.

If parallel computers were built with a single address space that was large enough to hold the full array yet provided equal-time access from any PE to any array element, we would not need to invest much time in how these arrays are handled. But processors are much faster than large memory subsystems, and networks connecting nodes are much slower than memory buses. The end result is usually a system in which access times vary substantially depending on which PE is accessing which array element.

The challenge is to organize the arrays so that the elements needed by each UE are nearby at the right time in the computation. In other words, the arrays must be distributed about the computer so that the array distribution matches the flow of the computation.

This pattern is important for any parallel algorithm involving large arrays in a parallel algorithm. It is particularly important when the algorithm uses the *Geometric Decomposition* pattern for its algorithm structure and the *SPMD* pattern for its program structure. Although this pattern is in some respects specific to distributed-memory environments in which global data structures must be somehow distributed among the ensemble of PEs, some of the ideas of this pattern apply if the single address space is implemented on a NUMA platform, in which all PEs have access to all memory locations, but access time varies. For such platforms, it is not necessary to explicitly decompose and distribute arrays, but it is still important to manage the memory hierarchy so that array elements stay close[9] to the PEs that need them. Because of this, on NUMA machines, MPI programs can sometimes outperform similar algorithms implemented using a native multithreaded API. Further, the ideas of this pattern can be used with a multithreaded API to keep memory pages close to the processors that will work with them. For example, if the target system uses a first touch page-management scheme, efficiency is improved if every array element is initialized by the PE that will be working with it. This strategy, however, breaks down if arrays need to be remapped in the course of the computation.

Forces

- **Load balance.** Because a parallel computation is not finished until all UEs complete their work, the computational load among the UEs must be distributed so each UE takes nearly the same time to compute.

---

[9]NUMA computers are usually built from hardware modules that bundle together processors and a subset of the total system memory. Within one of these hardware modules, the processors and memory are "close" together and processors can access this "close" memory in much less time than for remote memory.

- **Effective memory management.** Modern microprocessors are much faster than the computer's memory. To address this problem, high-performance computer systems include complex memory hierarchies. Good performance depends on making good use of this memory hierarchy, and this is done by ensuring that the memory references implied by a series of calculations are close to the processor making the calculation (that is, data reuse from the caches is high and needed pages stay accessible to the processor).

- **Clarity of abstraction.** Programs involving distributed arrays are easier to write, debug, and maintain if it is clear how the arrays are divided among UEs and mapped to local arrays.

Solution

Overview. The solution is simple to state at a high level; it is the details that make it complicated. The basic approach is to partition the global array into blocks and then map those blocks onto the UEs. This mapping onto UEs should be done so that, as the computation unfolds, each UE has an equal amount of work to carry out (that is, the load must be well balanced). Unless all UEs share a single address space, each UE's blocks will be stored in an array that is local to a single UE. Thus, the code will access elements of the distributed array using indices into a local array. The mathematical description of the problem and solution, however, is based on indices into the global array. Thus, it must be clear how to move back and forth between two views of the array, one in which each element is referenced by global indices and one in which it is referenced by a combination of local indices and UE identifier. Making these translations clear within the text of the program is the challenge of using this pattern effectively.

Array distributions. Over the years, a small number of array distributions have become standard.

- **One-dimensional (1D) block.** The array is decomposed in one dimension only and distributed one block per UE. For a 2D matrix, for example, this corresponds to assigning a single block of contiguous rows or columns to each UE. This distribution is sometimes called a *column block* or *row block* distribution depending on which single dimension is distributed among the UEs. The UEs are conceptually organized as a 1D array.

- **Two-dimensional (2D) block.** As in the 1D block case, one block is assigned to each UE, but now the block is a rectangular subblock of the original global array. This mapping views the collection of UEs as a 2D array.

- **Block-cyclic.** The array is decomposed into blocks (using a 1D or 2D partition) such that there are more blocks than UEs. These blocks are then assigned round-robin to UEs, analogous to the way a deck of cards is dealt out. The UEs may be viewed as either a 1D or 2D array.

$a_{0,0}$	$a_{0,1}$	$a_{0,2}$	$a_{0,3}$	$a_{0,4}$	$a_{0,5}$	$a_{0,6}$	$a_{0,7}$
$a_{1,0}$	$a_{1,1}$	$a_{1,2}$	$a_{1,3}$	$a_{1,4}$	$a_{1,5}$	$a_{1,6}$	$a_{1,7}$
$a_{2,0}$	$a_{2,1}$	$a_{2,2}$	$a_{2,3}$	$a_{2,4}$	$a_{2,5}$	$a_{2,6}$	$a_{2,7}$
$a_{3,0}$	$a_{3,1}$	$a_{3,2}$	$a_{3,3}$	$a_{3,4}$	$a_{3,5}$	$a_{3,6}$	$a_{3,7}$
$a_{4,0}$	$a_{4,1}$	$a_{4,2}$	$a_{4,3}$	$a_{4,4}$	$a_{4,5}$	$a_{4,6}$	$a_{4,7}$
$a_{5,0}$	$a_{5,1}$	$a_{5,2}$	$a_{5,3}$	$a_{5,4}$	$a_{5,5}$	$a_{5,6}$	$a_{5,7}$
$a_{6,0}$	$a_{6,1}$	$a_{6,2}$	$a_{6,3}$	$a_{6,4}$	$a_{6,5}$	$a_{6,6}$	$a_{6,7}$
$a_{7,0}$	$a_{7,1}$	$a_{7,2}$	$a_{7,3}$	$a_{7,4}$	$a_{7,5}$	$a_{7,6}$	$a_{7,7}$

Figure 5.49: Original square matrix *A*

Next, we explore these distributions in more detail. For illustration, we use a square matrix A of order 8, as shown in Fig. 5.49.[10]

1D block. Fig. 5.50 shows a column block distribution of A onto a linear array of four UEs. The matrix is decomposed along the column index only; the number of columns in each block, MB (2 here), is the matrix order divided by the number of UEs. Matrix element (i, j) is assigned to $UE(j \backslash MB)$.[11]

Mapping to UEs. More generally, we could have an $N \times M$ matrix where the number of UEs, P, need not divide the number of columns evenly. In this case, MB is the maximum number of columns mapped to a UE, and all UEs except $UE(P - 1)$ contain MB blocks. Then, $MB = \lceil M/P \rceil$, and elements of column j are mapped to $UE(\lfloor j/MB \rfloor)$.[12] (This reduces to the formula given earlier for the

---

[10]In this and the other figures in this pattern, we will use the following notational conventions: A matrix element will be represented as a lowercase letter with subscripts representing indices; for example, $a_{1,2}$ is the element in row 1 and column 2 of matrix A. A submatrix will be represented as an uppercase letter with subscripts representing indices; for example, $A_{0,0}$ is a submatrix containing the top-left corner of A. When we talk about assigning parts of A to UEs, we will reference different UEs using UE and an index or indices in parentheses; for example, if we are regarding UEs as forming a 1D array, $UE(0)$ is the conceptually leftmost UE, while if we are regarding UEs as forming a 2D array, $UE(0,0)$ is the conceptually top-left UE. Indices are all assumed to be zero-based (that is, the smallest index is 0).

[11]We will use the notation "$\backslash$" for integer division, and "$/$" for normal division. Thus $a \backslash b = \lfloor a/b \rfloor$. Also, $\lfloor x \rfloor$ (floor) is the largest integer at most x, and $\lceil x \rceil$ (ceiling) is the smallest integer at least x. For example, $\lfloor 4/3 \rfloor = 1$, and $\lfloor 4/2 \rfloor = 2$.

[12]Notice that this is not the only possible way to distribute columns among UEs when the number of UEs does not evenly divide the number of columns. Another approach, more complex to define but producing a more balanced distribution in some cases, is to first define the minimum number of columns per UE as $\lfloor M/P \rfloor$, and then increase this number by one for the first (M mod P) UEs. For example, for $M = 10$ and $P = 4$, $UE(0)$ and $UE(1)$ would have three columns each and $UE(2)$ and $UE(3)$ would have two columns each.

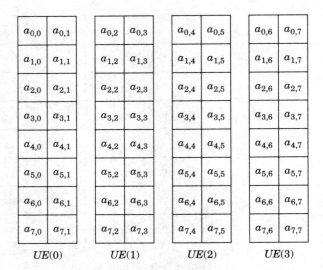

$a_{0,0}$	$a_{0,1}$	$a_{0,2}$	$a_{0,3}$	$a_{0,4}$	$a_{0,5}$	$a_{0,6}$	$a_{0,7}$
$a_{1,0}$	$a_{1,1}$	$a_{1,2}$	$a_{1,3}$	$a_{1,4}$	$a_{1,5}$	$a_{1,6}$	$a_{1,7}$
$a_{2,0}$	$a_{2,1}$	$a_{2,2}$	$a_{2,3}$	$a_{2,4}$	$a_{2,5}$	$a_{2,6}$	$a_{2,7}$
$a_{3,0}$	$a_{3,1}$	$a_{3,2}$	$a_{3,3}$	$a_{3,4}$	$a_{3,5}$	$a_{3,6}$	$a_{3,7}$
$a_{4,0}$	$a_{4,1}$	$a_{4,2}$	$a_{4,3}$	$a_{4,4}$	$a_{4,5}$	$a_{4,6}$	$a_{4,7}$
$a_{5,0}$	$a_{5,1}$	$a_{5,2}$	$a_{5,3}$	$a_{5,4}$	$a_{5,5}$	$a_{5,6}$	$a_{5,7}$
$a_{6,0}$	$a_{6,1}$	$a_{6,2}$	$a_{6,3}$	$a_{6,4}$	$a_{6,5}$	$a_{6,6}$	$a_{6,7}$
$a_{7,0}$	$a_{7,1}$	$a_{7,2}$	$a_{7,3}$	$a_{7,4}$	$a_{7,5}$	$a_{7,6}$	$a_{7,7}$
UE(0)		*UE*(1)		*UE*(2)		*UE*(3)	

Figure 5.50: 1D distribution of *A* onto four UEs

example, because in the special case where P evenly divides M, $\lceil M/P \rceil = M/P$ and $\lfloor j/MB \rfloor = j/MB$.) Analogous formulas apply for row distributions.

Mapping to local indices. In addition to mapping the columns to UEs, we also need to map the global indices to local indices. In this case, matrix element (i, j) maps to local element $(i, j \bmod MB)$. Given local indices (x, y) and $UE(w)$, we can recover the global indices $(x, wMB + y)$. Again, analogous formulas apply for row distributions.

2D block. Fig. 5.51 shows a 2D block distribution of A onto a two-by-two array of UEs. Here, A is being decomposed along two dimensions, so for each subblock, the number of columns is the matrix order divided by the number of columns of UEs, and the number of rows is the matrix order divided by the number of rows of UEs. Matrix element (i, j) is assigned to $UE(i\backslash 2, j\backslash 2)$.

Mapping to UEs. More generally, we map an $N \times M$ matrix to a $P_R \times P_C$ matrix of UEs. The maximum size of a subblock is $NB \times MB$, where $NB = \lceil N/P_R \rceil$ and $MB = \lceil M/P_C \rceil$. Then, element (i, j) in the global matrix is stored in $UE(\lfloor i/NB \rfloor, \lfloor j/MB \rfloor)$.

Mapping to local indices. Global indices (i, j) map to local indices $(i \bmod NB, j \bmod MB)$. Given local indices (x, y) on $UE(z, w)$ the corresponding global indices are $(zNB + x, wMB + y)$.

Block-cyclic. The main idea behind the block-cyclic distribution is to create more blocks than UEs and allocate them in a cyclic manner, similar to dealing

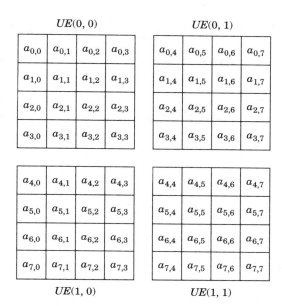

Figure 5.51: 2D distribution of *A* onto four UEs

out a deck of cards. Fig. 5.52 shows a 1D block-cyclic distribution of *A* onto a linear array of four UEs, illustrating how columns are assigned to UEs in a round-robin fashion. Here, matrix element (i, j) is assigned to $UE(j \bmod 4)$ (where 4 is the number of UEs).

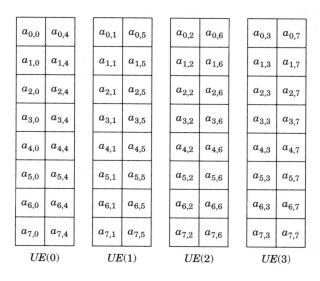

Figure 5.52: 1D block-cyclic distribution of *A* onto four UEs

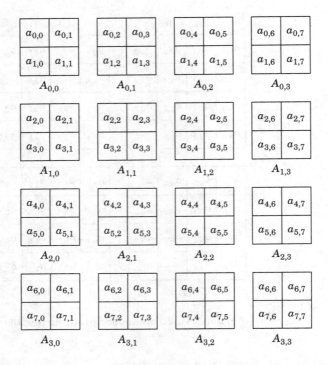

Figure 5.53: 2D block-cyclic distribution of *A* onto four UEs, part 1: Decomposing *A*

Fig. 5.53 and Fig. 5.54 show a 2D block-cyclic distribution of A onto a two-by-two array of UEs: Fig. 5.53 illustrates how A is decomposed into two-by-two submatrices. (We could have chosen a different decomposition, for example one-by-one submatrices, but two-by-two illustrates how this distribution can have both block and cyclic characteristics.) Fig. 5.54 then shows how these submatrices are assigned to UEs. Matrix element (i, j) is assigned to $UE(i \bmod 2, j \bmod 2)$.

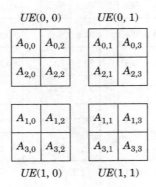

Figure 5.54: 2D block-cyclic distribution of *A* onto four UEs, part 2: Assigning submatrices to UEs

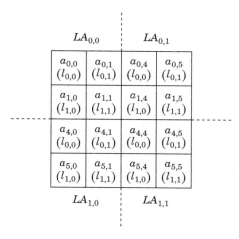

Figure 5.55: 2D block-cyclic distribution of A onto four UEs: Local view of elements of A assigned to $UE(0,0)$. $LA_{l,m}$ is the block with block indices (l, m). Each element is labeled both with its original global indices ($a_{i,j}$) and its indices within block $LA_{l,m}$ ($l_{x,y}$).

Mapping to UEs. In the general case, we have an $N \times M$ matrix to be mapped onto a $P_R \times P_C$ array of UEs. We choose block size $NB \times MB$. Element (i, j) in the global matrix will be mapped to $UE(z, w)$, where $z = \lfloor i/NB \rfloor \bmod P_R$ and $w = \lfloor j/MB \rfloor \bmod P_C$.

Mapping to local indices. Because multiple blocks are mapped to the same UE, we can view the local indexing blockwise or elementwise.

In the blockwise view, each element on a UE is indexed locally by block indices (l, m) and indices (x, y) into the block. To restate this: In this scheme, the global matrix element (i, j) will be found on the UE within the local (l, m) block at the position (x, y) where $(l, m) = (\lfloor i/(P_R\, NB) \rfloor, \lfloor j/(P_C\, MB) \rfloor)$ and $(x, y) = (i \bmod NB,\, j \bmod MB)$. Fig. 5.55 illustrates this for $UE(0,0)$.

For example, consider global matrix element $a_{5,1}$. Because $P_R = P_C = NB = MB = 2$, this element will map to $UE(0,0)$. There are four two-by-two blocks on this UE. From the figure, we see that this element appears in the block on the bottom left, or block $LA_{1,0}$ and indeed, from the formulas, we obtain $(l, m) = (\lfloor 5/(2 \times 2) \rfloor, \lfloor 1/(2 \times 2) \rfloor) = (1, 0)$. Finally, we need the local indices within the block. In this case, the indices within block are $(x, y) = (5 \bmod 2, 1 \bmod 2) = (1, 1)$.

In the elementwise view (which requires that all the blocks for each UE form a contiguous matrix), global indices (i, j) are mapped elementwise to local indices $(lNB + x, mMB + y)$, where l and m are defined as before. Fig. 5.56 illustrates this for $UE(0,0)$.

Again, looking at global matrix element $a_{5,1}$, we see that viewing the data as a single matrix, the element is found at local indices $(1 \times 2 + 1, 0 \times 2 + 1) = (3, 1)$. Local indices (x, y) in block (l, m) on $UE(z, w)$ correspond to global indices $((lP_R + z)NB + x, (mP_C + w)MB + y)$.

$a_{0,0}$ $(l_{0,0})$	$a_{0,1}$ $(l_{0,1})$	$a_{0,4}$ $(l_{0,2})$	$a_{0,5}$ $(l_{0,3})$
$a_{1,0}$ $(l_{1,0})$	$a_{1,1}$ $(l_{1,1})$	$a_{1,4}$ $(l_{1,2})$	$a_{1,5}$ $(l_{1,3})$
$a_{4,0}$ $(l_{2,0})$	$a_{4,1}$ $(l_{2,1})$	$a_{4,4}$ $(l_{2,2})$	$a_{4,5}$ $(l_{2,3})$
$a_{5,0}$ $(l_{3,0})$	$a_{5,1}$ $(l_{3,1})$	$a_{5,4}$ $(l_{3,2})$	$a_{5,5}$ $(l_{3,3})$

Figure 5.56: 2D block-cyclic distribution of A onto four UEs: Local view of elements of A assigned to $UE(0,0)$. Each element is labeled both with its original global indices $a_{i,j}$ and its local indices $l_{x',y'}$. Local indices are with respect to the contiguous matrix used to store all blocks assigned to this UE.

Choosing a distribution.   To select which distribution to use for a problem, consider how the computational load on the UEs changes as the computation proceeds. For example, in many single-channel signal-processing problems, the same set of operations is performed on each column of an array. The work does not vary as the computation proceeds, so a column block decomposition will produce both clarity of code and good load balance. If instead the amount of work varies by column, with higher-numbered columns requiring more work, a column block decomposition would lead to poor load balance, with the UEs processing lower-numbered columns finishing ahead of the UEs processing higher-numbered columns. In this case, a cyclic distribution would produce better load balance, because each UE is assigned a mix of low-numbered and high-numbered columns.

This same approach applies to higher dimensions as well. ScaLAPACK [Sca, BCC+97], the leading package of dense linear algebra software for distributed-memory computers, requires a 2D block-cyclic distribution. To see why this choice was made, consider Gaussian elimination, one of the more commonly used of the ScaLAPACK routines. In this algorithm, also known as LU decomposition, a dense square matrix is transformed into a pair of triangular matrices, an upper matrix U and a lower matrix L. At a high level, the algorithm proceeds from the upper-left corner and works its way down the diagonal of the global matrix, eliminating elements below the diagonal and transforming the remaining blocks to the right as needed. A block distribution would result in idle UEs as the processing marches down the diagonal. But with a 2D block-cyclic distribution such as the one shown in Fig. 5.54, each UE contains elements used both early and late in the algorithm, resulting in excellent load balance.

Mapping indices.   The examples in the preceding section illustrate how each element of the original (global) array is mapped to a UE and how each element in the global array, after distribution, is identified by both a set of global indices and a combination of UE identifier and local information. The original problem is typically stated in terms of global indices, but computation within each UE must be in terms of local indices. Applying this pattern effectively requires that the relationship between global indices and the combination of UE and local indices be as transparent as possible. In a quest for program efficiency, it is altogether too easy to bury these index mappings in the code in a way that makes the program painfully difficult to debug. A better approach is to use macros and inline functions to capture the index mappings; a human reader of the program then only needs to master the macro or function once. Such macros or functions also contribute to clarity of abstraction. The Examples section illustrates this strategy.

Aligning computation with locality.   One of the cardinal rules of performance-oriented computing is to maximize reuse of data close to a UE. That is, the loops that update local data should be organized in a way that gets as much use as possible out of each memory reference. This objective can also influence the choice of array distribution.

For example, in linear algebra computations, it is possible to organize computations on a matrix into smaller computations over submatrices. If these submatrices fit into cache, dramatic performance gains can result. Similar effects apply to other levels of the memory hierarchy: minimizing misses in the translation lookaside buffer (TLB), page faults, and so on. A detailed discussion of this topic goes well beyond the scope of this book. An introduction can be found in [PH98].

Examples

Transposing a matrix stored as column blocks.   As an example of organizing matrix computations into smaller computations over submatrices, consider transposing a square matrix distributed with a column block distribution. For simplicity, we will assume that the number of UEs evenly divides the number of columns, so that all blocks are the same size. Our strategy for transposing the matrix will be based on logically decomposing the matrix into square submatrices, as shown in Fig. 5.57. Each of the labeled blocks in the figure represents a square submatrix; labels show how the blocks of the transpose relate to the blocks of the

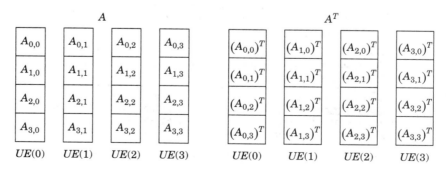

Figure 5.57: Matrix *A* and its transpose, in terms of submatrices, distributed among four UEs

original matrix. (For example, the block labeled $(A_{0,1})^T$ in the transpose is the transpose of the block labeled $A_{0,1}$ in the original matrix.) The algorithm proceeds in phases; the number of phases is the number of submatrices per UE (which is also the number of UEs). In the first phase, we transpose the submatrices on the diagonal of A, with each UE transposing one submatrix and no communication required. In successive phases, we transpose the submatrices one below the diagonal, then two below the diagonal, and so forth, wrapping around to the top of the matrix as necessary. In each of these phases, each UE must transpose one of its submatrices, send it to another UE, and receive a submatrix. For example, in the second phase, the UE labeled $UE(1)$ must compute $(A_{2,1})^T$, send it to $UE(2)$, and receive $(A_{0,1})^T$ from $UE(0)$. Figs. 5.58 and 5.59 show code to transpose such a matrix. This code represents a function that will transpose a square column-blocked array. We assume the blocks are distributed contiguously with one column block per UE. This function is intended as part of a larger program, so we assume the array has already been distributed prior to calling this function.

The program represents each local column block (one for A and one for the transposed result) as a 1D array. These arrays in turn consist of `Num_procs` submatrices each, each of size `block_size = Block_order * Block_order`, where

```
/*******************************************************************

NAME: trans_isend_ircv

PURPOSE: This function uses MPI Isend and Irecv to transpose
         a column-block distributed matrix.

*******************************************************************/

#include "mpi.h"
#include <stdio.h>

/*******************************************************************
** This function transposes a local block of a matrix. We don't
** display the text of this function as it is not relevant to the
** point of this example.
*******************************************************************/
void transpose(
    double* A, int Acols, /* input matrix */
    double* B, int Bcols, /* transposed mat */
    int sub_rows, int sub_cols); /* size of slice to transpose */

/*******************************************************************
** Define macros to compute process source and destinations and
** local indices
*******************************************************************/
#define TO(ID, PHASE, NPROC) ((ID + PHASE ) % NPROC)
#define FROM(ID, PHASE, NPROC) ((ID + NPROC - PHASE) % NPROC)
#define BLOCK(BUFF, ID) (BUFF + (ID * block_size))
/* continued in next figure */
```

Figure 5.58: Code to transpose a matrix (continued in Fig. 5.59)

```
/* continued from previous figure */

void trans_isnd_ircv(double *buff, double *trans, int Block_order,
                double *work, int my_ID, int num_procs)
{
   int iphase;
   int block_size;
   int send_to, recv_from;
   double *bblock; /* pointer to current location in buff */
   double *tblock; /* pointer to current location in trans */
   MPI_Status status;
   MPI_Request send_req, recv_req;

   block_size = Block_order * Block_order;

/*********************************************************************
** Do the transpose in num_procs phases.
**
** In the first phase, do the diagonal block. Then move out
** from the diagonal copying the local matrix into a communication
** buffer (while doing the local transpose) and send to process
** (diag+phase)%num_procs.
*********************************************************************/
   bblock = BLOCK(buff, my_ID);
   tblock = BLOCK(trans, my_ID);

   transpose(bblock, Block_order, tblock, Block_order,
           Block_order, Block_order);

   for (iphase=1; iphase<num_procs; iphase++){
      recv_from = FROM(my_ID, iphase, num_procs);
      tblock = BLOCK(trans, recv_from);
      MPI_Irecv (tblock, block_size, MPI_DOUBLE, recv_from,
              iphase, MPI_COMM_WORLD, &recv_req);

      send_to = TO(my_ID, iphase, num_procs);
      bblock = BLOCK(buff, send_to);
      transpose(bblock, Block_order, work, Block_order,
              Block_order, Block_order);
      MPI_Isend (work, block_size, MPI_DOUBLE, send_to,
                iphase, MPI_COMM_WORLD, &send_req);

      MPI_Wait(&recv_req, &status);
      MPI_Wait(&send_req, &status);
   }
}
```

Figure 5.59: Code to transpose a matrix (continued from Fig. 5.58)

`Block_order` is the number of columns per UE. We can therefore find the block indexed ID using the BLOCK macro:

```
#define BLOCK(BUFF, ID) (BUFF + (ID * block_size))
```

BUFF is the start of the 1D array (`buff` for the original array, `trans` for the transpose) and ID is the second index of the block. So for example, we find the diagonal block of both arrays as follows:

```
bblock = BLOCK(buff, my_ID);
tblock = BLOCK(trans, my_ID);
```

In succeeding phases of the algorithm, we must determine two things: (1) the index of the block we should transpose and send and (2) the index of the block we should receive. We do this with the TO and FROM macros:

```
#define TO(ID, PHASE, NPROC) ((ID + PHASE ) % NPROC)
#define FROM(ID, PHASE, NPROC) ((ID + NPROC - PHASE) % NPROC)
```

The TO index shows the progression through the off-diagonal blocks, working down from the diagonal and wrapping back to the top at the bottom of the matrix. At each phase of the algorithm, we compute which UE is to receive the block and then update the local pointer (bblock) to the block that will be sent:

```
send_to = TO(my_ID, iphase, num_procs);
bblock = BLOCK(buff, send_to);
```

Likewise, we compute where the next block is coming from and which local index corresponds to that block:

```
recv_from = FROM(my_ID, iphase, num_procs);
tblock = BLOCK(trans, recv_from);
```

This continues until all of the blocks have been transposed.

We use immediate (nonblocking) sends and receives in this example. (These primitives are described in more detail in the MPI appendix, Appendix B.) During each phase, each UE first posts a receive and then performs a transpose on the block it will send. After that transpose is complete, the UE sends the now-transposed block to the UE that should receive it. At the bottom of the loop and before moving to the next phase, functions are called to force the UE to wait until both the sends and receives complete. This approach lets us overlap communication and computation. More importantly (because in this case there isn't much computation to overlap with communication), it prevents deadlock: A more straightforward approach using regular sends and receives would be to first transpose the block to be sent, then send it, and then (wait to) receive a block from another UE. However, if the blocks to be sent are large, a regular send might block because there is insufficient buffer space for the message; in this case, such blocking could produce deadlock. By instead using nonblocking sends and receives and posting the receives first, we avoid this situation.

Known uses.   This pattern is used throughout the scientific-computing literature. The well-known ScaLAPACK package [Sca, BCC$^+$97] makes heavy use of the 2D block-cyclic distribution, and the documentation gives a thorough explanation of mapping and indexing issues for this distribution.

Several different array distributions were embedded into the HPF language [HPF97] definition.

Some of the most creative uses of this pattern can be found in quantum chemistry, particularly in the area of post Hartree Fock computations. The Global Arrays or GA package [NHL94, NHL96, NHK$^+$02, Gloa] was created specifically to address distributed-array problems in post Hartree Fock algorithms. A more recent approach is described in [NHL96, LDSH95].

The PLAPACK package [ABE$^+$97, PLA, vdG97] takes a different approach to array distribution. Rather than focusing on how to distribute the arrays, PLAPACK considers how the vectors operated upon by the arrays are organized. From these distributed vectors, the corresponding array distributions are derived. In many problems, these vectors correspond to the physical quantities in the problem domain, so the PLAPACK team refers to this as the physically based distribution.

Related Patterns

The *Distributed Array* pattern is often used together with the *Geometric Decomposition* and *SPMD* patterns.

5.11   OTHER SUPPORTING STRUCTURES

This pattern language (and hence the *Supporting Structures* patterns) is based on common practice among OpenMP, MPI, and Java programmers writing code for both shared-memory and distributed-memory MIMD computers. Parallel application programmers will in most cases find the patterns they need within this pattern language.

There are, however, additional patterns (with their own supporting structures) that have at various times been important in parallel programming. They are only rarely used at this time, but it is still important to be aware of them. They can provide insights into different opportunities for finding and exploiting concurrency. And it is possible that as parallel architectures continue to evolve, the parallel programming techniques suggested by these patterns may become important.

In this section, we will briefly describe some of these additional patterns and their supporting structures: *SIMD, MPMD, Client-Server,* and *Declarative Programming.* We close with a brief discussion of problem-solving environments. These are not patterns, but they help programmers work within a targeted set of problems.

5.11.1   SIMD

A SIMD computer has a single stream of instructions operating on multiple streams of data. These machines were inspired by the belief that programmers would find it too difficult to manage multiple streams of instructions. Many important problems are data parallel; that is, the concurrency can be expressed in terms of concurrent updates across the problem's data domain. Carried to its logical extreme, the SIMD approach assumes that it is possible to express *all* parallelism in terms of the data. Programs would then have single-thread semantics, making understanding and hence debugging them much easier. The basic idea behind the *SIMD* pattern can be summarized as follows.

- Define a network of virtual PEs to be mapped onto the actual PEs. These virtual PEs are connected according to a well-defined topology. Ideally the topology is (1) well-aligned with the way the PEs in the physical machine are connected and (2) effective for the communication patterns implied by the problem being solved.

- Express the problem in terms of arrays or other regular data structures that can be updated concurrently with a single stream of instructions.

- Associate these arrays with the local memories of the virtual PEs.

- Create a single stream of instructions that operates on slices of the regular data structures. These instructions may have an associated mask so they can be selectively skipped for subsets of array elements. This is critical for handling boundary conditions or other constraints.

When a problem is truly data parallel, this is an effective pattern. The resulting programs are relatively easy to write and debug [DKK90].

Unfortunately, most data problems contain subproblems that are not data parallel. Setting up the core data structures, dealing with boundary conditions, and post-processing after a core data parallel algorithm can all introduce logic that might not be strictly data parallel. Furthermore, this style of programming is tightly coupled to compilers that support data-parallel programming. These compilers have proven difficult to write and result in code that is difficult to optimize because it can be far removed from how a program runs on a particular machine. Thus, this style of parallel programming and the machines built around the SIMD concept have largely disappeared, except for a few special-purpose machines used for signal-processing applications.

The programming environment most closely associated with the *SIMD* pattern is High Performance Fortran (HPF) [HPF97]. HPF is an extension of the array-based constructs in Fortran 90. It was created to support portable parallel programming across SIMD machines, but also to allow the SIMD programming model to be used on MIMD computers. This required explicit control over data placement onto the PEs and the capability to remap the data during a calculation. Its dependence on a strictly data-parallel, SIMD model, however, doomed HPF by making it difficult to use with complex applications. The last large community of HPF users is in Japan [ZJS+02], where they have extended the language to relax the data-parallel constraints [HPF99].

5.11.2 MPMD

The *Multiple Program, Multiple Data (MPMD)* pattern, as the name implies, is used in a parallel algorithm when different programs run on different UEs. The basic approach is the following.

- Decompose the problem into a set of subproblems, where each subproblem maps onto a subset of UEs. Often each subset of UEs corresponds to the nodes of a different parallel computer.

- Create independent programs solving the appropriate subproblems and tuned to the relevant target UEs.

- Coordinate the programs running on distinct UEs as needed, typically through a message-passing framework.

In many ways, the MPMD approach is not too different from an SPMD program using MPI. In fact, the runtime environments associated with the two most common implementations of MPI, MPICH [MPI] and LAM/MPI [LAM], support simple MPMD programming.

Applications of the *MPMD* pattern typically arise in one of two ways. First, the architecture of the UEs may be so different that a single program cannot be used across the full system. This is the case when using parallel computing across some type of computational grid [Glob, FK03] using multiple classes of high-performance computing architectures. The second (and from a parallel-algorithm point of view more interesting) case occurs when completely different simulation programs are combined into a coupled simulation.

For example, climate emerges from a complex interplay between atmospheric and ocean phenomena. Well-understood programs for modeling the ocean and the atmosphere independently have been developed and highly refined over the years. Although an SPMD program could be created that implements a coupled ocean/ atmospheric model directly, a more effective approach is to take the separate, validated ocean and atmospheric programs and couple them through some intermediate layer, thereby producing a new coupled model from well-understood component models.

Although both MPICH and LAM/MPI provide some support for MPMD programming, they do not allow different implementations of MPI to interact, so only MPMD programs using a common MPI implementation are supported. To address a wider range of MPMD problems spanning different architectures and different MPI implementations, a new standard called interoperable MPI (iMPI) was created. The general idea of coordinating UEs through the exchange of messages is common to MPI and iMPI, but the detailed semantics are extended in iMPI to address the unique challenges arising from programs running on widely differing architectures. These multi-architecture issues can add significant communication overhead, so the part of an algorithm dependent on the performance of iMPI must be relatively coarse-grained.

MPMD programs are rare. As increasingly complicated coupled simulations grow in importance, however, use of the *MPMD* pattern will increase. Use of this pattern will also grow as grid technology becomes more robust and more widely deployed.

5.11.3 Client-Server Computing

Client-server architectures are related to MPMD. Traditionally, these systems have comprised two or three tiers where the front end is a graphical user interface executed on a client's computer and a mainframe back end (often with multiple processors) provides access to a database. The middle tier, if present, dispatches requests from the clients to (possibly multiple) back ends. Web servers are a familiar example of a client-server system. More generally, a server might offer a variety of services to clients, an essential aspect of the system being that services have well-defined interfaces. Parallelism can appear at the server (which can service many clients concurrently or can use parallel processing to obtain results more quickly for single requests) and at the client (which can initiate requests at more than one server simultaneously).

Techniques used in client-server systems are especially important in heterogeneous systems. Middleware such as CORBA [COR] provides a standard for service interface specifications, enabling new programs to be put together by composing existing services, even if those services are offered on vastly different hardware platforms and implemented in different programming languages. CORBA also provides facilities to allow services to be located. The Java J2EE (Java 2 Platform, Enterprise Edition) [Javb] also provides significant support for client-server applications. In both of these cases, interoperability was a major design force.

Client-server architectures have traditionally been used in enterprise rather than scientific applications. Grid technology, which is heavily used in scientific computing, borrows from client-server technology, extending it by blurring the distinction between clients and servers. All resources in a grid, whether they are computers, instruments, file systems, or anything else connected to the network, are peers and can serve as clients and servers. The middleware provides standards-based interfaces to tie the resources together into a single system that spans multiple administrative domains.

5.11.4 Concurrent Programming with Declarative Languages

The overwhelming majority of programming is done with imperative languages such as C++, Java, or Fortran. This is particularly the case for traditional applications in science and engineering. The artificial intelligence community and a small subset of academic computer scientists, however, have developed and shown great success with a different class of languages, the *declarative languages*. In these languages, the programmer describes a problem, a problem domain, and the conditions solutions must satisfy. The runtime system associated with the language then uses these to find valid solutions.

Declarative semantics impose a different style of programming that overlaps with the approaches discussed in this pattern language, but has some significant differences. There are two important classes of declarative languages: functional languages and logic programming languages.

Logic programming languages are based on formal rules of logical inference. The most common logic programming language by far is Prolog [SS94], a programming language based on first-order predicate calculus. When Prolog is extended to support expression of concurrency, the result is a concurrent logic programming language. Concurrency is exploited in one of three ways with these Prolog extensions: and-parallelism (execute multiple predicates), or-parallelism (execute multiple guards), or through explicit mapping of predicates linked together through single-assignment variables [CG86].

Concurrent logic programming languages were a hot area of research in the late 1980s and early 1990s. They ultimately failed because most programmers were deeply committed to more traditional imperative languages. Even with the advantages of declarative semantics and the value of logic programming for symbolic reasoning, the learning curve associated with these languages proved prohibitive.

The older and more established class of declarative programming languages is based on functional programming models [Hud89]. LISP is the oldest and best known of the functional languages. In pure functional languages, there are no side effects from a function. Therefore, functions can execute as soon as their input data is available. The resulting algorithms express concurrency in terms of the flow of data through the program leading, thereby resulting in "data-flow" algorithms [Jag96].

The best-known concurrent functional languages are Sisal [FCO90], Concurrent ML [Rep99, Con] (an extension to ML), and Haskell [HPF]. Because mathematical expressions are naturally written down in a functional notation, Sisal was particularly straightforward to work with in science and engineering applications and proved to be highly efficient for parallel programming. However, just as with the logic programming languages, programmers were unwilling to part with their familiar imperative languages, and Sisal essentially died. Concurrent ML and Haskell have not made major inroads into high-performance computing, although both remain popular in the functional programming community.

5.11.5   Problem-Solving Environments

A discussion of supporting structures for parallel algorithms would not be complete without mentioning problem-solving environments (PSE). A PSE is a programming environment specialized to the needs of a particular class of problems. When applied to parallel computing, PSEs also imply a particular algorithm structure as well.

The motivation behind PSEs is to spare the application programmer the low-level details of the parallel system. For example, PETsc (Portable, Extensible, Toolkit for Scientific Computation) [BGMS98] supports a variety of distributed data structures and functions required to use them for solving partial differential equations (typically for problems fitting the *Geometric Decomposition* pattern). The programmer needs to understand the data structures within PETSc, but is spared the need to master the details of how to implement them efficiently and portably. Other important PSEs are PLAPACK [ABE+97] (for dense linear algebra problems) and POOMA [RHC+96] (an object-oriented framework for scientific computing).

PSEs have not been very well accepted. PETSc is probably the only PSE that is heavily used for serious application programming. The problem is that by tying themselves to a narrow class of problems, PSEs restrict their potential audience and have a difficult time reaching a critical mass of users. We believe that over time and as the core patterns behind parallel algorithms become better understood, PSEs will be able to broaden their impact and play a more dominant role in parallel programming.

C H A P T E R 6

The *Implementation Mechanisms* Design Space

6.1 OVERVIEW
6.2 UE MANAGEMENT
6.3 SYNCHRONIZATION
6.4 COMMUNICATION

Up to this point, we have focused on designing algorithms and the high-level constructs used to organize parallel programs. With this chapter, we shift gears and consider a program's source code and the low-level operations used to write parallel programs.

What are these low-level operations, or *implementation mechanisms*, for parallel programming? Of course, there is the computer's instruction set, typically accessed through a high-level programming language, but this is the same for serial and parallel programs. Our concern is the implementation mechanisms unique to parallel programming. A complete and detailed discussion of these parallel programming "building blocks" would fill a large book. Fortunately, most parallel programmers use only a modest core subset of these mechanisms. These core implementation mechanisms fall into three categories:

- UE management

- Synchronization

- Communication

Within each of these categories, the most commonly used mechanisms are covered in this chapter. An overview of this design space and its place in the pattern language is shown in Fig. 6.1.

In this chapter we also drop the formalism of patterns. Most of the implementation mechanisms are included within the major parallel programming environments. Hence, rather than use patterns, we provide a high-level description of each implementation mechanism and then investigate how the mechanism maps onto our three target programming environments: OpenMP, MPI, and Java. This mapping will in some cases be trivial and require little more than presenting an existing construct in an API or language. The discussion will become interesting when we look at operations native to one programming model, but foreign to another. For

216

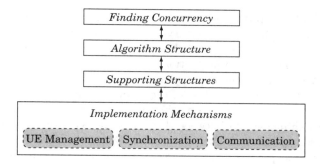

Figure 6.1: Overview of the *Implementation Mechanisms* design space and its place in the pattern language

example, it is possible to do message passing in OpenMP. It is not pretty, but it works and can be useful at times.

We assume that the reader is familiar with OpenMP, MPI, and Java and how they are used for writing parallel programs. Although we cover specific features of these APIs in this chapter, the details of using them are left to the appendixes.

6.1   OVERVIEW

Parallel programs exploit concurrency by mapping instructions onto multiple UEs. At a very basic level, every parallel program needs to (1) create the set of UEs, (2) manage interactions between them and their access to shared resources, (3) exchange information between UEs, and (4) shut them down in an orderly manner. This suggests the following categories of implementation mechanisms.

- **UE management.** The creation, destruction, and management of the processes and threads used in parallel computation.

- **Synchronization.** Enforcing constraints on the ordering of events occurring in different UEs. This is primarily used to ensure that shared resources are accessed by a collection of UEs in such a way that the program is correct regardless of how the UEs are scheduled.

- **Communication.** The exchange of information between UEs.

6.2   UE MANAGEMENT

Let us revisit the definition of unit of execution, or UE. A UE is an abstraction for the entity that carries out computations and is managed for the programmer by the operating system. In modern parallel programming environments, there are two types of UEs: processes and threads.

A process is a heavyweight object that carries with it the state or context required to define its place in the system. This includes memory, program counters, registers, buffers, open files, and anything else required to define its context within the operating system. In many systems, different processes can belong to different users, and thus processes are well protected from each other. Creating a new process and swapping between processes is expensive because all that state must be saved and restored. Communication between processes, even on the same machine, is also expensive because the protection boundaries must be crossed.

A thread, on the other hand, is a lightweight UE. A collection of threads is contained in a process. Most of the resources, including the memory, belong to the process and are shared among the threads. The result is that creating a new thread and switching context between threads is less expensive, requiring only the saving of a program counter and some registers. Communication between threads belonging to the same process is also inexpensive because it can be done by accessing the shared memory.

The mechanisms for managing these two types of UEs are completely different. We handle them separately in the next two sections.

6.2.1 Thread Creation/Destruction

Threads require a relatively modest number of machine cycles to create. Programmers can reasonably create and destroy threads as needed inside a program, and as long as they do not do so inside tight loops or time-critical kernels, the program's overall runtime will be affected only modestly. Hence, most parallel programming environments make it straightforward to create threads inside a program, and the API supports thread creation and destruction.

OpenMP: thread creation/destruction. In OpenMP, threads are created with the parallel pragma:

```
#pragma omp parallel
{ structured block }
```

Each thread will independently execute the code within the *structured block*. A structured block is just a block of statements with a single point of entry at the top and a single point of exit at the bottom.

The number of threads created in OpenMP can be either left to the operating system or controlled by the programmer (see the OpenMP appendix, Appendix A, for more details).

Destruction of threads occurs at the end of the structured block. The threads wait at the end of the structured block. After all threads have arrived, the threads are destroyed and the original or master thread continues.

Java: thread creation/destruction. In Java, threads are instances of the java.lang.Thread class or a subclass of the Thread class. A Thread object is instantiated in the usual way using the new keyword, and then the start method is invoked to launch the thread. The thread thus created can access any variable visible according to Java's scope rules.

There are two ways to specify the behavior of a thread. The first is to create a subclass of **Thread** and override the **run** method. The following shows how to do this to create a thread that, when launched, will execute **thread_body**.

```
class MyThread extends Thread
{ public void run(){ thread_body }}
```

To create and launch the thread one would write

```
Thread t = new MyThread(); //create thread object
t.start(); //launch the thread
```

To use the second approach, we define a class that implements the **java.lang. Runnable** interface, which contains a single method **public void run()**, and pass an instance of the **Runnable** class to the **Thread** constructor. For example, first we define the **Runnable** class:

```
class MyRunnable implements Runnable
{ public void run(){ thread_body }}
```

To create and execute the thread, we create a **Runnable** object and pass it to the **Thread** constructor. The thread is launched using the **start** method as before:

```
Thread t = new Thread(new MyRunnable()); //create Runnable
                                         //and Thread objects
t.start(); //start the thread
```

In most cases, the second approach is preferred.[1]

A thread terminates when the **run** method returns. The **Thread** object itself will be collected after termination by the garbage collector in the same way as any other object in a Java program.

The **java.util.concurrent** package defines the **Executor** and **Executor- Services** interfaces and provides several classes implementing them. These classes directly support higher-level structures such as the *Master/Worker* pattern by

---

[1]In Java, a class can implement any number of interfaces, but is only allowed to extend a single superclass. Thus, extending **Thread** in the first approach means that the class defining the **run** method cannot extend an application-specific class.

arranging for the execution of Runnables while hiding the details of thread creation and scheduling. More details are given in the Java appendix, Appendix C.

MPI: thread creation/destruction.   MPI is fundamentally based on processes. It is thread-aware in that the MPI 2.0 API [Mesa] defines different levels of thread safety and provides functions to query a system at runtime as to the level of thread safety that is supported. The API, however, has no concept of creating and destroying threads. To mix threads into an MPI program, the programmer must use a thread-based programming model in addition to MPI.

6.2.2 Process Creation/Destruction

A process carries with it all the information required to define its place in the operating system. In addition to program counters and registers, a process includes a large block of memory (its *address space*), system buffers, and everything else required to define its state to the operating system. Consequently, creating and destroying processes is expensive and not done very often.

MPI: process creation/destruction.   In older message-passing APIs such as PVM [Sun90], the capability to create new processes was embedded in the API. A programmer could issue a command called PVM_spawn to create a new process:

```
PVM_Spawn(node, program-executable)
```

This capability of PVM allowed programmers to control which executables ran on which nodes from inside a program. In MPI 1.1, however, this capability was not provided to the programmer and was left to the runtime environment. This decision might seem like a step backwards, but it was done for two reasons. One was the observation that the vast majority of PVM programs were based on the *SPMD* pattern, so it made sense to build this pattern into MPI. Second, it allowed the standard to be implemented on a wider range of parallel architectures. Many of the MPP computers available at the time the MPI Forum defined MPI could not easily handle a spawn statement.

For an example of process creation in MPI, consider an MPI program with an executable named foo. The programmer launches the job on multiple processors (four in this example) with the command:

```
mpirun -np 4 foo
```

In response to this command, the system goes to a standard file listing the names of the nodes to use, selects four of them, and launches the same executable on each one.

The processes are destroyed when the programs running on the nodes of the parallel computer exit. To make the termination clean, an MPI program has as its final executable statement:

```
MPI_Finalize()
```

The system attempts to clean up any processes left running after the program exits. If the exit is abnormal, such as can happen when an external interrupt occurs, it is possible for orphan child processes to be left behind. This is a major concern in large production environments where many large MPI programs come and go. Lack of proper cleanup can lead to an overly crowded system.

Java: process creation/destruction. Usually, one instance of a Java runtime (implementing the Java Virtual Machine, or JVM, specification) corresponds to a process, which will then contain all the threads created by the Java programs it supports. Limited facilities for creating new processes, and communicating and synchronizing with them, are found in the `java.lang.Process` and `java.lang.Runtime` classes in the standard API. These processes, however, are typically used to invoke non-Java programs from within a Java program, not for parallelism. Indeed, the specification does not even require that a new child process execute concurrently with the parent.

Java can also be used in distributed-memory machines; in this case, one starts a JVM instance on each machine using facilities of the operating system.

OpenMP: process creation/destruction. OpenMP is an API created to support multithreaded programming. These threads share a single process. There is no capability within OpenMP to create or destroy processes.

The extension of OpenMP to distributed-memory computers and hence to a multiprocess model is an active area of research [SLGZ99, BB99, Omn]. These systems usually adopt the technique used by MPI and leave process creation and destruction to the runtime environment.

6.3 SYNCHRONIZATION

Synchronization is used to enforce a constraint on the order of events occurring in different UEs. There is a vast body of literature on synchronization [And00], and it can be complicated. Most programmers, however, use only a few synchronization methods on a regular basis.

6.3.1 Memory Synchronization and Fences

In a simple, classical model of a shared-memory multiprocessor, each UE executes a sequence of instructions that can read or write atomically from the shared memory. We can think of the computation as a sequence of atomic events, with the events from different UEs interleaved. Thus, if UE A writes a memory location and then UE B reads it, UE B will see the value written by UE A.

Suppose, for example, that UE A does some work and then sets a variable **done** to true. Meanwhile, UE B executes a loop:

```
while (!done) {/*do something but don't change done*/}
```

In the simple model, UE A will eventually set **done**, and then in the next loop iteration, UE B will read the new value and terminate the loop.

In reality, several things could go wrong. First of all, the value of the variable may not actually be written by UE A or read by UE B. The new value could be held in a cache instead of the main memory, and even in systems with cache coherency, the value could be (as a result of compiler optimizations, say) held in a register and not be made visible to UE B. Similarly, UE B may try to read the variable and obtain a stale value, or due to compiler optimizations, not even read the value more than once because it isn't changed in the loop. In general, many factors—properties of the memory system, the compiler, instruction reordering etc.—can conspire to leave the contents of the memories (as seen by each UE) poorly defined.

A *memory fence* is a synchronization event that guarantees that the UEs will see a consistent view of memory. Writes performed before the fence will be visible to reads performed after the fence, as would be expected in the classical model, and all reads performed after the fence will obtain a value written no earlier than the latest write before the fence.

Clearly, memory synchronization is only an issue when there is shared context between the UEs. Hence, this is not generally an issue when the UEs are processes running in a distributed-memory environment. For threads, however, putting memory fences in the right location can make the difference between a working program and a program riddled with race conditions.

Explicit management of memory fences is cumbersome and error prone. Fortunately, most programmers, although needing to be aware of the issue, only rarely need to deal with fences explicitly because, as we will see in the next few sections, the memory fence is usually implied by higher-level synchronization constructs.

OpenMP: fences.   In OpenMP, a memory fence is defined with the **flush** statement:

```
#pragma omp flush
```

This statement affects every variable visible to the calling UE, causing them to be updated within the computer's memory. This is an expensive operation because guaranteeing consistency requires some of the cache lines and all system buffers and registers to be written to memory. A lower cost version of **flush** is provided where the programmer lists the variables to be flushed:

```
#pragma omp flush (flag)
```

OpenMP programmers only rarely use the `flush` construct because OpenMP's high-level synchronization constructs imply a flush where needed. When custom synchronization constructs are created, however, `flush` can be critical. A good example is pairwise synchronization, where the synchronization occurs between specific pairs of threads rather than among the full team. Because pairwise synchronization is not directly supported by the OpenMP API[2], when faced with an algorithm that demands it, programmers must create the pairwise synchronization construct on their own. The code in Fig. 6.2 shows how to safely implement pairwise synchronization in OpenMP using the `flush` construct.

In this program, each thread has two blocks of work to carry out concurrently with the other threads in the team. The work is represented by two functions: `do_a_whole_bunch()` and `do_more_stuff()`. The contents of these functions are irrelevant (and hence are not shown) for this example. All that matters is that for this example we assume that a thread cannot safely begin work on the second function—`do_more_stuff()`—until its neighbor has finished with the first function—`do_a_whole_bunch()`.

The program uses the *SPMD* pattern. The threads communicate their status for the sake of the pairwise synchronization by setting their value (indexed by the thread ID) of the `flag` array. Because this array must be visible to all of the threads, it needs to be a shared array. We create this within OpenMP by declaring the array in the sequential region (that is, prior to creating the team of threads). We create the team of threads with a parallel pragma:

```
#pragma omp parallel shared(flag)
```

When the work is done, the thread sets its flag to 1 to notify any interested threads that the work is done. This must be flushed to memory to ensure that other threads can see the updated value:

```
#pragma omp flush (flag)
```

---

[2]If a program uses synchronization among the full team, the synchronization will work independently of the size of the team, even if the team size is one. On the other hand, a program with pairwise synchronization will deadlock if run with a single thread. An OpenMP design goal was to encourage code that is equivalent whether run with one thread or many, a property called sequential equivalence. Thus, high-level constructs that are not sequentially equivalent, such as pairwise synchronization, were left out of the API.

```
#include <omp.h>
#include <stdio.h>
#define MAX 10 // max number of threads

// Functions used in this program: the details of these
// functions are not relevant so we do not include the
// function bodies.
extern int neighbor(int); // return the ID for a thread's neighbor
extern void do_a_whole_bunch(int);
extern void do_more_stuff();

int main() {
   int flag[MAX]; //Define an array of flags one per thread
   int i;

   for(i=0;i<MAX;i++)flag[i] = 0;

#pragma omp parallel shared (flag)
   {
   int ID;
   ID = omp_get_thread_num(); // returns a unique ID for each thread.

   do_a_whole_bunch(ID); // Do a whole bunch of work.

   flag[ID] = 1; // signal that this thread has finished its work
   #pragma omp flush (flag) // make sure all the threads have a chance to
                            // see the updated flag value

   while (!flag[neighbor(ID)]){ // wait to see if neighbor is done.
   #pragma omp flush(flag) // required to see any changes to flag
    }

    do_more_stuff(); // call a function that can't safely start until
                     // the neighbor's work is complete
   } // end parallel region
}
```

Figure 6.2: Program showing one way to implement pairwise synchronization in OpenMP. The flush construct is vital. It forces the memory to be consistent, thereby making the updates to the flag array visible. For more details about the syntax of OpenMP, see the OpenMP appendix, Appendix A.

The thread then waits until its neighbor is finished with `do_a_whole_bunch()` before moving on to finish its work with a call to `do_more_work()`:

```
while (!flag( neighbor(ID))){ // wait to see if neighbor is done.
#pragma omp flush(flag) // required to see any changes to flag
 }
```

The flush operation in OpenMP only affects the thread-visible variables for the calling thread. If another thread writes a shared variable and forces it to be available to the other threads by using a flush, the thread reading the variable still needs to execute a flush to make sure it picks up the new value. Hence, the body of the `while` loop must include a `flush(flag)` construct to make sure the thread sees any new values in the `flag` array.

As we mentioned earlier, knowing when a flush is needed and when it is not can be challenging. In most cases, the flush is built into the synchronization construct. But when the standard constructs aren't adequate and custom synchronization is required, placing memory fences in the right locations is essential.

Java: fences.   Java does not provide an explicit flush construct as in OpenMP. In fact, the Java memory model[3] is not defined in terms of flush operations, but in terms of constraints on visibility and ordering with respect to locking operations. The details are complicated, but the general idea is not: Suppose thread 1 performs some operations while holding lock L and then releases the lock, and then thread 2 acquires lock L. The rule is that all writes that occurred in thread 1 before thread 1 released the lock are visible in thread 2 after it acquires the lock. Further, when a thread is started by invoking its `start` method, the started thread sees all writes visible to the caller at the call point. Similarly, when a thread calls `join`, the caller will see all writes performed by the terminating thread.

Java allows variables to be declared as `volatile`. When a variable is marked volatile, all writes to the variable are guaranteed to be immediately visible, and all reads are guaranteed to obtain the last value written. Thus, the compiler takes care of memory synchronization issues for volatiles.[4] In a Java version of a program containing the fragment (where `done` is expected to be set by another thread)

```
while (!done) {.../*do something but don't change done*/}
```

we would mark `done` to be `volatile` when the variable is declared, as follows, and then ignore memory synchronization issues related to this variable in the rest of the program.

```
volatile boolean done = false;
```

Because the `volatile` keyword can be applied only to references to an array and not to the individual elements, the `java.util.concurrent.atomic` package introduced in Java 2 1.5 adds a notion of atomic arrays where the individual

---

[3] Java is one of the first languages where an attempt was made to specify its memory model precisely. The original specification has been criticized for imprecision as well as for not supporting certain synchronization idioms while at the same time disallowing some reasonable compiler optimizations. A new specification for Java 2 1.5 is described in [JSRa]. In this book, we assume the new specification.

[4] From the point of view of the rule stated previously, reading a volatile variable is defined to have the same effect with regard to memory synchronization as acquiring a lock associated with the variable, whereas writing has the same effect as releasing a lock.

elements are accessed with volatile semantics. For example, in a Java version of the OpenMP example shown in Fig. 6.2, we would declare the `flag` array to be of type `AtomicIntegerArray` and update and read with that class's `set` and `get` methods.

Another technique for ensuring proper memory synchronization is synchronized blocks. A synchronized block appears as follows:

```
synchronized(some_object){/*do something with shared variables*/}
```

We will describe synchronized blocks in more detail in Sec. 6.3.3 and the Java appendix, Appendix C. For the time being, it is sufficient to know that `some_object` is implicitly associated with a lock and the compiler will generate code to acquire this lock before executing the body of the synchronized block and to release the lock on exit from the block. This means that one can guarantee proper memory synchronization of access to a variable by ensuring that all accesses to the variable occur in synchronized blocks associated with the same object.

MPI: fences.　A fence only arises in environments that include shared memory. In MPI specifications prior to MPI 2.0, the API did not expose shared memory to the programmer, and hence there was no need for a user-callable fence. MPI 2.0, however, includes one-sided communication constructs. These constructs create "windows" of memory visible to other processes in an MPI program. Data can by pushed to or pulled from these windows by a single process without the explicit cooperation of the process owning the memory region in question. These memory windows require some type of fence, but are not discussed here because implementations of MPI 2.0 are not widely available at the time this was written.

6.3.2　Barriers

A *barrier* is a synchronization point at which every member of a collection of UEs must arrive before any members can proceed. If a UE arrives early, it will wait until all of the other UEs have arrived.

A barrier is one of the most common high-level synchronization constructs. It has relevance both in process-oriented environments such as MPI and thread-based systems such as OpenMP and Java.

MPI: barriers.　In MPI, a barrier is invoked by calling the function

```
MPI_Barrier(MPI_COMM)
```

where `MPI_COMM` is a communicator defining the process group and the communication context. All processes in the group associated with the communicator participate in the barrier. Although it might not be apparent to the programmer, the

```
#include <mpi.h> // MPI include file
#include <stdio.h>

extern void runit();

int main(int argc, char **argv) {
    int num_procs; // number of processes in the group
    int ID; // unique identifier ranging from 0 to (num_procs-1)
    double time_init, time_final, time_elapsed;
//
// Initialize MPI and set up the SPMD program
//
    MPI_Init(&argc,&argv);
    MPI_Comm_rank(MPI_COMM_WORLD, &ID);
    MPI_Comm_size (MPI_COMM_WORLD, &num_procs);
//
// Ensure that all processes are set up and ready to go before timing
// runit()
//
    MPI_Barrier(MPI_COMM_WORLD);

    time_init = MPI_Wtime();

    runit(); // a function that we wish to time on each process

    time_final = MPI_Wtime();

    time_elapsed = time_final - time_init;

    printf(" I am \%d and my computation took \%f seconds\n",
            ID, time_elapsed);

    MPI_Finalize();
    return 0;
}
```

Figure 6.3: MPI program containing a barrier. This program is used to time the execution of function runit().

barrier itself is almost always implemented with a cascade of pairwise messages using the same techniques as used in a reduction (see the discussion of reduction in Sec. 6.4.2).

As an example of a barrier, consider the program in Fig. 6.3. This simple program sets up the MPI environment and then records the execution time of a function called runit() (the code of which is not shown). The time itself is found using the MPI timing routine:

```
MPI_Wtime()
```

This function returns a double-precision value holding the elapsed time in seconds since some point in the past. The difference between the value returned after the function call and the value returned before the function call gives the elapsed time for the function's execution. This is *wall clock* time, that is, the time that would elapse on a clock external to the computer.

There can be considerable variation in process startup or the initialization of MPI. Thus, for the time to be consistent across all the processes, it is important that all processes enter the timed section of code together. To address this issue, we place a barrier before the timed section of code.

OpenMP: barriers.   In OpenMP, a simple pragma sets the barrier:

```
#pragma omp barrier
```

All threads in the team participate in the barrier. As an example of a barrier, consider the code in Fig. 6.4. This program is essentially the same as the MPI program. A barrier is used to ensure that all threads complete any startup activities

```
#include <omp.h>
#include <stdio.h>

extern void runit();

int main(int argc, char **argv) {
    double time_init, time_final, time_elapsed;

#pragma omp parallel private(time_init, time_final, time_elapsed)
{
    int ID;
    ID = omp_get_thread_num();
//
// ensure that all threads are set up and ready to go before timing runit()
//
    #pragma omp barrier

    time_init = omp_get_wtime();

    runit(); // a function that we wish to time on each thread

    time_final = omp_get_wtime();

    time_ elapsed = time_final - time_init;

    printf(" I am %d and my computation took \%f seconds\n",
        ID, time_elapsed);
}
return 0;
}
```

Figure 6.4: OpenMP program containing a barrier. This program is used to time the execution of function runit().

before the timing measurements are taken. The timing routine, `omp_Wtick()`, was modeled after the analogous MPI routine, `MPI_Wtime()`, and is defined in the same way.

In addition to an explicit barrier as shown in Fig. 6.4, OpenMP automatically inserts barriers at the end of the worksharing constructs (`for`, `single`, `section`, etc.). This implicit barrier can be disabled, if desired, by using the `nowait` clause.

The barrier implies a call to `flush`, so the OpenMP barrier creates a memory fence as well. These memory flushes, combined with any cycles wasted while UEs wait at the barrier, make it a potentially expensive construct. Barriers, which are expensive in any programming environment, must be used where required to ensure the correct program semantics, but for performance reasons should be used no more than absolutely required.

Java: barriers.   Java did not originally include a barrier primitive, although it is not difficult to create one using the facilities in the language, as was done in the public-domain `util.concurrent` package [Lea]. In Java 2 1.5, similar classes are provided in the `java.util.concurrent` package.

A `CyclicBarrier` is similar to the barrier described previously. The `Cyclic-Barrier` class contains two constructors: one that requires the number of threads that will synchronize on the barrier, and another that takes the number of threads along with a `Runnable` object whose `run` method will be executed by the last thread to arrive at the barrier. When a thread arrives at the barrier, it invokes the barrier's `await` method. If a thread "breaks" the barrier by terminating prematurely with an exception, the other threads will throw a `BrokenBarrierException`. A `CyclicBarrier` automatically resets itself when passed and can be used multiple times (in a loop, for example).

In Fig. 6.5, we provide a Java version of the barrier examples given previously using a `CyclicBarrier`.

The `java.util.concurrent` package also provides a related synchronization primitive `CountDownLatch`. A `CountDownLatch` is initialized to a particular value N. Each invocation of its `countDown` method decreases the count. A thread executing the `await` method blocks until the value of the latch reaches 0. The separation of `countDown` (analogous to "arriving at the barrier") and `await` (waiting for the other threads) allows more general situations than "all threads wait for all other threads to reach a barrier." For example, a single thread could wait for N events to happen, or N threads could wait for a single event to happen. A `CountDownLatch` cannot be reset and can only be used once. An example using a `CountDownLatch` is given in the Java appendix, Appendix C.

6.3.3   Mutual Exclusion

When memory or other system resources (for example, a file system) are shared, the program must ensure that multiple UEs do not interfere with each other. For example, if two threads try to update a shared data structure at the same time, a *race condition* results that can leave the structure in an inconsistent state. A *critical section* is a sequence of statements that conflict with a sequence of statements that may be executed by other UEs. Two sequences of statements conflict if both access the same data and at least one of them modifies the data. To protect the resources

```
import java.util.concurrent.*;

public class TimerExample implements Runnable {
   static int N;
   static CyclicBarrier barrier;
   final int ID;

   public void run()
   {
      //wait at barrier until all threads are ready
      System.out.println(ID + " at await");
      try{ barrier.await(); }
      catch (InterruptedException ex) { Thread.dumpStack();}
      catch (BrokenBarrierException ex){Thread.dumpStack();}

      //record start time
      long time_init = System.currentTimeMillis();

      //execute function to be timed on each thread
      runit();

      //record ending time
      long time_final = System.currentTimeMillis();

      //print elapsed time
      System.out.println("Elapsed time for thread "+ID+
         " = "+(time_final-time_init)+" msecs");
      return;
   }

   void runit(){...} //definition of runit()

   TimerExample(int ID){this.ID = ID;}

   public static void main(String[] args)
   { N = Integer.parseInt(args[0]); //read number of threads

      barrier = new CyclicBarrier(N); //instantiate barrier

      for(int i = 0; i!= N; i++) //create and start threads
      {new Thread(new TimerExample(i)).start(); }
   }
}
```

Figure 6.5: Java program containing a `CyclicBarrier`. This program is used to time the execution of function `runit()`.

accessed inside the critical section, the programmer must use some mechanism that ensures that only one thread at a time will execute the code within the critical section. This is called *mutual exclusion.*

When using mutual exclusion, it is easy to fall into a situation where one thread is making progress while one or more threads are blocked waiting for their turn to enter the critical section. This can be a serious source of inefficiency in a parallel program, so great care must be taken when using mutual-exclusion constructs. It is important to minimize the amount of code that is protected by mutual

```
#include <omp.h>
#include <stdio.h>
#define N 1000

extern double big_computation(int, int);
extern void consume_results(int, double, double *);

int main() {
   double global_result[N];

   #pragma omp parallel shared (global_result)
   {
     double local_result;
     int I;
     int ID = omp_get_thread_num(); // set a thread ID

     #pragma omp for
     for(i=0;i<N;i++){
         local_result = big_computation(ID, i); // carry out the UE's work
       #pragma omp critical
       {
           consume_results(ID, local_result, global_result);
       }
     }
   }
   return 0;
}
```

Figure 6.6: Example of an OpenMP program that includes a critical section

exclusion and, if possible, stagger the arrival at the mutual-exclusion construct by the members of a team of threads so a minimum number of threads are waiting to execute the protected code. The *Shared Data* pattern discusses the issue of what should be protected by mutual exclusion. Here we focus on the implementation mechanisms for protecting a critical section.

OpenMP: mutual exclusion.   In OpenMP, mutual exclusion is most easily accomplished using a construct called *critical section*. An example of using the critical section construct for OpenMP is shown in Fig. 6.6.

In this program, a team of threads is created to cooperatively carry out a series of N calls to `big_computation()`. The pragma

```
#pragma omp for
```

is the OpenMP construct that tells the compiler to distribute the iterations of the loop among a team of threads. After `big_computation()` is complete, the results need to be combined into the global data structure that will hold the result.

While we don't show the code, assume the update within `consume_results()` can be done in any order, but the update by one thread must complete before another thread can execute an update. The `critical` pragma accomplishes this for us. The first thread to finish its `big_computation()` enters the enclosed block of code and calls `consume_results()`. If a thread arrives at the top of the critical-section block while another thread is processing the block, it waits until the prior thread is finished.

The critical section is an expensive synchronization operation. Upon entry to a critical section, a thread flushes all visible variables to ensure that a consistent view of the memory is seen inside the critical section. At the end of the critical section, we need any memory updates occurring within the critical section to be visible to the other threads in the team, so a second flush of all thread-visible variables is required.

The critical section construct is not only expensive, it is not very general. It cannot be used among subsets of threads within a team or to provide mutual exclusion between different blocks of code. Thus, the OpenMP API provides a lower-level and more flexible construct for mutual exclusion called a *lock*.

Locks in different shared-memory APIs tend to be similar. The programmer declares the lock and initializes it. Only one thread at a time is allowed to hold the lock. Other threads trying to acquire the lock will block. Blocking while waiting for a lock is inefficient, so many lock APIs allow threads to test a lock's availability without trying to acquire it. Thus, a thread can opt to do useful work and come back to attempt to acquire the lock later.

Consider the use of locks in OpenMP. The example in Fig. 6.7 shows use of a simple lock to make sure only one thread at a time attempts to write to standard output.

The program first declares the lock to be of type `omp_lock_t`. This is an opaque object, meaning that as long as the programmer only manipulates lock objects through the OpenMP runtime library, the programmer can safely work with the locks without ever considering the details of the lock type. The lock is then initialized with a call to `omp_init_lock`.

```
#include <omp.h>
#include <stdio.h>

    int main() {
    omp_lock_t lock; // declare the lock using the lock
                     // type defined in omp.h

    omp_set_num_threads(5);
    omp_init_lock (&lock); // initialize the lock
#pragma omp parallel shared (lock)
    {
        int id = omp_get_thread_num();
        omp_set_lock (&lock);
        printf("\n only thread %d can do this print\n",id);
        omp_unset_lock (&lock);
    }
}
```

Figure 6.7: Example of using locks in OpenMP

To be of any use for managing concurrency, a lock must be shared between the individual members of the team of threads. Thus, the lock is defined prior to the `parallel` pragma and declared as a shared variable (which is the default, but we call the `shared` clause in this example just to emphasize the point). Inside the parallel region, a thread can set the lock, which causes any other threads attempting to set the same lock to block and wait until the lock has been unset.

Unlike the OpenMP critical section, an OpenMP lock does not define a memory fence. If the operations carried out by the thread holding the lock depend on any values from other threads, the program might fail because the memory might not be consistent. Managing memory consistency can be difficult for many programmers, so most OpenMP programmers opt to avoid locks and use the much safer critical sections.

Java: mutual exclusion.   The Java language provides support for mutual exclusion with the synchronized block construct and also, in Java 2 1.5, with new lock classes contained in the package `java.util.concurrent.lock`. Every object in a Java program implicitly contains its own lock. Each synchronized block has an associated object, and a thread must acquire the lock on that object before executing the body of the block. When the thread exits the body of the synchronized block, whether normally or abnormally by throwing an exception, the lock is released.

In Fig. 6.8, we provide a Java version of the example given previously. The work done by the threads is specified by the `run` method in the nested `Worker` class. Note that because N is declared to be `final` (and is thus immutable), it can safely be accessed by any thread without requiring any synchronization.

For the synchronized blocks to exclude each other, they must be associated with the same object. In the example, the synchronized block in the `run` method uses `this.getClass()` as an argument. This expression returns a reference to the runtime object representing the `Worker` class. This is a convenient way to ensure that all callers use the same object. We could also have introduced a global instance of `java.lang.Object` (or an instance of any other class) and used that as the argument to the synchronized block. What is important is that all the threads synchronize on the same object. A potential mistake would be to use, say, `this`, which would not enforce the desired mutual exclusion because each worker thread would be synchronizing on itself—and thus locking a different lock.

Because this is a very common misunderstanding and source of errors in multithreaded Java programs, we emphasize again that a synchronized block only protects a critical section from access by other threads whose conflicting statements are also enclosed in a synchronized block *with the same object* as an argument. Synchronized blocks associated with different objects do not exclude each other. (They also do not guarantee memory synchronization.) Also, the presence of a synchronized block in a method does not constrain code that is not in a synchronized block. Thus, forgetting a needed synchronized block or making a mistake with the argument to the synchronized block can have serious consequences.

The code in Fig. 6.8 is structured similarly to the OpenMP example. A more common approach used in Java programs is to encapsulate a shared data structure in a class and provide access only through synchronized methods. A synchronized method is just a special case of a synchronized block that includes an entire method.

```
public class Example {
static final int N = 10;
static double[] global_result = new double[N];

  public static void main(String[] args) throws InterruptedException
  {
    //create and start N threads
    Thread[] t = new Thread[N];
    for (int i = 0; i != N; i++)
      {t[i] = new Thread(new Worker(i)); t[i].start(); }

    //wait for all N threads to finish
    for (int i = 0; i != N; i++){t[i].join();}

    //print the results
    for (int i = 0; i!=N; i++)
      {System.out.print(global_result[i] + " ");}
    System.out.println("done");
  }

static class Worker implements Runnable
{
  double local_result;
  int i;
  int ID;

  Worker(int ID){this.ID = ID;}

  //main work of threads
  public void run()
  { //perform the main computation
    local_result = big_computation(ID, i);

    //update global variables in synchronized block
    synchronized(this.getClass())
     {consume_results(ID, local_result, global_result);}
  }

  //define computation
  double big_computation(int ID, int i){ . . . }

  //define result update
  void consume_results(int ID, double local_result,
                  double[] global_result){. . .}
  }
}
```

Figure 6.8: Java version of the OpenMP program in Fig. 6.6

It is implicitly synchronized on `this` for normal methods and the class object for static methods. This approach moves the responsibility for synchronization from the threads accessing the shared data structure to the data structure itself. Often this is a better-engineered approach. In Fig. 6.9, the previous example is rewritten to use this approach. Now the `global_result` variable is encapsulated in the `Example2` class and marked private to help enforce this. (To make the point, the `Worker` class is

```
public class Example2 {
   static final int N = 10;
   private static double[] global_result = new double[N];

   public static void main(String[] args) throws InterruptedException
   { //create and start N threads
      Thread[] t = new Thread[N];
      for (int i = 0; i != N; i++)
         {t[i] = new Thread(new Worker(i)); t[i].start(); }

      //wait for all threads to terminate
      for (int i = 0; i != N; i++){t[i].join();}

      //print results
      for (int i = 0; i!=N; i++)
         {System.out.print(global_result[i] + " ");}
      System.out.println("done");
   }

   //synchronized method serializing consume_results method
   synchronized static void consume_results(int ID, double local_result)
      { global_result[ID] = . . . }
}

class Worker implements Runnable
{
   double local_result;
   int i;
   int ID;

   Worker(int ID){this.ID = ID;}

   public void run()
   { //perform the main computation
      local_result = big_computation(ID, i); //carry out the UE's work

      //invoke method to update results
      Example2.consume_results(ID, local_result);
   }

   //define computation
   double big_computation(int ID, int i){ . . . }
}
```

Figure 6.9: Java program showing how to implement mutual exclusion with a synchronized method

no longer a nested class.) The only way for the workers to access the `global_result` array is through the `consume_results` method, which is now a synchronized method in the `Example2` class. Thus, the responsibility for synchronization has been moved from the class defining the worker threads to the class owning the `global_result` array.

The synchronized block construct in Java has some deficiencies. Probably the most important for parallel programmers is the lack of a way to find out whether a lock is available before attempting to acquire it. There is also no way to interrupt a thread waiting on a synchronized block, and the synchronized block construct forces the locks to be acquired and released in a nested fashion. This disallows certain kinds of programming idioms in which a lock is acquired in one block and released in another.

As a result of these deficiencies, many programmers have created their own lock classes instead of using the built-in synchronized blocks. For examples, see [Lea]. In response to this situation, in Java 2 1.5, package `java.util.concurrent.locks` provides several lock classes that can be used as an alternative to synchronized blocks. These are discussed in the Java appendix, Appendix C.

MPI: mutual exclusion. As is the case with most of the synchronization constructs, mutual exclusion is only needed when the statements execute within a shared context. Hence, a shared-nothing API such as MPI does not provide support for critical sections directly within the standard. Consider the OpenMP program in Fig. 6.6. If we want to implement a similar method in MPI with a complex data structure that has to be updated by one UE at a time, the typical approach is to dedicate a process to this update. The other processes would then send their contributions to the dedicated process. We show this situation in Fig. 6.10.

This program uses the *SPMD* pattern. As with the OpenMP program in Fig. 6.6, we have a loop to carry out N calls to `big_computation()`, the results of which are consumed and placed in a single global data structure. Updates to this data structure must be protected so that results from only one UE at a time are applied.

We arbitrarily choose the UE with the highest rank to manage the critical section. This process then executes a loop and posts N receives. By using the `MPI_ANY_SOURCE` and `MPI_ANY_TAG` values in the `MPI_Recv()` statement, the messages holding results from the calls to `big_computation()` are taken in any order. If the tag or ID are required, they can be recovered from the status variable returned from `MPI_Recv()`.

The other UEs carry out the N calls to `big_computation()`. Because one UE has been dedicated to managing the critical section, the effective number of processes in the computation is decreased by one. We use a cyclic distribution of the loop iterations as was described in the Examples section of the *SPMD* pattern. This assigns the loop iterations in a round-robin fashion. After a UE completes its computation, the result is sent to the process managing the critical section.[5]

---

[5] We used a synchronous send (`MPI_Ssend()`), which does not return until a matching MPI receive has been posted, to duplicate the behavior of shared-memory mutual exclusion as closely as possible. It is worth noting, however, that in a distributed-memory environment, making the sending process wait until the message has been received is only rarely needed and adds additional parallel overhead. Usually, MPI programmers go to great lengths to avoid parallel overheads and would only use synchronous message passing as a last resort. In this example, the standard-mode message-passing functions, `MPI_Send()` and `MPI_Recv()`, would be a better choice unless either (1) a condition external to the communication requires the two processes to satisfy an ordering constraint, hence forcing them to synchronize with each other, or (2) communication buffers or another system resource limit the capacity of the computer receiving the messages, thereby forcing the processes on the sending side to wait until the receiving side is ready.

```
#include <mpi.h> // MPI include file
#include <stdio.h>
#define N 1000
extern void consume_results(int, double, double * );
extern double big_computation(int, int);

int main(int argc, char **argv) {
    int Tag1 = 1; int Tag2 = 2; // message tags
    int num_procs; // number of processes in group
    int ID; // unique identifier from 0 to (num_procs-1)
    double local_result, global_result[N];
    int i, ID_CRIT;
    MPI_Status stat; // MPI status parameter

// Initialize MPI and set up the SPMD program
    MPI_Init(&argc,&argv);
    MPI_Comm_rank(MPI_COMM_WORLD, &ID);
    MPI_Comm_size (MPI_COMM_WORLD, &num_procs);

    // Need at least two processes for this method to work
    if(num_procs < 2) MPI_Abort(MPI_COMM_WORLD,-1);

// Dedicate the last process to managing update of final result
    ID_CRIT = num_procs-1;
    if (ID == ID_CRIT) {
        int ID_sender; // variable to hold ID of sender
        for(i=0;i<N;i++){
            MPI_Recv(&local_result, 1, MPI_DOUBLE, MPI_ANY_SOURCE,
                    MPI_ANY_TAG, MPI_COMM_WORLD, &stat);
            ID_sender = stat.MPI_SOURCE;
            consume_results(ID_sender, local_result, global_result);
        }
    }
    else {
        num_procs--;
        for(i=ID;i<N;i+=num_procs){ // cyclic distribution of loop iterations
            local_result = big_computation(ID, i); // carry out UE's work

// Send local result using a synchronous Send - a send that doesn't
// return until a matching receive has been posted.
            MPI_Ssend (&local_result, 1, MPI_DOUBLE, ID_CRIT, ID,
                    MPI_COMM_WORLD);
        }
    }
    MPI_Finalize();
    return 0;
}
```

Figure 6.10: Example of an MPI program with an update that requires mutual exclusion. A single process is dedicated to the update of this data structure.

6.4   COMMUNICATION

In most parallel algorithms, UEs need to exchange information as the computation proceeds. Shared-memory environments provide this capability by default, and the challenge in these systems is to synchronize access to shared memory so that the results are correct regardless of how the UEs are scheduled. In distributed-memory systems, however, it is the other way around: Because there are few, if any, shared resources, the need for explicit synchronization to protect these resources is rare. Communication, however, becomes a major focus of the programmer's effort.

6.4.1 Message Passing

A *message* is the most basic communication element. A message consists of a header containing data about the message (for example, source, destination, and a tag) and a series of bits to be communicated. Message passing is typically *two-sided,* meaning that a message is explicitly sent between a pair of UEs, from a specific source to a specific destination. In addition to direct message passing, there are communication events that involve multiple UEs (usually all of them) in a single communication event. We call this *collective communication.* These collective communication events often include computation as well, the classic example being a global summation where a set of values distributed about the system is summed into a single value on each node.

In the following sections, we will explore communication mechanisms in more detail. We start with basic message passing in MPI, OpenMP, and Java. Then, we consider collective communication, looking in particular at the reduction operation in MPI and OpenMP. We close with a brief look at other approaches to managing communication in parallel programs.

MPI: message passing. Message passing between a pair of UEs is the most basic of the communication operations and provides a natural starting point for our discussion. A message is sent by one UE and received by another. In its most basic form, the send and the receive operation are paired.

As an example, consider the MPI program in Figs. 6.11 and 6.12. In this program, a ring of processors work together to iteratively compute the elements within a field (`field` in the program). To keep the problem simple, we assume the dependencies in the update operation are such that each UE only needs information from its neighbor to the left to update the field.

We show only the parts of the program relevant to the communication. The details of the actual update operation, initialization of the field, or even the structure of the field and boundary data are omitted.

The program in Figs. 6.11 and 6.12 declares its variables and then initializes the MPI environment. This is an instance of the *SPMD* pattern where the logic within the parallel algorithm will be driven by the process rank `ID` and the number of processes in the team.

After initializing `field`, we set up the communication pattern by computing two variables, `left` and `right`, that identify which processes are located to the left and the right. In this example, the computation is straightforward and implements a ring communication pattern. In more complex programs, however, these index computations can be complex, obscure, and the source of many errors.

The core loop of the program executes a number of steps. At each step, the boundary data is collected and communicated to its neighbors by shifting around a ring, and then the local block of the field controlled by the process is updated.

```
#include <stdio.h>
#include "mpi.h" // MPI include file
#define IS_ODD(x) ((x)%2) // test for an odd int

// prototypes for functions to initialize the problem, extract
// the boundary region to share, and perform the field update.
// The contents of these functions are not provided.

extern void init (int, int, double *, double * , double *);
extern void extract_boundary (int, int, int, int, double *);
extern void update (int, int, int, int, double *, double *);
extern void output_results (int, double *);

int main(int argc, char **argv) {
    int Tag1 = 1; // message tag
    int nprocs; // the number of processes in the group
    int ID; // the process rank
    int Nsize; // Problem size (order of field matrix)
    int Bsize; // Number of doubles in the boundary
    int Nsteps; // Number of iterations
    double *field, *boundary, *incoming;

    int i, left, right;
    MPI_Status stat; // MPI status parameter
//
// Initialize MPI and set up the SPMD program
//
    MPI_Init(&argc,&argv);
    MPI_Comm_rank(MPI_COMM_WORLD, &ID);
    MPI_Comm_size(MPI_COMM_WORLD, &nprocs);

    init (Nsize, Bsize, field, boundary, incoming);

/* continued in next figure */
```

Figure 6.11: MPI program that uses a ring of processors and a communication pattern where information is shifted to the right. The functions to do the computation do not affect the communication itself so they are not shown. (Continued in Fig. 6.12.)

Notice that we had to explicitly switch the communication between odd and even processes. This ensures that the matching communication events are ordered consistently on the two processes involved. This is important because on systems with limited buffer space, a send may not be able to return until the relevant receive has been posted.

OpenMP: message passing. Message passing can be an effective strategy in OpenMP. One use of message passing in OpenMP is to emulate an MPI algorithm, for example when porting a working MPI program to a system where only OpenMP is available. Another case is when using NUMA machines where data locality is important. By using the *SPMD* pattern and message passing, the programmer can more precisely control how the program data is aligned with the system's memory hierarchy, thereby resulting in better performance.

```
/* continued from previous figure */

// assume a ring of processors and a communication pattern
// where boundaries are shifted to the right.

left = (ID+1); if(left>(nprocs-1)) left = 0;
right = (ID-1); if(right<0)right = nprocs-1;

for(i = 0; i < Nsteps; i++){

  extract_boundary(Nsize, Bsize, ID, nprocs, boundary);
  if(IS_ODD(ID)){
    MPI_Send (boundary, Bsize, MPI_DOUBLE, right, Tag1,
            MPI_COMM_WORLD);
    MPI_Recv (incoming, Bsize, MPI_DOUBLE, left, Tag1,
            MPI_COMM_WORLD, &stat);
  }
  else {
    MPI_Recv (incoming, Bsize, MPI_DOUBLE, left, Tag1,
            MPI_COMM_WORLD, &stat);
    MPI_Send (boundary, Bsize, MPI_DOUBLE, right, Tag1,
            MPI_COMM_WORLD);
  }
  update(Nsize, Bsize, ID, nprocs, field, incoming);
}
output_results(Nsize, field);
MPI_Finalize();
return 0;
}
```

Figure 6.12: MPI program that uses a ring of processors and a communication pattern where information is shifted to the right (continued from Fig. 6.11)

A particularly easy way to use message passing within OpenMP is shown in Figs. 6.13 and 6.14. This program is basically the same as the MPI program in Figs. 6.11 and 6.12. As before, we hide details of the problem not relevant to a discussion of the parallel algorithm.

Message passing is accomplished in OpenMP by the receiving process reading the message from a shared data structure. In MPI, the synchronization required by the problem is implied by the message-passing functions. In OpenMP, the synchronization is explicit. We start with a **barrier** to make sure all threads are at the same point (that is, ready to fill the **boundary** they will share). A second **barrier** ensures that all the threads have finished filling their **boundary** before the receiving side uses the data.

This strategy is extremely effective for problems that involve the same amount of work on each thread. When some threads are faster than other threads, because either the hardware is less loaded or perhaps the data is not evenly distributed, the use of barriers leads to excessive parallel overhead as threads wait at the barrier. The solution is to more finely tune the synchronization to the needs of the problem, which, in this case, would indicate that pairwise synchronization should be used.

The "message-passing" OpenMP program in Fig. 6.15 shows a simple way to introduce pairwise synchronization in OpenMP. This code is much more

```
#include <stdio.h>
#include <omp.h> // OpenMP include file
#define MAX 10 // maximum number of threads
//
// prototypes for functions to initialize the problem,
// extract the boundary region to share, and perform the
// field update. Note: the initialize routine is different
// here in that it sets up a large shared array (that is, for
// the full problem), not just a local block.
//
extern void init (int, int, double *, double * , double *);
extern void extract_boundary (int, int, double *, double *);
extern void update (int, int, double *, double *);
extern void output_results (int, double *);

int main(int argc, char **argv) {
    int Nsize; // Problem size (order of field matrix)
    int Bsize; // Number of doubles in the boundary
    double *field;
    double *boundary[MAX]; // array of pointers to a buffer to hold
                           // boundary data
//
// Create Team of Threads
//

    init (Nsize, Bsize, field, boundary, incoming);
/* continued in next figure */
```

Figure 6.13: OpenMP program that uses a ring of threads and a communication pattern where information is shifted to the right (continued in Fig. 6.14)

complicated than the OpenMP program in Fig. 6.13 and Fig. 6.14. Basically, we have added an array called **done** that a thread uses to indicate that its buffer (that is, the **boundary** data) is ready to use. A thread fills its buffer, sets the flag, and then flushes it to make sure other threads can see the updated value. The thread then checks the flag for its neighbor and waits (using a so-called *spin lock*) until the buffer from its neighbor is ready to receive.

This code is significantly more complex, but it can be more efficient on two counts. First, barriers cause all threads to wait for the full team. If any one thread is delayed for whatever reason, it slows down the entire team. This can be disastrous for performance, especially if the variability between threads' workloads is high. Second, we've replaced two barriers with one barrier and a series of flushes. A flush is expensive, but notice that each of these flushes only flushes a single small array (**done**). It is likely that multiple calls to a flush with a single array will be much faster than the single flush of all thread-visible data implied by a barrier.

Java: message passing. The Java language definition does not specify message passing (as it does facilities for concurrent programming with threads). Similar techniques to those discussed for message passing in OpenMP could be used. However, the standard class libraries provided with the Java distribution provide extensive support for various types of communication in distributed environments. Rather

```
/* continued from previous figure */

#pragma omp parallel shared(boundary, field, Bsize, Nsize)

//
// Set up the SPMD program. Note: by declaring ID and Num_threads
// inside the parallel region, we make them private to each thread.
//
    int ID, nprocs, i, left;

    ID = omp_get_thread_num();
    nprocs = omp_get_num_threads();

    if (nprocs > MAX) {
       exit (-1);
    }


    //
    // assume a ring of processors and a communication pattern
    // where boundaries are shifted to the right.
    //
    left = (ID-1); if(left<0) left = nprocs-1;

    for(i = 0; i < Nsteps; i++){

#pragma omp barrier

        extract_boundary(Nsize, Bsize, ID, nprocs, boundary[ID]);

#pragma omp barrier

        update(Nsize, Bsize, ID, nprocs, field, boundary[left]);
    }
    output_results(Nsize, field);
    return 0;
}
```

Figure 6.14: OpenMP program that uses a ring of threads and a communication pattern where information is shifted to the right (continued from Fig. 6.13)

than provide examples of those techniques, we will provide an overview of the available facilities.

Java provides significant support for client-server distributed computing in heterogeneous environments. It is very easy to set up a TCP socket connection between two PEs and send and receive data over the connection. The relevant classes are found in packages `java.net` and `java.io`. The serialization facilities (see the `java.io.Serializable` interface) support converting a possibly complex data structure into a sequence of bytes that can be transmitted over a network (or written to a file) and reconstructed at the destination. The RMI (remote method invocation) packages `java.rmi.*` provide a mechanism enabling an object on one JVM to invoke methods on an object in another JVM, which may be running on a different computer. Serialization is used by the RMI packages to marshal the arguments to the method and return the result to the caller.

```
    int done[MAX]; // an array of flags dimensioned for the
                    // boundary data
//
// Create Team of Threads
//
    init (Nsize, Bsize, field, boundary, incoming);

#pragma omp parallel shared(boundary, field, Bsize, Nsize)

//
// Set up the SPMD program. Note: by declaring ID and Num_threads
// inside the parallel region, we make them private to each thread.
//
    int ID, nprocs, i, left;

    ID = omp_get_thread_num();
    nprocs = omp_get_num_threads();
    if (nprocs > MAX) { exit (-1); }

    //
    // assume a ring of processors and a communication pattern
    // where boundaries are shifted to the right.
    //
    left = (ID-1); if(left<0) left = nprocs-1;

    done[ID] = 0; // set flag stating "buffer ready to fill"
    for(i = 0; i < Nsteps; i++){

    #pragma omp barrier // all visible variables flushed, so we
                        // don't need to flush "done".
      extract_boundary(Nsize, Bsize, ID, num_procs, boundary[ID]);

      done[ID] = 1; // flag that the buffer is ready to use

    #pragma omp flush (done)

      while (done[left] != 1){
        #pragma omp flush (done)
      }

      update(Nsize, Bsize, ID, num_procs, field, boundary[left]);

      done[left] = 0; // set flag stating "buffer ready to fill"
    }
    output_results(Nsize, field);
```

Figure 6.15: The message-passing block from Fig. 6.13 and Fig. 6.14, but with more careful synchronization management (pairwise synchronization)

Although the java.io, java.net, and java.rmi.* packages provide very convenient programming abstractions and work very well in the domain for which they were designed, they incur high parallel overheads and are considered to be inadequate for high-performance computing. High-performance computers typically use homogeneous networks of computers, so the general-purpose distributed computing approaches supported by Java's TCP/IP support result in data conversions and checks that are not usually needed in high-performance computing. Another source of parallel overhead is the emphasis in Java on portability. This led to lowest-common-denominator facilities in the design of Java's networking support. A major problem is blocking I/O. This means, for example, that a read operation on a socket will block until data is available. Stalling the application is usually avoided in practice by creating a new thread to perform the read. Because a read operation can be applied to only one socket at a time, this leads to a cumbersome and nonscalable programming style with separate threads for each communication partner.

To remedy some of these deficiencies, (which were also affecting high-performance enterprise servers) new I/O facilities in the `java.nio` packages were introduced in Java 2 1.4. Because the Java specification has now been split into three separate versions (enterprise, core, and mobile), the core Java and enterprise Java APIs are no longer restricted to supporting only features that can be supported on the least capable devices. Results reported by Pugh and Sacco [PS04] indicate that the new facilities promise to provide sufficient performance to make Java a reasonable choice for high-performance computing in clusters.

The `java.nio` packages provide nonblocking I/O and selectors so that one thread can monitor several socket connections. The mechanism for this is a new abstraction, called a *channel,* that serves as an open connection to sockets, files, hardware devices, etc. A `SocketChannel` is used for communication over TCP or UDP connections. A program may read or write to or from a `SocketChannel` into a `ByteBuffer` using nonblocking operations. Buffers are another new abstraction introduced in Java 2 1.4. They are containers for linear, finite sequences of primitive types. They maintain a state containing a current position (along with some other information) and are accessed with "put" and "get" operations that put or get an element in the slot indicated by the current position. Buffers may be allocated as direct or indirect. The space for a direct buffer is allocated outside of the usual memory space managed by the JVM and subject to garbage collection. As a result, direct buffers are not moved by the garbage collector, and references to them can be passed to the system-level network software, eliminating a copying step by the JVM. Unfortunately, this comes at the price of more complicated programming, because put and get operations are not especially convenient to use. Typically, however, one would not use a `Buffer` for the main computation in the program, but would use a more convenient data structure such as an array that would be bulk copied to or from the `Buffer`.[6]

Many parallel programmers desire higher-level, or at least more familiar, communication abstractions than those supported by the standard packages in Java. Several groups have implemented MPI-like bindings for Java using various approaches. One approach uses the JNI (Java Native Interface) to bind to existing MPI libraries. JavaMPI [Min97] and mpiJava [BCKL98] are examples. Other approaches use new communication systems written in Java. These are not widely used and are in various states of availability. Some [JCS98] attempt to provide an

---

[6]Pugh and Sacco [PS04] have reported that it is actually more efficient to do bulk copies between buffers and arrays before a send than to eliminate the array and perform the calculation updates directly on the buffers using put and get.

MPI-like experience for the programmer following proposed standards described in [BC00], while others experiment with alternative models [Man]. An overview is given in [AJMJS02]. These systems typically use the old `java.io` because the `java.nio` package has only recently become available. An exception is the work reported by Pugh and Sacco [PS04]. Although they have not, at this writing, provided downloadable software, they describe a package providing a subset of MPI with performance measurements that suggests an optimistic outlook for the potential of Java with `java.nio` for high-performance computing in clusters. One can expect that in the near future more packages built on `java.nio` that simplify parallel programming will become available.

6.4.2   Collective Communication

When multiple (more than two) UEs participate in a single communication event, the event is called a *collective communication operation*. MPI, as a message-passing library, includes most of the major collective communication operations.

- **Broadcast.** A mechanism to send a single message to all UEs.

- **Barrier.** A point within a program at which all UEs must arrive before any UEs can continue. This is described earlier in this chapter with the other synchronization mechanisms, but it is mentioned again here because in MPI it is implemented as a collective communication.

- **Reduction.** A mechanism to take a collection of objects, one on each UE, and combine them into a single object on one UE (`MPI_Reduce`) or combine them such that the combined value is left on each of the UEs (`MPI_Allreduce`).

Of these, reduction is the most commonly used. It plays such an important role in parallel algorithms that it is included within most parallel programming APIs (including shared-memory APIs such as OpenMP). We will focus on reduction in this discussion because the communication patterns and techniques used with reduction are the same as those used with any of the global communication events.

Reduction.   A *reduction operation* reduces a collection of data items to a single data item by repeatedly combining the data items pairwise with a binary operator, usually one that is associative and commutative. Examples of reductions include finding the sum, product, or maximum of all elements in an array. In general, we can represent such an operation as the calculation of

$$v_0 \circ v_1 \circ \cdots \circ v_{m-1} \tag{6.1}$$

where $\circ$ is a binary operator. The most general way to implement a reduction is to perform the calculation serially from left to right, an approach that offers no potential for concurrent execution. If $\circ$ is associative, however, the calculation in Eq. 6.1 contains exploitable concurrency, in that partial results over subsets of $v_0, \cdots, v_{m-1}$ can be calculated concurrently and then combined. If $\circ$ is also commutative, the calculation can be not only regrouped, but also reordered, opening up additional possibilities for concurrent execution, as described later.

Not all reduction operators have these useful properties, however, and one question to be considered is whether the operator can be treated as if it were associative and/or commutative without significantly changing the result of the calculation. For example, floating-point addition is not strictly associative (because the finite precision with which numbers are represented can cause round-off errors, especially if the difference in magnitude between operands is large), but if all the data items to be added have roughly the same magnitude, it is usually close enough to associative to permit the parallelization strategies discussed next. If the data items vary considerably in magnitude, this may not be the case.

Most parallel programming environments provide constructs that implement reduction.

- MPI provides general-purpose functions `MPI_Reduce` and `MPI_Allreduce` as well as support for several common reduction operations (`MPI_MIN`, `MPI_MAX`, and `MPI_SUM`).

- OpenMP includes a `reduction` clause that can be applied on a parallel section or a workshare construct. It provides for addition, subtraction, multiplication, and a number of bitwise and logical operators.

As an example of a reduction, consider the MPI program in Fig. 6.16. This is a continuation of our earlier example where we used a barrier to enforce consistent timing (Fig. 6.3). The timing is measured for each UE independently. As an indication of the load imbalance for the program, it is useful to report the time as a minimum time, a maximum time, and an average time. We do this in Fig. 6.16 with three calls to `MPI_Reduce`—one with the `MPI_MIN` function, one with the `MPI_MAX` function, and one with the `MPI_SUM` function.

An example of reduction in OpenMP can be found in Fig. 6.17. This is an OpenMP version of the program in Fig. 6.16. The variables for the number of threads (`num_threads`) and the average time (`ave_time`) are declared prior to the parallel region so they can be visible both inside and following the parallel region. We use a `reduction` clause on the `parallel` pragma to indicate that we will be doing a reduction with the + operator on the variable `ave_time`. The compiler will create a local copy of the variable and initialize it to the value of the identity of the operator in question (zero for addition). Each thread sums its values into the local copy. Following the close of the parallel region, all the local copies are combined with the global copy to produce the final value.

Because we need to compute the average time, we need to know how many threads were used in the parallel region. The only way to safely determine the number of threads is by a call to the `omp_num_threads()` function inside the parallel region. Multiple writes to the same variable can interfere with each other, so we place the call to `omp_num_threads()` inside a `single` construct, thereby ensuring that only one thread will assign a value to the shared variable `num_threads`. A `single` in OpenMP implies a barrier, so we do not need to explicitly include one to make sure all the threads enter the timed code at the same time. Finally, note that we compute only the average time in Fig. 6.17 because min and max operators are not included in the C/C++ OpenMP version 2.0.

```
#include "mpi.h" // MPI include file
#include <stdio.h>

int main(int argc, char**argv) {
    int num_procs; // the number of processes in the group
     int ID; // a unique identifier ranging from 0 to (num_procs-1)
    double local_result;
    double time_init, time_final, time_elapsed;
    double min_time, max_time, ave_time;
//
// Initialize MPI and set up the SPMD program
//
    MPI_Init(&argc,&argv);
    MPI_Comm_rank(MPI_COMM_WORLD, &ID);
    MPI_Comm_size (MPI_COMM_WORLD, &num_procs);

//
// Ensure that all processes are set up and ready to go before timing
// runit()
//
    MPI_Barrier(MPI_COMM_WORLD);

    time_init = MPI_Wtime();

    runit(); // a function that we wish to time on each process

    time_final = MPI_Wtime();

    time_elapsed = time_final - time_init;

    MPI_Reduce (&time_elapsed, &min_time, 1, MPI_DOUBLE, MPI_MIN, 0,
                                        MPI_COMM_WORLD);
    MPI_Reduce (&time_elapsed, &max_time, 1, MPI_DOUBLE, MPI_MAX, 0,
                                        MPI_COMM_WORLD);
    MPI_Reduce (&time_elapsed, &ave_time, 1, MPI_DOUBLE, MPI_SUM, 0,
                                        MPI_COMM_WORLD);
    if (ID == 0){
       ave_time = ave_time /(double)num_procs;
       printf(" min, ave and max times (secs): %f, %f, %f\n",
              min_time, ave_time,max_time);
    }

     MPI_Finalize();
     return 0;
}
```

Figure 6.16: MPI program to time the execution of a function called `runit()`. We use `MPI_Reduce` to find minimum, maximum, and average runtimes.

Implementing reduction operations.   Most programmers will never implement their own reductions because the reduction mechanisms available with most parallel programming environments meet their needs. Java, however, does not provide a reduction operator, so Java programmers might need to implement their own parallel reductions. In any case, the algorithms used for reductions are instructive and well worth the effort to understand.

```
#include <stdio.h>
#include <omp.h> // OpenMP include file

extern void runit();

int main(int argc, char**argv) {
    int num_threads; // the number of processes in the group
    double ave_time=0.0;

#pragma omp parallel reduction(+ : ave_time) num_threads(10)
{
    double local_result;
    double time_init, time_final, time_elapsed;

// The single construct causes one thread to set the value of
// the num_threads variable. The other threads wait at the
// barrier implied by the single construct.
    #pragma omp single
        num_threads = omp_get_num_threads();

    time_init = omp_get_wtime();

    runit(); // a function that we wish to time on each process

    time_final = omp_get_wtime();

    time_elapsed = time_final - time_init;

    ave_time += time_elapsed;
}
    ave_time = ave_time/(double)num_threads;
    printf(" ave time (secs): %f\n", ave_time);
    return 0;
}
```

Figure 6.17: OpenMP program to time the execution of a function called `runit()`. We use a reduction clause to find sum of the runtimes.

We consider tree-based reductions in the following discussion. These are the simplest of the scalable parallel reduction algorithms and although not optimal, they expose most of the issues addressed in the more optimal reduction algorithms [CKP+93].

Serial computation. If the reduction operator is not associative, or cannot be treated as associative without significantly affecting the result, it will likely be necessary to perform the entire reduction serially in a single UE, as sketched in Fig. 6.18. If only one UE needs the result of the reduction, it is probably simplest to have that UE perform the operation; if all UEs need the result, the reduction operation can be followed by a broadcast operation to communicate the result to other UEs. For simplicity, the figure shows a situation in which there are as many UEs as data items. The solution can be extended to situations in which there are more data items than UEs, but the requirement that all the actual computation be done in a single UE still holds because of the lack of associativity. (Clearly this

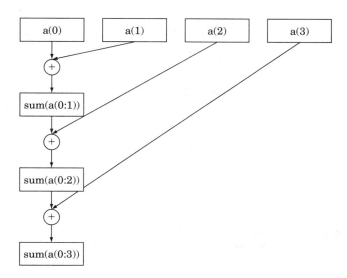

Figure 6.18: Serial reduction to compute the sum of `a(0)` through `a(3)`. `sum(a(i:j))` denotes the sum of elements `i` through `j` of array `a`.

solution completely lacks concurrency; we mention it for the sake of completeness and because it might still be useful and appropriate if the reduction operation represents only a relatively small part of a computation whose other parts *do* have exploitable concurrency.)

In this approach, the individual combine-two-elements operations must be performed in sequence, so it is simplest to have them all performed by a single task. Because of the data dependencies (indicated by the arrows in the figure), however, some caution is required if the reduction operation is performed as part of a larger calculation involving multiple concurrent UEs; the UEs not performing the reduction can continue with other work only if they can do so without affecting the computation of the reduction operation (for example, if multiple UEs share access to an array and one of them is computing the sum of the elements of the array, the others should not be simultaneously modifying elements of the array). In a message-passing environment, this can usually be accomplished using message passing to enforce the data-dependency constraints (that is, the UEs not performing the reduction operation send their data to the single UE actually doing the computation). In other environments, the UEs not performing the reduction operation can be forced to wait by means of a barrier.

Tree-based reduction.   If the reduction operator is associative or can be treated as such, then the tree-based reduction shown in Fig. 6.19 is appropriate. The algorithm proceeds through a series of stages; at each stage half the UEs pass their data to another UE. At the beginning, all of the UEs are actively involved in the reduction, but at each stage, half the UEs drop out, and finally we are left with a single UE holding the reduced value.

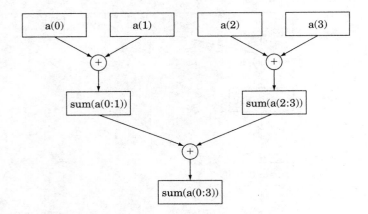

Figure 6.19: Tree-based reduction to compute the sum of a(0) through a(3) on a system with 4 UEs. sum(a(i:j)) denotes the sum of elements i through j of array a.

For simplicity, the figure shows the case where there are as many UEs as data items. The solution can be extended to situations in which there are more data items than UEs by first having each UE perform a serial reduction on a subset of the data items and then combining the results as shown. (The serial reductions, one per UE, are independent and can be done concurrently.)

In a tree-based reduction algorithm some, but not all, of the combine-two-elements operations can be performed concurrently (for example, in the figure, we can compute sum(a(0:1)) and sum(a(2:3)) concurrently, but the computation of sum(a(0:3)) must occur later). A more general sketch for performing a tree-based reduction using 2^n UEs similarly breaks down into n steps, with each step involving half as many concurrent operations as the previous step. As with the serial strategy, caution is required to make sure that the data dependencies shown in the figure are honored. In a message-passing environment, this can usually be accomplished by appropriate message passing; in other environments, it could be implemented using barrier synchronization after each of the n steps.

Using the tree-based reduction algorithm is particularly attractive if only one UE needs the result of the reduction. If other UEs also need the result, the reduction operation can be followed by a broadcast operation to communicate the result to other UEs. Notice that the broadcast is just the inverse of the reduction shown in Fig. 6.19; that is, at each stage, a UE passes the value to two UEs, thereby doubling the number of UEs with the broadcast value.

Recursive doubling. If all of the UEs must know the result of the reduction operation, then the recursive-doubling scheme of Fig. 6.20 is better than the tree-based approach followed by a broadcast.

As with the tree-based code, if the number of UEs is equal to 2^n, then the algorithm proceeds in n steps. At the beginning of the algorithm, every UE has some number of values to contribute to the reduction. These are combined locally to a single value to contribute to the reduction. In the first step, the even-numbered UEs

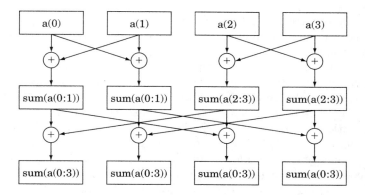

Figure 6.20: Recursive-doubling reduction to compute the sum of `a(0)` through `a(3)`. `sum(a(i:j))` denotes the sum of elements `i` through `j` of array `a`.

exchange their partial sums with their odd-numbered neighbors. In the second stage, instead of immediate neighbors exchanging values, UEs two steps away interact. At the next stage, UEs four steps away interact, and so forth, doubling the reach of the interaction at each step until the reduction is complete.

At the end of n steps, each UE has a copy of the reduced value. Comparing this to the previous strategy of using a tree-based algorithm followed by a broadcast, we see the following: The reduction and the broadcast take n steps each, and the broadcast cannot begin until the reduction is complete, so the elapsed time is $O(2n)$, and during these $2n$ steps many of the UEs are idle. The recursive-doubling algorithm, however, involves all the UEs at each step and produces the single reduced value at every UE after only n steps.

6.4.3   Other Communication Constructs

We have looked at only the most common message-passing constructs: point-to-point message passing and collective communication. There are many important variations in message passing. In MPI, it is possible to fine-tune performance by changing how the communication buffers are handled or to overlap communication and computation. Some of these mechanisms are described in the MPI appendix, Appendix B.

Notice that in our discussion of communication, there is a receiving UE and a sending UE. This is called *two-sided communication*. For some algorithms (as discussed in the *Distributed Array* pattern), the calculations involved in computing indices into a distributed data structure and mapping them onto the process owning the desired data can be very complicated and difficult to debug. Some of these problems can be avoided by using *one-sided communication*.

One-sided communication occurs when a UE manages communication with another UE without the explicit involvement of the other UE. For example, a message can be directly "put" into a buffer on another node without the involvement of the receiving UE. The MPI 2.0 standard includes a one-sided communication API. Another example of one-sided communication is an older system called GA or Global Arrays [NHL94, NHL96, NHK$^+$02, Gloa]. GA provides a simple one-sided communication environment specialized to the problem of distributed-array algorithms.

Another option is to replace explicit communication with a virtual shared memory, where the term "virtual" is used because the physical memory could be distributed. An approach that was popular in the early 1990s was Linda [CG91]. Linda is based on an associative virtual shared memory called a tuple space. The operations in Linda "put", "take", or "read" a set of values bundled together into an object called a *tuple*. Tuples are accessed by matching against a template, making the memory content-addressable or *associative*. Linda is generally implemented as a coordination language, that is, a small set of instructions that extend a normal programming language (the so-called computation language). Linda is no longer used to any significant extent, but the idea of an associative virtual shared memory inspired by Linda lives on in JavaSpaces [FHA99].

More recent attempts to hide message passing behind a virtual shared memory are the collection of languages based on the Partitioned Global Address Space Model: UPC [UPC], Titanium [Tita], and Co-Array Fortran [Co]. These are explicitly parallel dialects of C, Java, and Fortran (respectively) based on a virtual shared memory. Unlike other shared-memory models, such as Linda or OpenMP, the shared memory in the Partitioned Global Address Space model is partitioned and includes the concept of affinity of shared memory to particular processors. UEs can read and write each others' memory and perform bulk transfers, but the programming model takes into account nonuniform memory access, allowing the model to be mapped onto a wide range of machines, from SMP to NUMA to clusters.

APPENDIX A

A Brief Introduction to OpenMP

A.1 CORE CONCEPTS
A.2 STRUCTURED BLOCKS AND DIRECTIVE FORMATS
A.3 WORKSHARING
A.4 DATA ENVIRONMENT CLAUSES
A.5 THE OpenMP RUNTIME LIBRARY
A.6 SYNCHRONIZATION
A.7 THE SCHEDULE CLAUSE
A.8 THE REST OF THE LANGUAGE

OpenMP [OMP] is a collection of compiler directives and library functions that are used to create parallel programs for shared-memory computers. OpenMP is combined with C, C++, or Fortran to create a multithreading programming language; that is, the language model is based on the assumption that the UEs are threads that share an address space.

The formal definition of OpenMP is contained in a pair of specifications, one for Fortran and the other for C and C++. They differ in some minor details, but for the most part, a programmer who knows OpenMP for one language can pick up the other language with little additional effort.

OpenMP is based on the fork/join programming model. An executing OpenMP program starts as a single thread. At points in the program where parallel execution is desired, the program *forks* additional threads to form a team of threads. The threads execute in parallel across a region of code called a *parallel region*. At the end of the parallel region, the threads wait until the full team arrives, and then they *join* back together. At that point, the original or *master* thread continues until the next parallel region (or the end of the program).

The goal of OpenMP's creators was to make OpenMP easy for application programmers to use. Ultimate performance is important, but not if it would make the language difficult for software engineers to use, either to create parallel programs or to maintain them. To this end, OpenMP was designed around two key concepts: *sequential equivalence* and *incremental parallelism*.

A program is said to be *sequentially equivalent* when it yields the same[1] results whether it executes using one thread or many threads. A sequentially equivalent program is easier to maintain and, in most cases, much easier to understand (and hence write).

---

[1]The results may differ slightly due to the nonassociativity of floating-point operations.

```
program simple
print *,"E pur si muove"
stop
end
```

```
#include <stdio.h>
int main()
{
    printf("E pur si muove \n");
}
```

Figure A.1: Fortran and C programs that print a simple string to standard output

Incremental parallelism refers to a style of parallel programming in which a program evolves from a sequential program into a parallel program. A programmer starts with a working sequential program and block by block finds pieces of code that are worthwhile to execute in parallel. Thus, parallelism is added incrementally. At each phase of the process, there is a working program that can be verified, greatly increasing the chances that the project will be successful.

It is not always possible to use incremental parallelism or to create sequentially equivalent OpenMP programs. Sometimes a parallel algorithm requires complete restructuring of the analogous sequential program. In other cases, the program is constructed from the beginning to be parallel and there is no sequential program to incrementally parallelize. Also, there are parallel algorithms that do not work with one thread and hence cannot be sequentially equivalent. Still, incremental parallelism and sequential equivalence guided the design of the OpenMP API and are recommended practices.

A.1 CORE CONCEPTS

We will start our review of the core concepts behind OpenMP by considering a simple program that prints a string to the standard output device. Fortran and C versions of this program are given in Fig. A.1.

We will write a version of this program that creates multiple threads, each of which will print "E pur si muove."[2]

OpenMP is an explicitly parallel programming language. The compiler doesn't guess how to exploit concurrency. Any parallelism expressed in a program is there because the programmer directed the compiler to "put it there". To create threads in OpenMP, the programmer designates blocks of code that are to run in parallel. This is done in C and C++ with the pragma

```
#pragma omp parallel
```

---

[2]These words are attributed to Giordano Bruno on February 16, 1600, as he was burned at the stake for insisting that the earth orbited the Sun. This Latin phrase roughly translates as "And nonetheless, it moves."

or in Fortran with the directive

```
C$OMP PARALLEL
```

Modern languages such as C and C++ are block structured. Fortran, however, is not. Hence, the Fortran OpenMP specification defines a directive to close the parallel block:

```
C$OMP END PARALLEL
```

This pattern is used with other Fortran constructs in OpenMP; that is, one form opens the structured block, and a matching form with the word END inserted after the OMP closes the block.

In Fig. A.2, we show parallel programs in which each thread prints a string to the standard output.

When this program executes, the OpenMP runtime system creates a number of threads, each of which will execute the instructions inside the parallel construct. If the programmer doesn't specify the number of threads to create, a default number is used. We will later show how to control the default number of threads, but for the sake of this example, assume it was set to three.

OpenMP requires that I/O be thread safe. Therefore, each output record printed by one thread is printed completely without interference from other threads. The output from the program in Fig. A.2 would then look like:

```
E pur si muove
E pur si muove
E pur si muove
```

In this case, each output record was identical. It is important to note, however, that although each record prints as a unit, the records can be interleaved in any

```
      program simple
C$OMP PARALLEL
      print *,"E pur si muove"
C$OMP END PARALLEL
      stop
      end
```

```
#include <stdio.h>
#include "omp.h"
int main()
{
#pragma omp parallel
    {
      printf("E pur si muove\n");
    }
}
```

Figure A.2: Fortran and C programs that print a simple string to standard output

```fortran
        program simple
        integer i
        i = 5
C$OMP PARALLEL
        print *,"E pur si muove",i
C$OMP END PARALLEL
        stop
        end
```

```c
#include <stdio.h>
#include "omp.h"

int main()
{
  int i=5;

  #pragma omp parallel
  {
    printf("E pur si muove %d\n",i);
  }
}
```

Figure A.3: Fortran and C programs that print a simple string to standard output

way, so a programmer cannot depend on the threads writing their records in a particular order.

OpenMP is a shared-memory programming model. The details of the memory model will be discussed later, but a good rule that holds in most cases is this: *A variable allocated prior to the parallel region is shared between the threads.* So the program in Fig. A.3 would print:

```
E pur si muove 5
E pur si muove 5
E pur si muove 5
```

If a variable is declared inside a parallel region, it is said to be *local* or *private* to a thread. In C, a variable declaration can occur in any block. In Fortran, however, declarations can only occur at the beginning of a subprogram.

Fig. A.4 shows a C program with a local variable. We have also included a call to a function called `omp_get_thread_num()`. This integer function is part of

```c
#include <stdio.h>
#include <omp.h>
int main()
{

  int i=5; // a shared variable

#pragma omp parallel
  {
    int c; // a variable local or private to each thread
    c = omp_get_thread_num();
    printf("c = %d, i = %d\n",c,i);
  }

}
```

Figure A.4: Simple program to show the difference between shared and local (or private) data

the OpenMP standard runtime library (described later in this appendix). It returns an integer unique to each thread that ranges from zero to the number of threads minus one. If we assume the default number of threads is three, then the following lines (interleaved in any order) will be printed:

```
c = 0, i = 5
c = 2, i = 5
c = 1, i = 5
```

The first value printed is the private variable, `c`, where each thread has its own private copy holding a unique value. The second variable printed, `i`, is shared, and thus all the threads display the same value for `i`.

In each of these examples, the runtime system is allowed to select the number of threads. This is the most common approach. It is possible to change the operating system's default number of threads to use with OpenMP applications by setting the `OMP_NUM_THREADS` environment variable. For example, on a Linux system with `csh` as the shell, to use three threads in our program, prior to running the program one would issue the following command:

```
setenv OMP_NUM_THREADS 3
```

The number of threads to be used can also be set inside the program with the `num_threads` clause. For example, to create a parallel region with three threads, the programmer would use the pragma

```
#pragma omp parallel num_threads(3)
```

In each of these cases, the number of threads should be thought of as a request for a certain number of threads. The system in certain circumstances may provide fewer threads than the number requested. Hence, if an algorithm must know the actual number of threads being used, the program must query the system for this number inside the parallel region. We discuss how to do this later when we describe OpenMP's runtime library.

A.2   STRUCTURED BLOCKS AND DIRECTIVE FORMATS

An *OpenMP construct* is defined to be a directive (or pragma) plus a block of code. Not just any block of code will do. It must be a *structured block;* that is, a block with one point of entry at the top and a single point of exit at the bottom.

An OpenMP program is not allowed to branch into or out of a structured block. To attempt to do so is a fatal error generally caught at compile time. Likewise, the structured block cannot contain a `return` statement. The only branch statements allowed are those that shut down the entire program (`STOP` in Fortran or `exit()` in C). When the structured block contains only a single statement, it is not necessary to include the brackets (in C) or the `end construct` directives.

As we saw in our simple example, an OpenMP directive in C or C++ has the form

```
#pragma omp directive-name [clause[ clause] ... ]
```

where `directive-name` identifies the construct and the optional clauses[3] modify the construct. Some examples of OpenMP pragmas in C or C++ follow:

```
#pragma omp parallel private(ii, jj, kk)
#pragma omp barrier
#pragma omp for reduction(+:result)
```

For Fortran, the situation is more complicated. We will consider only the simplest case, fixed-form[4] Fortran code. In this case, an OpenMP directive has the following form:

```
sentinel directive-name [clause[[,]clause] ... ]
```

where `sentinel` can be one of:

```
C$OMP
C!OMP
*!OMP
```

The rules concerning fixed-form source lines apply. Spaces within the constructs are optional, and continuation is indicated by a character in column six. For

---

[3]Throughout this appendix, we will use square brackets to indicate optional syntactic elements.

[4]Fixed form refers to the fixed-column conventions for statements in older versions of Fortran (Fortran77 and earlier).

example, the following three OpenMP directives are equivalent:

```
C$OMP PARALLEL DO PRIVATE(I,J)
```

```
*!OMP PARALLEL
*!OMP1 DOPRIVATE(I,J)
```

```
C!OMP PARALLEL DO PRIVATE(I,J)
```

A.3   WORKSHARING

When using the parallel construct alone, every thread executes the same block of statements. There are times, however, when we need different code to map onto different threads. This is called *worksharing*.

The most commonly used worksharing construct in OpenMP is the construct to split loop iterations between different threads. Designing a parallel algorithm around parallel loops is an old tradition in parallel programming [X393]. This style is sometimes called *loop splitting* and is discussed at length in the *Loop Parallelism* pattern. In this approach, the programmer identifies the most time-consuming loops in the program. Each loop is restructured, if necessary, so the loop iterations are largely independent. The program is then parallelized by mapping different groups of loop iterations onto different threads.

For example, consider the program in Fig. A.5. In this program, a computationally intensive function `big_comp()` is called repeatedly to compute results that

```fortran
program loop
real *8 answer, res
real *8 big_comp
integer i, N
N = 1000
answer = 0.0;
do i=1,N
   res = big_comp(i)
   call combine(answer, res)
end do
print *,answer
stop
end
```

```c
#include <stdio.h>
#define N 1000
extern void combine(double, double);
extern double big_comp(int);

int main() {
  int i;
  double answer, res;
  answer = 0.0;
  for (i=0;i<N;i++){
    res = big_comp(i);
    combine(answer,res);
  }
  printf("%f\n", answer);
}
```

Figure A.5: Fortran and C examples of a typical loop-oriented program

```
program loop                          #include <stdio.h>
real *8 answer, res(1000)             extern void combine(double, double);
real *8 big_comp                      extern double big_comp(int);
integer i, N                          #define N 1000
N = 1000
answer = 0.0;                         int main() {
do i=1,N                                int i;
  res(i) = big_comp(i)                  double answer, res[N];
end do                                  answer = 0.0;
                                        for(i=0;i<N;i++)
do i=1,N                                  res[i] = big_comp(i);
  call combine(answer,res(i))
end do                                  for (i=0;i<N;i++){
                                          combine(answer,res[i]);
print *,answer                          }
stop                                    printf("%f\n", answer);
end                                   }
```

Figure A.6: Fortran and C examples of a typical loop-oriented program. In this version of the program, the computationally intensive loop has been isolated and modified so the iterations are independent.

are then combined into a single global answer. For the sake of this example, we assume the following.

- The combine() routine does not take much time to run.

- The combine() function must be called in the sequential order.

The first step is to make the loop iterations independent. One way to accomplish this is shown in Fig. A.6. Because the combine() function must be called in the same order as in the sequential program, there is an extra ordering constraint introduced into the parallel algorithm. This creates a dependency between the iterations of the loop. If we want to run the loop iterations in parallel, we need to remove this dependency.

In this example, we've assumed the combine() function is simple and doesn't take much time. Hence, it should be acceptable to run the calls to combine() outside the parallel region. We do this by placing each intermediate result computed by big_comp() into an element of an array. Then the array elements can be passed to the combine() function in the sequential order in a separate loop. This code transformation preserves the meaning of the original program (that is, the results are identical between the parallel code and the original version of the program).

With this transformation, the iterations of the first loop are independent and they can be safely computed in parallel. To divide the loop iterations among multiple threads, an OpenMP *worksharing* construct is used. This construct assigns loop iterations from the immediately following loop onto a team of threads. Later we will discuss how to control the way the loop iterations are scheduled, but for now, we leave it to the system to figure out how the loop iterations are to be mapped onto the threads. The parallel versions are shown in Fig. A.7.

```
      program loop
      real *8 answer, res(1000)
      real *8 big_comp()
      integer i,N
      N = 1000
      answer = 0.0;
C$OMP PARALLEL
C$OMP DO
      do i=1,N
        res(i) = big_comp(i)
      end do
C$OMP END DO
C$OMP END PARALLEL

      do i=1,N
        call combine(answer,res)
      end do

      print *,answer
      stop
      end
```

```
#include <stdio.h>
#include <omp.h>
#define N 1000
extern void combine(double,double);
extern double big_comp(int);

int main() {
  int i;
  double answer, res[N];
  answer = 0.0;

  #pragma omp parallel
  {
    #pragma omp for
    for(i=0;i<N;i++) {
      res[i] = big_comp(i);
    }
  }

  for (i=0;i<N;i++){
    combine(answer,res[i]);
  }
  printf("%f\n", answer);
}
```

Figure A.7: Fortran and C examples of a typical loop-oriented program parallelized with OpenMP

The OpenMP `parallel` construct is used to create the team of threads. This is followed by the worksharing construct to split up loop iterations among the threads: a `DO` construct in the case of Fortran and a `for` construct for C/C++. The program runs correctly in parallel and preserves sequential equivalence because no two threads update the same variable and any operations (such as calls to the `combine()` function) that do not commute or are not associative are carried out in the sequential order. Notice that, according to the rules we gave earlier concerning the sharing of variables, the loop control variable `i` would be shared between threads. The OpenMP specification, however, recognizes that it never makes sense to share the loop control index on a parallel loop, so it automatically creates a private copy of the loop control index for each thread.

By default, there is an implicit barrier at the end of any OpenMP workshare construct; that is, all the threads wait at the end of the construct and only proceed after all of the threads have arrived. This barrier can be removed by adding a `nowait` clause to the worksharing construct:

```
#pragma omp for nowait
```

One should be very careful when using a `nowait` because, in most cases, these barriers are needed to prevent race conditions.

There are two other commonly used types of worksharing constructs in OpenMP: the `single` construct and the `sections` construct. The `single` construct defines a block of code that will be executed by the first thread that encounters the construct. The other threads skip the construct and wait at the implicit barrier at the end of the `single` (unless the `nowait` clause is used). We used this construct in the OpenMP reduction example in the *Implementation Mechanisms* design space. We needed to copy the number of threads used in a parallel region into a shared variable. To make sure only one thread wrote into this shared variable, we placed it in a `single` construct:

```
#pragma omp single
    num_threads = omp_get_num_threads();
```

The `sections` construct is used to set up a region of the program where distinct blocks of code are to be assigned to different threads. Each block is defined with a `section` construct. We do not use `sections` in any of our examples, so we will not discuss them in detail here.

Finally, it is very common in an OpenMP program to have a parallel construct immediately followed by a worksharing construct. For example, in Fig. A.7, we had

```
#pragma omp parallel
{
    #pragma omp for
    ...
}
```

As a shortcut, OpenMP defines a combined construct:

```
#pragma omp parallel for
    ...
```

This is identical to the case where the `parallel` and `for` constructs are placed within separate pragmas.

A.4 DATA ENVIRONMENT CLAUSES

OpenMP is a relatively simple API. Most of the challenges in working with OpenMP arise from the details of how data is shared between threads and how data initialization interacts with OpenMP. We will address some of the more common issues here, but to thoroughly understand the data environment associated with OpenMP, one should read the OpenMP specification [OMP]. Details of memory synchronization are discussed in the section on synchronization (Sec. 6.3) in the *Implementation Mechanisms* design space.

We begin by defining the terms we will use to describe the data environment in OpenMP. In a program, a *variable* is a container (or more concretely, a storage location in memory) bound to a name and holding a *value*. Variables can be read and written as the program runs (as opposed to *constants* that can only be read).

In OpenMP, the variable that is bound to a given name depends on whether the name appears prior to a parallel region, inside a parallel region, or following a parallel region. When the variable is declared prior to a parallel region, it is by default shared and the name is always bound to the same variable.

OpenMP, however, includes clauses that can be added to **parallel** and to the worksharing constructs to control the data environment. These clauses affect the variable bound to a name. A **private(list)** clause directs the compiler to create, for each thread, a *private* (or *local*) variable for each name included in the list. The names in the private list must have been defined and bound to shared variables prior to the parallel region. The initial values of these new private variables are undefined, so they must be explicitly initialized. Furthermore, after the parallel region, the value of a variable bound to a name appearing in a **private** clause for the region is undefined.

For example, in the *Loop Parallelism* pattern we presented a program to carry out a simple trapezoid integration. The program consists of a single main loop in which values of the integrand are computed for a range of x values. The x variable is a temporary variable set and then used in each iteration of the loop. Hence, any dependencies implied by this variable can be removed by giving each thread its own copy of the variable. This can be done simply with the **private (x)** clause, as shown in Fig. A.8. (The **reduction** clause in this example is discussed later.)

```c
#include <stdio.h>
#include <math.h>
#include <omp.h>

int main () {
   int i;
   int num_steps = 1000000;
   double x, pi, step, sum = 0.0;

   step = 1.0/(double) num_steps;

#pragma omp parallel for private(x) reduction(+:sum)
   for (i=0;i< num_steps; i++)
   {
      x = (i+0.5)*step;
      sum += 4.0/(1.0+x*x);
   }
   pi = step * sum;
   printf("pi %lf\n",pi);
   return 0;
}
```

Figure A.8: C program to carry out a trapezoid rule integration to compute $\int_0^1 \frac{4}{1+x^2}\,dx$

Several other clauses change how variables are shared between threads. The most commonly used ones follow.

- `firstprivate(list)`. Just as with `private`, for each name appearing in the list, a new private variable for that name is created for each thread. Unlike `private`, however, the newly created variables are initialized with the value of the variable that was bound to the name in the region of code preceding the construct containing the `firstprivate` clause. This clause can be used on both `parallel` and the worksharing constructs.

- `lastprivate(list)`. Once again, private variables for each thread are created for each name in the `list`. In this case, however, the value of the private variable from the sequentially last loop iteration is copied out into the variable bound to the name in the region following the OpenMP construct containing the `lastprivate` clause. This clause can only be used with the loop-oriented workshare constructs.

Variables generally can appear in the list of only a single data clause. The exception is with `lastprivate` and `firstprivate`, because it is quite possible that a private variable will need both a well-defined initial value and a value exported to the region following the OpenMP construct in question.

An example using these clauses is provided in Fig. A.9. We declare four variables private to each thread and assign values to three of them: h = 1, j = 2, and k = 0. Following the parallel loop, we print the values of h, j, and k. The variable k is well defined. As each thread executes a loop iteration, the variable k is incremented. It is therefore a measure of how many iterations each thread handled.

```c
#include <stdio.h>
#include <omp.h>
#define N 1000

int main()
{
   int h, i, j, k;
   h = 1; j = 2; k = 0;
#pragma omp parallel for private(h) firstprivate(j,k) \
                          lastprivate(j,k)
   for(i=0;i<N;i++) {
        k++;
        j = h + i; //ERROR: h, and therefore j, is undefined
   }

   printf("h = %d, j = %d, k = %d\n",h, j, k); //ERROR j and h
                                 //are undefined
}
```

Figure A.9: C program showing use of the `private`, `firstprivate`, and `lastprivate` clauses. This program is incorrect in that the variables h and j do not have well-defined values when the `printf` is called. Notice the use of a backslash to continue the OpenMP pragma onto a second line.

The value passed outside the loop because of the `lastprivate` clause is the value of k for whichever thread executed the sequentially last iteration of the loop (that is, the iteration for which i = 999). The values of both h and j are undefined, but for different reasons. The variable j is undefined because it was assigned the value from a sum with an uninitialized variable (h) inside the parallel loop. The problem with the variable h is more subtle. It was declared as a `private` variable, but its value was unchanged inside the parallel loop. OpenMP stipulates, however, that after a name appears in any of the private clauses, the variable associated with that name in the region of code following the OpenMP construct is undefined. Hence, the print statement following the `parallel for` does not have a well-defined value of h to print.

A few other clauses affect the way variables are shared, but we do not use them in this book and hence will not discuss them here.

The final clause we will discuss that affects how data is shared is the `reduction` clause. Reductions were discussed at length in the *Implementation Mechanisms* design space. A reduction is an operation that, using a binary, associative operator, combines a set of values into a single value. Reductions are very common and are included in most parallel programming environments. In OpenMP, the reduction clause defines a list of variable names and a binary operator. For each name in the list, a private variable is created and initialized with the value of the identity element for the binary operator (for example, zero for addition). Each thread carries out the reduction into its copy of the local variable associated with each name in the list. At the end of the construct containing the `reduction` clause, the local values are combined with the associated value prior to the OpenMP construct in question to define a single value. This value is assigned to the variable with the same name in the region following the OpenMP construct containing the reduction.

An example of a reduction was given in Fig. A.8. In the example, the `reduction` clause was applied with the + operator to compute a summation and leave the result in the variable `sum`.

Although the most common reduction involves summation, OpenMP also supports reductions in Fortran for the operators +, *, -, .AND., .OR., .EQV., .NEQV., MAX, MIN, IAND, IOR, and IEOR. In C and C++, OpenMP supports reduction with the standard C/C++ operators *, -, &, |, ^, &&, and ||. C and C++ do not include a number of useful intrinsic functions such as "min" or "max" within the language definition. Hence, OpenMP cannot provide reductions in such cases; if they are required, the programmer must code them explicitly by hand. More details about reduction in OpenMP are given in the OpenMP specification [OMP].

A.5   THE OpenMP RUNTIME LIBRARY

As much as possible, the syntax of OpenMP is expressed through compiler directives. Certain features of the language, however, can only be handled with runtime library functions. Of the functions within the runtime library, the most commonly used functions are the following.

- `omp_set_num_threads()` takes an integer argument and requests that the operating system provide that number of threads in subsequent parallel regions.

```
#include <stdio.h>
#include <omp.h>

int main() {

    int id, numb;

    omp_set_num_threads(3);

 #pragma omp parallel private (id, numb)
    {
     id = omp_get_thread_num();
     numb = omp_get_num_threads();
     printf(" I am thread %d out of %d \n",id,numb);
    }
}
```

Figure A.10: C program showing use of the most common runtime library functions

- `omp_get_num_threads()` (integer function) returns the actual number of threads in the current team of threads.

- `omp_get_thread_num()` (integer function) returns the ID of a thread, where the ID ranges from 0 to the number of threads minus 1. The thread with ID of 0 is the master thread.

- The lock functions create, use, and destroy locks. These are described later with the other synchronization constructs.

We provide a simple example of how these functions are used in Fig. A.10. The program prints the thread ID and the number of threads to the standard output. The output from the program in Fig. A.10 would look something like this:

```
I am thread 2 out of 3
I am thread 0 out of 3
I am thread 1 out of 3
```

The output records would be complete and nonoverlapping because OpenMP requires that the I/O libraries be thread-safe. Which thread prints its record when, however, is not specified, and any valid interleaving of the output records can occur.

A.6 SYNCHRONIZATION

Many OpenMP programs can be written using only the `parallel` and `parallel for` (`parallel do` in Fortran) constructs. There are algorithms, however, where one needs more careful control over how variables are shared. When multiple threads read and write shared data, the programmer must ensure that the threads do not interfere with each other, so that the program returns the same results regardless of how the threads are scheduled. This is of critical importance since as a multi-threaded program runs, any semantically allowed interleaving of the instructions could actually occur. Hence, the programmer must manage reads and writes to shared variables to ensure that threads read the correct value and that multiple threads do not try to write to a variable at the same time.

Synchronization is the process of managing shared resources so that reads and writes occur in the correct order regardless of how the threads are scheduled. The concepts behind synchronization are discussed in detail in the section on synchronization (Sec. 6.3) in the *Implementation Mechanisms* design space. Our focus here will be on the syntax and use of synchronization in OpenMP.

Consider the loop-based program in Fig. A.5 earlier in this chapter. We used this example to introduce worksharing in OpenMP, at which time we assumed the combination of the computed results (`res`) did not take much time and had to occur in the sequential order. Hence, it was no problem to store intermediate results in a shared array and later (within a serial region) combine the results into the final answer.

In the more common case, however, results of `big_comp()` can be accumulated in any order as long as the accumulations do not interfere. To make things more interesting, we will assume that the `combine()` and `big_comp()` routines are both time-consuming and take unpredictable and widely varying amounts of time to execute. Hence, we need to bring the `combine()` function into the parallel region and use synchronization constructs to ensure that parallel calls to the `combine()` function do not interfere.

The major synchronization constructs in OpenMP are the following.

- `flush` defines a synchronization point at which memory consistency is enforced. This can be subtle. Basically, a modern computer can hold values in registers or buffers that are not guaranteed to be consistent with the computer's memory at any given point. Cache coherency protocols guarantee that all processors ultimately see a single address space, but they do not guarantee that memory references will be up to date and consistent at every point in time. The syntax of `flush` is

```
#pragma omp flush [(list)]
```

where `list` is a comma-separated list of variables that need to be flushed. If the list is omitted, all variables visible to the calling thread will be flushed. Programmers only rarely need to call `flush` because it is automatically inserted at most points where it is needed. Typically it is needed only by programmers building their own low-level synchronization primitives.

- `critical` implements a critical section for mutual exclusion. In other words, only one thread at a time will execute the structured block within a critical section. The other threads will wait their turn at the top of the construct.

The syntax of a critical section is

```
#pragma omp critical [(name)]
{ a structured block }
```

where **name** is an identifier that can be used to support disjoint sets of critical sections. A critical section implies a call to **flush** on entry to and on exit from the critical section.

- **barrier** provides a synchronization point at which the threads wait until every member of the team has arrived before any threads continue. The syntax of a barrier is

```
#pragma omp barrier
```

A barrier can be added explicitly, but it is also implied where it makes sense (such as at the end of parallel or worksharing constructs). A barrier implies a flush.

Critical sections, barriers, and flushes are discussed further in the *Implementation Mechanisms* design space.

Returning to our example in Fig. A.5, we can safely include the call to the **combine()** routine inside the parallel loop if we enforce mutual exclusion. We will do this with the **critical** construct as shown in Fig. A.11. Notice that we had to create a private copy of the variable **res** to prevent conflicts between iterations of the loop.

```
#include <stdio.h>
#include <omp.h>
#define N 1000
extern void combine(double,double);
extern double big_comp(int);

int main() {
   int i;
   double answer, res;
   answer = 0.0;
#pragma omp parallel for private (res)
   for (i=0;i<N;i++){
      res = big_comp(i);
#pragma omp critical
      combine(answer,res);
   }
   printf("%f\n", answer);
}
```

Figure A.11: Parallel version of the program in Fig. A.5. In this case, however, we assume that the calls to combine() can occur in any order as long as only one thread at a time executes the function. This is enforced with the critical construct.

For most programmers, the high-level synchronization constructs in OpenMP are sufficient. There are cases, however, where the high-level synchronization constructs cannot be used. Two common cases where this situation comes up are the following.

- The synchronization protocols required by a problem cannot be expressed with OpenMP's high-level synchronization constructs.

- The parallel overhead incurred by OpenMP's high-level synchronization constructs is too large.

To address these problems, the OpenMP runtime library includes low-level synchronization functions that provide a lock capability. The prototypes for lock functions are included in the `omp.h` include file. The locks use an opaque data type `omp_lock_t` defined in the `omp.h` include file. The key functions follow.

- `void omp_init_lock(omp_lock_t *lock)`. Initialize the lock.

- `void omp_destroy_lock(omp_lock_t *lock)`. Destroy the lock, thereby freeing any memory associated with the lock.

- `void omp_set_lock(omp_lock_t *lock)`. Set or acquire the lock. If the lock is free, then the thread calling `omp_set_lock()` will acquire the lock and continue. If the lock is held by another thread, the thread calling `omp_set_lock()` will wait on the call until the lock is available.

- `void omp_unset_lock(omp_lock_t *lock)`. Unset or release the lock so some other thread can acquire it.

- `int omp_test_lock(omp_lock_t *lock)`. Test or inquire if the lock is available. If it is, then the thread calling this function will acquire the lock and continue. The test and acquisition of the lock is done atomically. If it is not, the function returns false (nonzero) and the calling thread continues. This function is used so a thread can do useful work while waiting for a lock.

The lock functions guarantee that the lock variable itself is consistently updated between threads, but do not imply a flush of other variables. Therefore, programmers using locks must call **flush** explicitly as needed. An example of a program using OpenMP locks is shown in Fig. A.12. The program declares and then initializes the lock variables at the beginning of the program. Because this occurs prior to the parallel region, the lock variables are shared between the threads. Inside the parallel region, the first lock is used to make sure only one thread at a time tries to print a message to the standard output. The lock is needed to ensure that the two **printf** statements are executed together and not interleaved with those of other threads. The second lock is used to ensure that only one thread at a time executes the `go_for_it()` function, but this time, the `omp_test_lock()` function is used so a thread can do useful work while waiting for the lock. After the parallel region completes, the memory associated with the locks is freed by a call to `omp_lock_destroy()`.

```
#include <stdio.h>
#include <omp.h>

extern void do_something_else(int); extern void go_for_it(int);

int main() {
   omp_lock_t lck1, lck2; int id;

   omp_init_lock(&lck1);
   omp_init_lock(&lck2);

#pragma omp parallel shared(lck1, lck2) private(id)
   {
      id = omp_get_thread_num();

      omp_set_lock(&lck1);
      printf("thread %d has the lock \n", id);
      printf("thread %d ready to release the lock \n", id);
      omp_unset_lock(&lck1);

      while (! omp_test_lock(&lck2)) {

        do_something_else(id); // do something useful while waiting
                               // for the lock
      }
      go_for_it(id); // Thread has the lock

      omp_unset_lock(&lck2);
   }
   omp_destroy_lock(&lck1);
   omp_destroy_lock(&lck2);
}
```

Figure A.12: Example showing how the lock functions in OpenMP are used

A.7 THE SCHEDULE CLAUSE

The key to performance in a loop-based parallel algorithm is to schedule the loop iterations onto threads such that the load is balanced between threads. OpenMP compilers try to do this for the programmer. Although compilers are excellent at managing data dependencies and are very effective at generic optimizations, they do a poor job of understanding, for a particular algorithm, memory access patterns and how execution times vary from one loop iteration to the next. To get the best performance, programmers need to tell the compiler how to divide the loop iterations among the threads.

This is accomplished by adding a **schedule** clause to the **for** or **do** worksharing constructs. In both C and Fortran, the schedule clause takes the form

```
schedule( sched [,chunk])
```

where `sched` is either `static`, `dynamic`, `guided`, or `runtime` and `chunk` is an optional integer parameter.

- `schedule (static [,chunk])`. The iteration space is divided into blocks of size `chunk`. If `chunk` is omitted, then the block size is selected to provide one approximately equal-sized block per thread. The blocks are dealt out to the threads that make up a team in a round-robin fashion. For example, a chunk size of 2 for 3 threads and 12 iterations will create 6 blocks containing iterations (0,1), (2,3), (4,5), (6,7), (8,9), and (10,11) and assign them to threads as [(0,1), (6,7)] to one thread, [(2,3), (8,9)] to another thread and [(4,5), (10,11)] to the last thread.

- `schedule(dynamic [,chunk])`. The iteration space is divided into blocks of size `chunk`. If `chunk` is omitted, the block size is set to 1. Each thread is initially given one block of iterations to work with. The remaining blocks are placed in a queue. When a thread finishes with its current block, it pulls the next block of iterations that need to be computed off the queue. This continues until all the iterations have been computed.

- `schedule(guided [,chunk])`. This is a variation of the dynamic schedule optimized to decrease scheduling overhead. As with dynamic scheduling, the loop iterations are divided into blocks, and each thread is assigned one block initially and then receives an additional block when it finishes the current one. The difference is the size of the blocks: The size of the first block is implementation-dependent, but large; block size is decreased rapidly for subsequent blocks, down to the value specified by `chunk`. This method has the benefits of the `dynamic` schedule, but by starting with large block sizes, the number of scheduling decisions at runtime, and hence the parallel overhead, is greatly reduced.

- `schedule(runtime)`. The `runtime` schedule stipulates that the actual schedule and chunk size for the loop is to be taken from the value of the environment variable `OMP_SCHEDULE`. This lets a programmer try different schedules without having to recompile for each trial.

Consider the loop-based program in Fig. A.13. Because the `schedule` clause is the same for both Fortran and C, we will only consider the case for C. If the runtime associated with different loop iterations changes unpredictably as the program runs, a static schedule is probably not going to be effective. We will therefore use the dynamic schedule. Scheduling overhead is a serious problem, however, so to minimize the number of scheduling decisions, we will start with a block size of 10 iterations per scheduling decision. There are no firm rules, however, and OpenMP programmers usually experiment with a range of schedules and chunk sizes until the optimum values are found. For example, parallel loops in programs such as the one in Fig. A.13 can also be effectively scheduled with a static schedule as long as the chunk size is small enough that work is equally distributed among threads.

```
#include <stdio.h>
#include <omp.h>
#define N 1000
extern void combine(double,double);
extern double big_comp(int);

int main() {
    int i;
    double answer, res;
    answer = 0.0;
#pragma omp parallel for private(res) schedule(dynamic,10)
  for (i=0;i<N;i++){
      res = big_comp(i);
#pragma omp critical
      combine(answer,res);
  }
  printf("%f\n", answer);
}
```

Figure A.13: Parallel version of the program in Fig. A.11, modified to show the use of the schedule clause

A.8 THE REST OF THE LANGUAGE

This discussion has addressed only the features of OpenMP used in this book. Although we have covered the most commonly used constructs in OpenMP, a programmer interested in working with the OpenMP language should obtain the complete specification [OMP]. The definition of the full API is only 50 pages of text. The specification also includes more than 25 pages of examples. A book about the language is available [CDK+00], and a description of the abstractions behind OpenMP and some ideas about future directions are presented in [Mat03]. There is a growing body of literature about OpenMP; many OpenMP applications are described in the proceedings of the various OpenMP workshops [VJKT00, EV01, EWO01].

A Brief Introduction to MPI

B.1 CONCEPTS
B.2 GETTING STARTED
B.3 BASIC POINT-TO-POINT MESSAGE PASSING
B.4 COLLECTIVE OPERATIONS
B.5 ADVANCED POINT-TO-POINT MESSAGE PASSING
B.6 MPI AND FORTRAN
B.7 CONCLUSION

MPI (Message Passing Interface) is the standard programming environment for distributed-memory parallel computers. The central construct in MPI is message passing: One process[1] packages information into a message and sends that message to another process. MPI, however, includes far more than simple message passing. MPI includes routines to synchronize processes, sum numbers distributed among a collection of processes, scatter data across a collection of processes, and much more.

MPI was created in the early 1990s to provide a common message-passing environment that could run on clusters, MPPs, and even shared-memory machines. MPI is distributed in the form of a library, and the official specification defines bindings for C and Fortran, although bindings for other languages have been defined as well. The overwhelming majority of MPI programmers today use MPI version 1.1 (released in 1995). The specification of an enhanced version, MPI 2.0, with parallel I/O, dynamic process management, one-sided communication, and other advanced features was released in 1997. Unfortunately, it was such a complex addition to the standard that at the time this is being written (more than six years after the standard was defined), only a handful of MPI implementations support MPI 2.0. For this reason, we will focus on MPI 1.1 in this discussion.

There are several implementations of MPI in common use. The two most common are LAM/MPI [LAM] and MPICH [MPI]. Both may be downloaded free of charge and are straightforward to install using the instructions that come with them. They support a wide range of parallel computers, including Linux clusters, NUMA computers, and SMPs.

B.1 CONCEPTS

The basic idea of passing a message is deceptively simple: One process sends a message and another one receives it. Digging deeper, however, the details behind

---

[1] The UEs are processes in MPI.

message passing become much more complicated: How are messages buffered within the system? Can a process do useful work while it is sending or receiving messages? How can messages be identified so that sends are always paired with their intended receives?

The long-term success of MPI is due to its elegant solution to these (and other) problems. The approach is based on two core elements of MPI: *process groups* and a *communication context*. A process group is a set of processes involved in a computation. In MPI, all the processes involved in the computation are launched together when the program starts and belong to a single group. As the computation proceeds, however, the programmer can divide the processes into subgroups and precisely control how the groups interact.

A *communication context* provides a mechanism for grouping together sets of related communications. In any message-passing system, messages must be labeled so they can be delivered to the intended destination or destinations. The message labels in MPI consist of the ID of the sending process, the ID of the intended receiver, and an integer tag. A receive statement includes parameters indicating a source and tag, either or both of which may be wild cards. The result, then, of executing a receive statement at process i is the delivery of a message with destination i whose source and tag match those in the receive statement.

While straightforward, identifying messages with source, destination, and tag may not be adequate in complex applications, particularly those that include libraries or other functions reused from other programs. Often, the application programmer doesn't know any of the details about this borrowed code, and if the library includes calls to MPI, the possibility exists that messages in the application and the library might accidentally share tags, destinations IDs, and source IDs. This could lead to errors when a library message is delivered to application code, or vice versa. One way to deal with this problem is for library writers to specify reserved tags that users must avoid in their code. This approach has proved cumbersome, however, and is prone to error because it requires programmers to carefully read and follow the instructions in the documentation.

MPI's solution to this problem is based on the notion of *communication contexts*.[2] Each send (and its resulting message) and receive belong to a communication context, and only those communication events that share a communication context will match. Hence, even if messages share a source, a destination, and a tag, they will not be confused with each other as long as they have different contexts. Communication contexts are dynamically created and guaranteed to be unique.

In MPI, the process group and communication context are combined into a single object called a *communicator*. With only a few exceptions, the functions in MPI include a reference to a communicator. At program startup, the runtime system creates a common communicator called

```
MPI_COMM_WORLD
```

---

[2]The Zipcode message passing library [SSD+94] was the only message-passing library in use prior to MPI that included distinct communication contexts.

In most cases, MPI programmers only need a single communicator and just use `MPI_COMM_WORLD`. While creating and manipulating communicators is straightforward, only programmers writing reusable software components need to do so. Hence, manipulating communicators is beyond the scope of this discussion.

B.2   GETTING STARTED

The MPI standard does not mandate how a job is started, so there is considerable variation between different MPI implementations and in different situations (for example, jobs started interactively versus jobs started by a batch scheduler). For starting a job interactively with MPI 1.1, the most common method launches all the processes involved in the MPI program together on nodes obtained from a list in a configuration file. All processes execute the same program. The command that accomplishes this is usually called `mpirun` and takes the name of the program as a parameter. Unfortunately, the MPI standard does not define the interface to `mpirun`, and it varies between MPI implementations. Details can be found in each implementation's documentation [LAM, MPI].

All MPI programs include a few basic elements. Consider the program in Fig. B.1.

We will explore the elements of MPI required to turn this into a parallel program where multiple processes execute the function. First, the function prototypes for MPI need to be defined. This is done with the MPI include file:

```
#include <mpi.h>
```

Next, the MPI environment must be initialized. As part of the initialization, the communicator shared by all the processes is created. As mentioned earlier, this is called `MPI_COMM_WORLD`:

```
MPI_Init(&argc, &argv);
```

The command-line arguments are passed into `MPI_Init` so the MPI environment can influence the behavior of the program by adding its own command-line

```
#include <stdio.h>
int main(int argc, char **argv) {
    printf("\n Never miss a good chance to shut up \n");
}
```

Figure B.1: Program to print a simple string to standard output

```
#include <stdio.h>
#include "mpi.h"

int main(int argc, char **argv) {
    int num_procs; // the number of processes in the group
    int ID; // a unique identifier ranging from 0 to (num_procs-1)

    if (MPI_Init(&argc, &argv) != MPI_SUCCESS) {
      // print error message and exit
    }

    MPI_Comm_size (MPI_COMM_WORLD, &num_procs);
    MPI_Comm_rank (MPI_COMM_WORLD, &ID);
    printf("\n Never miss a good chance to shut up %d \n",ID);

    MPI_Finalize();
}
```

Figure B.2: Parallel program in which each process prints a simple string to the standard output

arguments (transparently to the programmer). This function returns an integer status flag used to indicate success or failure of the function call. With very few exceptions, all MPI functions return this flag. Possible values of this flag are described in the MPI include file, `mpi.h`.

Although not required, almost every MPI program uses the number of processes in the group and the rank[3] of each process in the group to guide the computation, as described in the *SPMD* pattern. This information is found through calls to the functions `MPI_Comm_size` and `MPI_Comm_rank`:

```
int num_procs; // the number of processes in the group
int ID;// a unique identifier ranging from 0 to (num_procs-1)

MPI_Comm_size(MPI_COMM_WORLD, &num_procs);
MPI_Comm_rank(MPI_COMM_WORLD, &ID);
```

When the MPI program finishes running, the environment needs to be cleanly shut down. This is done with this function:

```
MPI_Finalize();
```

Using these elements in our simple example program, we arrive at the parallel program in Fig. B.2.

---

[3]The *rank* is an integer ranging from zero to the number of processes in the group minus one. It indicates the position of each process within the process group.

If at any point within a program a fatal condition is detected, it might be necessary to shut down the program. If this is not done carefully, processes can be left on some of the nodes. These processes, called *orphan processes*, can in principle stay around "forever" waiting for interaction with other processes within the group. The following function tells the MPI runtime environment to make a best-effort attempt to shut down all the processes in the MPI program:

```
MPI_Abort();
```

B.3   BASIC POINT-TO-POINT MESSAGE PASSING

The point-to-point message-passing routines in MPI send a message from one process to another. There are more than 21 functions in MPI 1.1 for point-to-point communication. This large set of message-passing functions provides the controls needed to optimize the use of communication buffers and specify how communication and computation overlap.

The most commonly used message-passing functions in MPI 1.1 are the blocking send/receive functions defined in Fig. B.3. The MPI_Send() function returns

```
int MPI_Send (buff, count, MPI_type, dest, tag, Comm);

int MPI_Recv (buff, count, MPI_type, source, tag, Comm, &stat);
```

buff	Pointer to a buffer with a type compatible with MPI_type.
int count	The number of items of the indicated type contained in buff.
MPI_type	The type of the items in the buffers. The most commonly used types are MPI_DOUBLE, MPI_INT, MPI_LONG, and MPI_FLOAT.
int source	The rank for the process sending the message. The constant MPI_ANY_SOURCE can be used by MPI_Recv to accept a message from any source.
int dest	The rank of the process receiving the message.
int tag	An integer to identify the message involved in the communication. The constant MPI_ANY_TAG is a wild card that matches with any tag value.
MPI_Status stat	A structure holding status information on receipt of the message.
MPI_COMM COMM	The MPI communicator; this is usually the default MPI_COMM_WORLD.

Figure B.3: The standard blocking point-to-point communication routines in the C binding for MPI 1.1

when the buffer (`buff`) has been transmitted into the system and can safely be reused. On the receiving side, the `MPI_Recv()` function returns when the buffer (`buff`) has received the message and is ready to use.

The `MPI_Status` data type is defined in `mpi.h`. The status variable is used to characterize a received message. If `MPI_ANY_TAG` was used by `MPI_Recv()`, for example, the actual tag for the message can be extracted from the status variables as `status.MPI_TAG`.

The program in Fig. B.4 provides an example of how to use the basic message-passing functions. In this program, a message is bounced between two processes.

```
#include <stdio.h> // standard I/O include file
#include "memory.h" // standard include file with function
                    // prototypes for memory management
#include "mpi.h" // MPI include file

int main(int argc, char **argv) {
  int Tag1 = 1; int Tag2 = 2; // message tags
  int num_procs; // the number of processes in the group
  int ID; // a unique identifier ranging from 0 to (num_procs-1)
  int buffer_count = 100; // number of items in message to bounce
  long *buffer; // buffer to bounce between processes
  int i;
  MPI_Status stat; // MPI status parameter

  MPI_Init(&argc,&argv); // Initialize MPI environment
  MPI_Comm_rank(MPI_COMM_WORLD, &ID); // Find Rank of this
                                      // process in the group
  MPI_Comm_size (MPI_COMM_WORLD, &num_procs); // Find number of
                                              // processes in the group

  if (num_procs != 2) MPI_Abort(MPI_COMM_WORLD, 1);

  buffer = (long *)malloc(buffer_count* sizeof(long));

  for (i=0; i<buffer_count; i++) // fill buffer with some values
    buffer[i] = (long) i;

  if (ID == 0) {
    MPI_Send (buffer, buffer_count, MPI_LONG, 1, Tag1,
              MPI_COMM_WORLD);
    MPI_Recv (buffer, buffer_count, MPI_LONG, 1,
              Tag2, MPI_COMM_WORLD, &stat);
  }
  else {
    MPI_Recv (buffer, buffer_count, MPI_LONG, 0, Tag1,
              MPI_COMM_WORLD,&stat);
    MPI_Send (buffer, buffer_count, MPI_LONG, 0, Tag2,
              MPI_COMM_WORLD);
  }

  MPI_Finalize();
}
```

Figure B.4: MPI program to "bounce" a message between two processes using the standard blocking point-to-point communication routines in the C binding to MPI 1.1

This program (sometimes called a "ping pong" program) is frequently used as a performance metric for communication systems in parallel computers.

The program opens with the regular include files and declarations. We initialize MPI as the first executable statement in the program. This could be done later, the only firm requirement being that initialization must occur before any MPI routines are called. Next, we determine the rank of each process and the size of the process group. To keep the example short and simple, the program has been written assuming there will only be two processes in the group. We verify this fact (aborting the program if necessary) and then allocate memory to hold the buffer.

The communication itself is split into two parts. In the process with rank equal to 0, we send and then receive. In the other process, we receive and then send. Matching up sends and receives in this way (sending and then receiving on one side of a pairwise exchange of messages while receiving and then sending on the other) can be important with blocking sends and large messages. To understand the issues, consider a problem where two processes (ID 0 and ID 1) both need to send a message (from buffer **outgoing**) and receive a message (into buffer **incoming**). Because this is an SPMD program, it is tempting to write this as

```
int neigh; // the rank of the neighbor process

If (ID == 0) neigh = 1; else neigh = 0;

MPI_Send (outgoing, buffer_count, MPI_LONG, neigh, Tag1,
        MPI_COMM_WORLD);

// ERROR: possibly deadlocking program
MPI_Recv (incoming, buffer_count, MPI_LONG, neigh, Tag2,
        MPI_COMM_WORLD, &stat);
```

This code is simple and compact. Unfortunately, in some cases (large message sizes), the system can't free up the system buffers used to send the message until they have been copied into the incoming buffer on the receiving end of the communication. Because the sends block until the system buffers can be reused, the receive functions are never called and the program deadlocks. Hence, the safest way to write the previous code is to split up the communications as we did in Fig. B.4.

B.4   COLLECTIVE OPERATIONS

In addition to the point-to-point message-passing routines, MPI includes a set of operations in which all the processes in the group work together to carry out a complex communication. These collective communication operations are extremely important in MPI programming. In fact, many MPI programs consist primarily of collective operations and completely lack pairwise message passing.

The most commonly used collective operations include the following.

- **MPI_Barrier**. A barrier defines a synchronization point at which all processes must arrive before any of them are allowed to proceed. For MPI, this means that every process using the indicated communicator must call the barrier function before any of them proceed. This function is described in detail in the *Implementation Mechanisms* design space.

- **MPI_Bcast.** A broadcast sends a message from one process to all the processes in a group.

- **MPI_Reduce.** A reduction operation takes a set of values (in the buffer pointed to by `inbuff`) spread out around a process group and combines them using the indicated binary operation. To be meaningful, the operation in question must be associative. The most common examples for the binary function are summation and finding the maximum or minimum of a set of values. Notice that the final reduced value (in the buffer pointed to by `outbuff`) is only available in the indicated destination process. If the value is needed by all processes, there is a variant of this routine called `MPI_All_reduce()`. Reductions are described in detail in the *Implementation Mechanisms* design space.

The syntax of these functions is defined in Fig. B.5.

In Figs. B.6 and B.7 we present a program that uses these three functions. In this program, we wish to time a function that passes a message around a ring of processes. The code for the ring communication function is not relevant for this discussion, but for completeness, we provide it in Fig. B.8. The runtime for any parallel program is the time taken by the slowest process. So we need to find the

```
int MPI_Barrier (COMM);

int MPI_Bcast (outbuff, count, MPI_type, source, COMM);

int MPI_Reduce (inbuff, outbuff, count, MPI_type, OP, dest, COMM);
```

`inbuff, outbuff`	Pointers to buffers with a type compatible with `MPI_type`.
`int count`	The number of items of the indicated type contained in buff.
`MPI_type`	The type of the items in the buffers as defined in `mpi.h`.
`int source`	The rank for the process sending the message.
`int dest`	The process that will hold the final output value from the reduction.
`MPI_COMM COMM`	The MPI communicator; this is usually the default `MPI_COMM_WORLD`.
`OP`	The operation used in the reduction as defined in `mpi.h`. Common values are `MPI_MIN`, `MPI_MAX`, and `MPI_SUM`.

Figure B.5: The major collective communication routines in the C binding to MPI 1.1 (`MPI_Barrier`, `MPI_Bcast`, and `MPI_Reduce`)

```
//
// Ring communication test.
// Command-line arguments define the size of the message
// and the number of times it is shifted around the ring:
//
// a.out msg_size num_shifts
//
#include "mpi.h"
#include <stdio.h>
#include <memory.h>

int main(int argc, char **argv) {
  int num_shifts = 0; // number of times to shift the message
  int buff_count = 0; // number of doubles in the message
  int num_procs = 0; // number of processes in the ring
  int ID; // process (or node) id
  int buff_size_bytes; // message size in bytes
  int i;

  double t0; // wall-clock time in seconds
  double ring_time; // ring comm time - this process
  double max_time; // ring comm time - max time for all processes
  double *x; // the outgoing message
  double *incoming; // the incoming message

  MPI_Status stat;

// Initialize the MPI environment
  MPI_Init(&argc,&argv);
  MPI_Comm_rank(MPI_COMM_WORLD, &ID);
  MPI_Comm_size(MPI_COMM_WORLD, &num_procs);

// Process, test, and broadcast input parameters
  if(ID == 0){
     if (argc != 3){
        printf("Usage: %s <size of message> <Num of shifts> \n",*argv);
        fflush(stdout);
        MPI_Abort(MPI_COMM_WORLD, 1);
     }
     buff_count = atoi(*++argv); num_shifts = atoi(*++argv);

     printf(": shift %d doubles %d times \n",buff_count, num_shifts);
     fflush(stdout);
  }

// Continued in the next figure
```

Figure B.6: Program to time the `ring` function as it passes messages around a ring of processes (continued in Fig. B.7). The program returns the time from the process that takes the longest elapsed time to complete the communication. The code to the `ring` function is not relevant for this example, but it is included in Fig. B.8.

time consumed in each process and then find the maximum across all the processes. The time is measured using the standard MPI timing function:

```
double MPI_Wtime();
```

```
// Continued from the previous figure

// Broadcast data from rank 0 process to all other processes
  MPI_Bcast (&buff_count, 1, MPI_INT, 0, MPI_COMM_WORLD);
  MPI_Bcast (&num_shifts, 1, MPI_INT, 0, MPI_COMM_WORLD);

// Allocate space and fill the outgoing ("x") and "incoming" vectors.
  buff_size_bytes = buff_count * sizeof(double);

  x = (double*)malloc(buff_size_bytes);
  incoming = (double*)malloc(buff_size_bytes);

  for(i=0;i<buff_count;i++){
     x[i] = (double) i;
     incoming[i] = -1.0;
  }

// Do the ring communication tests.
  MPI_Barrier(MPI_COMM_WORLD);

  t0 = MPI_Wtime();
  /* code to pass messages around a ring */
  ring (x,incoming,buff_count,num_procs,num_shifts,ID);
  ring_time = MPI_Wtime() - t0;

// Analyze results
  MPI_Barrier(MPI_COMM_WORLD);

  MPI_Reduce(&ring_time, &max_time, 1, MPI_DOUBLE, MPI_MAX, 0,
                                    MPI_COMM_WORLD);
  if(ID == 0){
    printf("\n Ring test took %f seconds", max_time);
  }
  MPI_Finalize();
}
```

Figure B.7: Program to time the `ring` function as it passes messages around a ring of processes (continued from Fig. B.6)

MPI_Wtime() returns the time in seconds since some arbitrary point in the past. Usually the time interval of interest is computed by calling this function twice.

This program begins as most MPI programs do, with declarations, MPI initialization, and finding the rank and number of processes. We then process the command-line arguments to determine the message size and number of times to shift the message around the ring of processes. Every process will need these values, so the MPI_Bcast() function is called to broadcast these values.

We then allocate space for the outgoing and incoming vectors to be used in the ring test. To produce consistent results, every process must complete the initialization before any processes enter the timed section of the program. This is guaranteed by calling the MPI_Barrier() function just before the timed section of code. The time function is then called to get an initial time, the ring test itself is called, and then the time function is called a second time. The difference between

```
/****************************************************************
NAME: ring
PURPOSE: This function does the ring communication, with the
         odd numbered processes sending then receiving while the even
         processes receive and then send.
         The sends are blocking sends, but this version of the ring
         test still is deadlock-free since each send always has a
         posted receive.
 ****************************************************************/
#define IS_ODD(x) ((x)%2) /* test for an odd int */
#include "mpi.h"
 ring(
         double *x, /* message to shift around the ring */
         double *incoming, /* buffer to hold incoming message */
         int buff_count, /* size of message */
         int num_procs, /* total number of processes */a
         int num_shifts, /* numb of times to shift message */
         int my_ID) /* process id number */
{
   int next; /* process id of the next process */
   int prev; /* process id of the prev process */
   int i;
   MPI_Status stat;
/****************************************************************
** In this ring method, odd processes snd/rcv and even processes
rcv/snd.
 ****************************************************************/
   next = (my_ID +1 )%num_procs;
   prev = ((my_ID==0)?(num_procs-1):(my_ID-1));
   if( IS_ODD(my_ID) ){

      for(i=0;i<num_shifts; i++){
        MPI_Send (x, buff_count, MPI_DOUBLE, next, 3,
                MPI_COMM_WORLD);
         MPI_Recv (incoming, buff_count, MPI_DOUBLE, prev, 3,
                MPI_COMM_WORLD, &stat);
      }
   }
   else{
      for(i=0;i<num_shifts; i++){
        MPI_Recv (incoming, buff_count, MPI_DOUBLE, prev, 3,
                MPI_COMM_WORLD, &stat);
         MPI_Send (x, buff_count, MPI_DOUBLE, next, 3,
                MPI_COMM_WORLD);
      }
   }
}
```

Figure B.8: Function to pass a message around a ring of processes. It is deadlock-free because the sends and receives are split between the even and odd processes.

these two calls to the time functions is the elapsed time this process spent passing messages around the ring.

The total runtime for an MPI program is given by the time required by the slowest processor. So to report a single number for the time, we need to determine

```
int MPI_Isend(outbuff, count, MPI_type, dest, tag, MPI_COMM, request);

int MPI_Irecv (inbuff, count, MPI_type, source, tag, MPI_COMM, request);

int MPI_Wait(request, status);

int MPI_Test(request, flag, status);
```

`inbuff, outbuff`	Pointers to a buffer with a type compatible with `MPI_type`.
`int count`	The number of items of the indicated type contained in `buff`.
`MPI_type`	The type of the items in the buffers as defined in `mpi.h`.
`int source`	The rank for the process sending the message.
`int tag`	A label for the message.
`int dest`	The process that will hold the final output value from the reduction.
`MPI_COMM COMM`	The MPI communicator; this is usually the default `MPI_COMM_WORLD`.
`MPI_Request request`	A handle used to interact with the communication.
`int flag`	A flag set to nonzero (true) if the message has completed.

Figure B.9: The nonblocking or asynchronous communication functions

the maximum of the times taken by each processors. We do this with a single call to `MPI_Reduce()` with `MPI_MAX`.

B.5   ADVANCED POINT-TO-POINT MESSAGE PASSING

Most MPI programmers use only the standard point-to-point message-passing functions. MPI includes additional message-passing functions, however, giving programmers more control over the details of the communication. Probably the most important of these advanced message-passing routines are the *nonblocking* or *asynchronous* communication functions.

Nonblocking communication can sometimes be used to decrease parallel overhead by overlapping computation and communication. The nonblocking communication functions return immediately, providing "request handles" that can be waited on and queried. The syntax of these functions is presented in Fig. B.9. To understand how these functions are used, consider the program in Fig. B.10.

After initializing the MPI environment, memory is allocated for the field (`U`) and the buffers used to communicate the edges of `U` (`B` and `inB`). The ring communication pattern is then established for each process by computing the IDs for the processes to the left and to the right. Entering the main processing loop, each iteration begins by posting the receive:

```
MPI_Irecv(inB, N, MPI_DOUBLE, left, i, MPI_COMM_WORLD, &req_recv);
```

```
#include <stdio.h>
#include <mpi.h>
// Update a distributed field with a local N by N block on each process
// (held in the array U). The point of this example is to show
// communication overlapped with computation, so code for other
// functions is not included.

#define N 100 // size of an edge in the square field.
void extern initialize(int, double*);
void extern extract_boundary(int, double*, double*);
void extern update_interior(int, double*);
void extern update_edge(int,double*, double*);

int main(int argc, char **argv) {
  double *U, *B, *inB;
  int i, num_procs, ID, left, right, Nsteps = 100;
  MPI_Status status;
  MPI_Request req_recv, req_send;

  // Initialize the MPI environment
  MPI_Init(&argc,&argv);
  MPI_Comm_rank(MPI_COMM_WORLD, &ID);
  MPI_Comm_size(MPI_COMM_WORLD, &num_procs);

  // allocate space for the field (U), and the buffers
  // to send and receive the edges (B, inB)
  U = (double*)malloc(N*N * sizeof(double));
  B = (double*)malloc(N * sizeof(double));
  inB = (double*)malloc(N * sizeof(double));

  // Initialize the field and set up a ring communication pattern
  initialize (N, U);
  right = ID + 1; if (right > (num_procs-1)) right = 0;
  left = ID - 1; if (left < 0 ) left = num_procs-1;

  // Iteratively update the field U
  for(i=0; i<Nsteps; i++){
    MPI_Irecv(inB, N, MPI_DOUBLE, left, i, MPI_COMM_WORLD, &req_recv);
    extract_boundary(N, U, B); //Copy the edge of U into B
    MPI_Isend(B, N, MPI_DOUBLE, right, i, MPI_COMM_WORLD, &req_send);
    update_interior(N, U);
    MPI_Wait(&req_recv, &status); MPI_Wait(&req_send, &status);
    update_edge(ID, inB, U);
  }
  MPI_Finalize();
}
```

Figure B.10: Program using nonblocking communication to iteratively update a field using an algorithm that requires only communication around a ring (shifting messages to the right)

The function returns as soon as the system sets up resources to hold the message incoming from the left. The handle `req_recv` provides a mechanism to inquire about the status of the communication. The edge of the field is then extracted and sent to the neighbor on the right:

```
MPI_Isend(B, N, MPI_DOUBLE, right, i, MPI_COMM_WORLD, &req_send);
```

While the communication is taking place, the program updates the interior of the field (the interior refers to that part of the update that does not require edge information from the neighboring processes). After that work is complete, each process must wait until the communication is complete

```
MPI_Wait(&req_send, &status);
MPI_Wait(&req_recv, &status);
```

at which point, the field edges are updated and the program continues to the next iteration.

Another technique for reducing parallel overhead in an MPI program is *persistent communication*. This approach is used when a problem is dominated by repeated use of a communication pattern. The idea is to set up the communication once and then use it multiple times to pass the actual messages. The functions used in persistent communication are

```
MPI_Send_init(outbuff, count, MPI_type, dest, tag, MPI_COMM, &request);
MPI_Recv_init(inbuff, count, MPI_type, src, tag, MPI_COMM, &request);
MPI_Start(&request);
MPI_Wait(&request, &status);
```

`MPI_Send_init` and `MPI_Recv_init` are called to set up the communication. A request handle is returned to manipulate the actual communication events. The communication is initiated with a call to `MPI_Start`, at which point, the process is free to continue with any computation. When no further work can be done until the communication is complete, the processes can wait on a call to `MPI_Wait`. A function using persistent communication for the ring communication pattern used in Fig. B.8 is shown in Fig. B.11.

In addition to nonblocking and persistent communication, MPI defines several communication modes corresponding to different ways the sends work with the communication buffers:

- **Standard mode** (`MPI_Send`). The standard MPI send; the send will not complete until the send buffer is empty and ready to reuse.

- **Synchronous mode** (`MPI_Ssend`). The send does not complete until after a matching receive has been posted. This makes it possible to use the communication as a pairwise synchronization event.

- **Buffered mode** (`MPI_Bsend`). User-supplied buffer space is used to buffer the messages. The send will complete as soon as the send buffer is copied to the system buffer.

```
/******************************************************************
NAME: ring_persistent
PURPOSE: This function uses the persistent communication request
         mechanism to implement the ring communication in MPI.
******************************************************************/

#include "mpi.h"
#include <stdio.h>

ring_persistent(
        double *x, /* message to shift around the ring */
        double *incoming, /* buffer to hold incoming message */
        int buff_count, /* size of message */
        int num_procs, /* total number of processes */
        int num_shifts, /* numb of times to shift message */
        int my_ID) /* process id number */
{
   int next; /* process id of the next process */
   int prev; /* process id of the prev process */
   int i;
   MPI_Request snd_req; /* handle to the persistent send */
   MPI_Request rcv_req; /* handle to the persistent receive */
   MPI_Status stat;

/******************************************************************
** In this ring method, first post all the sends and then pick up
** the messages with the receives.
******************************************************************/
   next = (my_ID +1 )%num_procs;
   prev = ((my_ID==0)?(num_procs-1):(my_ID-1));

   MPI_Send_init(x, buff_count, MPI_DOUBLE, next, 3,
                           MPI_COMM_WORLD, &snd_req);
   MPI_Recv_init(incoming, buff_count, MPI_DOUBLE, prev, 3,
                           MPI_COMM_WORLD, &rcv_req);
   for(i=0;i<num_shifts; i++){

     MPI_Start(&snd_req);
     MPI_Start(&rcv_req);

     MPI_Wait(&snd_req, &stat);
     MPI_Wait(&rcv_req, &stat);

   }
}
```

Figure B.11: Function to pass a message around a ring of processes using persistent communication

- **Ready mode** (`MPI_Rsend`). The send will transmit the message immediately under the assumption that a matching receive has already been posted (an erroneous program otherwise). On some systems, ready mode communication is more efficient.

Most of the MPI examples in this book use standard mode. We used the synchronous-mode communication to implement mutual exclusion in the

Implementation Mechanisms design space. Information about the other modes can be found in the MPI specification [Mesb].

B.6   MPI AND FORTRAN

The formal MPI definition includes language bindings for C and Fortran. Bindings for MPI and Java have been defined as well [BC00, Min97, BCKL98, AJMJS02]. Up

---

In C, a reduction is accomplished with the following function:

```
int MPI_Reduce (inbuff, outbuff, count, MPI_type, OP, dest, COMM);
```

`inbuff, outbuff`	Pointers to a buffer with a type compatible with `MPI_type`.
`int count`	The number of items of the indicated type contained in the buffer.
`MPI_type`	The type of the items in the buffers as defined in `mpi.h`.
`OP`	The operation used in the reduction as defined in `mpi.h`. Common values are `MPI_MIN`, `MPI_MAX`, and `MPI_SUM`.
`int dest`	The process that will hold the final output value from the reduction.
`MPI_COMM COMM`	The MPI communicator; this is usually the default `MPI_COMM_WORLD`.

The analogous routine in Fortran is the following subroutine:

```
subroutine MPI_REDUCE (inbuff, outbuff, count, MPI_type, OP, dest,
                       COMM, ierr)
```

`inbuff, outbuff`	Arrays of the appropriate size and type.
`integer count`	The number of items of the indicated type contained in the buffer.
`MPI_type`	The type of the items in the buffers as defined in `mpif.h`.
`OP`	The operation used in the reduction as defined in `mpif.h`. Common values are `MPI_MIN`, `MPI_MAX`, and `MPI_SUM`.
`integer dest`	The process that will hold the final output value from the reduction.
`MPI_COMM COMM`	The MPI communicator; this is usually the default `MPI_COMM_WORLD`.
`integer ierr`	An integer to hold the error code as defined in `mpif.h`.

Figure B.12: Comparison of the C and Fortran language bindings for the reduction routine in MPI 1.1

to this point, we have focused on C. Translating from C to Fortran, however, is straightforward and based on a few simple rules.

- The include file in Fortran containing constants, error codes, etc., is called `mpif.h`.

- MPI routines essentially have the same names in the two languages. Whereas the MPI functions in C are case-sensitive, the MPI subprograms in Fortran are case-insensitive.

- In every case except for the timing routines, Fortran uses subroutines while C uses functions.

- The arguments to the C functions and Fortran subroutines are the same with the obvious mappings onto Fortran's standard data types. There is one additional argument added to most Fortran subroutines. This is an integer parameter, `ierr`, that holds the MPI error return code.

For example, we show C and Fortran version of MPI's reduction routine in Fig. B.12.

Opaque objects (such as `MPI_COMM` or `MPI_Request`) are of type `INTEGER` in Fortran (with the exception of Boolean-valued variables, which are of type `LOGICAL`).

A simple Fortran program using MPI is shown in Fig. B.13. This program shows how the basic setup and finalization subroutines work in MPI Fortran. The direct analogy with the MPI C language binding should be clear from this figure. Basically, if a programmer understands MPI with one language, then he or she knows MPI for the other language. The basic constructs are the same between language bindings; however, programmers must be careful when mixing Fortran-MPI and C-MPI because the MPI specifications do not guarantee interoperability between languages.

```fortran
program firstprog
include "mpif.h"
integer ID, Nprocs, ierr

call MPI_INIT( ierr )
call MPI_COMM_RANK ( MPI_COMM_WORLD, ID, ierr)
call MPI_COMM_SIZE ( MPI_COMM_WORLD, Nprocs, ierr )

print *, "Process ", ID, " out of ", Nprocs

call MPI_FINALIZE( ierr )

end
```

Figure B.13: Simple Fortran MPI program where each process prints its ID and the number of processes in the computation

B.7 CONCLUSION

MPI is by far the most commonly used API for parallel programming. It is often called the "assembly code" of parallel programming. MPI's low-level constructs are closely aligned to the MIMD model of parallel computers. This allows MPI programmers to precisely control how the parallel computation unfolds and write highly efficient programs. Perhaps even more important, this lets programmers write *portable* parallel programs that run well on shared-memory machines, massively parallel supercomputers, clusters, and even over a grid.

Learning MPI can be intimidating. It is huge, with more than 125 different functions in MPI 1.1. The large size of MPI does make it complex, but most programmers avoid this complexity and use only a small subset of MPI. Many parallel programs can be written with just six functions: `MPI_Init`, `MPI_Comm_Size`, `MPI_Comm_Rank`, `MPI_Send`, `MPI_Recv`, and `MPI_Finalize`. Good sources of more information about MPI include [Pac96], [GLS99], and [GS98]. Versions of MPI are available for most computer systems, usually in the form of open-source software readily available on-line. The most commonly used versions of MPI are LAM/MPI [LAM] and MPICH [MPI].

A Brief Introduction to Concurrent Programming in Java

Java is an object-oriented programming language that provides language support for expressing concurrency in shared-memory programs. Java's support for polymorphism can be exploited to write frameworks directly supporting some of the patterns described in this book. The framework provides the infrastructure for the pattern; the application programmer adds subclasses containing the application-specific code. An example is found in the Examples section of the *Pipeline* pattern. Because Java programs are typically compiled to an intermediate language called Java bytecode, which is then compiled and/or interpreted on the target machine, Java programs enjoy a high degree of portability.

Java can also be used for distributed computing, and the standard libraries provide support for several mechanisms for interprocess communication in distributed systems. A brief overview of these is given in the *Implementation Mechanisms* design space. In addition, there is an ever-growing collection of packages that allow concurrency and interprocess communication to be expressed at higher levels than with the facilities provided by the language and core packages. Currently, the most common type of applications that exploit Java's facilities for concurrency are multithreaded server-side applications, graphical user interfaces, and programs that are naturally distributed due to their use of data and/or resources in different locations.

The performance available from current implementations of Java is not as good as that from programming languages more typically used in high-performance scientific computing. However, the ubiquity and portability of Java, along with the language support for concurrency, make it an important platform. For many people,

```
/*class holding two objects of arbitrary type providing swap and
accessor methods. The generic type variable name is enclosed in
angle brackets*/

class Pair<Gentype>
//Gentype is a type variable
{ private Gentype x,y;
  void swap(){Gentype temp = x; x=y; y=temp;}
  public Gentype getX(){return x;}
  public Gentype getY(){return y;}
  Pair(Gentype x, Gentype y){this.x = x; this.y = y;}
  public String toString(){return "(" + x + "," + y + ")";}

}

/*The following method, defined in some class, instantiates two
Pair objects, replacing the type variable in angle brackets with
the actual type the object should contain. */

  public static void test()
  { /*create a Pair holding Strings.*/
    Pair<String> p1 = new Pair<String>("hello","goodbye");

    /*create a Pair holding Integers. Autoboxing automatically
    creates Integer objects from the given int parameters,
    saving the programmer from writing
    new Pair<Integer>(new Integer(1), new Integer(2));*/
    Pair<Integer> p2 = new Pair<Integer>(1,2);

    /*do something with the Pairs.*/
    System.out.println(p1); p1.swap(); System.out.println(p1);
    System.out.println(p2); p2.swap(); System.out.println(p2);
  }
```

Figure C.1: A class holding pairs of objects of an arbitrary type. Without generic types, this would have been done by declaring x and y to be of type Object, requiring casting the returned values of getX and getY. In addition to less-verbose programs, this allows type errors to be found by the compiler rather than throwing a ClassCastException at runtime.

a Java program may be their first concurrent program. In addition, continually improving compiler technology and libraries should reduce the performance gap in the future.

In this appendix, we describe Java 2 1.5[1] [Java], which, compared with earlier versions, includes several additions to the programming language and standard libraries. Additions to the programming language include support for generic types, autoboxing (which provides automatic conversion between primitive and object types such as int and Integer), and enhanced for loops. The example in Fig. C.1 illustrates generic types, the only language addition used in this book.

Java 2 1.5 also provides significantly enhanced support for concurrent programming via several changes in the java.lang and java.util packages and the

---

[1]The version available at press time was J2SE 1.5.0 Beta 1.

introduction of new packages `java.util.concurrent`, `java.util.concurrent.`
`atomic`, and `java.util.concurrent.locks`. A new, more precise specification of
the memory model has also been incorporated. The facilities for concurrent programming are described in [JSRb, JSRc] and the new memory model is described
in [JSRa].

It isn't feasible to give a complete introduction to Java in this appendix.
Hence, we assume that the reader has some familiarity with the language and focus
on those aspects that are most relevant to shared-memory parallel programming,
including new features introduced in Java 2 1.5. Introductions to Java and its
(pre-Java 2 1.5) libraries can be found in [AGH00, HC02, HC01]. An excellent discussion of concurrent programming in Java is [Lea00a].

C.1   CREATING THREADS

In Java, an application always has at least one thread, the one that executes the
main method. A new thread is created by instantiating and starting a `thread`
object; the code to be executed is provided in a `run` method, as described later.
A thread terminates when its `run` method returns. A thread can be normal or
marked as a daemon thread. Each thread runs independently of the other threads
in an application, and the application terminates when all of its nondaemon threads
have terminated.

A thread can access all variables visible to its `run` method according to the
usual Java scope rules. Thus, by making variables visible to multiple threads, memory can be shared between them. By encapsulating variables, memory can be protected from access by other threads. In addition, a variable can be marked `final`,
which means that, once initialized, its value will not change. Provided the initialization is done properly, final variables can be accessed by multiple threads without
requiring synchronization. (However, marking a reference `final` does not guarantee immutability of the referenced object; care must be taken to ensure that it is
thread-safe as well.)

There are two different ways to specify the `run` method that a thread will
execute. One is to extend the `Thread` class and override its `run` method. Then, one
simply instantiates an object of the subclass and calls its inherited `start` method.
The more common approach is to instantiate a `Thread` object using the constructor that takes a `Runnable` object as a parameter. As before, invoking the `Thread`
object's `start` method begins the thread's execution. The `Runnable` interface contains a `public void run` method; the newly created thread executes the `Runnable`
object's `run` method. Because the `run` method is parameterless, information is typically passed to the thread via data members of the `Thread` subclass or the `Runnable`.
These are typically set in the constructor.

In the following example, the class `ThinkParallel` implements the `Runnable`
interface (that is, it declares that it implements the interface and provides a `public`
`void run()` method). The main method creates and starts four `Thread` objects.
Each of these is passed a `ThinkParallel` object, whose `id` field has been set to the
value of loop counter `i`. This causes four threads to be created, each executing the
`run` method of the `ThinkParallel` class.

```
class ThinkParallel implements Runnable
{
    int id; //thread-specific variable containing thread ID

    /*The run method defines the thread's behavior*/
    public void run()
    { System.out.println(id + ": Are we there yet?");
    }

    /*Constructor sets id*/
    ThinkParallel(int id){this.id = id;}

    /*main method instantiates and starts the threads*/
    public static void main(String[] args)

    { /*create and start 4 Thread objects,
        passing each a ThinkParallel object
      */

    for(int i = 0; i != 4; i++)
        { new Thread(new ThinkParallel(i)).start(); }
    }
}
```

Figure C.2: Program to create four threads, passing a `Runnable` in the `Thread` constructor. Thread-specific data is held in a field of the `Runnable` object.

C.1.1 Anonymous Inner Classes

A common programming idiom found in several of the examples uses an anonymous class to define the `Runnables` or `Threads` at the point where they are created. This often makes reading the source code more convenient and avoids file and class clutter. We show how to rewrite the example of Fig. C.2 using this idiom in Fig. C.3. Variables that are local to a method cannot be mentioned in an anonymous class unless declared `final`, and are thus immutable after being assigned a value. This is the reason for introducing the seemingly redundant variable j.

C.1.2 Executors and Factories

The `java.util.concurrent` package provides the `Executor` interface and its subinterface `ExecutorServices` along with several implementations. An `Executor` executes `Runnable` objects while hiding the details of thread creation and scheduling.[2] Thus, instead of instantiating a `Thread` object and passing it a `Runnable` to execute a task, one would instantiate an `Executor` object and then use the `Executor`'s `execute` method to execute the `Runnable`. For example, a `ThreadPoolExecutor` manages a pool of threads and arranges for the execution of submitted `Runnables` using one of the pooled threads. The classes implementing the interfaces provide adjustable parameters, but the `Executors` class provides factory methods that

---

[2]The `ExecutorServices` interface provides additional methods to manage thread termination and support `Futures`. The implementations of `Executor` in `java.util.concurrent` also implement the `ExecutorServices` interface.

```
class ThinkParallelAnon {

  /*main method instantiates and starts the threads*/

  public static void main(String[] args)

  { /*create and start 4 Thread objects,
      passing each a Runnable object defined by an anonymous class
    */

    for(int i = 0; i != 4; i++)
    { final int j = i;
       new Thread( new Runnable() //define Runnable objects
                                  // anonymously
                       { int id = j; //references
                         public void run()
                         { System.out.println(id + ":
                                       Are we there yet?");}
                       }
                 ).start();

    }
  }
}
```

Figure C.3: Program similar to the one in Fig. C.2, but using an anonymous class to define the `Runnable` object

create various `ExecutorService`s preconfigured for the most common scenarios. For example, the factory method `Executors.newCachedThreadPool()` returns an `ExecutorService` with an unbounded thread pool and automatic thread reclamation. This will attempt to use a thread from the pool if one is available, and, if not, create a new thread. Idle threads are removed from the pool after a certain amount of time. Another example is `Executors.newFixedThreadPool(int nThreads)`, which creates a fixed-size thread pool containing `nThreads` threads. It contains an unbounded queue for waiting tasks. Other configurations are possible, both using additional factory methods not described here and also by directly instantiating a class implementing `ExecutorService` and adjusting the parameters manually.

As an example, we could rewrite the previous example as shown in Fig. C.4. Note that to change to a different thread-management policy, we would only need to invoke a different factory method for the instantiation of the `Executor`. The rest of the code would remain the same.

The `run` method in the `Runnable` interface does not return a value and cannot be declared to throw exceptions. To correct this deficiency, the `Callable` interface, which contains a method `call` that throws an `Exception` and returns a result, was introduced. The interface definition exploits the new support for generic types. `Callable`s can arrange execution by using the `submit` method of an object that implements the `ExecutorService` interface. The `submit` method returns a `Future` object, which represents the result of an asynchronous computation. The `Future`

```
import java.util.concurrent.*;

class ThinkParalleln implements Runnable {

    int id; //thread-specific variable containing thread ID

    /*The run method defines the tasks behavior*/
    public void run()
    { System.out.println(id + ": Are we there yet?");
    }

    /*Constructor sets id*/
    ThinkParalleln(int id){this.id = id;}

    /*main method creates an Executor to manage the tasks*/
    public static void main(String[] args)

    { /*create an Executor using a factory method in Executors*/
      ExecutorService executor = Executors.newCachedThreadPool();

      // send each task to the executor
      for(int i = 0; i != 4; i++)
        { executor.execute(new ThinkParalleln(i)); }


      /*shuts down after all queued tasks handled*/
      executor.shutdown();

    }
}
```

Figure C.4: Program using a `ThreadPoolExecutor` instead of creating threads directly

object provides methods to check whether the computation is complete, to wait for completion, and to get the result. The type enclosed within angle brackets specifies that the class is to be specialized to that type.

As an example, we show in Fig. C.5 a code fragment in which the main thread submits an anonymous `Callable` to an `Executor`. The `Executor` arranges for the

```
/*execute a Callable that returns a Double.
The notation Future<Double> indicates a (generic) Future that
has been specialized to be a <Double>.
*/
Future<Double> future = executor.submit(
    new Callable<Double>() {
        public Double call() { return result_of_long_computation; }
});
do_something_else(); /* do other things while long
  computation proceeds in another thread */
try {
  Double d = (future.get()); /* get results of long
    computation, waiting if necessary*/
} catch (ExecutionException ex) { cleanup(); return; }
```

Figure C.5: Code fragment illustrating use of `Callable` and `Future`

call method to be executed in another thread. Meanwhile, the original thread performs some other work. When finished with the other work, it uses the get method to obtain the result of the Callable's execution. If necessary, the main thread will block on the get method until the result is available.

C.2   ATOMICITY, MEMORY SYNCHRONIZATION, AND THE volatile KEYWORD

The Java Virtual Machine (JVM) specification requires that reads and writes of all the primitive types, except long and double, be atomic. Thus, a statement such as done = true will not be interfered with by another thread. Unfortunately, as was explained in the *Implementation Mechanisms* design space, more than just atomicity is needed. We also need to ensure that the write is made visible to other threads and that values that are read are the freshest values. In Java, a variable marked volatile is guaranteed to have memory synchronized on each access. The volatile keyword applied to long and double guarantees, in addition, atomicity.

The java.util.concurrent.atomic package provides extended support for atomicity and memory synchronization. For example, the package includes a variety of classes that provide atomic compareAndSet operations on their types. On many systems, such operations can be implemented with a single machine instruction. Where it makes sense, other operations such as atomic increment may be provided. The package also provides array classes where the individual array elements have volatile semantics.[3] The classes in the java.util.concurrent.atomic package are only useful when critical updates for an object are limited to a single variable. As a result, they are most commonly used as building blocks for higher-level constructs.

The following code uses the getAndIncrement method of the AtomicLong class to implement a thread-safe sequencer. The getAndIncrement method atomically obtains the value of the variable, increments it, and returns the original value. Such a sequencer could be used to implement a task queue in some master/worker designs.

```
class Sequencer
{
  private AtomicLong sequenceNumber = new AtomicLong(0);
  public long next() { return sequenceNumber.getAndIncrement(); }
}
```

C.3   SYNCHRONIZED BLOCKS

When variables can be accessed by multiple threads, care must be taken to ensure that data-corrupting race conditions cannot occur. Java provides a construct called *synchronized blocks* to allow the programmer to ensure mutually exclusive access to shared variables. Synchronized blocks also serve as implicit memory fences, as described in the *Implementation Mechanisms* design space (Sec. 6.3).

---

[3]In the Java language, declaring an array to be volatile only makes the *reference* to the array volatile, not the individual elements.

Every class in a Java program is a direct or indirect subclass of class `Object`. Every `Object` instance implicitly contains a lock. A synchronized block is always associated with an object: Before a thread can enter a synchronized block, it must acquire the lock associated with that object. When the thread leaves the synchronized block, whether normally or because an exception was thrown, the lock is released. At most one thread can hold the lock at the same time, so synchronized blocks can be used to ensure mutually exclusive access to data. They are also used to synchronize memory.

A synchronized block is specified in code as

```
synchronized(object_ref){...body of block....}
```

The curly braces delimit the block. The code for acquiring and releasing the lock is generate by the compiler.

Suppose we add a variable `static int count` to the `ThinkParallel` class to be incremented by each thread after it prints its message. This is a static variable, so there is one per class (not one per object), and it is visible and thus shared by all the threads. To avoid race conditions, `count` could be accessed in a synchronized block.[4] To provide protection, all threads must use the same lock, so we use the object associated with the class itself. For any class `X`, `X.class` is a reference to the unique object representing class `X`, so we could write the following:

```
public void run()
{ System.out.println(id + ": Are we there yet?");
  synchronized(ThinkParallel.class){count++;}
}
```

It is important to emphasize that only synchronized blocks associated with the same object exclude each other. Two synchronized blocks associated with different objects could execute concurrently. For example, a common programming error would be to write the previous code as

```
public void run()
{ System.out.println(id + ": Are we there yet?");
  synchronized(this){count++;} //WRONG!
}
```

---

[4]Of course, for this particular situation, one could instead use an atomic variable as defined in the `java.util.concurrent.atomic` package.

In the buggy version, each thread would be synchronizing on the lock associated with the "self" or `this` object. This would mean that each thread locks a different lock (the one associated with the thread object itself) as it enters the synchronized block, so none of them would exclude each other. Also, a synchronized block does not constrain the behavior of a thread that references a shared variable in code that is not in a synchronized block. It is up to the programmer to carefully ensure that *all* mentions of shared variables are appropriately protected.

Special syntax is provided for the common situation in which the entire method body should be inside a synchronized block associated with the `this` object. In this case, the `synchronized` keyword is used to modify the method declaration. That is,

```
public synchronized void updateSharedVariables(...)
{....body.... }
```

is shorthand for

```
public void updateSharedVariables(...)
{ synchronized(this){....body....} }
```

C.4   WAIT AND NOTIFY

It is sometimes the case that a thread needs to check to see whether some condition holds. If it holds, then the thread should perform some action; if not, it should wait until some other thread established the condition. For example, a thread might check a buffer to see whether it contains an item. If it does, then an item is removed. If not, the thread should wait until a different thread has inserted one. It is important that checking the condition and performing the action be done atomically. Otherwise, one thread could check the condition (that is, find the buffer nonempty), another thread could falsify it (by removing the only item), and then the first thread would perform an action that depended on the condition (which no longer holds) and corrupt the program state. Thus, checking the condition and performing the action need to be placed inside a synchronized block. On the other hand, the thread cannot hold the lock associated with the synchronized block while waiting because this would block other threads from access, preventing the condition from ever being established. What is needed is a way for a thread waiting on a condition to release the lock and then, after the condition has been satisfied, reacquire the lock before rechecking the condition and performing its action. Traditional monitors [Hoa74] were proposed to handle this situation. Java provides similar facilities.

The `Object` class, along with the previously mentioned lock, also contains an implicit *wait set* that serves as a condition variable. The `Object` class provides

```
synchronized(lockObject)
{ while( ! condition ){ lockObject.wait();}
   action;
}
```

Figure C.6: Basic idiom for using wait. Because wait throws an InterruptedException, it should somehow be enclosed in a try-catch block, omitted here.

several versions of wait methods that cause the calling thread to implicitly release the lock and add itself to the wait set. Threads in the wait set are suspended and not eligible to be scheduled to run.

The basic idiom for using wait is shown in Fig. C.6. The scenario is as follows: The thread acquires the lock associated with lockObject. It checks condition. If the condition does not hold, then the body of the while loop, the wait method, is executed. This causes the lock to be released, suspends the thread, and places it in the wait set belonging to lockObject. If the condition does hold, the thread performs action and leaves the synchronized block. On leaving the synchronized block, the lock is released.

Threads leave the wait set in one of three ways. First, the Object class methods notify and notifyAll awaken one or all threads, respectively, in the wait set of that object. These methods are intended to be invoked by a thread that establishes the condition being waited upon. An awakened thread leaves the wait set and joins the threads waiting to reacquire the lock. The awakened thread will reacquire the lock before it continues execution. The wait method may be called without parameters or with timeout values. A thread that uses one of the timed wait methods (that is, one that is given a timeout value) may be awakened by notification as just described, or by the system at some point after the timeout has expired. Upon being reawakened, it will reacquire the lock and continue normal execution. Unfortunately, there is no indication of whether a thread was awakened by a notification or a timeout. The third way that a thread can leave the wait set is if it is interrupted. This causes an InterruptedException to be thrown, whereupon the control flow in the thread follows the normal rules for handling exceptions.

We now continue describing the scenario started previously for Fig. C.6, at the point at which the thread has waited and been awakened. When awakened by some other thread executing notify or notifyAll on lockObject (or by a timeout), the thread will be removed from the wait set. At some point, it will be scheduled for execution and will attempt to reacquire the lock associated with lockObject. After the lock has been reacquired, the thread will recheck the condition and either release the lock and wait again or, if the condition holds, execute action without releasing the lock.

It is the job of the programmer to ensure that waiting threads are properly notified after the condition has been established. Failure to do so can cause the program to stall. The following code illustrates using the notifyAll method after statements in the program that establish the condition:

```
synchronized(lockObject) {
  establish_the_condition;
  lockObject.notifyAll()
}
```

In the standard idiom, the call to `wait` is the body of a `while` loop. This ensures that the condition will always be rechecked before performing the action and adds a considerable degree of robustness to the program. One should never be tempted to save a few CPU cycles by changing the `while` loop to an `if` statement. Among other things, the `while` loop ensures that an extra `notify` method can never cause an error. Thus, as a first step, one can use `notifyAll` at any point that might possibly establish the condition. Performance of the program might be improved by careful analysis that would eliminate spurious `notifyAll`s, and in some programs, it may be possible to replace `notifyAll` with `notify`. However, these optimizations should be done carefully. An example illustrating these points is found in the *Shared Queue* pattern.

C.5   LOCKS

The semantics of synchronized blocks together with `wait` and `notify` have certain deficiencies when used in the straightforward way described in the previous section. Probably the worst problem is that there is no access to information about the state of the associated implicit lock. This means that a thread cannot determine whether or not a lock is available before attempting to acquire it. Further, a thread blocked waiting for the lock associated with a synchronized block cannot be interrupted.[5] Another problem is that only a single (implicit) condition variable is associated with each lock. Thus, threads waiting for different conditions to be established share a wait set, with `notify` possibly waking the wrong thread (and forcing the use of `notifyAll`).

For this reason, in the past many Java programmers implemented their own locking primitives or used third-party packages such as `util.concurrent` [Lea]. Now, the `java.util.concurrent.locks` package provides `ReentrantLock`,[6] which is similar to synchronized blocks, but with extended capabilities. The lock must be explicitly instantiated

```
//instantiate lock
private final ReentrantLock lock = new ReentrantLock();
```

---

[5] This is discussed further in the next section.

[6] A lock is reentrant if it can be acquired multiple times by the same thread without causing deadlock.

```
import java.util.*;
import java.util.concurrent.*;
import java.util.concurrent.locks.*;

class SharedQueue2 {
  class Node
  { Object task;
    Node next;

    Node(Object task)
    {this.task = task; next = null;}
  }

  private Node head = new Node(null);
  private Node last = head;

  Lock lock = new ReentrantLock();
  final Condition notEmpty = lock.newCondition();

  public void put(Object task)
  { //cannot insert null
    assert task != null: "Cannot insert null task";
    lock.lock();
    try{ Node p = new Node(task); last.next = p; last = p;
        notEmpty.signalAll();
    } finally{lock.unlock();}
  }

  public Object take()
  { //returns first task in queue, waits if queue is empty
    Object task = null;
    lock.lock();
    try {
    while (isEmpty())
      { try{ notEmpty.await(); }
        catch(InterruptedException error)
        { assert false:"sq2: no interrupts here";}
      }
    Node first = head.next; task = first.task; first.task = null;
    head = first;
    } finally{lock.unlock();}
    return task;
  }

  private boolean isEmpty(){return head.next == null;}
}
```

Figure C.7: A version of `SharedQueue2` (see the *Shared Queue* pattern) using a `Lock` and `Condition` instead of synchronized blocks with `wait` and `notify`

and should always be used in a try-catch block, such as

```
//critical section
lock.lock(); // block until lock acquired
try { critical_section }
finally { lock.unlock(); }
```

Other methods allow information about the state of the lock to be acquired. These locks trade syntactic convenience and a certain amount of support by the compiler (it is impossible for the programmer to forget to release the lock associated with a synchronized block) for greater flexibility.

In addition, the package provides implementations of the new `Condition` interface that implements a condition variable. This allows multiple condition variables to be associated with a single lock. A `Condition` associated with a lock is obtained by calling the lock's `newCondition` method. The analogues of `wait`, `notify`, and `notifyAll` are `await`, `signal`, and `signalAll`. An example of using these new classes to implement a shared queue (as described in the *Shared Queue* pattern) is shown in Fig. C.7.

C.6   OTHER SYNCHRONIZATION MECHANISMS AND SHARED DATA STRUCTURES

A comparison with OpenMP reveals that OpenMP has constructs analogous to synchronized blocks (locks and critical sections), but lacks features similar to `wait` and `notify`. This is because OpenMP offers higher-level constructs typically used in parallel programming rather than the more general approach in Java. One can easily implement a variety of higher-level constructs using the available features. Also, the `java.util.concurrent` package provides several higher-level synchronization primitives and shared data structures. The synchronization primitives include `CountDownLatch` (a simple single-use barrier that causes threads to block until a given number of threads have reached the latch), `CyclicBarrier` (a cyclic barrier that automatically resets when it has been passed and thus is convenient to use multiple times, for example, in a loop), and `Exchanger` (which allows two threads to exchange objects at a synchronization point). `CountDownLatch` and `CyclicBarrier` are also discussed in the *Implementation Mechanisms* design space in Sec. 6.3.2.

In Fig. C.8, we show a very simple loop-based program along with a parallel version in Fig. C.9. This is similar to the example in the OpenMP appendix, Appendix A.

```
class SequentialLoop {
   static int num_iters = 1000;
   static double[] res = new double[num_iters];
   static double answer = 0.0;

   static void combine(int i){.....}
   static double big_comp(int i){.....}

   public static void main(String[] args)
   { for (int i = 0; i < num_iters; i++){ res[i] = big_comp(i); }
     for (int i = 0; i < num_iters; i++){ combine(i);}
     System.out.println(answer));
   }
}
```

Figure C.8: Simple sequential loop-based program similar to the one in Fig. A.5

```
import java.util.concurrent.*;

class ParallelLoop {

    static ExecutorService exec;
    static CountDownLatch done;
    static int num_iters = 1000;
    static double[] res = new double[num_iters];
    static double answer = 0.0;

    static void combine(int i){.....}
    static double big_comp(int i){.....}

    public static void main(String[] args) throws InterruptedException
    { /*create executor with pool of 10 threads */
        exec = Executors.newFixedThreadPool(10);

        /*create and initialize the countdown latch*/
        done = new CountDownLatch(num_iters);

        long startTime = System.nanoTime();
        for (int i = 0; i < num_iters; i++)
        { //only final local vars can be referenced in an anonymous class
          final int j = i;
          /*pass the executor a Runnable object to execute the loop
          body and decrement the CountDownLatch */
          exec.execute(new Runnable(){
            public void run()
            { res[j] = big_comp(j);
              done.countDown(); /*decrement the CountDownLatch*/
            }
          });
        }
        done.await(); //wait until all tasks have completed

        /*combine results using sequential loop*/
        for (int i = 0; i < num_iters; i++){ combine(i); }
        System.out.println(answer);

        /*cleanly shut down thread pool*/
        exec.shutdown();
    }
}
```

Figure C.9: Program showing a parallel version of the sequential program in Fig. C.8 where each iteration of the big_comp loop is a separate task. A thread pool containing ten threads is used to execute the tasks. A CountDownLatch is used to ensure that all of the tasks have completed before executing the (still sequential) loop that combines the results.

The java.util.concurrent package also provides several implementations of the *Shared Queue* pattern as well as some thread-safe Collection classes, including ConcurrentHashMap, CopyOnWriteArrayList, and CopyOnWriteArraySet.

C.7 INTERRUPTS

Part of the state of a thread is its interrupt status. A thread can be interrupted using the interrupt method. This sets the interrupt status of the thread to interrupted.

If the thread is suspended (that is, it has executed a `wait`, `sleep`, `join`, or other command that suspends the thread), the suspension will be interrupted and an `InterruptedException` thrown. Because of this, the methods that can cause blocking, such as `wait`, throw this exception, and thus must either be called from a method that declares itself to throw the exception, or the call must be enclosed within a try-catch block. Because the signature of the `run` method in class `Thread` and interface `Runnable` does not include throwing this exception, a try-catch block must enclose, either directly or indirectly, any call to a blocking method invoked by a thread. This does not apply to the main thread, because the `main` method can be declared to throw an `InterruptedException`.

The interrupt status of a thread can be used to indicate that the thread should terminate. To enable this, the thread's `run` method should be coded to periodically check the interrupt status (using the `isInterrupted` or the `interrupted` method); if the thread has been interrupted, the thread should return from its `run` method in an orderly way. `InterruptedExceptions` can be caught and the handler used to ensure graceful termination if the thread is interrupted when waiting. In many parallel programs, provisions to externally stop a thread are not needed, and the catch blocks for `InterruptedExceptions` can either provide debugging information or simply be empty.

The `Callable` interface was introduced as an alternative to `Runnable` that allows an exception to be thrown (and also, as discussed previously, allows a result to be returned). This interface exploits the support for generic types.

Glossary

- **Abstract data type (ADT).** A data type given by its set of allowed values and the available operations on those values. The values and operations are defined independently of a particular representation of the values or implementation of the operations. In a programming language that directly supports ADTs, the interface of the type reveals the operations on it, but the implementation is hidden and can (in principle) be changed without affecting clients that use the type. The classic example of an ADT is a stack, which is defined by its operations, typically including `push` and `pop`. Many different internal representations are possible.

- **Abstraction.** Abstraction can have several meanings depending on the context. In software, it often means combining a set of small operations or data items and giving them a name. For example, control abstraction takes a group of operations, combines them into a procedure, and gives the procedure a name. As another example, a class in object-oriented programming is an abstraction of both data and control. More generally, an abstraction is a representation that captures the essential character of an entity, but hides the specific details. Often we will talk about a named abstraction without concern for the actual details, which may not be determined.

- **Address space.** The range of memory locations that a process or processor can access. Depending on context, this could refer to either physical or virtual memory.

- **ADT.** See *abstract data type*.

- **Amdahl's law.** A law stating that (under certain assumptions, as described in Sec. 2.5) the maximum *speedup* that can be obtained by running an algorithm on a system of P processors is

$$S(P) = \frac{T(1)}{(\gamma + \frac{1-\gamma}{P}) \, T(1)}$$
$$= \frac{1}{\gamma + \frac{1-\gamma}{P}}$$

where γ is the *serial fraction* of the program, and $T(n)$ is the total execution time running on n processors. See *speedup* and *serial fraction*.

- **AND parallelism.** This is one of the main techniques for introducing parallelism into a logic language. Consider the goal `A: B,C,D` (read "A follows from B and C and D"), which means that goal `A` succeeds if and only if all three subgoals—B and C and D—succeed. In AND parallelism, subgoals B, C, and D are evaluated in parallel.

- **API.** See *application programming interface.*

- **Application Programming Interface (API).** An API defines the calling conventions and other information needed for one software module (typically an application program) to utilize the services provided by another software module. MPI is an API for parallel programming. The term is sometimes used more loosely to define the notation used by programmers to express a particular functionality in a program. For example, the OpenMP specification is referred to as an API. An important aspect of an API is that any program coded to it can be recompiled to run on any system that supports that API.

- **Atomic.** *Atomic* has slightly different meanings in different contexts. An atomic operation at the hardware level is uninterruptible, for example load and store, or atomic test-and-set instructions. In the database world, an atomic operation (or transaction) is one that appears to execute completely or not at all. In parallel programming, an atomic operation is one for which sufficient synchronization has been provided that it cannot be interfered with by other UEs. Atomic operations also must be guaranteed to terminate (for example, no infinite loops).

- **Autoboxing.** A language feature, available in Java 2 1.5, that provides automatic conversion of data of a primitive type to the corresponding wrapper type—for example, from `int` to `Integer`.

- **Bandwidth.** The capacity of a system, usually expressed as items per second. In parallel computing, the most common usage of the term "bandwidth" is in reference to the number of bytes per second that can be moved across a network link. A parallel program that generates relatively small numbers of huge messages may be limited by the bandwidth of the network, in which case it is called a *bandwidth-limited* program. See *bisection bandwidth.*

- **Barrier.** A synchronization mechanism applied to groups of UEs, with the property that no UE in the group can pass the barrier until all UEs in the group have reached the barrier. In other words, UEs arriving at the barrier suspend or block until all UEs have arrived; they can then all proceed.

- **Beowulf cluster.** A *cluster* built from PCs running the Linux operating system. Clusters were already well established when Beowulf clusters were first built in the early 1990s. Prior to Beowulf, however, clusters were built from workstations running UNIX. By dropping the cost of cluster hardware, Beowulf clusters dramatically increased access to cluster computing.

- **Bisection bandwidth.** The bidirectional capacity of a network between two equal-sized partitions of nodes. The cut across the network is taken at the narrowest point in each bisection of the network.

- **Broadcast.** Sending a message to all members of a group of recipients, usually all UEs participating in a computation.

- **Cache.** A relatively small region of memory that is local to a processor and is considerably faster than the computer's main memory. Cache hierarchies consisting of one or more levels of cache are essential in modern computer systems. Because processors are so much faster than the computer's main memory, a processor can run at a significant fraction of full speed only if the data can be loaded into cache before it is needed and that data can be reused during a calculation. Data is moved between the cache and the computer's main memory in small blocks of bytes called *cache lines*. An entire cache line is moved when any byte within the memory mapped to the cache line is accessed. Cache lines are removed from the cache according to some protocol when the cache becomes full and space is needed for other data, or when they are accessed by some other processor. Usually each processor has its own cache (though sometimes multiple processors share a level of cache), so keeping the caches coherent (that is, ensuring that all processors have the same view of memory through their distinct caches) is an issue that must be dealt with by computer architects and compiler writers. Programmers must be aware of caching issues when optimizing the performance of software.

- **ccNUMA.** Cache-coherent NUMA. A NUMA model where data is coherent at the level of the cache. See *NUMA*.

- **Cluster.** Any collection of distinct computers that are connected and used as a parallel computer, or to form a redundant system for higher availability. The computers in a cluster are not specialized to cluster computing and could, in principle, be used in isolation as standalone computers. In other words, the components making up the cluster, both the computers and the networks connecting them, are not custom-built for use in the cluster. Examples include Ethernet-connected workstation networks and rack-mounted workstations dedicated to parallel computing. See *workstation farm*.

- **Collective communication.** A high-level operation involving a group of UEs and having at its core the cooperative exchange of information between the UEs. The high-level operation might be a pure communication event (for example, a broadcast) or it might include some computation (for example, a reduction). See *broadcast, reduction*.

- **Concurrent execution.** A condition in which two or more UEs are active and making progress simultaneously. This can be either because they are being executed at the same time on different PEs, or because the actions of the UEs are interleaved on the same PE.

- **Concurrent program.** A program with multiple loci of control (threads, processes, etc.).

- **Condition variable.** Condition variables are part of the *monitor* synchronization mechanism. A condition variable is used by a process or thread to delay until the monitor's state satisfies some condition; it is also used to awaken a delayed process when the condition becomes true. Associated with each condition variable is a wait set of suspended (delayed) processes or threads. Operations on a condition variable include `wait` (add this process or thread to the wait set for this variable) and `signal` or `notify` (awaken a process or thread on the wait set for this variable). See *monitor*.

- **Copy on write.** A technique that ensures, using minimal synchronization, that concurrent threads will never see a data structure in an inconsistent state. To update the structure, a copy is made, modifications are made on the copy, and then the reference to the old structure is atomically replaced with a reference to the new. This means that a thread holding a reference to the old structure may continue to read an old (consistent) version, but no thread will ever see the structure in an inconsistent state. Synchronization is only needed to acquire and update the reference to the structure, and to serialize the updates.

- **Counting semaphore.** Counting semaphores are semaphores whose state can represent any integer. Some implementations allow the P and V operations to take an integer parameter and increment or decrement the state (atomically) by that value. See *semaphore*.

- **Cyclic distribution.** A distribution of data (for example, components of arrays) or tasks (for example, loop iterations) produced by dividing the set into a number of blocks greater than the number of UEs and then allocating those blocks to UEs in a cyclic manner analogous to dealing a deck of cards.

- **Data parallel.** A type of parallel computing in which the concurrency is expressed by applying a single stream of instructions simultaneously to the elements of a data structure.

- **Deadlock.** An error condition common in parallel programming in which the computation has stalled because a group of UEs are blocked and waiting for each other in a cyclic configuration.

- **Design pattern.** A design pattern is a "solution to a problem in context"; that is, it represents a high-quality solution to a recurring problem in design.

- **Distributed computing.** A type of computing in which a computational task is divided into subtasks that execute on a collection of networked computers. The networks are general-purpose networks (LANs, WANs, or the Internet) as opposed to dedicated cluster interconnects.

- **Distributed shared memory (DSM).** An address space shared among multiple UEs that is constructed from memory subsystems that are distinct and distributed about the system. There may be operating-system and hardware support for the distributed shared memory system, or the shared memory may be implemented entirely in software as a separate middleware layer (see *Virtual shared memory.*)

- **DSM.** See *distributed shared memory.*

- **Eager evaluation.** A scheduling strategy where the evaluation of an expression, or execution of a procedure, can occur as soon as (but not before) all of its arguments have been evaluated. Eager evaluation is typical for most programming environments and contrasts with *lazy evaluation.* Eager evaluation can sometimes lead to extra work (or even nontermination) when an argument that will not actually be needed in a computation must be computed anyway.

- **Efficiency.** The efficiency E of a computation is the *speedup* normalized by the number of PEs (P). It is given by

$$E(P) = \frac{S(P)}{P}$$

and indicates how effectively the resources in a parallel computer are used.

- **Embarrassingly parallel.** A task-parallel algorithm in which the tasks are completely independent. See the *Task Parallelism* pattern.

- **Explicitly parallel language.** A parallel programming language in which the programmer fully defines the concurrency and how it will be exploited in a parallel computation. OpenMP, Java, and MPI are explicitly parallel languages.

- **Factory.** A class with methods to create objects, usually instances of any one of several subclasses of an abstract base class. Design patterns for factory classes (*Abstract Factory* and *Factory Method*) were given in [GHJV95].

- **False sharing.** False sharing occurs when two semantically independent variables reside in the same cache line and UEs running on multiple processors modify these variables. They are semantically independent so memory conflicts are avoided, but the cache line holding the variables must be shuffled between the processors, and the performance suffers.

- **Fork.** See *fork/join.*

- **Fork/join.** A programming model used in multithreaded APIs such as OpenMP. A thread executes a *fork* and creates additional threads. The threads (called a *team* in OpenMP) execute concurrently. When the members of the team complete their concurrent tasks, they execute *joins* and suspend until every member of the team has arrived at the join. At that point, the members of the team are destroyed and the original thread continues.

- **Framework.** A reusable, partially complete program that embodies a design for applications in a particular domain. Programmers complete the program by providing application-specific components.

- **Future variable.** A mechanism used in some parallel programming enviroments for coordinating the execution of UEs. The *future variable* is a special variable that will eventually hold the result from an asynchronous computation. For example, Java (in package `java.util.concurrent`) contains a class `Future` to hold future variables.

- **Generics.** Programming language features that allow programs to contain placeholders for certain entities, typically types. The generic component's definition is completed before it is used in a program. Generics are included in Ada, C++ (via templates), and Java.

- **Grid.** A grid is an architecture for distributed computing and resource sharing. A grid system is composed of a heterogeneous collection of resources connected by local-area and/or wide-area networks (often the Internet). These individual resources are general and include compute servers, storage, application servers, information services, or even scientific instruments. Grids are often implemented in terms of Web services and integrated middleware components that provide a consistent interface to the grid. A grid is different from a cluster in that the resources in a grid are not controlled through a single point of administration; the grid middleware manages the system so control of resources on the grid and the policies governing use of the resources remain with the resource owners.

- **Heterogeneous.** A heterogeneous system is constructed from components of more than one kind. An example is a distributed system with a variety of processor types.

- **Homogeneous.** The components of a homogeneous system are all of the same kind.

- **Hypercube.** A multicomputer in which the nodes are placed at the vertices of a d-dimensional cube. The most frequently used configuration is a binary hypercube where each of 2^n nodes is connected to n others.

- **Implicitly parallel language.** A parallel programming language in which the details of what can execute concurrently and how that concurrency is implemented is left to the compiler. Most parallel functional and dataflow languages are implicitly parallel.

- **Incremental parallelism.** Incremental parallelism is a technique for parallelizing an existing program, in which the parallelization is introduced as a sequence of incremental changes, parallelizing one loop at a time. Following each transformation, the program is tested to ensure that its behavior is the same as the original program, greatly decreasing the chances of introducing undetected bugs. See *refactoring*.

- **Java Virtual Machine (JVM).** An abstract stack-based computing machine whose instruction set is called *Java bytecode*. Typically, Java programs are compiled into class files containing bytecode, a symbol table, and other information. The purpose of the JVM is to provide a consistent execution environment for class files regardless of the underlying platform.

- **Join.** See *fork/join.*

- **JVM.** See *Java Virtual Machine.*

- **Latency.** The fixed cost of servicing a request, such as sending a message or accessing information from a disk. In parallel computing, the term most often is used to refer to the time it takes to send an empty message over the communication medium, from the time the send routine is called to the time the empty message is received by the recipient. Programs that generate large numbers of small messages are sensitive to the latency and are called *latency-bound* programs.

- **Lazy evaluation.** A scheduling policy that does not evaluate an expression (or invoke a procedure) until the results of the evaluation are needed. Lazy evaluation may avoid some unnecessary work and in some situations may allow a computation to terminate that otherwise would not. Lazy evaluation is often used in functional and logic programming.

- **Linda.** A coordination language for parallel programming. See *tuple space.*

- **Load balance.** In a parallel computation, tasks are assigned to UEs, which are then mapped onto PEs for execution. The net work carried out by the collection of PEs is the "load" associated with the computation. Load balance refers to how that load is distributed among the PEs. In an efficient parallel program, the load is balanced so each PE spends about the same amount of time on the computation. In other words, in a program with good load balance, each PE finishes with its share of the load at about the same time.

- **Load balancing.** The process of distributing work to UEs such that each UE involved in a parallel computation takes approximately the same amount of time. There are two major forms of load balancing. In *static* load balancing, the distribution of work is determined before the computation starts. In *dynamic* load balancing, the load is modified as the computation proceeds (that is, during runtime).

- **Locality.** The extent to which the computations carried out by a PE use data that is associated with (that is, *is close to*) that PE. For example, in many dense linear algebra problems, the key to high performance is to decompose matrices into blocks and then structure the calculations in terms of these blocks so data brought into a processor's cache is used many times. This is an example of an algorithm transformation that increases locality in a computation.

- **Massively parallel processor (MPP).** A distributed-memory parallel computer designed to scale to hundreds if not thousands of processors. To better support high scalability, the computer elements or *nodes* in the MPP machine are custom-designed for use in a scalable computer. This typically includes tight integration between the computing elements and the scalable network.

- **Message Passing Interface (MPI).** A standard message passing interface adopted by most *MPP* vendors as well as by the cluster-computing community. The existence of a widely supported standard enhances program portability; an MPI-based program developed for one platform should also run on any other platform for which an implementation of MPI exists.

- **MIMD (Multiple Instruction, Multiple Data).** One of the categories of architectures in Flynn's taxonomy of computer architectures. In a MIMD system, each PE has its own stream of instructions operating on its own data. The vast majority of modern parallel systems use the MIMD architecture.

- **Monitor.** Monitors are a synchronization mechanism originally proposed by Hoare [Hoa74]. A monitor is an ADT implementation that guarantees mutually exclusive access to its internal data. Conditional synchronization is provided by condition variables (see *condition variable*).

- **MPI.** See *Message Passing Interface.*

- **MPP.** See *massively parallel processor.*

- **Multicomputer.** A parallel computer based on a distributed-memory, MIMD parallel architecture. The system appears to the user as a single computer.

- **Multiprocessor.** A parallel computer with multiple processors that share an address space.

- **Mutex.** A mutual exclusion lock. A mutex serializes the execution of multiple threads.

- **Node.** Common term for the computational elements that make up a distributed-memory parallel machine. Each node has its own memory and at least one processor; that is, a node can be a uniprocessor or some type of multiprocessor.

- **NUMA.** This term is used to describe a shared-memory computer system where not all memory is equidistant from all processors. Thus, the time required to access memory locations is not uniform, and for good performance the programmer usually needs to be concerned with the placement of data in the memory.

- **Opaque type.** A type that can be used without knowledge of the internal representation. Instances of the opaque type can be created and manipulated via a well-defined interface. The data types used for MPI communicators and OpenMP locks are examples.

- **OpenMP.** A specification defining compiler directives, library routines, and environment variables that can be used to express shared-memory parallelism in Fortran and C/C++ programs. OpenMP implementations exist for a large variety of platforms.

- **OR parallelism.** An execution technique in parallel logic languages in which multiple clauses can be evaluated in parallel. For example, consider a problem with two clauses: `A: B,C` and `A: E,F`. The clauses can execute in parallel until one of them succeeds.

- **Parallel file system.** A file system that is visible to any processor in the system and can be read and written by multiple UEs simultaneously. Although a parallel file system appears to the computer system as a single file system, it is physically distributed among a number of disks. To be effective, the aggregate throughput for read and write must be scalable.

- **Parallel overhead.** The time spent in a parallel computation managing the computation rather than computing results. Contributors to parallel overhead include thread creation and scheduling, communication, and synchronization.

- **PE.** See *processing element*.

- **Peer-to-peer computing.** A distributed computing model in which each node has equal standing among the collection of nodes. In the most typical usage of this term, the same capabilities are offered by each node, and any node can initiate a communication session with another node. This contrasts with, for example, client-server computing. The capabilities that are shared in peer-to-peer computing include file-sharing as well as computation.

- **POSIX.** The Portable Operating System Interface as defined by the Portable Applications Standards Committee (PASC) of the IEEE Computer Society. Whereas other operating systems follow some of the POSIX standards, the primary use of this term refers to the family of standards that define the interfaces in UNIX and UNIX-like (for example, Linux) operating systems.

- **Precedence graph.** A way of representing the order constraints among a collection of statements. The nodes of the graph represent the statements, and there is a directed edge from node A to node B if statement A must be executed before statement B. A precedence graph with a cycle represents a collection of statements that cannot be executed without deadlock.

- **Process.** A collection of resources that enable the execution of program instructions. These resources can include virtual memory, I/O descriptors, a runtime stack, signal handlers, user and group IDs, and access control tokens. A more high-level view is that a process is a "heavyweight" UE with its own address space. See *unit of execution, thread*.

- **Process migration.** Changing the processor responsible for running a process during execution. Process migration is commonly used to dynamically balance the load on multiprocessor systems. It is also used to support fault-tolerant computing by moving processes away from failing processors.

- **Processing element (PE).** A generic term used to reference a hardware element that executes a stream of instructions. The context defines what unit of hardware is considered a PE. Consider a cluster of SMP workstations. In some programming environments, each workstation is viewed as executing a single instruction stream; in this case, a PE is a workstation. A different programming environment running on the same hardware, however, might view each *processor* of the individual workstations as executing an individual instruction stream; in this case, the PE is the processor rather than the workstation.

- **Programming environment.** Programming environments provide the basic tools and APIs needed to construct programs. A programming environment implies a particular abstraction of the computer system called a *programming model*.

- **Programming model.** Abstraction of a computer system, for example the von Neumann model used in traditional sequential computers. For parallel computing, there are many possible models typically reflecting different ways processors can be interconnected. The most common are based on shared memory, distributed memory with message passing, or a hybrid of the two.

- **Pthreads.** Another name for POSIX threads, that is, the definition of threads in the various POSIX standards. See *POSIX*.

- **PVM (Parallel Virtual Machine).** A message-passing library for parallel computing. PVM played an important role in the history of parallel computing as it was the first portable message-passing programming environment to gain widespread use in the parallel computing community. It has largely been superseded by MPI.

- **Race condition.** An error condition peculiar to parallel programs in which the outcome of a program changes as the relative scheduling of UEs varies.

- **Reader/writer locks.** This pair of locks is similar to mutexes except that multiple UEs can hold a read lock, whereas a write lock excludes both other writers and all readers. Reader/writer locks are often effective when resources protected by the lock are read far more often than they are written.

- **Reduction.** An operation that takes a collection of objects (usually one on each UE) and combines them into a single object on one UE or combines them such that each UE has a copy of the combined object. Reductions typically involve combining a set of values pairwise using an associative, commutative operator, such as addition or `max`.

- **Refactoring.** Refactoring is a software engineering technique in which a program is restructured carefully so as to alter its internal structure without changing its external behavior. The restructuring occurs through a series of small transformations (called *refactorings*) that can be verified as preserving behavior following each transformation. The system is fully working and verifiable following each transformation, greatly decreasing the chances of introducing serious, undetected bugs. Incremental parallelism can be viewed as an application of refactoring to parallel programming. See *incremental parallelism.*

- **Remote procedure call (RPC).** A procedure invoked in a different address space than the caller, often on a different machine. Remote procedure calls are a popular approach for interprocess communication and launching remote processes in distributed client-server computing environments.

- **RPC.** See *remote procedure call.*

- **Semaphore.** An ADT used to implement certain kinds of synchronization. A semaphore has a value that is constrained to be a nonnegative integer and two *atomic* operations. The allowable operations are V (sometimes called **up**) and P (sometimes called **down**). A V operation increases the value of the semaphore by one. A P operation decreases the value of the semaphore by one, provided that can be done without violating the constraint that the value be nonnegative. A P operation that is initiated when the value of the semaphore is 0 suspends. It may continue when the value is positive.

- **Serial fraction.** Most computations consist of parts that contain exploitable concurrency and parts that must be executed serially. The *serial fraction* is that fraction of the program's execution time taken up by the parts that must execute serially. For example, if a program decomposes into *setup, compute,* and *finalization,* we could write

$$T_{total} = T_{setup} + T_{compute} + T_{finalization}$$

If the *setup* and *finalization* phases must execute serially, then the serial fraction would be

$$\gamma = \frac{T_{setup} + T_{finalization}}{T_{total}}$$

- **Shared address space.** An addressable block of memory that is shared between a collection of UEs.

- **Shared memory.** A term applied to both hardware and software indicating the presence of a memory region that is shared between system components. For programming environments, the term means that memory is shared between processes or threads. Applied to hardware, it means that the architectural feature tying processors together is shared memory. See *shared address space.*

- **Shared nothing.** A distributed-memory MIMD architecture where nothing other than the local-area network is shared between the nodes.

- **Simultaneous multithreading (SMT).** An architectural feature of some processors that allows multiple threads to issue instructions on each cycle.

In other words, SMT allows the functional units that make up the processor to work on behalf of more than one thread at the same time. Examples of systems utilizing SMT are microprocessors from Intel Corporation that use Hyper-Threading Technology.

- **SIMD (Single Instruction, Multiple Data).** One of the categories in Flynn's taxonomy of computer architectures. In a SIMD system, a single instruction stream runs synchronously on multiple processors, each with its own data stream.

- **Single-assignment variable.** A special kind of variable to which a value can be assigned only once. The variable initially is in an unassigned state. After a value has been assigned, it cannot be changed. These variables are commonly used with programming environments that employ a dataflow control strategy, with tasks waiting to fire until all input variables have been assigned.

- **SMP.** See *symmetric multiprocessor.*

- **SMT.** See *simultaneous multithreading.*

- **Speedup.** Speedup, S, is a multiplier indicating how many times faster the parallel program is than its sequential counterpart. It is given by

$$S(P) = \frac{T(1)}{T(P)}$$

where $T(n)$ is the total execution time on a system with n PEs. When the speedup equals the number of PEs in the parallel computer, the speedup is said to be perfectly linear.

- **Single Program, Multiple Data (SPMD).** This is the most common way to organize a parallel program, especially on *MIMD* computers. The idea is that a single program is written and loaded onto each node of a parallel computer. Each copy of the single program runs independently (aside from coordination events), so the instruction streams executed on each node can be completely different. The specific path through the code is in part selected by the node ID.

- **SPMD.** See *single program, multiple data.*

- **Stride.** The increment used when stepping through a structure in memory. The precise meaning of stride is context dependent. For example, in an $M \times N$ array stored in a column-major order in a contiguous block of memory, traversing the elements of a column of the matrix involves a stride of one. In the same example, traversing across a row requires a stride of M.

- **Symmetric multiprocessor (SMP).** A shared-memory computer in which every processor is functionally identical and has equal-time access to every memory address. In other words, both memory addresses and operating system services are equally available to every processor.

- **Synchronization.** Enforcing constraints on the ordering of events occurring in different UEs. This is primarily used to ensure that shared resources are accessed by a collection of UEs in such a way that the program is correct regardless of how the UEs are scheduled.

- **Systolic array.** A parallel architecture consisting of an array of processors with each processor connected to a small number of its nearest neighbors. Data flows through the array. As data arrives at a processor, it carries out its assigned operations and then passes the output to one or more of its nearest neighbors. Although each processor in a systolic array can run a distinct stream of instructions, they progress in lock-step, alternating between computation and communication phases. Hence, systolic arrays have a great deal in common with the SIMD architecture.

- **Systolic algorithm.** A parallel algorithm where tasks operate synchronously with a regular nearest-neighbor communication pattern. Many computational problems can be formulated as systolic algorithms by reformulating as a certain type of recurrence relation.

- **Task.** A task is a sequence of instructions that operate together as a group. This group corresponds to some logical part of an algorithm or program.

- **Task queue.** A queue that holds tasks for execution by one or more UEs. Task queues are commonly used to implement dynamic scheduling algorithms in programs using the *Task Parallelism* pattern, particularly when used with the *Master/Worker* pattern.

- **Thread.** A fundamental unit of execution on certain computers. In a UNIX context, threads are associated with a process and share the process's environment. This makes the threads lightweight (that is, a context switch between threads is cheap). A more high-level view is that a thread is a "lightweight" unit of execution that shares an address space with other threads. See *unit of execution, process*.

- **Transputer.** The transputer is a microprocessor developed by Inmos Ltd. with on-chip support for parallel processing. Each processor contains four high-speed communication links that are easily connected to the links of other transputers and a very efficient built-in scheduler for multiprocessing.

- **Tuple space.** A shared-memory system where the elements held in the memory are compound objects known as *tuples*. A tuple is a small set of fields holding values or variables, as in the following examples:

$$(3, \texttt{"the larch"}, 4)$$
$$(X, 47, [2, 4, 89, 3])$$
$$(\texttt{"done"})$$

As seen in these examples, the fields making up a tuple can hold integers, strings, variables, arrays, or any other value defined in the base programming language. Whereas traditional memory systems access objects through an address, tuples are accessed by association. The programmer working with a tuple space defines a template and asks the system to deliver tuples matching the template. Tuple spaces were created as part of the Linda coordination language [CG91]. The Linda language is small, with only a handful of primitives to insert tuples, remove tuples, and fetch a copy of a tuple. It is combined with a base language, such as C, C++, or Fortran, to create a combined parallel programming language. In addition to its original implementations on machines with a shared address space, Linda was also implemented with a virtual shared memory and used to communicate between UEs running on the nodes of distributed-memory computers. The idea of an associative virtual shared memory as inspired by Linda has been incorporated into JavaSpaces [FHA99].

- **UE.** See *unit of execution.*

- **Unit of execution (UE).** Generic term for one of a collection of concurrently-executing entities, usually either processes or threads. See *process, thread.*

- **Vector supercomputer.** A supercomputer with a vector hardware unit as an integral part of its central processing unit boards. The vector hardware processes arrays in a pipeline fashion.

- **Virtual shared memory.** A system that provides the abstraction of shared memory, allowing programmers to write to a shared memory even when the underlying hardware is based on a distributed-memory architecture. Virtual shared memory systems can be implemented within the operating system or as part of the programming environment.

- **Workstation farm.** A *cluster* constructed from workstations typically running some version of UNIX. In some cases, the term "farm" is used to imply that the system will be used to run large numbers of independent sequential jobs as opposed to parallel computing.

Bibliography

[ABE+97]   Philip Alpatov, Greg Baker, Carter Edwards, John Gunnels, Greg Morrow, James Overfelt, Robert van de Geijn, and Yuan-Jye J. Wu. PLAPACK: Parallel linear algebra package design overview. In *Proceedings of the 1997 ACM/IEEE Conference on Supercomputing*, pages 1–16. ACM Press, 1997.

[ABKP03]   Mark F. Adams, Harun H. Bayraldar, Tony M. Keaveny, and Panayiotis Papadopoulos. Applications of algebraic multigrid to large-scale finite element analysis of whole bone micro-mechanics on the IBM SP. In *Proceedings SC'03*. IEEE Press, 2003. Also available at http://www.sc-conference.org/sc2003.

[ACC+90]   Robert Alverson, David Callahan, Daniel Cummings, Brian Koblenz, Allan Porterfield, and Burton Smith. The Tera computer system. In *Proceedings of the 4th International Conference on Supercomputing*, pages 1–6. ACM Press, June 1990.

[ACK+02]   David P. Anderson, Jeff Cobb, Eric Korpela, Matt Lebofsky, and Dan Werthimer. SETI@home: An experiment in public-resource computing. *Communications of the ACM*, 45(11):56–61, November 2002.

[ADE+01]   V. Aslot, M. Domeika, R. Eigenmann, G. Gaertner, W. B. Jones, and B. Parady. SPEC OMP: A new benchmark suite for measuring parallel computer performance. In *OpenMP Shared Memory Parallel Programming*, volume 2104 of *Lecture Notes in Computer Science*, pages 1–10. Springer-Verlag, 2001.

[AE03]   Vishal Aslot and Rudolf Eigenmann. Quantitative performance analysis of the SPEC OMP 2001 benchmarks. *Scientific Programming*, 11:105–124, 2003.

[AGH00]   Ken Arnold, James Gosling, and David Holmes. *The Java Programming Language*. Addison-Wesley, 3rd edition, 2000.

[AIS77]   Christopher Alexander, Sara Ishikawa, and Murray Silverstein. *A Pattern Language: Towns, Buildings, Construction*. Oxford University Press, 1977.

[AJMJS02]   J. Al-Jaroodi, N. Mohamed, H. Jiang, and D. Swanson. A comparative study of parallel and distributed Java projects for heterogeneous systems. In *Proceedings of the IPDPS'02 4th International Workshop on Java for Parallel and Distributed Computing (JavaPDC2002)*. IEEE, 2002.

[AML+99]   E. Ayguade, X. Martorell, J. Labarta, M. Gonzalez, and N. Navarro. Exploiting multiple levels of parallelism in OpenMP: a case study. In *Proceedings of the 1999 International Conference on Parallel Processing*, pages 172–180. IEEE Computer Society, 1999.

[And00]   Gregory R. Andrews. *Foundations of Multithreaded, Parallel, and Distributed Programming*. Addison-Wesley, 2000.

[ARv03]   C. Addison, Y. Ren, and M. van Waveren. OpenMP issues arising in the development of parallel BLAS and LAPACK libraries. *Scientific Programming*, 11(2):95–104, 2003.

[BB99]   Christian Brunschen and Mats Brorsson. OdinMP/CCP: A portable imple-
            mentation of OpenMP for C. In *Proceedings of the European Workshop on
            OpenMP,* 1999. Also available at `http://www.community.org/eayguade/`
            `resPub/papers/ewomp99/brunschen.pdf`.

[BBC⁺03]   Christian Bell, Dan Bonachea, Yannick Cote, Jason Duell, Paul Hargrove,
            Parry Husbands, Costin Iancu, Michael Welcome, and Katherine A. Yelick.
            An evaluation of current high-performance networks. In *Proceedings of the
            17th IPDPS.* IEEE, 2003.

[BBE⁺99]   Steve Bova, Clay Beshears, Rudolf Eigenmann, Henry Gabb, Greg Gaertner,
            Bob Kuhn, Bill Magro, Stefano Salvini, and Veer Vatsa. Combining
            message-passing and directives in parallel applications. *SIAM,* 32(9),
            November 1999.

[BC87]   K. Beck and W. Cunningham. Using pattern languages for object-oriented
            programs. Presented at Workshop on Specification and Design, held in
            connection with OOPSLA 1987. Also available at `http://c2.com/doc/`
            `oopsla87.html`.

[BC00]   M. A. Baker and D. B. Carpenter. A proposed Jini infrastructure to sup-
            port a Java message passing implementation. In *Proceedings of the 2nd
            Annual Workshop on Active Middleware Services.* Kluwer Academic Pub-
            lishers, 2000. Held at HPDC-9.

[BCC⁺97]   L. S. Blackford, J. Choi, A. Cleary, E. D'Azevedo, J. Demmel, I. Dhillon,
            J. Dongarra, S. Hammarling, G. Henry, A. Petitet, K. Stanley, D. Walker,
            and R. C. Whaley. *ScaLAPACK Users' Guide.* Society for Industrial and
            Applied Mathematics, 1997.

[BCKL98]   Mark Baker, Bryan Carpenter, Sung Hoon Ko, and Xinying Li. mpi-
            Java: A Java interface to MPI. Presented at First UK Workshop on Java
            for High Performance Network Computing, Europar 1998. Available at
            `http://www.hpjava.org/papers/mpiJava/mpiJava.pdf`, 1998.

[BCM⁺91]   R. Bjornson, N. Carriero, T. G. Mattson, D. Kaminsky, and A. Sherman.
            Experience with Linda. Technical Report RR-866, Yale University Com-
            puter Science Department, August 1991.

[BDK95]   A. Baratloo, P. Dasgupta, and Z. M. Kedem. CALYPSO: a novel software
            system for fault-tolerant parallel processing on distributed platforms. In
            *Proceedings of the 4th IEEE International Symposium on High Performance
            Distributed Computing.* IEEE, 1995.

[Beo]   Beowulf.org: The Beowulf cluster site. `http://www.beowulf.org`.

[BGMS98]   Satish Balay, William D. Gropp, Lois Curfman McInnes, and Barry
            F. Smith. PETSc home page. `http://www.mcs.anl.gov/petsc`, 1998.

[BH86]   Josh Barnes and Piet Hut. A hierarchical O(N log N) force calculation
            algorithm. *Nature,* 324(4), December 1986.

[BJK⁺96]   Robert D. Blumofe, Christopher F. Joerg, Bradley C. Kuszmaul, Charles E.
            Leiserson, Keith H. Randall, and Yuli Zhou. Cilk: An efficient multithreaded
            runtime system. *Journal of Parallel and Distributed Computing,* 37(1):
            55–69, August 1996.

[BKS91]   R. Bjornson, C. Kolb, and A. Sherman. Ray tracing with network Linda.
            SIAM News, 24(1), January 1991.

[BMR+96]   Frank Buschmann, Regine Meunier, Hans Rohnert, Peter Sommerlad, and Michael Stal. *Pattern-Oriented Software Architecture, Volume 1: A System of Patterns*. John Wiley & Sons, 1996.

[BP99]   Robert D. Blumofe and Dionisios Papadopoulos. Hood: A user-level threads library for multiprogrammed multiprocessors. Technical Report, University of Texas, 1999. See also `http://www.cs.utexas.edu/users/hood/`.

[BT89]   D. P. Bertsekas and J. N. Tsitsiklis. *Parallel and Distributed Computation Numerical Methods*. Prentice Hall, 1989.

[But97]   David R. Butenhof. *Programming with POSIX Threads*. Addison-Wesley, 1st edition, 1997.

[CD97]   A. Cleary and J. Dongarra. Implementation in ScaLAPACK of divide-and-conquer algorithms for banded and tridiagonal linear systems. Technical Report CS-97-358, University of Tennessee, Knoxville, 1997. Also available as LAPACK Working Note #124 from `http://www.netlib.org/lapack/lawns/`.

[CDK+00]   Rohit Chandra, Leonardo Dagum, Dave Kohr, Dror Maydan, Jeff McDonald, and Ramesh Menon. *Parallel Programming in OpenMP*. Morgan Kaufmann Publishers, 2000.

[Cen]   The Center for Programming Models for Scalable Parallel Computing. `http://www.pmodels.org`.

[CG86]   K. L. Clark and S. Gregory. PARLOG: Parallel programming in logic. *ACM Trans. Programming Language Systems*, 8(1):1–49, 1986.

[CG91]   N. Carriero and D. Gelernter. *How to Write Parallel Programs: A First Course*. MIT Press, 1991.

[CGMS94]   N. J. Carriero, D. Gelernter, T. G. Mattson, and A. H. Sherman. The Linda alternative to message-passing systems. *Parallel Computing*, 20:633–655, 1994.

[CKP+93]   David Culler, Richard Karp, David Patterson, Abhijit Sahay, Klaus Erik Schauser, Eunice Santos, Ramesh Subramonian, and Thorsten von Eicken. LogP: Toward a realistic model of parallel computation. In *ACM SIGPLAN Symposium on Principles and Practice of Parallel Programming*, pages 1–12. May 1993.

[CLL+99]   James Cowie, Hongbo Liu, Jason Liu, David M. Nicol, and Andrew T. Ogielski. Towards realistic million-node Internet simulations. In *Proceedings of the International Conference on Parallel and Distributed Processing Techniques and Applications (PDPTA 1999)*. CSREA Press, 1999. See also `http://www.ssfnet.org`.

[CLW+00]   A. Choudhary, W. Liao, D. Weiner, P. Varshney, R. Linderman, and R. Brown. Design, implementation, and evaluation of parallel pipelined STAP on parallel computers. *IEEE Transactions on Aerospace and Electronic Systems*, 36(2):528–548, April 2000.

[Co]   Co-Array Fortran. `http://www.co-array.org`.

[Con]   Concurrent ML. `http://cml.cs.uchicago.edu`.

[COR]   CORBA FAQ. `http://www.omg.org/gettingstarted/corbafaq.htm`.

[CPP01]   Barbara Chapman, Amit Patil, and Achal Prabhakar. Performance-oriented programming for NUMA architectures. In R. Eigenmann and M. J. Voss, editors, *Proceedings of WOMPAT 2001 (LNCS 2104)*, pages 137–154. Springer-Verlag, 2001.

[CS95]   J. O. Coplien and D. C. Schmidt, editors. *Pattern Languages of Program Design.* Addison-Wesley, 1995.

[DD97]   J. J. Dongarra and T. Dunigan. Message-passing performance of various computers. *Concurrency: Practice and Experience,* 9(10):915–926, 1997.

[DFF+02]   Jack Dongarra, Ian Foster, Geoffrey Fox, Ken Kennedy, Andy White, Linda Torczon, and William Gropp, editors. *The Sourcebook of Parallel Computing.* Morgan Kaufmann Publishers, 2002.

[DFP+94]   S. Das, R. M. Fujimoto, K. Panesar, D. Allison, and M. Hybinette. GTW: A Time Warp system for shared memory multiprocessors. In *Proceedings of the 1994 Winter Simulation Conference,* pages 1332–1339. Society for Computer Simulation International, 1994.

[DGO+94]   P. Dinda, T. Gross, D. O'Hallaron, E. Segall, J. Stichnoth, J. Subhlok, J. Webb, and B. Yang. The CMU task parallel program suite. Technical Report CMU-CS-94-131, School of Computer Science, Carnegie Mellon University, March 1994.

[DKK90]   Jack Dongarra, Alan H. Karp, and David J. Kuck. 1989 Gordon Bell prize. *IEEE Software,* 7(3):100–104, 110, 1990.

[Dou86]   A. Douady. Julia sets and the Mandelbrot set. In H.-O. Peitgen and D. H. Richter, editors, *The Beauty of Fractals: Images of Complex Dynamical Systems,* page 161. Springer-Verlag, 1986.

[DS80]   E. W. Dijkstra and C. S. Scholten. Termination detection for diffusing computations. *Information Processing Letters,* 11(1), August 1980.

[DS87]   J. J. Dongarra and D. C. Sorensen. A fully parallel algorithm for the symmetric eigenvalue problem. *SIAM J. Sci. and Stat. Comp.,* 8:S139–S154, 1987.

[EG88]   David Eppstein and Zvi Galil. Parallel algorithmic techniques for combinatorial computation. *Annual Reviews in Computer Science,* 3:233–283, 1988.

[Ein00]   David Einstein. Compaq a winner in gene race. *Forbes.com,* June 26, 2000. http://www.forbes.com/2000/06/26/mu7.html.

[EM]   Rudolf Eigenmann and Timothy G. Mattson. OpenMP tutorial, part 2: Advanced OpenMP. Tutorial presented at SC'2001 in Denver, Colorado, USA, 2001. Available at http://www.cise.ufl.edu/research/ParallelPatterns/sc01-omp-tut-advanced.ppt.

[EV01]   Rudolf Eigenmann and Michael J. Voss, editors. *OpenMP Shared Memory Parallel Programming,* volume 2104 of *Lecture Notes in Computer Science.* Springer-Verlag, 2001.

[EWO01]   Selected papers from the Second European Workshop on OpenMP (EWOMP 2000). Special issue. *Scientific Programming,* 9(2–3), 2001.

[FCO90]   J. T. Feo, D. C. Cann, and R. R. Oldehoeft. A report on the SISAL language project. *Journal of Parallel and Distributed Computing,* 12:349, 1990.

[FHA99]   Eric Freeman, Susanne Hupfer, and Ken Arnold. *JavaSpaces: Principles, Patterns, and Practice.* Addison-Wesley, 1999.

[FJL⁺88]   G. Fox, M. Johnson, G. Lyzenga, S. Otto, J. Salmon, and D. Walker. *Solving Problems on Concurrent Processors, Volume I: General Techniques and Regular Problems.* Prentice Hall, 1988.

[FK03]   Ian Foster and Carl Kesselman. *The Grid 2: Blueprint for a New Computing Infrastructure,* 2nd edition. Morgan Kaufmann Publishers, 2003.

[FLR98]   Matteo Frigo, Charles Leiserson, and Keith Randall. The implementation of the Cilk-5 multithreaded language. In *Proceedings of 1998 ACM SIGPLAN Conference on Programming Language Design and Implementation (PLDI).* ACM Press, 1998.

[Fly72]   M. J. Flynn. Some computer organizations and their effectiveness. *IEEE Transactions on Computers,* C-21(9), 1972.

[GAM⁺00]   M. Gonzalez, E. Ayguade, X. Martorell, J. Labarta, N. Navarro, and J. Oliver. NanosCompiler: Supporting flexible multilevel parallelism in OpenMP. *Concurrency: Practice and Experience, Special Issue on OpenMP,* 12(12):1205–1218, October 2000.

[GG90]   L. Greengard and W. D. Gropp. A parallel version for the fast multipole method. *Computers Math. Applic.,* 20(7), 1990.

[GGHvdG01]   John A. Gunnels, Fred G. Gustavson, Greg M. Henry, and Robert A. van de Geijn. FLAME: Formal linear algebra methods environment. *ACM Trans. Math. Soft.,* 27(4):422–455, December 2001. Also see `http://www.cs.utexas.edu/users/flame/`.

[GHJV95]   Erich Gamma, Richard Helm, Ralph Johnson, and John Vlissides. *Design Patterns: Elements of Reusable Object-Oriented Software.* Addison-Wesley, 1995.

[GL96]   Gene H. Golub and Charles F. Van Loan. *Matrix Computations.* Johns Hopkins University Press, 3rd edition, 1996.

[Gloa]   Global Arrays. `http://www.emsl.pnl.gov/docs/global/ga.html`.

[Glob]   The Globus Alliance. `http://www.globus.org/`.

[GLS99]   William Gropp, Ewing Lusk, and Anthony Skjellum. *Using MPI: Portable Parallel Programming with the Message-Passing Interface,* 2nd edition. The MIT Press, 1999.

[GOS94]   Thomas Gross, David R. O'Hallaron, and Jaspal Subhlok. Task parallelism in a High Performance Fortran framework. *IEEE Parallel & Distributed Technology,* 2(3):16–26, 1994. Also see `http://www.cs.cmu.edu/afs/cs.cmu.edu/project/iwarp/member/fx/public/www/fx.html`.

[GS98]   William Gropp and Marc Snir. *MPI: The Complete Reference,* 2nd edition. MIT Press, 1998.

[Gus88]   John L. Gustafson. Reevaluating Amdahl's law. *Commun. ACM,* 31(5): 532–533, 1988.

[Har91]   R. J. Harrison. Portable tools and applications for parallel computers. *Int. J. Quantum Chem.,* 40(6):847–863, 1991.

[HC01]   Cay S. Horstmann and Gary Cornell. *Core Java 2, Volume II: Advanced Features,* 5th edition. Prentice Hall PTR, 2001.

[HC02]   Cay S. Horstmann and Gary Cornell. *Core Java 2, Volume I: Fundamentals,* 6th edition. Prentice Hall PTR, 2002.

[HFR99]   N. Harrison, B. Foote, and H. Rohnert, editors. *Pattern Languages of Program Design 4.* Addison-Wesley, 1999.

[HHS01]   William W. Hargrove, Forrest M. Hoffman, and Thomas Sterling. The do-it-yourself supercomputer. *Scientific American,* 285(2):72–79, August 2001.

[Hil]   Hillside Group. `http://hillside.net`.

[HLCZ99]   Y. Charlie Hu, Honghui Lu, Alan L. Cox, and Willy Zwaenepoel. OpenMP for networks of SMPs. In *Proceedings of 13th International Parallel Processing Symposium and 10th Symposium on Parallel and Distributed Processing,* pages 302–310. IEEE Computer Society, 1999.

[Hoa74]   C. A. R. Hoare. Monitors: An operating system structuring concept. *Communications of the ACM,* 17(10):549–557, 1974. Also available at `http://www.acm.org/classics/feb96`.

[HPF]   Paul Hudak, John Peterson, and Joseph Fasel. A Gentle Introduction to Haskell Version 98. Available at `http://www.haskell.org/tutorial`.

[HPF97]   High Performance Fortran Forum: High Performance Fortran Language specification, version 2.0. `http://dacnet.rice.edu/Depts/CRPC/HPFF`, 1997.

[HPF99]   Japan Association for High Performance Fortran: HPF/JA language specification, version 1.0. `http://www.hpfpc.org/jahpf/spec/jahpf-e.html`, 1999.

[HS86]   W. Daniel Hillis and Guy L. Steele, Jr. Data parallel algorithms. *Communications of the ACM,* 29(12):1170–1183, 1986.

[Hud89]   P. Hudak. Conception, evolution, and application of functional programming languages. *ACM Computing Surveys,* 21(3):359–411, 1989.

[IBM02]   The IBM BlueGene/L team. An overview of the BlueGene/L supercomputer. In *Proceedings of SC'2002.* 2002. `http://sc-2002.org/paperpdfs/pap.pap207.pdf`.

[IEE]   IEEE. The Open Group Base Specifications, Issue 6, IEEE Std 1003.1, 2004 edition. Available at `http://www.opengroup.org/onlinepubs/009695399/toc.htm`.

[J92]   J. JáJá. *An Introduction to Parallel Algorithms.* Addison-Wesley, 1992.

[Jag96]   R. Jagannathan. Dataflow models. In A. Y. H. Zomaya, editor, *Parallel and Distributed Computing Handbook,* Chapter 8. McGraw-Hill, 1996.

[Java]   Java 2 Platform. `http://java.sun.com`.

[Javb]   Java 2 Platform, Enterprise Edition (J2EE). `http://java.sun.com/j2ee`.

[JCS98]   Glenn Judd, Mark J. Clement, and Quinn Snell. DOGMA: distributed object group metacomputing architecture. *Concurrency: Practice and Experience* 10(11–13):977–983, 1998.

[Jef85]   David R. Jefferson. Virtual time. *ACM Transactions on Programming Languages and Systems (TOPLAS),* 7(3):404–425, 1985.

[JSRa]   JSR 133: Java memory model and thread specification revision. `http://www.jcp.org/en/jsr/detail?id=133`.

[JSRb]   JSR 166: Concurrency utilities. `http://www.jcp.org/en/jsr/detail?id=166`.

[JSRc]   Concurrency JSR-166 interest site. `http://gee.cs.oswego.edu/dl/concurrency-interest/index.html`.

[KLK⁺03]   Seung Jo Kim, Chang Sung Lee, Jeong Ho Kim, Minsu Joh, and Sangsan Lee. IPSAP: A high-performance parallel finite element code for large-scale structural analysis based on domain-wise multifrontal technique. In *Proceedings SC'03*. IEEE Press, 2003. Also available at `http://www.sc-conference.org/sc2003`.

[LAM]   LAM/MPI parallel computing. `http://www.lam-mpi.org/`.

[Lam78]   Leslie Lamport. Time, clocks, and the ordering of events in a distributed system. *Communications of the ACM,* 21(7):558–565, 1978.

[LDSH95]   Hans Lischka, Holger Dachsel, Ron Shepard, and Robert J. Harrison. The parallelization of a general ab initio multireference configuration interaction program: The COLUMBUS program system. In T. G. Mattson, editor, *Parallel Computing in Computational Chemistry, ACS Symposium Series 592,* pages 75–83. American Chemical Society, 1995.

[Lea]   Doug Lea. Overview of package `util.concurrent`. `http://gee.cs.oswego.edu/dl/classes/EDU/oswego/cs/dl/util/concurrent/intro.html`.

[Lea00a]   Doug Lea. *Concurrent Programming in Java: Design Principles and Patterns,* 2nd edition. Addison-Wesley, 2000.

[Lea00b]   Doug Lea. A Java fork/join framework. In *Proceedings of the ACM 2000 conference on Java Grande,* pages 36–43. ACM Press, 2000.

[LK98]   Micheal Ljungberg and M. A. King, editors. *Monte Carlo Calculations in Nuclear Medicine: Applications in Diagnostic Imaging.* Institute of Physics Publishing, 1998.

[Man]   Manta: Fast parallel Java. `http://www.cs.vu.nl/manta/`.

[Mas97]   M. Mascagni. Some methods of parallel pseudorandom number generation. In Michael T. Heath, Abhiram Ranade, and Robert S. Schreiber, editors, *Algorithms for Parallel Processing,* volume 105 of *IMA Volumes in Mathematics and Its Applications,* pages 277–288. Springer-Verlag, 1997.

[Mat87]   F. Mattern. Algorithms for distributed termination detection. *Distributed Computing,* 2(3):161–175, 1987.

[Mat94]   T. G. Mattson. The efficiency of Linda for general purpose scientific programming. *Scientific Programming,* 3:61–71, 1994.

[Mat95]   T. G. Mattson, editor. *Parallel Computing in Computational Chemistry, ACS Symposium Series 592.* American Chemical Society, 1995.

[Mat96]   T. G. Mattson. Scientific computation. In A. Zomaya, editor, *Parallel and Distributed Computing Handbook,* pages 981–1002. McGraw-Hill, 1996.

[Mat03]   T. G. Mattson. How good is OpenMP? *Scientific Programming,* 11(3): 81–93, 2003.

[Mesa]   MPI (Message Passing Interface) 2.0 Standard. `http://www.mpi-forum.org/docs/docs.html`.

[Mesb]   Message Passing Interface Forum. `http://www.mpi-forum.org`.

[Met]   Metron, Inc. SPEEDES (Synchronous Parallel Environment for Emulation and Discrete-Event Simulation). http://www.speedes.com.

[MHC⁺99]   A. A. Mirin, R. H. Cohen, B. C. Curtis, W. P. Dannevik, A. M. Dimits, M. A. Duchaineau, D. E. Eliason, D. R. Schikore, S. E. Anderson, D. H. Porter, P. R. Woodward, L. J. Shieh, and S. W. White. Very high resolution simulation of compressible turbulence on the IBM-SP system. In *Proceedings of the 1999 ACM/IEEE Conference on Supercomputing*. ACM Press, 1999.

[Min97]   S. Mintchev. Writing programs in JavaMPI. Technical Report MAN-CSPE-02, School of Computer Science, University of Westminster, London, UK, 1997.

[Mis86]   J. Misra. Distributed discrete-event simulation. *ACM Computing Surveys*, 18(1):39–65, 1986.

[MPI]   MPICH—a portable implementation of MPI. http://www-unix.mcs.anl.gov/mpi/mpich/.

[MPS02]   W. Magro, P. Petersen, and S. Shah. Hyper-threading technology: Impact on computer-intensive workloads. *Intel Technology Journal*, 06(01), 2002.

[MR95]   T. G. Mattson and G. Ravishanker. Portable molecular dynamics software for parallel computing. In T. G. Mattson, editor, *Parallel Computing in Computational Chemistry, ACS Symposium Series 592*, page 133. American Chemical Society, 1995.

[MRB97]   R. C. Martin, D. Riehle, and F. Buschmann, editors. *Pattern Languages of Program Design 3*. Addison-Wesley, 1997.

[MSW96]   Timothy G. Mattson, David Scott, and Stephen R. Wheat. A TeraFLOP supercomputer in 1996: the ASCI TeraFLOP system. In *Proceedings of IPPS'96, The 10th International Parallel Processing Symposium*. IEEE Computer Society, 1996.

[NA01]   Dimitrios S. Nikolopoulos and Eduard Ayguadé. A study of implicit data distribution methods for OpenMP using the SPEC benchmarks. In Rudolf Eigenmann and Michael J. Voss, editors, *OpenMP Shared Memory Parallel Programming*, volume 2104 of *Lecture Notes in Computer Science*, pages 115–129. Springer-Verlag, 2001.

[NBB01]   Jeffrey S. Norris, Paul G. Backes, and Eric T. Baumgartner. PTEP: The parallel telemetry processor. In *Proceedings IEEE Aerospace Conference*, volume 7, pages 7–3339 – 7–3345. IEEE, 2001. Also see http://wits.jpl.nasa.gov:8080/WITS/publications/2001-ptep-ieee-as.pdf.

[NHK⁺02]   J. Nieplocha, R. J. Harrison, M. K. Kumar, B. Palmer, V. Tipparaju, and H. Trease. Combining distributed and shared memory models: Approach and evolution of the Global Arrays toolkit. In *Proceedings of Workshop on Performance Optimization for High-Level Languages and Libraries (ICS'2002)*. ACM Press, 2002.

[NHL94]   Jaroslaw Nieplocha, Robert J. Harrison, and Richard J. Littlefield. Global Arrays: a portable "shared-memory" programming model for distributed memory computers. In *Proceedings of the 1994 ACM/IEEE Conference on Supercomputing*, pages 340–349. ACM Press, 1994.

[NHL96]   J. Nieplocha, R. J. Harrison, and R. J. Littlefield. Global Arrays: A nonuniform memory access programming model for high-performance computers. *The Journal of Supercomputing,* 10(2):169–189, 1996.

[NM92]   Robert H. B. Netzer and Barton P. Miller. What are race conditions?: Some issues and formalizations. *ACM Lett. Program. Lang. Syst.,* 1(1):74–88, 1992.

[Omn]   Omni OpenMP compiler. `http://phase.hpcc.jp/Omni/home.html`.

[OMP]   OpenMP: Simple, portable, scalable SMP programming. `http://www.openmp.org`.

[OSG03]   Ryan M. Olson, Michael W. Schmidt, and Mark S. Gordon. Enabling the efficient use of SMP clusters: the GAMESS/DDI model. In *Proceedings SC'03*. IEEE Press, 2003. Also available at `http://www.sc-conference.org/sc2003/paperpdfs/pap263.pdf`.

[Pac96]   Peter Pacheco. *Parallel Programming with MPI*. Morgan Kaufmann, 1996.

[Pat]   The Pattern Languages of Programs Conference. `http://www.hillside.net/conferences/plop.htm`.

[PH95]   S. J. Plimpton and B. A. Hendrickson. Parallel molecular dynamics algorithms for simulation of molecular systems. In T. G. Mattson, editor, *Parallel Computing in Computational Chemistry, ACS Symposium Series 592,* pages 114–132. American Chemical Society, 1995.

[PH98]   David A. Patterson and John L. Hennessy. *Computer Organization and Design: The Hardware/Software Interface*. Morgan Kaufmann Publishers, 2nd edition, 1998.

[PLA]   PLAPACK: Parallel linear algebra package. `http://www.cs.utexas.edu/users/plapack`.

[Pli95]   S. J. Plimpton. Fast parallel algorithms for short-range molecular dynamics. *J Comp Phys,* 117(1):1–19, 1995.

[PS00]   Tom Porter and Galyn Susman. On site: Creating lifelike characters in Pixar movies. *Communications of the ACM,* 43(1):25–29, 2000.

[PS04]   Bill Pugh and Jaime Spacco. MPJava: high-performance message passing in Java using java.nio. In Lawrence Rauchwerger, editor, *Languages and Compilers for Parallel Computing, 16 International Workshop (LCPC 2003), Revised Papers,* volume 2958 of *Lecture Notes in Computer Science.* Springer, 2004. Also appeared in the Proceedings of MASPLAS'03. `http://www.cs.haverford.edu/masplas/masplas03-01.pdf`.

[PTV93]   William H. Press, Saul A. Teukolsky, and William T. Vetterling. *Numerical Recipes in C: The Art of Scientific Computing,* 2nd edition. Cambridge University Press, 1993.

[Rep99]   John H. Reppy. *Concurrent Programming in ML*. Cambridge University Press, 1999.

[RHB03]   John W. Romein, Jaap Heringa, and Henri E. Bal. A million-fold speed improvement in genomic repeats detection. In *Proceedings SC'03*. IEEE Press, 2003. `http://www.sc-conference.org/sc2003/paperpdfs/pap189.pdf`.

[RHC⁺96]   J. V. W. Reynders, P. J. Hinker, J. C. Cummings, S. R. Atlas, S. Banerjee, W. F. Humphrey, S. R. Karmesin, K. Keahey, M. Srikant, and M. Tholburn. POOMA. In *Parallel Programming Using C++*. The MIT Press, 1996.

[RMC+98]   Radharamanan Radhakrishnan, Dale E. Martin, Malolan Chetlur, Dhananjai Madhava Rao, and Philip A. Wilsey. An object-oriented Time Warp simulation kernel. In *Proceedings of the Second International Symposium on Computing in Object-Oriented Parallel Environments.* Springer-Verlag, 1998. Also available at `http://www.ececs.uc.edu/~paw/lab/papers/warped/iscope98.ps.gz`. See also `http://www.ece.uc.edu/~paw/warped`.

[Sca]   The ScaLAPACK project. `http://www.netlib.org/scalapack/`.

[Sci03]   Special issue on OpenMP and its applications. *Scientific Programming,* 11(2), 2003.

[SER]   Java Servlet Technology. `http://java.sun.com/products/servlet/`.

[SET]   SETI@home: The search for extraterrestrial intelligence. `http://setiathome.ssl.berkeley.edu/`.

[SHPT00]   S. Shah, G. Haab, P. Petersen, and J. Throop. Flexible control structures for parallelism in OpenMP. *Concurrency: Practice and Experience,* 12:1219–1239, 2000.

[SHTS01]   Mitsuhisa Sato, Motonari Hirano, Yoshio Tanaka, and Satoshi Sekiguchi. OmniRPC: A grid RPC facility for cluster and global computing in OpenMP. In Rudolf Eigenmann and Michael J. Voss, editors, *OpenMP Shared Memory Parallel Programming,* volume 2104 of *Lecture Notes in Computer Science,* pages 130–136. Springer-Verlag, 2001.

[SLGZ99]   Alex Scherer, Honghui Lu, Thomas Gross, and Willy Zwaenepoel. Transparent adaptive parallelism on NOWS using OpenMP. *ACM SIGPLAN Notices (ACM Special Interest Group on Programming Languages),* 34(8):96–106, August 1999.

[SN90]   Xian-He Sun and Lionel M. Ni. Another view on parallel speedup. In *Proceedings of the 1990 Conference on Supercomputing,* pages 324–333. IEEE Computer Society Press, 1990.

[SR98]   Daryl A. Swade and James F. Rose. OPUS: A flexible pipeline data-processing environment. In *Proceedings of the AIAA/USU Conference on Small Satellites.* September 1998. See also `http://www.smallsat.org/proceedings/12/ssc98/2/sscii6.pdf`.

[SS94]   Leon Sterling and Ehud Shapiro. *The Art of Prolog: Advanced Programming Techniques,* 2nd edition. MIT Press, 1994.

[SSD+94]   Anthony Skjellum, Steven G. Smith, Nathan E. Doss, Alvin P. Leung, and Manfred Morari. The design and evolution of Zipcode. *Parallel Computing,* 20(4):565–596, 1994.

[SSGF00]   C. P. Sosa, C. Scalmani, R. Gomperts, and M. J. Frisch. Ab initio quantum chemistry on a ccNUMA architecture using OpenMP III. *Parallel Computing,* 26(7–8):843–856, July 2000.

[SSOG93]   Jaspal Subhlok, James M. Stichnoth, David R. O'Hallaron, and Thomas Gross. Exploiting task and data parallelism on a multicomputer. In *Proceedings of the Fourth ACM SIGPLAN Symposium on Principles and Practice of Parallel Programming.* ACM Press, May 1993.

[Sun90]   V. S. Sunderam. PVM: A framework for parallel distributed computing. *Concurrency: Practice and Experience,* 4(2):315–339, 1990.

[Tho95]   John Thornley. Performance of a class of highly-parallel divide-and-conquer algorithms. Technical report, Caltech, 1995. `http://resolver.caltech.edu/CaltechCSTR:1995.cs-tr-95-10`.

[Tita]   Titanium home page. `http://titanium.cs.berkeley.edu/intro.html`.

[Top]   TOP500 supercomputer sites. `http://www.top500.org`.

[UPC]   Unified Parallel C. `http://upc.gwu.edu`.

[VCK96]   J. M. Vlissides, J. O. Coplien, and N. L. Kerth, editors. *Pattern Languages of Program Design 2*. Addison-Wesley, 1996.

[vdG97]   Robert A. van de Geijn. *Using PLAPACK*. MIT Press, 1997.

[vdSD03]   Aad J. van der Steen and Jack J. Dongarra. Overview of recent supercomputers. 2003. `http://www.top500.org/ORSC/`.

[VJKT00]   M. Valero, K. Joe, M. Kitsuregawa, and H. Tanaka, editors. *High Performance Computing: Third International Symposium,* volume 1940 of *Lecture Notes in Computer Science*. Springer-Verlag, 2000.

[vRBH+98]   Robbert van Renesse, Ken Birman, Mark Hayden, Alexey Vaysburd, and David Karr. Building adaptive systems using Ensemble. *Software—Practice and Experience,* 28(9):963–979, August 1998. See also `http://www.cs.cornell.edu/Info/Projects/Ensemble`.

[Wie01]   Frederick Wieland. Practical parallel simulation applied to aviation modeling. In *Proceedings of the Fifteenth Workshop on Parallel and Distributed Simulation,* pages 109–116. IEEE Computer Society, 2001.

[Win95]   A. Windemuth. Advanced algorithms for molecular dynamics simulation: The program PMD. In T. G. Mattson, editor, *Parallel Computing in Computational Chemistry, ACS Symposium Series 592*. American Chemical Society, 1995.

[WSG95]   T. L. Windus, M. W. Schmidt, and M. S. Gordon. Parallel implementation of the electronic structure code GAMESS. In T. G. Mattson, editor, *Parallel Computing in Computational Chemistry, ACS Symposium Series 592,* pages 16–28. American Chemical Society, 1995.

[WY95]   Chin-Po Wen and Katherine A. Yelick. Portable runtime support for asynchronous simulation. In *Proceedings of the 1995 International Conference on Parallel Processing, Volume II: Software*. CRC Press, August 1995.

[X393]   Accredited Standards Committee X3. Parallel extensions for Fortran. Technical Report X3H5/93-SDI revision M, American National Standards Institute, April 1993.

[YWC+96]   Katherine A. Yelick, Chih-Po Wen, Soumen Chakrabarti, Etienne Deprit, Jeff A. Jones, and Arvind Krishnamurthy. Portable parallel irregular applications. In Takayasu Ito, Robert H. Halstead Jr., and Christian Queinnec, editors, *Parallel Symbolic Languages and Systems, International Workshop (PSLS'95),* volume 1068 of *Lecture Notes in Computer Science,* pages 157–173. Springer, 1996.

[ZJS+02]   Hans P. Zima, Kazuki Joe, Mitsuhisa Sato, Yoshiki Seo, and Masaaki Shimasaki, editors. *Proceedings HPF International Workshop: Experiences and Progress (HiWEP 2002),* volume 2327 of *Lecture Notes in Computer Science*. Springer-Verlag, 2002.

About the Authors

TIMOTHY G. MATTSON

Timothy G. Mattson earned a Ph.D. in chemistry from the University of California at Santa Cruz for his work on quantum molecular scattering theory. This was followed by a postdoc at Caltech where he ported his molecular scattering software to the Caltech/JPL hypercubes. Since then, he has held a number of commercial and academic positions with computational science on high-performance computers as the common thread. He has been involved with a number of noteworthy projects in parallel computing, including the ASCI Red project (the first TeraFLOP MPP), the creation of OpenMP, and OSCAR (a popular package for cluster computing). Currently he is responsible for Intel's strategy for the life sciences market and is Intel's chief spokesman to the life sciences community.

BEVERLY A. SANDERS

Beverly A. Sanders received a Ph.D. in applied mathematics from Harvard University. She has held faculty positions at the University of Maryland, the Swiss Federal Institute of Technology (ETH Zürich), and Caltech, and is currently with the Department of Computer and Information Science and Engineering at the University of Florida. A main theme of her teaching and research has been the development and application of techniques, including design patterns, formal methods, and programming language concepts, to help programmers construct high-quality, correct programs, particularly programs involving concurrency.

BERNA L. MASSINGILL

Berna L. Massingill earned a Ph.D. in computer science from Caltech. This was followed by a postdoc at the University of Florida, where she and the other authors began their work on design patterns for parallel computing. She currently holds a faculty position in the Department of Computer Science at Trinity University (San Antonio, Texas). She also spent more than ten years as a working programmer, first in mainframe systems programming and later as a developer for a software company. Her research interests include parallel and distributed computing, design patterns, and formal methods, and a goal of her teaching and research has been applying ideas from these fields to help programmers construct high-quality, correct programs.

Index

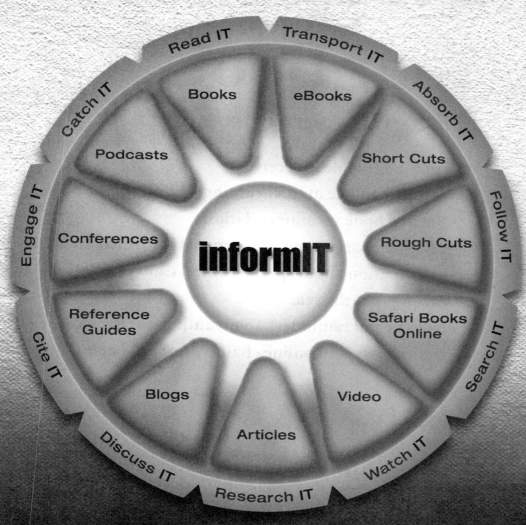

Learn at InformIT

Go Beyond the Book

informIT

- Read IT — Books
- Transport IT — eBooks
- Absorb IT — Short Cuts
- Follow IT — Rough Cuts
- Search IT — Safari Books Online
- Watch IT — Video
- Research IT — Articles
- Discuss IT — Blogs
- Cite IT — Reference Guides
- Engage IT — Conferences
- Catch IT — Podcasts

11 WAYS TO LEARN IT at **www.informIT.com/learn**

The online portal of the information technology
publishing imprints of Pearson Education